Frommer's®
Toronto

My Toronto
by Hilary Davidson

THERE WAS A TIME WHEN I LONGED TO ESCAPE FROM TORONTO.
Growing up there in the 1980s, I remember locals calling it a "World Class
City." Like any cynical teenager, I wondered, *if Toronto's so great, why do
people sound so lame saying so?*

It wasn't until spending some time away that I fell in love with Toronto.
There was no one attribute that won me over, but rather a collection of
charms: architecture that spans the Victorian and modern eras; parks, gardens, greenhouses, and gazebos, spread throughout the downtown district;
neighborhoods that fit together like a patchwork quilt of ethnic groups that
have settled here—Little Italy, Little India, Chinatown, Greektown.

Toronto is big enough to contain major art venues and countless independent galleries, international boutiques and cutting-edge young fashion
designers, brash Broadway musicals and experimental theater. The juxtaposi-
tion of elegance and innovation is exactly what makes my heart beat faster.

What's hard to reconcile is that Toronto is dynamic and dramatic, and yet
remains a place accurately described by words like nice. It's friendly, it's safe,
it's walkable, and it's livable. Now that I don't live in Toronto, I long to return.
I hope the photos in these pages will help you understand why.

© Larry Fisher/Masterfile

CASA LOMA (left) is Toronto's dream house. My friend Stephanie and I used to come here to look for secret passageways (of which it has plenty). As we got older, we came back to see the elegant conservatory, the Norman and Scottish towers, the blooming gardens, and the awe-inspiring library.

I started shopping in **KENSINGTON MARKET (above)** when I was 14 years old and realized that my lust for satin, chiffon, and marabou would never be bankrolled by my paltry allowance and part-time job proceeds . . . unless I bought vintage. You do need patience and a willingness to dig, however.

I'm not the only one who's been besot-
ted by Toronto; the artist Henry Moore
felt the same way, and made a gift of
more than 800 of his works to the city.
The collection is housed at the **ART
GALLERY OF ONTARIO (left).**

If I could listen to music in only one
place, it would be **ROY THOMSON HALL
(above).** In 2002, it underwent a major
overhaul, and the result is acoustic per-
fection. The hall is home to the Toronto
Symphony Orchestra, but everyone
from Ray Charles to Ravi Shankar has
performed here.

Toronto has several **CHINATOWNS (above)**, but the one at Dundas and Spadina was the first. I love discovering this neighborhood's produce markets, tearooms, and herbalists. When you're tired of walking, stop at one of the many excellent but cheap dining options.

While studying at the University of Toronto, I walked through **QUEEN'S PARK (right)** almost every day. The rose-tinted building is home to the Ontario Legislature. In May and June, you'll see the tulips in bloom—the people of Holland send thousands of bulbs every year to thank Canadians for their assistance during World War II.

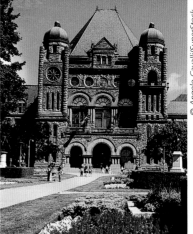

Whenever people tease me about my obsessive love of shoes, I blame Sonja Bata, who founded the **BATA SHOE MUSEUM (right),** and who just might be a bigger footwear fanatic than I. Her collection includes articles worn by Elton John (like the silver platforms shown here), Marilyn Monroe, and John Lennon.

The highlights of my elementary school years were visits to the **ONTARIO SCIENCE CENTRE (below).** Every exhibit here is hands-on, interactive, and educational. The permanent exhibits, such as the rainforest re-creation, still keep me enthralled, but the best thing is watching kids play and learn.

Oscar Wilde ridiculed **NIAGARA FALLS** **(left)** as a honeymoon destination, dubbing it a bride's "*second* great disappointment." Personally, I love the falls, and the best way to experience them up close is aboard the mighty *Maid of the Mist*. Oscar never got a chance to do that.

Summer wouldn't be summer for me without a day trip to **STRATFORD** **(above).** This scenic town 90 miles northwest of Toronto is set on a river (yes, it's called the Avon, and it has swans), and it is home to the Stratford Festival, one of the best theater festivals in the world.

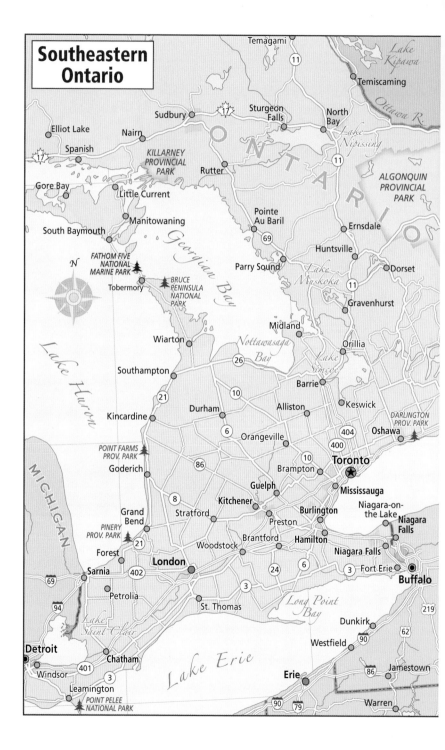

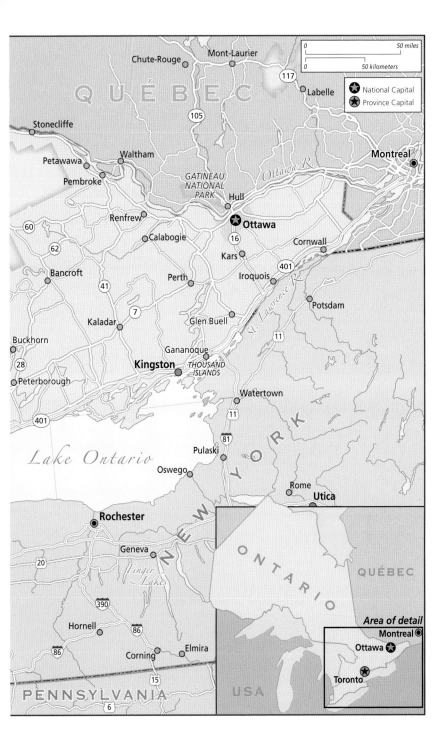

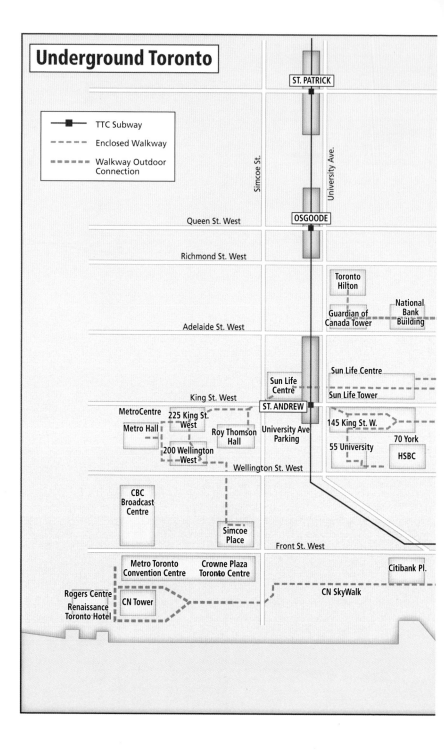

Underground Toronto

- ■— TTC Subway
- - - - - Enclosed Walkway
- ▬ ▬ ▬ Walkway Outdoor Connection

ST. PATRICK

Simcoe St.

University Ave.

OSGOODE

Queen St. West

Richmond St. West

Toronto Hilton

Guardian of Canada Tower

National Bank Building

Adelaide St. West

Sun Life Centre

Sun Life Tower

Sun Life Centre

King St. West

ST. ANDREW

MetroCentre

225 King St. West

Metro Hall

Roy Thomson Hall

University Ave Parking

200 Wellington West

145 King St. W.

55 University

70 York

HSBC

Wellington St. West

CBC Broadcast Centre

Simcoe Place

Front St. West

Metro Toronto Convention Centre

Crowne Plaza Toronto Centre

Citibank Pl.

Rogers Centre

CN Tower

CN SkyWalk

Renaissance Toronto Hotel

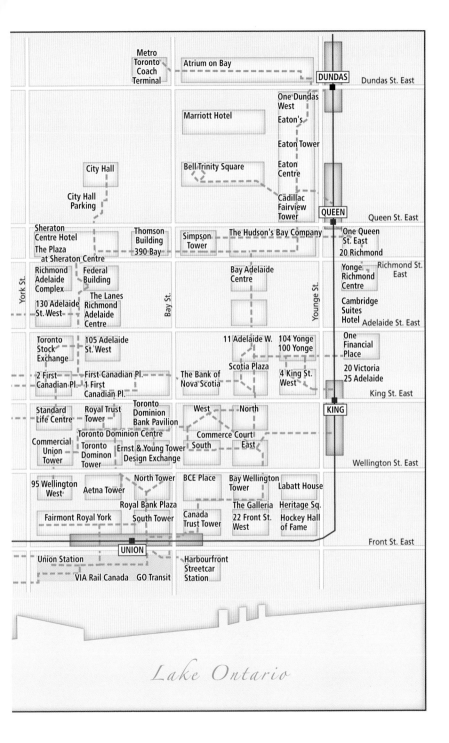

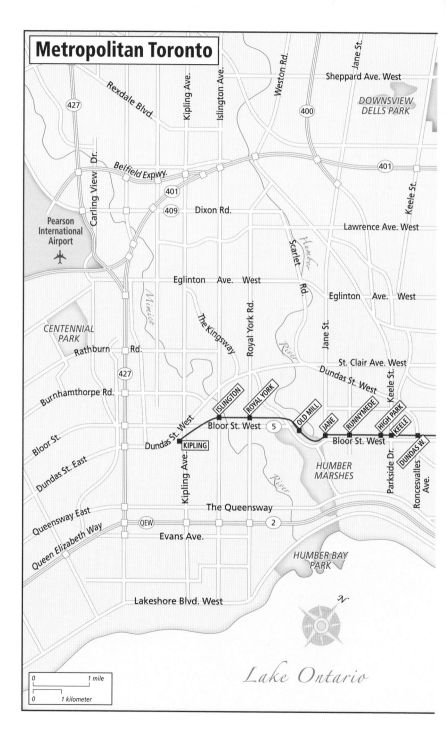

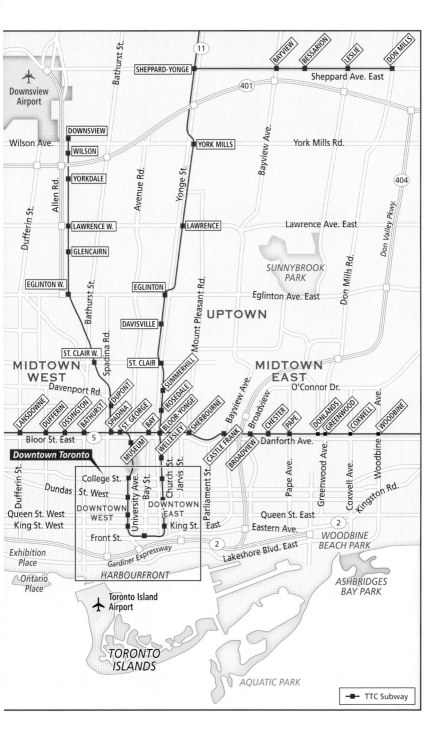

Downsview
Airport

Wilson Ave.

DOWNSVIEW
WILSON
YORKDALE
LAWRENCE W.
GLENCAIRN
EGLINTON W.

Allen Rd.
Dufferin St.
Bathurst St.

Bathurst St.

Avenue Rd.

Yonge St.

11
SHEPPARD-YONGE

401
Sheppard Ave. East

BAYVIEW BESSARION LESLIE DON MILLS

YORK MILLS

York Mills Rd.

Bayview Ave.

LAWRENCE

Lawrence Ave. East

404
Don Valley Pkwy.

SUNNYBROOK
PARK

EGLINTON

Mount Pleasant Rd.

Eglinton Ave. East

UPTOWN

Don Mills Rd.

DAVISVILLE

ST. CLAIR W.

Spadina Rd.

ST. CLAIR

Summerhill

MIDTOWN
WEST

Davenport Rd.

LANSDOWNE DUFFERIN OSSINGTON BATHURST

DUPONT
SPADINA
ST. GEORGE
BAY
BLOOR-YONGE
WELLESLEY

ROSEDALE

SHERBOURNE

MIDTOWN
EAST

O'Connor Dr.

Bayview Ave.

Broadview

CHESTER PAPE

DONLANDS GREENWOOD COXWELL WOODBINE

Bloor St. East

5

MUSEUM

CASTLE FRANK

BROADVIEW

Danforth Ave.

Downtown Toronto

Dufferin St.

Dundas

College St.
St. West

DOWNTOWN
WEST

Queen St. West
King St. West

Front St.

University Ave.
Bay St.

Church St.
Jarvis St.

DOWNTOWN
EAST

King St. East

Parliament St.

Queen St. East

Eastern Ave.

Pape Ave.

Greenwood Ave.

Coxwell Ave.

Woodbine

Kingston Rd.

2

WOODBINE
BEACH PARK

Exhibition
Place

Ontario
Place

Gardiner Expressway

2
Lakeshore Blvd. East

HARBOURFRONT

ASHBRIDGES
BAY PARK

Toronto Island
Airport

TORONTO
ISLANDS

AQUATIC PARK

TTC Subway

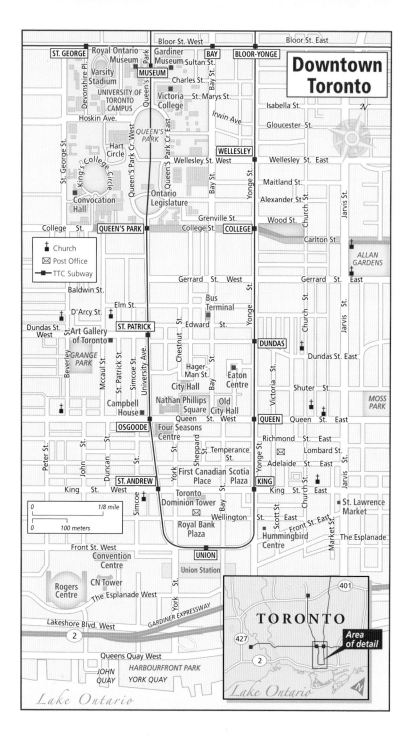

Downtown Toronto

Church
Post Office
TTC Subway

Bloor St. West
Bloor St. East

ST. GEORGE
Royal Ontario Museum
Gardiner Museum
BAY
BLOOR-YONGE
MUSEUM
Sultan St.

Varsity Stadium
Charles St.
Victoria College
St. Marys St.
Isabella St.

UNIVERSITY OF TORONTO CAMPUS

Devonshire Pl.
Queen's Park
Irwin Ave.
Gloucester St.

Hoskin Ave.

Hart Circle

QUEEN'S PARK

WELLESLEY
Wellesley St. East

St. George St.
King's College Circle
Wellesley St. West
Bay St.
Yonge St.
Maitland St.

Queen's Park Cr. West
Queen's Park Cr. East
Alexander St.
Church St.
Jarvis St.

Convocation Hall
Ontario Legislature
Wood St.

College St.
Grenville St.
College St.
COLLEGE
Carlton St.
ALLAN GARDENS

QUEEN'S PARK

Baldwin St.
Gerrard St. West
Yonge St.
Gerrard St. East

Elm St.
Bus Terminal

D'Arcy St.
ST. PATRICK
Edward St.
Church St.
Jarvis St.

Dundas St. West
Art Gallery of Toronto
Chestnut St.
DUNDAS
Dundas St. East

GRANGE PARK
Beverley St.
Mccaul St.
St. Patrick St.
Simcoe St.
University Ave.
Hager-Man St.
Bay St.
Victoria St.
Shuter St.
MOSS PARK

Eaton Centre

City Hall
Nathan Phillips Square
Old City Hall
QUEEN
Queen St. East

Campbell House
OSGOODE
Queen St. West
Richmond St. East
Lombard St.

Four Seasons Centre
Sheppard St.
Temperance St.
Adelaide St. East

Peter St.
John St.
Duncan St.
Widmer St.
York St.
First Canadian Place
Scotia Plaza
KING
King St. East
Jarvis St.

ST. ANDREW
King St. West
Toronto Dominion Tower
Bay St.
Yonge St.
Church St.

Simcoe St.
Wellington
Royal Bank Plaza
St. Lawrence Market

Front St. West
Scott St. East
Front St. East
Market St.
The Esplanade

Convention Centre
Hummingbird Centre

UNION

Rogers Centre
CN Tower
Union Station

The Esplanade West
York St.

Lakeshore Blvd. West
GARDINER EXPRESSWAY
2

Queens Quay West

JOHN QUAY
HARBOURFRONT PARK
YORK QUAY

Lake Ontario

0   1/8 mile
0   100 meters

TORONTO
401
427
2
Area of detail
Lake Ontario

Frommer's®

Toronto 2009

by Hilary Davidson

Here's what the critics say about Frommer's:

"Amazingly easy to use. Very portable, very complete."
—**BOOKLIST**

"Detailed, accurate, and easy-to-read information for all price ranges."
—**GLAMOUR MAGAZINE**

"Hotel information is close to encyclopedic."
—**DES MOINES SUNDAY REGISTER**

"Frommer's Guides have a way of giving you a real feel for a place."
—**KNIGHT RIDDER NEWSPAPERS**

WILEY

Wiley Publishing, Inc.

ABOUT THE AUTHOR

Toronto native **Hilary Davidson** now calls New York City home, thanks to her persuasive Manhattan-born husband, Daniel. She is the author of *Frommer's New York City Day by Day,* First Edition, a contributor to *Frommer's Canada,* and the founder of www.Gluten FreeGuidebook.com, a website for travelers with gluten intolerance and food allergies. She has also written for *American Archaeology, Discover, Fitness, Glow, House & Home, Martha Stewart Weddings,* and *Today's Parent.* Visit her website at www.hilarydavidson.com.

Published by:

WILEY PUBLISHING, INC.

111 River St.
Hoboken, NJ 07030-5774

ISBN 978-0-470-39906-4

Editor: Jennifer Polland
Production Editor: Michael Brumitt
Cartographer: Andy Dolan
Photo Editor: Richard Fox
Production by Wiley Indianapolis Composition Services

Front cover photo: Sea-kayaking around Center Island in the Toronto Harbour, Lake Ontario
Back cover photo: Kensington: Colorful architecture, exterior of houses

For information on our other products and services or to obtain technical support, please contact our Customer Care Department within the U.S. at 800/762-2974, outside the U.S. at 317/572-3993 or fax 317/572-4002.

Wiley also publishes its books in a variety of electronic formats. Some content that appears in print may not be available in electronic formats.

Manufactured in the United States of America
5 4 3 2 1

CONTENTS

4 SUGGESTED TORONTO ITINERARIES   58

5 WHERE TO STAY   72

6 WHERE TO DINE   91

7 WHAT TO SEE & DO   125

LIST OF MAPS

ACKNOWLEDGMENTS

Many thanks to my editor, Jennifer Polland, and to the rest of the Frommer's team, who worked their usual magic in transforming a manuscript into a book. I am also grateful to my mother, Sheila Davidson, whose eagle eye is always on the lookout for what's new in Toronto. I owe a heartfelt thanks to my husband, Dan, whose sense of humor and tireless enthusiasm carried me throughout this project. Finally, deepest thanks to my wonderful friends in Toronto who are always so generous in sharing their observations and opinions.

AN INVITATION TO THE READER

In researching this book, we discovered many wonderful places—hotels, restaurants, shops, and more. We're sure you'll find others. Please tell us about them, so we can share the information with your fellow travelers in upcoming editions. If you were disappointed with a recommendation, we'd love to know that, too. Please write to:

Frommer's Toronto 2009
Wiley Publishing, Inc. • 111 River St. • Hoboken, NJ 07030-5774

AN ADDITIONAL NOTE

Please be advised that travel information is subject to change at any time—and this is especially true of prices. We therefore suggest that you write or call ahead for confirmation when making your travel plans. Because the Canadian dollar is roughly on par with the US dollar as press time, the US dollar conversions have been omitted in this edition. The authors, editors, and publisher cannot be held responsible for the experiences of readers while traveling. Your safety is important to us, however, so we encourage you to stay alert and be aware of your surroundings. Keep a close eye on cameras, purses, and wallets, all favorite targets of thieves and pickpockets.

Other Great Guides for Your Trip:

Frommer's Canada
Frommer's Montréal & Quebec City
Frommer's Nova Scotia, New Brunswick & Prince Edward Island
Frommer's Vancouver & Victoria
Frommer's Ottawa

FROMMER'S STAR RATINGS, ICONS & ABBREVIATIONS

Every hotel, restaurant, and attraction listing in this guide has been ranked for quality, value, service, amenities, and special features using a **star-rating system.** In country, state, and regional guides, we also rate towns and regions to help you narrow down your choices and budget your time accordingly. Hotels and restaurants are rated on a scale of zero (recommended) to three stars (exceptional). Attractions, shopping, nightlife, towns, and regions are rated according to the following scale: zero stars (recommended), one star (highly recommended), two stars (very highly recommended), and three stars (must-see).

In addition to the star-rating system, we also use **seven feature icons** that point you to the great deals, in-the-know advice, and unique experiences that separate travelers from tourists. Throughout the book, look for:

Finds	Special finds—those places only insiders know about
Fun Facts	Fun facts—details that make travelers more informed and their trips more fun
Kids	Best bets for kids, and advice for the whole family
Moments	Special moments—those experiences that memories are made of
Overrated	Places or experiences not worth your time or money
Tips	Insider tips—great ways to save time and money
Value	Great values—where to get the best deals

The following abbreviations are used for credit cards:

AE	American Express	**DISC**	Discover	**V**	Visa
DC	Diners Club	**MC**	MasterCard		

FROMMERS.COM

Now that you have this guidebook to help you plan a great trip, visit our website at **www. frommers.com** for additional travel information on more than 4,000 destinations. We update features regularly to give you instant access to the most current trip-planning information available. At Frommers.com, you'll find scoops on the best airfares, lodging rates, and car rental bargains. You can even book your travel online through our reliable travel booking partners. Other popular features include:

- Online updates of our most popular guidebooks
- Vacation sweepstakes and contest giveaways
- Newsletters highlighting the hottest travel trends
- Podcasts, interactive maps, and up-to-the-minute events listings
- Opinionated blog entries by Arthur Frommer himself
- Online travel message boards with featured travel discussions

What's New in Toronto

When you're strolling around Toronto these days, you may feel that you should have packed a hardhat. The city is caught up in renovating its art institutions and building new skyscrapers. Here's a quick look at what's new.

PLANNING YOUR TRIP With the cost of fuel making airfares soar, it's good to note that there's a new option for flying into Toronto from the U.S. A relatively new airline, **Porter** (℗ 888/619-8622 or 416/619-8622; www.flyporter.com), has several daily flights from New York City to the Toronto Island Airport; there are plans to expand its service to other U.S. cities, including Chicago. See chapter 3.

WHERE TO STAY The **Hazelton Hotel** (118 Yorkville Ave., ℗ 866/473-6301; www.thehazeltonhotel.com) recently opened with a splash. It's a lovely space—and it boasts its own private screening room—but it's proud of having the priciest room rates in the city. Neighboring luxury hotels, such as the **Park Hyatt** (℗ 800/233-1234; www.parktoronto.hyatt.com) and the **Four Seasons** (℗ 800/268-6282; www.fourseasons.com/toronto), look like a steal by comparison.

While you're in town, you may notice that there are some new hotel-construction projects going on. The city is set to get its first-ever **Ritz Carlton,** the **Trump** empire is building a tower, and the **Four Seasons** plans to open a new property. However, none of these options will be available anytime soon (some are still on the drawing board at press time).

WHERE TO DINE Toronto's most famous chef, Susur Lee, has left for New York (with promises to open a new restaurant in Toronto down the road), but the city is studded with culinary gems. There's **Amuse-Bouche,** 96 Tecumseth St. (℗ 416/913-5830), an elegant bistro on a quiet side street downtown; **Four,** 187 Bay St. (℗ 416/368-1444), is located in the Financial District, in what used to be a subterranean watering hole; and **Greg Couillard's Spice Room & Chutney Bar,** 55 Avenue Rd. (℗ 416/935-0000), is an opulent dining room hidden inside—surprise!—an upscale mall. There are also some changes with well-established Toronto restaurants: **Le Papillon,** the Quebecois creperie, is in a new location at 69 Front St. E. (℗ 416/367-0303) and will open a second spot at 1001 Eastern Ave. in 2009.

WHAT TO SEE & DO The **CN Tower** lost its title as the world's tallest freestanding structure in 2008, but that doesn't make visiting it any less breathtaking. As a matter of fact, its newest attraction—an incredible glass-*floored* elevator—just opened in the summer; see p. 132. The transformation of the **Royal Ontario Museum (ROM)** is finally complete. The Daniel Libeskind-designed galleries—which included the dinosaurs and the new costume gallery—are located inside the Michael Lee-Chin Crystal, which dominates Bloor Street West. See p. 134. The **Ontario Science Centre** has also completed its major makeover, adding even more hands-on galleries and creating a new outdoor exhibition space. The highlight is the new KidSpark gallery, designed for kids 8 and under. See p. 134.

At press time, the Frank Gehry-designed renovation at the **Art Gallery of Ontario (AGO)** is ongoing. If all goes according to plan, it should reopen in November 2008, with 40% more viewing space than it had before the renovation. There will also be newly acquired pieces in the collection, including Peter Paul Reubens's masterpiece, "The Massacre of the Innocents," new galleries of African and Australian aboriginal art and a permanent photography installation. For details, see chapter 7.

SHOPPING I know that many travelers head to the Eaton Centre to get their retail fix. I drop by, too (hey, there's an Apple store there now, after all), but Toronto has so many great shopping neighborhoods that it's a shame to focus on chain stores. The **Art & Design District** along Queen St. West and the **Distillery District** near King St. East and Parliament St. are both great areas to find unique boutiques. See chapter 9 for details.

Visitors familiar with the legendary Canadian department store **The Bay** will be in for a shock: they may see **Lord & Taylor** signs in some of its stores. The Bay was purchased by the same company that owns the American retailer in the summer of 2008, and while plans are still developing, it sounds like some Bay stores with be operating under a different banner.

Unfortunately for American shoppers, the Canadian dollar has gotten so strong that it's roughly on par with the U.S. dollar (that's why prices in this volume are listed in Canadian dollars and British pounds). However Toronto remains a great shopping destination. The "Shopping" chapter veers away from nationally known retailers to focus on unique local shops

that sell things you won't find anywhere else.

AFTER DARK If you're an opera lover who's visiting Toronto, buy your tickets for the **Canadian Opera Company** right now. Its performances at the **Four Seasons Centre for the Performing Arts** have been at 99% capacity this past year, making it one tough "get." Of course, since Toronto is such an opera-loving city, there are plenty of other opera companies to check out: see "Opera Obsessed" on p. 212.

Toronto's dance clubs run the gamut. Some of the newest, like **Park Lane,** are expensive and all about the velvet rope; others, like the massive **Circa,** run by club king Peter Gatien, are big enough to offer something for everyone. See chapter 10 for more.

The **Sony Centre for the Performing Arts**—formerly known as the Hummingbird Centre—will be dark in 2009. Architect Daniel Libeskind, the man responsible for the Royal Ontario Museum's crystal galleries, has designed a 49-story residential tower that will loom over the theater, which will also be completely overhauled. At press time, there's no information about when the theater will reopen.

SIDE TRIPS **Niagara Falls** is in the middle of upgrading some of its attractions and introducing new ones (believe it or not, it's just not enough to have the famous falls anymore). The **Table Rock Centre,** essentially the "gateway" to the falls, is getting a $32 million upgrade. Its new star is **Niagara's Fury,** which opened on June 27, 2008. Visitors are invited to "experience" the creation of the falls in a chamber that swirls visual images over a 360-degree screen, has the ground shake beneath them, envelops them in a blizzard, and makes the temperature drop from 75°F to 40°F (24°C to 4°C) in 3 seconds. See p. 242.

The Best of Toronto

When I was growing up in Toronto in the 1980s, there were three little words that I dreaded. I heard them on a regular basis, almost daily. And while it's true that plenty of things make an adolescent recoil, the phrase "World-Class City" was my personal horror. It was a mantra that was repeated by Toronto politicians ad nauseam, and it ended up on other people's lips (my friends from Montréal found it endlessly amusing). The fact that local boosters had to prop up Toronto with a meaningless moniker just made me cringe.

Looking back now, it's easier to understand where those three little words came from. Have you been to Toronto? Chances are that even if you've never set foot here, you've seen the city a hundred times over. Known for the past several years as "Hollywood North," Toronto has been a stand-in for international centers from European capitals to New York—but rarely does it play itself. Self-deprecating Torontonians embody a paradox: Proud of their city's architectural, cultural, and culinary charms, they are unsure whether it's all up to international snuff.

After spending a single afternoon wandering around Toronto, you might wonder why this is a question at all. The sprawling city boasts lush parks, renowned architecture, and excellent galleries. There's no shortage of skyscrapers, particularly in the downtown core. Still, many visitors marvel at the number of Torontonians who live in houses on tree-lined boulevards that are a walk or a bike ride away from work.

Out-of-towners can see the fun side of the place, but Torontonians aren't so sure. They recall the stuffiness of the city's past. Often called "Toronto the Good," it was a town where you could walk down any street in safety, but you couldn't get a drink on Sunday.

Then a funny thing happened on the way through the 1970s. Canada loosened its immigration policies and welcomed waves of Italians, Greeks, Chinese, Vietnamese, Jamaicans, Indians, Somalians, and others, many of whom settled in Toronto. Political unrest in Québec drove out Anglophones, many into the waiting arms of Toronto (that's how my Montréal friends arrived in Toronto in the first place). The city's economy flourished, which in turn gave its cultural side a boost.

Natives and visitors alike enjoy the benefits of this rich cultural mosaic. More than 7,000 restaurants are scattered across the city, serving everything from simple Greek souvlakia to Asian-accented fusion cuisine. Festivals such as Caribana and Caravan draw tremendous crowds to celebrate heritage through music and dance. Its newfound cosmopolitanism has made Toronto a key player on the arts scene, too. The Toronto International Film Festival in September and the International Festival of Authors in October draw top stars of the movie and publishing worlds. The theater scene rivals London's and New York's.

By any measure, Toronto is a great place to be. It has accomplished something rare, expanding and developing its daring side while holding on to its traditional strengths. The World-Class City campaign may have been a world-class flop, but maybe that lingering insecurity is exactly what propels Toronto forward.

Metropolitan Toronto

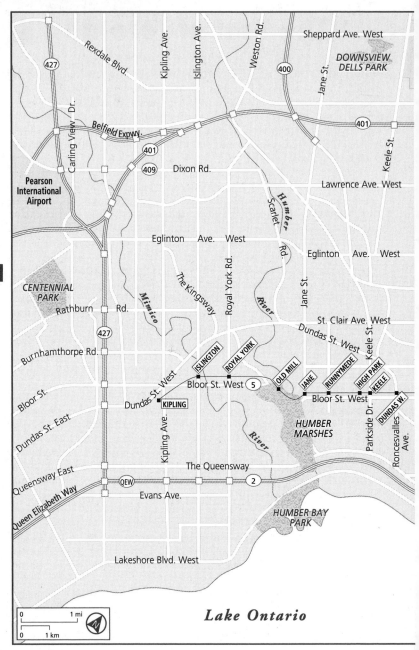

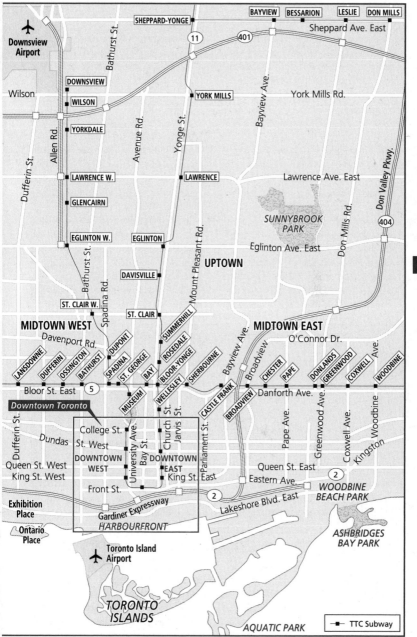

1 THE MOST UNFORGETTABLE TRAVEL EXPERIENCES

- **Exploring the Distillery District:** Not only is this recently restored area a gorgeous example of 19th-century industrial architecture, but it's also a hive of activity. In addition to the art galleries, shops, and restaurants, you can hear live music or visit the farmers' market. See p. 132.

- **Taking in the Art Galleries and Boutiques on West Queen West:** The stretch of Queen that runs west of Bathurst Avenue is known as the Art & Design District, with good reason. This is the home of the Museum of Contemporary Canadian Art and the place to visit for cutting-edge style. See chapter 7.

- **Checking Out Local Theater and Music:** Sure, Toronto likes its blockbuster shows. However, the offerings from the Canadian Stage Company,

Soulpepper, Opera Atelier, Tafelmusik, and the Lorraine Kimsa Theatre for Young People are innovative and consistently excellent, too. And seeing the Canadian Opera Company onstage at the Four Seasons Centre for the Performing Arts is breathtaking. See "The Performing Arts," in chapter 10.

- **Cafe Hopping at Trattorias in Little Italy:** Trendy, yes, but it's also a fun area for stopping by the many cafes and wine bars and for dining on outstanding food. See chapter 6.

- **Viewing the City from the Roof Bar at the Park Hyatt:** Unfortunately, the famous CN Tower gives you a better view of Niagara Falls than it does of Toronto itself. To truly appreciate the city's dramatic architecture, there's no better spot than the Roof.

2 THE BEST SPLURGE HOTELS

- **Park Hyatt Toronto,** 4 Avenue Rd. (© 800/233-1234): Talk about having it all—the Park Hyatt boasts a beautifully renovated Art Deco building, topnotch service, and one of the best views in the city from the rooftop terrace lounge. This is a place to relax and let yourself be pampered. See p. 85.

- **The Gladstone Hotel,** 1214 Queen St. W. (© 416/531-4635): This hotel is moderately priced overall, but its

double-decker "Rock Star Suite," located in the hotel's Gothic tower, is a unique splurge—and its view makes the downtown Toronto core look like a faraway metropolis. See p. 78.

- **Hôtel Le Germain,** 30 Mercer St. (© 866/345-9501): Edgy yet elegant, this is one of Toronto's most beautifully designed hotels. Attention is paid to the smallest details—even the elevators are wrapped in poetry! See p. 76.

3 THE BEST MODERATELY PRICED HOTELS

- **Delta Chelsea,** 33 Gerrard St. W. (© 800/243-5732): This is a longtime favorite with budget-minded families. Perks include a playroom with live bunnies and fish, a video arcade, and a waterslide. It also offers children's

programs, a day-care center, and kid-friendly restaurants. Many rooms have fridges or kitchenettes. See p. 77.

- **Hotel Victoria,** 56 Yonge St. (© 800/363-8228): This property offers the best value in town. Double rooms start at C$120 (£60) per night, and for this you get excellent service; a smallish but well-appointed room; and proximity to the Eaton Centre, Chinatown, and the Financial District. See p. 80.

- **Clarion Hotel & Suites Selby,** 592 Sherbourne St. (© **800/4-CHOICE**): Ornate chandeliers, stucco moldings, and high ceilings make the 1890s Victorian building an absolute stunner. History buffs will love the fact that Ernest Hemingway lived here for a couple of years while he was on staff at the *Toronto Star* newspaper (and yes, there's a Hemingway suite). See p. 88.

4 THE MOST UNFORGETTABLE DINING EXPERIENCES

- **Amuse-Bouche,** 96 Tecumseth St. (© **416/913-5830**): Dining at this downtown restaurant, located on a quiet, mostly residential street, would be a highlight of any trip to Toronto. Simply put: Great chef plus great food plus great service equal one magical meal. See p. 102.
- **Jamie Kennedy Wine Bar,** 9 Church St. (© **416/362-1957**): My favorite wine bar is always one of the best bets in Toronto. All of the plates are delicious and moderately priced. See p. 111.
- **Edward Levesque's Kitchen,** 1290 Queen St. E. (© **416/465-3600**): Located in Leslieville, an up-and-coming neighborhood, this small, unpretentious bistro offers cooking so sophisticated and service so smooth that it caught the attention of the *New York Times*. See p. 110.
- **Canoe Restaurant & Bar,** in the Toronto Dominion Tower, 66 Wellington St. W. (© **416/364-0054**): Defining Canadian cuisine is a tricky task because the country has absorbed a wealth of cooking styles and techniques from around the world. Come to Canoe to see how these are blended with Canadian produce; it's a recipe for a perfect meal. See p. 100.
- **Four,** 187 Bay St. (© **416/368-1444**): Located in the heart of the Financial District, this moderately priced restaurant serves up healthful food (no entrée is more than 650 calories) that tastes divinely decadent. See p. 104.

5 THE BEST THINGS TO DO FOR FREE (OR ALMOST)

- **Picnicking on Centre Island:** Hop on the ferry and escape to the islands. From across the water, you'll see the city in an entirely new light. See "The Toronto Islands," on p. 130.
- **Listening to a Concert at the Toronto Music Garden:** Cellist Yo-Yo Ma co-designed this serene space that's intended to evoke Bach's First Suite for Unaccompanied Cello. It's easy on the eyes, but the best time to come here is for a summertime concert. Pure bliss. See p. 151.
- **Wandering through Riverdale Farm:** In case you need more proof that Toronto is a very green city, it has a working farm in its midst. Cows, sheep, pigs, goats, and other critters call it home. See p. 155.
- **Visiting Ireland Park:** This memorial to the Irish Famine features the "Arrival" figures created by Rowan Gillespie

(they're related to his "Departure" series in Dublin). See p. 151.

- **Treasure Hunting for Vintage Clothing in Kensington Market:** How can one small area have a dozen vintage-clothing vendors? And how do they keep prices low and quality good? Haphazard Kensington Market is a joy for bargain hunters. See "Walking Tour 1: Chinatown & Kensington Market," in chapter 8 and "Hunting for Vintage," in chapter 9.

6 THE BEST MUSEUMS

- **Royal Ontario Museum,** 100 Queen's Park (© **416/586-8000**): The ROM is quite possibly the best museum in the country. Its major renovation now complete, the whole family can go back to admiring its dinosaurs, Chinese temple art, Roman statues, and Middle Eastern mosaics. See p. 134.
- **Harbourfront Centre,** 235 Queens Quay W. (© **416/973-4000**): While it isn't exactly a museum, this waterfront complex has art exhibits, musical performances, cultural celebrations, outdoor Artists' Gardens, and many special events. The highlight of its calendar is the International Festival of Authors. See p. 127.
- **Ontario Science Centre,** 770 Don Mills Rd. (© **416/696-3127**): You don't have to be a tyke to appreciate the amazing interactive displays about biology, ecology, and technology here. See p. 134.
- **University of Toronto Art Centre,** 15 King's College Circle (© **416/978-1838**): This intimate gallery is one of the city's secret treasures. Visit it for the special exhibits or for the stunning permanent collection of Byzantine art. See p. 140.
- **Casa Loma,** 1 Austin Terrace (© **416/923-1171**): Toronto has its own castle, and it's a smashing example of architecture. Perhaps the man who built it was a little obsessive, but how can you not admire the fact that it has both a Scottish *and* a Norman tower? See p. 143.

7 THE BEST PLACES TO HANG WITH THE LOCALS

- **The Drake Hotel,** 1150 Queen St. W. (© **416/531-5042**): Set in the middle of the Art & Design District, this hotel fosters a sense of community by hosting music events, literary readings, and other festivities. If you hate feeling like a tourist, this place is for you. See p. 77.
- **The Rogers Centre or the Air Canada Centre:** The Rogers Centre is home base for the Toronto Blue Jays baseball team. The Air Canada Centre is where the Maple Leafs (hockey) and the Raptors (basketball) play. Torontonians come out to support them in droves. See p. 150.
- **Day Spas:** For many Torontonians, taking care of their well-being involves a little indulgence. After all, Toronto is home to some of the best day spas in North America, including the Victoria Spa, the Stillwater Spa, and the HealthWinds Spa. See "Spas & the City," p. 158.
- **Comedy Clubs:** Maybe it's something in the water: Toronto has produced more than its share of top-notch comedians, including the shagadelic Mike Myers, Jim Carrey, Dan Aykroyd, and the late John Candy. Checking out local talent or international stand-up stars at one of the many comedy clubs is a favorite pastime for Torontonians. See p. 216.

Toronto in Depth

"Toronto will be a fine town when it is finished," quipped Irish playwright Brendan Behan in the mid–20th century. Fast forward to 2009, and Canada's largest city remains a work in progress. Visitors will notice that it's still perpetually under construction as they tuck under scaffolding and crane their necks up at new skyscrapers unfurling toward the heavens all over this sprawling metropolis.

Some of these projects have the imprimatur of world-famous architects, such as the Sony Centre, the performing arts venue where a 49-story residential tower designed by Daniel Libeskind will dwarf the historic stage where Mikhail Baryshnikov defected to the West (the architect's plans for the center will also reshape the stage itself). Libeskind also designed the new crystal galleries at the Royal Ontario Museum, a project that is still controversial among locals. The city's long-awaited opera house (designed by Jack Diamond) opened a couple of years ago to rave reviews. The Art Gallery of Ontario is finishing up its own Frank Gehry–designed renovations. Donald Trump has discovered Toronto and is building a luxury tower (of course), and Ritz-Carlton suddenly realized that the city is a prime spot for a towering new hotel (Toronto was long overdue for a Ritz).

Ironically, while Torontonians seem eager to show off what's shiny and new in town, many of the most popular attractions have been there for decades. The city's extensive green spaces, which include High Park, Trinity-Bellwoods, Queen's Park, Sunnybrook, and Edwards Gardens, are inspired retreats from the concrete city. For an unforgettable experience, take the short ferry ride to the Toronto Islands and picnic there in full view of the jutting skyline. The writer and urban-planning guru Jane Jacobs—an American who chose to make Toronto her home—liked to say "Eyes on the street," and that's exactly where Toronto thrives. The city is still a patchwork of village-like neighborhoods, and its strength—from Parkdale to the Annex, from Little Italy to Little India, and from Chinatown to Rosedale—is its rich diversity. Sipping a cappuccino on a Little Italy patio, strolling through Cabbagetown's narrow streets, and exploring historic Kensington Market (especially on a summer Sunday, when it's closed to cars) are among Toronto's finest pleasures. Successive waves of immigration have shaped the city (as you'll read in this chapter), and you'll experience this rich heritage best on foot, exploring Toronto's ethnic neighborhoods.

1 TORONTO TODAY

Toronto's downtown core is thriving. It was never abandoned like the city centers of so many American cities, but many outlying areas had been neglected. In the past few years, that has changed for the better as they have been revitalized. Parkdale, a once-gloomy neighborhood west of the downtown core has been reclaimed by young families and gentrified, and the search for housing within reach of downtown has led to the gentrification of neighborhoods in the western and eastern parts of the city (Leslieville is the most notable recent example).

Toronto is still the Canadian city of choice for arriving immigrants; almost half

SARSapalooza

Toronto has a talent for reinvention that would be the envy of any pop star. After the "SARS crisis" of 2003—and by *crisis,* I mean that the international media treated the few SARS cases in the city like the return of the plague—the city's image was in tatters and its tourism trade sank very low. Instead of trying to quietly fold up the memory of the SARS panic, Toronto hosted a blockbuster event to herald the city's comeback. Dubbed **SARSapalooza** by local wags, the event was headlined by the Rolling Stones and turned into Canada's largest rock concert in history.

of Canada's new immigrants now come to Toronto. Roughly 300,000 Hong Kong émigrés have joined Toronto's Chinese community, and there have been influxes from Somalia, Eastern Europe, India, Pakistan, and Central America. Neighborhoods around town preserve these cultures. While their influence is strong in many areas, it is perhaps most visible to a short-term visitor in the city's diverse dining options and in Toronto's many cultural festivals.

Life in Toronto sounds pretty sweet, but there's trouble under that smooth, polite surface. To understand the problems, you need to go back to 1998. That's when the Conservative provincial government—ignoring countless petitions, protests, and public opinion—forced through the megacity merger, making six municipalities unite under the name "Toronto." At the same time, the provincial government cut social spending. This is incredibly frustrating to most Torontonians, because the city has long been the engine of financial growth for the rest of the country (though with Alberta awash in oil money these days, that may change). The most frequent complaint heard in Toronto is that the city's municipal taxes aren't reinvested in its infrastructure, but end up being funneled to other places. What that translates into is that the city doesn't have the resources to take care of its own people. The city's homeless problem has only grown over the past several years.

In 2003, Ontario elected a Liberal government, which is still in power. Its relationship with the municipal government has been far more cordial than the previous government's, but that hasn't made Torontonians any happier. The provincial government agreed that Toronto needed to keep more of its tax revenue for itself, but it couldn't part with the great gobs of money it got from the city. So, in 2006, the City of Toronto Act was created. This allowed the municipal government to charge new and greater taxes (on things such as alcohol and land-transfer agreements), and to keep those revenues for its own coffers. Unfortunately, this has driven people and businesses out of Toronto; the surrounding Greater Toronto Area (GTA), is the main beneficiary (the GTA has its own municipal governments, and they keep the area a low-taxation haven). People in Toronto are paying more taxes than ever, yet getting fewer services than before.

Toronto managed to get over the fact that it lost the 2008 Olympics to Beijing (many locals never wanted the Games in their town, actually). At the time, some claimed that Toronto was being "strongly encouraged" to go after the 2012 Summer Olympic Games. However, the fact that Vancouver won the 2010 Winter Games quashed that dream. Unfortunately, the dream may have died a little too hard: there were some terrific plans that were drawn up to win over the International

Olympic Committee (such as a public-transit link to Pearson International Airport) but there has been no movement on those fronts. However, Toronto put forward a bold new face in other ways. Suddenly it seemed like the right time to re-create its key arts institutions: Frank Gehry was tapped to design an expanded space for the **Art Gallery of Ontario,** and the **Royal Ontario Museum** tore down its charming Terrace Galleries to make way for the prominent crystal galleries envisioned by Daniel Libeskind. Toronto also finally built its long-awaited opera house (the **Four Seasons Centre for the Performing Arts**), which became the permanent home of the Canadian Opera Company and the National Ballet of Canada. Toronto also opened new attractions such as the **Distillery District** (and by "new," I mean that a complex of Victorian industrial buildings was redeveloped, not newly built), and **Ireland Park,** an impressive memorial to the 38,000 Irish immigrants who arrived during the Great Famine.

2 LOOKING BACK AT TORONTO

EARLY SETTLEMENT IN "MUDDY YORK"

Native Canadians had long stopped here—at the entrance to the Toronto Trail, a short route between the Lower and Upper lakes. In 1615, French fur trader Étienne Brûlé was the first European to travel the trail. It wasn't until 1720 that the French established the first trading post, known as Fort Toronto (the Huron word *Toronton* meant "place of meetings"), to intercept the furs that were being taken across Lake Ontario to New York State by English rivals. Fort Rouillé, built on the site of today's CNE grounds, replaced the trading post in 1751. When the 1763 Treaty of Paris ended the Anglo-French War after the fall of Québec, French rule in North America effectively ended, and the city's French antecedents were all but forgotten.

In the wake of the American Revolution, the Loyalists fled north and the British decided it was time to carve a capital city out of the northern wilderness. In 1791, the British established Upper Canada (modern-day Ontario) as a province, and its first lieutenant governor, John Graves Simcoe, decided that Toronto's location made it strategically and militarily important. Further sealing the deal, the British had already purchased a vast tract of land from the Mississauga tribe for the paltry sum of £1,700, plus blankets, guns, rum, and tobacco. In 1793, Simcoe, his wife, Elizabeth, and the Queen's Rangers arrived in Toronto, which Simcoe immediately renamed "York" in honor of Frederick, Duke of York (one of George III's sons). Simcoe ordered a garrison built and laid it out in a 10-block rectangle around King, Front, George, and Berkeley streets. Beyond stretched a series of 40-hectare (100-acre) lots from Queen to Bloor, which were granted to mollify government officials who resented having to move to the mosquito-plagued, marshy outpost. York was notorious for its always-muddy streets, earning it the nickname "Muddy York."

By 1796, the hamlet had grown, and the first parliament buildings were erected. Simcoe also surveyed Yonge Street, which would eventually become the longest street in the world (in Simcoe's time, it facilitated trade by fur-trappers and farmers, and offered an escape route in the case of an American attack). The first Parliament meeting confirmed York as the capital of Upper Canada.

THE WAR OF 1812 & ITS AFTERMATH

When America declared war on Britain in the War of 1812 (actually 1812–15),

(Fun Facts) **Muddy York**

Just how muddy was the early settlement of Muddy York? It was a subject of continuous complaint by early settlers. One apocryphal story tells of a man who saw a hat lying in the middle of a street and went to pick it up. When he did, he found the head of a live man submerged in the muck below it.

President Madison assumed it would be simple to invade and hold Canada. The opposite proved to be true. In April 1813, 14 ships carrying 1,700 American troops invaded York (population 625), looting and destroying the Parliament buildings, the Fort York garrison, and much of the settlement. It was a Pyrrhic victory, because the Americans suffered heavy losses and failed to take any more Canadian territory. In retaliation, British and Canadian troops marched on Washington, D.C. in 1814 and burned all government buildings, including the American president's residence. (The Americans later whitewashed it to hide the charred wood—hence, the White House.)

Perhaps unsurprisingly given the events of the war, York's ruling oligarchy shared a conservative pro-British outlook. Called the Family Compact, the group consisted of William Jarvis, a New England Loyalist who became provincial secretary; John Beverley Robinson, son of a Virginia Loyalist, who became attorney general at age 22 and, later, chief justice of Upper Canada; and Scottish-educated Dr. John Strachan, a schoolmaster who became an Anglican rector and, eventually, the most powerful figure in York. Anglo-Irish Dr. William Warren Baldwin, doctor, lawyer, architect, judge, and parliamentarian, laid out Spadina Avenue as a thoroughfare leading to his country house; the Boultons were prominent lawyers, judges, and politicians—Judge D'Arcy Boulton built a mansion, the Grange, which later became the core of the art museum and still stands today.

THE EARLY 1800s: REBELLION & IMMIGRATION

In 1834, the city was incorporated, and York became Toronto, a city bounded by Parliament Street to the east, Bathurst to the west, the lakefront to the south, and 366m (1,200 ft.) north of the current Queen Street (then called Lot) on the northern edge. Outside this area—west to Dufferin Street, east to the Don River, and north to Bloor Street—laid the "liberties," out of which the city would later carve new wards. North of Bloor, local brewer Joseph Bloor and Sheriff William Jarvis were already drawing up plans for the village of Yorkville. In 1843 the University of Toronto opened; this was an intellectual achievement but also an aesthetic one, since the university added new and beautiful architecture to the city.

As increasing numbers of immigrants arrived, demands arose for democracy and reform. Among the reformers were such leaders as Francis Collins, who launched the radical paper *Canadian Freeman* in 1825; lawyer William Draper; and, most famous of all, fiery William Lyon Mackenzie, who was elected Toronto's first mayor in 1834.

Immigration was changing Toronto more than anything else. During the 1820s, 1830s, and 1840s, immigrants— Irish Protestants and Catholics, Scots, Presbyterians, Methodists, and other nonconformists—arrived in droves. In 1822, York got its first Catholic church, St. Paul's, built on the eastern outskirts of town. By 1832, York had become the largest urban community in the province, with a population of 1,600. Slavery was outlawed throughout the British empire in 1834; by the 1850s, roughly 3% of Toronto's population was black. But the biggest change was the arrival of the Irish. In early 1847, Toronto's population stood at 20,000. That summer 38,000 Irish immigrants fleeing the Great Famine landed in Toronto, forever changing the city. Many were sick with typhus, and more than 1,000 perished after arriving in Toronto. While some of the Irish settlers were Ulster Protestants, many more were Catholics, and the old-country Orange and Green conflicts flared into mob violence every year on July 12th.

CANADIAN CONFEDERATION & THE LATE VICTORIAN ERA

During the 1850s, the building of the railroads accelerated Toronto's booming economy. By 1860, it was the trading hub for lumber and grain imports and exports. Merchant empires were founded, railroad magnates emerged, and institutions such as the Bank of Toronto were established. The foundations of an industrial city were laid: Toronto gained a waterworks, gas, and public transportation. Many municipal facilities were built, including a city hall, the Royal Lyceum Theatre (1848), St. Lawrence Hall (1851), and the Toronto Stock Exchange (1852).

Despite its wealth, Toronto lagged behind Montréal, which had twice Toronto's population in 1861. But Toronto increasingly took advantage of its superior links to the south, and that edge eventually helped it overtake its rival. Under the Confederation of 1867, the city was guaranteed another advantage: As the capital of the newly created Ontario province, Toronto in effect controlled the minerals and timber of the north.

By 1891, Toronto's population was 181,000. The business of the city was business, and amassing wealth was the pastime of such figures as Henry Pellatt, stockbroker, president of the Electrical Development Company, and builder of Casa Loma; E. B. Osler; George Albertus Cox; and A. R. Ames. Although these men were self-made entrepreneurs, not Family Compact officials, they formed a traditional, socially conservative elite linked by money, tastes, investments, and religious affiliation. And they were staunchly British. They, and the rest of the citizens, celebrated the Queen's Jubilee in 1897 with gusto and gave Toronto boys a rousing send-off to fight in the Boer War in 1899.

The Toronto Rebellion

William Lyon Mackenzie, Toronto's first mayor, founded the *Colonial Advocate* to crusade against the narrow-minded Family Compact, calling for reform and challenging their power to such an extent that some of them broke into his office and dumped his presses into the lake. By 1837, Mackenzie, undaunted, was calling for open rebellion. The city's financial turmoil in the wake of some bank failures made his wish come true. On December 5, 1837, 700 rebels gathered at Montgomery's Tavern outside the city (near modern-day Eglinton Ave.). Led by Mackenzie on a white mare, they marched on the city. But Sheriff Jarvis was waiting for them, and his militia crushed the rebellion. Mackenzie fled to the United States, but two other rebellion leaders were hanged (their graves are in the Toronto Necropolis). Mackenzie was later pardoned, returned to Toronto in 1849, and was elected to the Upper Canada legislature.

Revolutionary Shopping

Toronto's burgeoning urban market helped spawn two great Toronto merchants—Timothy Eaton and Robert Simpson—who moved to Toronto from Ontario towns to open stores at Queen and Yonge streets in 1869 and 1872, respectively. Eaton developed his reputation on fixed prices, cash sales only, and promises of refunds if the customer wasn't satisfied—all unique gambits at the time. Simpson copied Eaton and competed by providing better service, such as two telephones to take orders instead of one. Both enterprises developed into full-fledged department stores, and both entered the mail-order business, conquering the country with their catalogs.

The prominent businessmen also had a fondness for clubs—the Albany Club for the Conservatives and the National Club for the Liberals. As in England, their sports clubs (notably the Royal Yacht Club, the Toronto Cricket Club, the Toronto Golf Club, and the Lawn Tennis Club) carried a certain cachet.

The boom spurred new commercial and residential construction. Projects included the first steel-frame building—the Board of Trade Building (1889) at Yonge and Front—George Gooderham's Romanesque-style mansion (1890) at St. George and Bloor (now the York Club), the provincial parliament buildings in Queen's Park (1886–92), and the city hall (1899) at Queen and Bay. Public transit improved, and by 1891, the city had 109km (68 miles) of tracks for horse-drawn cars. Electric lights, telephones, and electric streetcars appeared in the 1890s.

FROM BOOMTOWN TO THE GREAT DEPRESSION

Toronto's Great Fire of 1904 demolished 5.6 hectares (14 acres) of downtown, and the damage was an estimated $10,000,000 (in 1904 dollars). Miraculously, no one died in the fire, the cause of which was never discovered. Less impressively, insurance companies raised all premiums for businesses in the torched area by 75%, retroactive to the night of the fire, April 19th.

Between 1901 and 1921, Toronto population more than doubled, climbing from 208,000 to 521,893. The economy continued to expand, fueled by the lumber, mining, wholesale, and agricultural machinery industries, and, after 1911, by hydroelectric power. Much of the new wealth went into construction, and three marvelous buildings from this era can still be seen today: the Horticultural Building at the Exhibition Grounds (1907), the King Edward Hotel (1903), and Union Station (1914–19).

The booming economy and its factories attracted a wave of new immigrants—mostly Italians and Jews from Russia and Eastern Europe—who settled in the city's emerging ethnic enclaves. By 1912, Kensington Market was well established, and the garment center and Jewish community were firmly ensconced around King and Spadina. Little Italy clustered around College and Grace. By 1911, more than 30,000 Torontonians were foreign-born, and the slow march to change the English character of the city had begun.

Increased industrialization brought social problems, largely concentrated in Cabbagetown and the Ward, a large area that stretched west of Yonge and north of Queen. Here, poor people lived in crowded, wretched conditions: Housing was inadequate; health conditions were poor; and rag picking, or sweatshop labor, was the only employment.

As industry grew, unionism also increased, but the movement, as in the United States, failed to organize politically. Two major strikes—at Bell, in 1907, and in the garment industry, in 1912—were easily broken.

As it became larger and wealthier, Toronto also became an intellectual and cultural magnet. Artists such as Charles Jefferys, J. H. MacDonald, Arthur Lismer, Tom Thomson, Lawren Harris, Frederick Varley, and A. Y. Jackson, most associated with the Group of Seven, set up studios in Toronto. Their first group show opened in 1920. Toronto also became the English-language publishing center of the nation, and such national magazines as *Maclean's* (1896) and *Saturday Night* (1887) were launched. The Art Gallery of Ontario, the Royal Ontario Museum, the Toronto Symphony Orchestra, and the Royal Alexandra Theatre all opened before 1914.

Women advanced, too, at the turn of the 20th century. In 1880, Emily Jennings Stowe became the first Canadian woman authorized to practice medicine. In 1886, the University of Toronto began to accept women. Clara Brett Martin was the first woman admitted to the law courts. The women's suffrage movement gained strength, led by Dr. Stowe, Flora McDonald Denison, and the Women's Christian Temperance Union.

When Britain entered World War I, Canada was immediately pulled into it as well. During the war, Toronto sent 70,000 men to the trenches; about 13,000 were killed. At home, the war had a great impact economically and socially: Toronto became Canada's chief aviation center; factories, shipyards, and power facilities expanded to meet the needs of war; and women entered the workforce in great numbers.

After the war, the city took on much more of the aspect and tone that characterize it today. Automobiles appeared on the streets—the Canadian Cycle and Motor Company began manufacturing them in 1906 (the first parking ticket was given in 1908), and one or two skyscrapers appeared. Although 80% of the population was of British origin, ethnic enclaves were clearly defined.

The 1920s roared along, fueled by a mining boom that saw Bay Street turned into a veritable gold-rush alley where everyone was pushing something hot. The Great Depression followed, inflicting 30% unemployment in 1933. The only distraction from its bleakness was the opening of Maple Leaf Gardens in 1931. Besides being an ice-hockey center, it was host to large protest rallies during the Depression and later to such diverse entities as the Jehovah's Witnesses, Billy Graham, the

"Toronto the Good"

Toronto's reputation for conservatism was well deserved. While the city was blessed with many beautiful churches, its nickname, "Toronto the Good," had less to do with religion and more to do with legislation against fun. This was, after all, the city that, in 1912, banned tobogganing on Sunday. As late as 1936, 30 men were arrested at the lakeshore resort of Sunnyside because they exposed their chests—even though the temperature was 105°F (41°C)! In 1947, cocktail lounges were approved, but it wasn't until 1950 that playing sports on Sunday became legal. Leopold Infeld, a University of Toronto physicist who worked with Einstein, famously said: "I dreaded the Sundays and prayed to God that if he chose for me to die in Toronto he would let it be on a Saturday afternoon to save me from one more Toronto Sunday."

Impressions

In the eyes of the rest of the country, Toronto is a kind of combination Sodom and Mecca.

—Pierre Berton, 1961

Ringling Bros. Circus, and the Metropolitan Opera.

As in the United States, hostility toward new immigrants was rife during the '20s. It reached a peak in 1923, when the Chinese Exclusion Act was passed, banning Chinese immigration. In the 1930s, antagonism toward Jews intensified. Signs such as NO JEWS, NIGGERS, OR DOGS were posted occasionally at Balmy and Kew beaches. In August 1933, the display of a swastika at Christie Pits Park caused a battle between Nazis and Jews. As if things weren't bad enough, a polio epidemic broke out in 1936.

WORLD WAR II & BEYOND

Unlike World War I, Canada wasn't automatically bound to enter World War II by Britain's declaration of war. However, the Canadian parliament voted to declare war on Germany on September 10, 1939, a move that was widely supported by Canadians.

The Second World War brought new life to Toronto—literally. Toronto men rushed to volunteer to serve while women took their place in the factories. At the same time, 8,000 British children were sent to Toronto by their parents, to keep them safe from the war. Toronto became a major aviation center, manufacturing roughly 3,000 planes, as well as weapons including machine guns. Torontonians endured rationing—one bottle of liquor a month, and limited supplies of sugar, tea, and other staples—while they listened to the war-front news delivered by future *Bonanza* star Lorne Greene.

After World War II, prosperous Toronto continued to expand. The suburbs alone added more than 200,000 to the population between 1940 and 1953. By the 1950s, the urban area had grown so large, disputes between city and suburbs were so frequent, and the need for social and other services was so great that an effective administrative solution was needed. In 1953, the Metro Council, composed of equal numbers of representatives from the city and the suburbs, was established.

Toronto became a major city in the 1950s, with Metro providing a structure for planning and growth. The Yonge subway opened, and a network of highways was constructed. It linked the city to the affluent suburbs. Don Mills, the first new town, was built between 1952 and 1962; Yorkdale Center, a mammoth shopping center, followed in 1964. American companies began locating branch plants in the area, fueling much of the growth.

The city also began to loosen up. While the old social elite continued to dominate the boardrooms, politics, at least, had become more accessible and fluid. In 1954, Nathan Phillips became the first Jewish mayor, signifying how greatly the population had changed. In 1947, the Chinese Exclusion Act of 1923 was repealed, opening the door to relatives of Toronto's then-small Chinese community. After 1950, the door swung open farther. Germans and Italians were allowed to enter, adding to the communities that were already established; then, under pressure from the United Nations, Poles, Ukrainians, Central European and Russian Jews, Yugoslavs, Estonians, Latvians, and other East Europeans poured in. Most arrived at Union Station, having journeyed from the ports of Halifax, Québec City, and Montréal. At the beginning of the 1950s, the foreign-born were 31% of the population; by 1961, they were 42%, and the number of people claiming British descent had fallen from 73% to 59%. The 1960s brought an even richer mix of people—Portuguese, Greeks, West Indians, South Asians, Chinese, Vietnamese, and Chilean refugees—changing the city's character forever.

In the 1960s, the focus shifted from the suburbs to the city. People moved back downtown, renovating the handsome brick Victorians so characteristic of today's downtown. Yorkville emerged briefly as the hippie capital—the Haight-Ashbury of Canada. Gordon Lightfoot and Joni Mitchell sang in the coffeehouses, and a group called the Toronto Anti-Draft Programme helped many Americans fleeing the Vietnam draft settle in Toronto.

During the 1970s, the provincial government also helped develop attractions that would polish Toronto's patina and lure visitors: Ontario Place in 1971, Harbourfront in 1972, and the Metro Zoo and the Ontario Science Centre in 1974. The CN Tower is another development from that era, and for more than 3 decades it was the tallest free-standing structure in the world (now surpassed by the Burj Dubai tower). Unfortunately, in spite of stiring efforts by preservationists, Toronto lost many historic buildings in the 1960s and 70s, (a few, such as the Royal Alexandra Theatre, were recognized for their historic importance in this period).

The 1980s were an interesting time in Toronto. On the one hand, the city fell into the habit of conspicuous consumption that seemed to define the era. Yorkville was transformed from hippie coffeehouse central into a hive of chic boutiques (a trend that has only continued in the years since, in spite of the closing of Creeds, its most famous shop). But on a more positive note, previously neglected neighborhoods such as the Annex and Cabbagetown were revitalized, the grand mansions being brought back to life by a new wave of residents. In fairness to the oft-mocked 1980s, this was a time when people began to appreciate Toronto's historic architecture, working to restore it rather than tear it down as they had in the 1970s. The Elgin and Winter Garden theaters were fully renovated and reopened, as was the Pantages Theatre (now called the Canon). In 1986, Toronto's Mirvish family (of "Honest Ed's" fame) created Mirvish Productions, which (along with the now-defunct Livent group) ushered in a renaissance on the Toronto theater scene. There was also important new construction in the city: Roy Thomson Hall opened in 1982, and SkyDome (now called the Rogers Centre) debuted in 1989.

In the 1990's, the municipalities around Toronto (known as the Greater Toronto Area, or GTA), really began to boom, fueled in part by rising immigration to the city. In 1998, the despised megacity merger

Montreal's Loss, Toronto's Gain

In the 1970s, Toronto became the fastest-growing city in North America. For years, it had competed with Montréal for first-city status, but it was the election of the Parti Québécois, in 1976, that boosted Toronto over the top. Montreal's loss was Toronto's gain, as English-speaking families and large companies resettled in Toronto. The city overtook Montréal as a financial center, boasting more corporate headquarters. Its stock market was more important, and it remained the country's prime publishing center.

was forced through by the provincial government. Toronto was forced into a union with five previously independent boroughs, causing cuts in public services and misery all around.

The past decade has been a boom time for construction in the city, particularly since the SARS outbreak in 2003. Developments include the **Four Seasons Centre for the Performing Arts** (the new opera house), which opened in 2006. Also, the **Royal Ontario Museum, the Art Gallery of Ontario, the Ontario Science Centre,** and the **Gardiner Museum of Ceramic Art** have all undergone extensive renovations. By 2008, Toronto had become North America's largest condo market, with towers going up all over the city. Preservationists are fighting hard against some of the developments (for example, the Kensington Market neighborhood has rallied to save the historic church of St.-Stephen-in-the-Fields). However, with so many new arrivals coming to Toronto and wanting to live downtown, it doesn't look like there's anywhere to build but up.

3 TORONTO'S ARCHITECTURE

Toronto contains a wealth of architectural styles, from Gothic Revival churches to Romanesque civic buildings and the towering skyscrapers off the Financial District. Toronto's history stretches over 200 years, and what its citizens built tells visitors a lot about the mindset of the city in a particular era.

THE SETTLING OF YORK (1793–1837)

There was a settlement on the shore of Lake Ontario before 1793, but it was only after John Simcoe arrived that year and named it "York," that the town grew rapidly and became the capital of Upper Canada (modern-day Ontario). While there aren't many examples of the era's architecture still standing in Toronto, the ones that do exist show just how deeply York's early settlers were still connected to the motherland. The flourishing town took not only its name from England (it was renamed Toronto in 1834), but its architectural direction as well. The most notable style of the era was:

GEORGIAN These buildings are characterized by their formal, symmetrical design, and by their classically inspired details, such as columns and pediments. There are few examples in Toronto, but an outstanding one is **Campbell House** at 160 Queen St. West (p. 147). Built for Sir William Campbell in 1822 (he was a Loyalist and a chief justice of Upper Canada), it was moved $1^1/2$km from its original location in 1972 to save it from being demolished in favor of a parking lot. Campbell House is currently a museum. Another example of Georgian architecture is **The Grange** (p. 164), which is part of the Art Gallery of Ontario and sits behind the AGO's Dundas St. West main building. Built in 1817, The Grange isn't currently open to the public.

EARLY VICTORIAN (1837–1860)

The Victorian era in Toronto was a creative time in which a variety of different architectural styles were employed. There was a strong tendency to look at the styles of the past and reinterpret them for the present. The chief ones were:

GOTHIC REVIVAL This fanciful style was part of a literary and aesthetic movement in England in the 1830s and 1840s, and became incredibly popular in Toronto. Gothic Revival design was asymmetrical, with pointed arches and windows, extensive ornamentation, and steeply pitched roofs; towers were often incorporated into the design. While the inspiration for Gothic Revival buildings was the great churches of the past, the style was applied to many types of buildings in Toronto. **St. James' Cathedral** (p. 146), built between 1850 and 1874, is a perfect example of the style with its hundred-foot-tall bell tower and its Romantic-inspired stained glass windows. **St. Michael's Cathedral** (p. 146) and the **Church of St.-Stephen-in-the-Fields** (p. 167) are also prime examples of Gothic Revival religious architecture. The **Toronto Necropolis** (p. 152), a cemetery that was established in 1850, is one of the best examples of Gothic Revival architecture in Toronto, with its recently restored entryway: the chapel boasts an asymmetrical tower, and the porte-cochere has steep peaks and extensive gabling. One great secular example of the style is **Hart House** (p. 139) at the University of Toronto (note that it was built much later than the others, completed during the First World War).

GREEK REVIVAL Influenced by Greece's fight for independence in the 1820s (in which the Romantic poet Lord Byron famously perished), there was a revival in interest in the country's history, arts, and architecture. Picture the classical columns, friezes, and low-pitch pediment of a Greek temple, and you have a general outline of the style. Few Greek Revival buildings have survived in Toronto. One example stands at **15 Wellington Street West,** an 1845 bank building now stripped of its signage. A smaller example is **Mackenzie House** (p. 148), where the would-be revolutionary William Lyon Mackenzie lived after returning from his exile in America. The house, built in the 1850s, is an elegant Greek Revival row house with a decorative frieze.

RENAISSANCE REVIVAL Just as ancient Greece fascinated the Victorian mind, so did the ideals of the Italian Renaissance. Buildings designed in this style tended to be large, impressive, and formal, with a symmetrical arrangement of the façade, quoins (cornerstones that give an impression of strength and solidity), columns separating windows, and large blocks of masonry on the lowest floor. Toronto's **St. Lawrence Hall** (next to the St. Lawrence Market, p. 150), built in 1850, is a textbook example of Renaissance Revival.

VICTORIAN CLASSICAL Some buildings in Toronto were constructed in the spirit of several different revivals (an eclectic approach to architecture that is still relevant today). They don't fit well into any particular style, and so are grouped together as Victorian Classical. **Osgoode Hall** (p. 148), which was built, re-built, and expanded multiple times between 1829 and 1858, is referred to this way for its unique design.

LATE VICTORIAN (1860–1901)

Later in the Victorian period, Toronto was still being influenced by Britain, but the city was also becoming more original in its design:

RICHARDSONIAN ROMANESQUE Arguably old Toronto's most beloved architectural style. In England, there was a Romanesque Revival, though the style was usually called Norman, calling on elements of 11th- and 12th-century castle and church design. Toronto's Richardson Romanesque buildings were influenced by the American architect Henry Hobson Richardson. The style is immediately identifiable by its massive scale, rounded archways, belt courses (continuous rows of bricks in a wall), decorative arcading, and large towers. The **Ontario Legislature** at Queen's Park (p. 145), built in 1893, is a Richardsonian Romanesque masterpiece in rose-tinted sandstone and granite. So is **Old Toronto City Hall** (p. 144), though its design is less orthodox with its two-tone sandstone exterior and prominent gargoyles.

2

Impressions

You build your stations like we build our cathedrals.

—The Prince of Wales, speaking at the official opening
of Toronto's Union Station in 1927

BAY-AND-GABLE Closely related to Gothic Revival architecture, this is a style that is considered unique to Toronto. It applies some of the most visually spectacular elements of Gothic Revival to single-family homes. Lots in 19th-century Toronto were oddly long and narrow (20 feet by 13 feet), and the Bay-and-Gable style, with its sharply peaked roofs, large bay windows (often filled with stained glass), and extensive decorative gabling managed to fit into these lots perfectly (most stand three storeys tall). There are excellent examples of Bay-and-Gable in **Cabbagetown** (see Walking Tour 4 on p. 175), as well as in the **Annex** and in **Little Italy.**

EARLY & MID-20TH CENTURY (1901–1970)

Toronto erected its first skyscraper in 1894—the Beard Building—but unfortunately it has been demolished. In the first decades of the 20th century, the city became less interested in looking back at the past and more intrigued by the future. When the decision was made to create a new city hall in the 1950s, Torontonians voted down a classically designed city hall in a general plebiscite, eventually favoring a modern building based on International Style (see below).

EARLY SKYSCRAPER The **Royal Bank Building** at the corner of King and Yonge streets was the tallest building in the British Commonwealth when it was completed in 1914. The **Royal York Hotel** (now called the Fairmont Royal York, p. 74) was even taller, but by the time it opened, there was more competition (it was the tallest building in Toronto from the year it opened, 1929, until 1931).

BEAUX ARTS Taking its name from the Ecole des Beaux-Arts in Paris, this style was an idealization of classical Greek and Roman architecture. These grand buildings featured sweeping staircases and archways, classical columns, and frequently classical decoration (including statues and friezes). Toronto's most beloved example of Beaux Arts style is **Union Station** (p. 171), which was built between 1914 and 1921, but not used as a rail station until 1927 because of a legal dispute.

INTERNATIONAL STYLE In the 1930s, this was modern architecture. These stark, rectangular buildings, which frequently were surfaced with glass, were influenced by Germany's Bauhaus School. They were simple in design (as least to the naked eye), unornamented, and seriously functional. The **Toronto-Dominion Bank Tower** at 66 Wellington Street West was designed by Mies van der Rohe, perhaps the most famous of the Bauhaus architects. Built in 1967, it is distinctive for its black steel structure and black-glazed glass. **New Toronto City Hall** (p. 144), built in 1965, is another fine example.

LATE 20TH CENTURY & BEYOND (1970–PRESENT)

Toronto architecture in the past 4 decades has veered from the Postmodern to the wildly eclectic. It's hard to group works together in a cohesive style, though they do share elements of whimsy and improbability. The glass-and-steel International Style left a lot of people cold eventually. In the 1970s, a postmodern approach, in which classical or historical references were incorporated into the design of a building, became popular.

Impressions

It's a beautiful city, and the waterfront area is fantastic. I haven't had time to visit the theater, but I find it remarkable that Toronto has the third-largest English-speaking theater district in the world, after New York and London. I once noticed a fellow sitting on a bench, then I realized it was a statue of Glenn Gould. It's very realistic.

—Donald Trump

There was a great deal of leeway in terms of the overall shape of a building, rather than using a simple rectangle. The **Toronto Reference Library** (p. 147) and the **Bata Shoe Museum** (p. 138), both designed by Toronto architect Raymond Moriyama, are two visually stunning counterpoints within walking distance of each other. The Bata is shaped like a shoebox, which seems appropriate given the museum's central theme. The **Royal Ontario Museum** (p. 134) and the **Art Gallery of Ontario** (p. 131) have engaged high-profile architects to reinvent their traditional spaces, with eye-popping results. The **Sharp Centre for Design** (p. 145), which opened in 2004, still shocks many visitors. Best described as a checkerboard on stilts, it was designed by the renowned Will Alsop and has won a major design award.

4 TORONTO IN POPULAR CULTURE

Though it hasn't always played itself in the movies (doubling often as other major cities instead), Toronto does have quite a literary legacy to call its own. It's the hometown of authors Margaret Atwood, Michael Ondaatje, and media theorist and writer Marshall McLuhan. McLuhan is famous for his maxim "The medium is the message," and his works include *Understanding Media: The Extensions of Man* and *War & Peace in the Global Village.* There's also a volume called *The Essential McLuhan* to consider if you're a fan.

Atwood's *The Robber Bride* pays homage to her hometown with a story that covers 3 decades of life in the city. Some of her other novels—such as *The Edible Woman, Cat's Eye,* and *The Blind Assassin*—also use Toronto as a backdrop. Her futuristic 2003 novel *Oryx and Crake* isn't set in any recognizable place, but it's such a brilliant read that it deserves a mention anyway. *In the Skin of a Lion,* by Michael Ondaatje, the celebrated author of *The English Patient,* is a moving love story that brings the city's landmarks to life. Carol Shields, who died in 2003, set her final novel, *Unless,* in Toronto's streets.

Another notable novel is *Cabbagetown,* by Hugh Garner, the story of the fight to survive in a Toronto slum in the 1930s. (Cabbagetown was famous as the largest Anglo-Saxon slum in North America.) Anyone who is partial to mysteries and thrillers should read Lawrence Block's *The Girl with the Long Green Heart,* in which two American con artists set up shop in Toronto to fleece a wealthy American in the 1960s.

For those more interested in possible futures than the past, there's an Afrofuturist/sci-fi novel called *Brown Girl in the Ring,* by Nalo Hopkinson. Some other books to consider: *Noise* and *How Insensitive,* by Russell Smith; *Headhunter,* by Timothy Findley; *Then Again* by Elyse Friedman; *Lost Girls,* by Andrew Pyper; and *The Origin of Waves,* by Austin Clarke.

Cabbagetown

"A few houses on almost every street were as verminous and tumbledown as any in the city, but next door or across the street was the same type of house, clean and in good repair, reflecting the decency or pride of the occupants, or reflecting the fact that the tenant was buying it. In 1929 most Cabbagetowners rented their homes, from the ingrained habit of generations or because they refused to tie themselves down to the district. This was a neighborhood almost without tenements, and the streets were lined with single-family houses, many of whose upper stories accommodated a second family.

The citizens of Cabbagetown believed in God, the Royal Family, the Conservative Party and private enterprise. They were suspicious and a little condescending towards all heathen religions, higher education, 'foreigners' and social reformers. They were generally unskilled working people, among whom were scattered, like raisins in a ten-cent cake, representatives of the State—such as postmen, civic employees, streetcar conductors and even a policeman or two."

—From *Cabbagetown* by Hugh Garner, 1950

Clarke has also written three novels that are collectively known as the Toronto Trilogy: *The Meeting Point* (1967), *Storm of Fortune* (1973), and *The Bigger Light* (1975). The literary legend Robertson Davies was working on the third novel in his own Toronto Trilogy when he died in 1995. The first two books, *Murther and Walking Spirits* and *The Cunning Man*, were published in 1991 and 1994, respectively.

If you're interested in architecture, an especially good read is *Emerald City: Toronto Revisited,* by John Bentley Mays. *Emerald City* explores all of Toronto's special places, from the majesty of Casa Loma to the colorful bedlam of Kensington Market. Speaking of craziness, another nonfiction book to check out is *In the Mad Water: Two Centuries of Adventure and Lunacy at Niagara Falls,* by T. W. Kriner. Finally, travel writer Jan Morris is always a delight to read, and her book *O Canada! Travels in an Unknown Country* is no exception.

5 EATING & DRINKING IN TORONTO

Dining out is nothing short of a passion in Toronto. It's not that residents are too lazy to cook, but we are spoiled by the embarrassment of edible riches in all parts of the city. The city is a restaurant-goer's nirvana for a wealth of reasons. For starters, there are more than 7,000 places to choose from. They represent cooking styles from any country or nationality you can name, making Toronto's culinary scene both eclectic and palate-teasing. Eating out is also remarkably affordable: While the most expensive restaurants have broken the C$50-an-entree mark, there are many, many reasonably priced options that offer inventive cooking and attentive service. (Keep in mind, too, that for many international visitors, even the most expensive Toronto restaurants aren't so pricey given the Canadian dollar's value compared to the pound or the euro.)

Toronto is a place where chefs can become stars. Perhaps the most internationally recognized name, Susur Lee, left Toronto for New York in 2008 (though he has promised to return to create a new restaurant—devoted foodies may want to check for updates on this). But there are so many star chefs in the Toronto firmament—Jamie Kennedy of the **Jamie Kennedy Wine Bar** (p. 111), Mark McEwan of **North 44** (p. 120), Marc Thuet of **Thuet,** Edward Levesque of **Edward Levesque's Restaurant** (p. 110), Greg Couillard of **Spice Room & Chutney Bar** (p. 113), Chris McDonald of **Cava** (p. 122)—that it's a tough challenge to figure out where to dine if you have only a long weekend in the city.

Generally, Mediterranean and Asian cuisines dominate the scene—and often appear on the same plate. Fusion cooking caught on big here and has never lost its steam. Many restaurants that started out as, say, Italian have incorporated ingredients and cooking styles from Southeast Asia and North Africa, among other regions. Each wave of immigration has carried new ideas and flavors to the city. Some of the newest restaurants, such as **Amuse-Bouche** (p. 102) are mixing powerful flavors in unexpected ways.

While restaurants of all descriptions are found across the city, certain neighborhoods are renowned for their specialties: Little Italy for its trattorias, Chinatown for its Chinese and Vietnamese eateries, and the Danforth for its Greek tavernas. King Street West has, in the past several years, unexpectedly become a magnet for gourmet restaurants, offering a bevy of bistros and boîtes. One thing that's particularly wonderful about Toronto's dining scene is that it's entirely possible to have a great meal at a bargain price. Restaurants such as **Torito Tapas Bar** (p. 109), and **Four** (p. 104), let you dine well without breaking the bank.

Icewine & Other Ontario Whites

Ontario vintners' greatest successes so far have been with white wines. Delicious, crisp, and complex, they're impossible to resist, whether we're talking about Riesling, Gewürztraminer, pinot gris, or chardonnay. You don't have to take my word for it: These wines are taking home gold medals at international competitions. The red wines aren't as consistent. There are some terrific cabernet sauvignons, pinot noirs, and cabernet francs from Ontario, but I have yet to encounter a local merlot I've liked.

The *coup de grâce* comes at dessert time, when you can try an Ontario icewine. Before you appreciate the final product, take a moment to consider what it takes to create it. It's a long shot that would test any gambler's nerves: Grapes are left on the vine through December and most or all of January, and then the ripe berries that weren't lost to hungry birds or wind damage are dehydrated by the one-two punch of freezing and thawing. The process concentrates the sugars and acids, giving icewine its great complexity. But the grapes can't be harvested until temperatures hit at least 17°F (–8°C)—which means they must be harvested in the middle of the night. Still, such risk can pay off in huge rewards, as it did for Inniskillin in 1991, when the Ontario winery won the Grand Prix d'Honneur for its 1989 Vidal icewine. Since then, other vintners—such as Hillebrand, Pillitteri, Magnotta, and Stoney Ridge—have produced award-winning icewines. To learn more about Ontario wine before your visit, check out the Ontario Wine Council at **www.winesofontario.org**.

Here's one more indulgence, if you have the time for a day trip. Just south and west of Toronto is the Niagara region, which is the best wine country in Canada. Follow its Wine Route to discover for yourself why local vintners such as Inniskillin, Henry of Pelham, and Pillitteri are winning international competitions. Niagara's wineries use imported European vines, and because the region lies on the same latitude as France's Burgundy region, this meeting of Old and New World results in bottles of Riesling, Sauvignon Blanc, Chardonnay, Pinot Noir, and Cabernet Sauvignon that are consistently excellent.

On second thought, even if you don't have the time for a day trip, you can try many of these wines at the local restaurants. Even those who don't normally save room for dessert won't be able to resist a small glass of Niagara icewine to polish off a perfect meal. Bon appetit.

3

Planning Your Trip to Toronto

Whether you're traveling on a whim or charting your course months in advance, some planning will help you make the most of your trip. This chapter will help you prepare for your trip to Toronto.

For additional assistance and on-the-ground resources in Toronto, please turn to the "Fast Facts, Toll-Free Numbers, & Websites," appendix on p. 256.

1 VISITOR INFORMATION

FROM NORTH AMERICA

The best source for Toronto-specific information is **Tourism Toronto** (© 800/499-2514 from North America, or 416/203-2600; www.seetorontonow.com). The new website includes sections on accommodations, sights, shopping, and dining, plus up-to-the-minute events information. There's also a "Special Offers" section, which has package deals for hotels and attractions or shows.

For information about traveling in the province of Ontario, contact **Tourism Ontario** (© 800/ONTARIO; www.ontario travel.net), or visit its information center in the **Atrium on Bay** (street level) at 20 Dundas St. W.—it's just across Dundas from the Sears store at the northern edge of the Eaton Centre. It's open daily from 8:30am to 5pm; hours are extended during the summer, often to 8pm.

Canadian consulates in the United States do not provide tourist information.

FROM ABROAD

The following consulates can provide information or refer you to the appropriate offices. Consult Tourism Toronto (see "From North America," above) for general information. For a list of Canadian consular offices around the world, visit **www. dfait-maeci.gc.ca/world/embassies/ cra-en.asp**.

U.K. and Ireland: The **Canadian High Commission,** MacDonald House, 1 Grosvenor Sq., London W1X 0AB (© 0207/258-6600; fax 0207/258-6333).

Australia: The **Canadian High Commission,** Commonwealth Avenue, Canberra, ACT 2600 (© 02/6273-3844), or the **Consulate General of Canada,** Level 5, Quay West, 111 Harrington St., Sydney, NSW 2000 (© 02/9364-3000). The consulate general also has offices in Melbourne and Perth.

New Zealand: The **Canadian High Commission,** 61 Molesworth St., third floor, Thorndon, Wellington (© 04/473-9577).

South Africa: The **Canadian High Commission,** 1103 Arcadia St., Hatfield 0083, Pretoria (© 012/422-3000). The commission also has offices in Cape Town and Johannesburg.

TORONTO PRINT & ONLINE MEDIA

Toronto has four daily newspapers: the *Globe and Mail* (www.globeandmail.com), the *National Post* (www.nationalpost. com), the *Toronto Star* (www.thestar.com), and the *Toronto Sun* (www.torontosun.

com). All have local listings, but the best are in the *Star,* which lists events, concerts, theater performances, and first-run films.

Even better bets are the free weeklies *Now* (www.nowtoronto.com) and *Eye* (www.eyeweekly.com), both published on Thursday and available in news boxes and at cafes and shops around town. *Xtra!* (www.xtra.ca) is another biweekly freebie; it lists events, seminars, and performances, particularly those of interest to the gay and lesbian community. A free annual directory called *The Pink Pages* targets Torontonians, but out-of-towners will find the information about gay- and lesbian-friendly restaurants, bars, and other businesses quite useful. It's available at shops, restaurants, and bars along Church Street.

Where Toronto (www.where.ca/toronto) is a glossy monthly magazine that lists events, attractions, restaurants, and shops; it's available free at most hotels in the city and at some restaurants in the Theater District. *Toronto Life* (www.torontolife.com) is an award-winning lifestyle magazine that has excellent listings of kids' events, theater,

speeches, and art exhibitions; the April issue contains a dining guide. *Fashion* magazine (formerly *Toronto Life Fashion*) will be of interest to serious shoppers.

Toronto.com (www.toronto.com), operated by the *Toronto Star,* offers extensive restaurant reviews, events listings, and feature articles. A couple of other great sources for local goings-on and news: the **Torontoist** blog (www.torontoist.com) and **blogTO** (www.blogto.com). If you love to shop, check out **SweetSpot** (www.sweetspot.ca) for its extensive Toronto coverage of local designers and boutiques. The **Gridskipper** blog (www.gridskipper.com) covers some Toronto news, too.

BlogTO produces some of my favorite local maps: You can pick them up for free at shops and restaurants around town. At press time, they have produced maps for West Queen West, Leslieville, Parkdale, and Little Italy. *Where Toronto* also prints good neighborhood maps in the magazine. Online, take a look at **Maporama** (www.maporama.com) for details on getting from point A to B.

2 ENTRY REQUIREMENTS

PASSPORTS

For citizens of many countries, only a passport is required to visit Canada for up to 90 days; no visas or proof of vaccinations are necessary. This is true for citizens of Andorra, Antigua and Barbuda, Australia, Austria, Bahamas, Belgium, Botswana, Brunei, Czech Republic, Denmark, Estonia, Finland, France, Germany, Iceland, Ireland, Israel, Italy, Japan, Korea, Lithuania, Liechtenstein, Luxembourg, Malta, Mexico, Monaco, Namibia, the Netherlands, New Zealand, Norway, Papua New Guinea, Poland, Portugal, St. Kitts and Nevis, St. Lucia, St. Vincent, San Marino, Singapore, Slovakia, Slovenia, Solomon Islands, Spain, Swaziland, Sweden, Switzerland, the United Kingdom, and the United

States. For the most up-to-date list of visitor visa exemptions, visit Citizenship and Immigration Canada at www.cic.gc.ca.

What's new is that all U.S. travelers need to bring a passport, even if you're just driving over the border for a day trip to Toronto. For information on how to obtain a passport, go to "Passports" in the "Fast Facts" appendix (p. 260).

VISAS

In addition to the list of countries above, no visas are required to enter Canada for people who have permanent resident status in the U.S., provided that they are in possession of their alien registration card ("Green Card"). For information about obtaining a visa to visit Canada, visit Citizenship and Immigration Canada at www.cic.gc.ca.

Cut to the Front of the Airport Security Line as a Registered Traveler

In 2003, the **Transportation Security Administration** (**TSA;** www.tsa.gov) approved a pilot program to help ease the time spent in line for airport security screenings. In exchange for information and a fee, persons can be pre-screened as registered travelers, granting them a front-of-the-line position when they fly. The program is run through private firms—the largest and most well-known is Steven Brill's **Clear** (www.flyclear.com), and it works like this: travelers complete an online application providing specific points of personal information including name, addresses for the previous 5 years, birth date, social security number, driver's license number, and a valid credit card (you're not charged the **$99 fee** until your application is approved). Print out the completed form and take it, along with proper ID, to an "enrollment station" (this can be found in over 20 participating airports and in a growing number of American Express offices around the country, for example). It's at this point where it gets seemingly sci-fi. At the enrollment station, a Clear representative will record your biometrics necessary for clearance; in this case, your fingerprints and your irises will be digitally recorded.

Once your application has been screened against no-fly lists, outstanding warrants, and other security measures, you'll be issued a clear plastic card that holds a chip containing your information. Each time you fly through participating airports (and the numbers are steadily growing), go to the Clear Pass station located next to the standard TSA screening line. Here you'll insert your card into a slot and place your finger on a scanner to read your print—when the information matches up, you're cleared to cut to the front of the security line. You'll still have to follow all the procedures of the day like removing your shoes and walking through the x-ray machine, but Clear promises to cut 30 minutes off your wait time at the airport.

On a personal note: Each time I've used my Clear Pass, my travel companions are still waiting to go through security while I'm already sitting down, reading the paper and sipping my overpriced smoothie. Granted, registered traveler programs are not for the infrequent traveler, but for those of us who fly on a regular basis, it's a perk I'm willing to pay for.

—David A. Lytle, Frommers.com

MEDICAL REQUIREMENTS

Unless you're arriving from an area known to be suffering from an epidemic (particularly cholera or yellow fever), inoculations or vaccinations are not required for entry into Canada.

CUSTOMS
What You Can Bring into Canada

Generally speaking, Canadian Customs regulations are generous, but they get complicated when it comes to firearms, plants, meat, and pets. Visitors can bring rifles into Canada during hunting season;

handguns and automatic rifles are not permitted. Fishing tackle poses no problem (provided the lures are not made of restricted materials—specific feathers, for example), but the bearer must possess a nonresident license for the province or territory where he or she plans to use it. You can bring in free of duty up to 50 cigars, 200 cigarettes, and 200 grams of tobacco, provided you're at least 18 years of age. You are also allowed 40 ounces (1.14 liters) of liquor or 1.5 liters of wine as long as you're of age in the province you're visiting (19 in Ontario). There are no restrictions on what you can take out (but if you're thinking of bringing Cuban cigars back to the United States, beware—they can be confiscated, and you could face a fine). In terms of pets, visitors from the U.S., the U.K., Ireland, Australia, and New Zealand can bring a cat or dog without quarantine. For more information (and for updates on these policies), check with the **Canada Border Services Agency** (© **204/983-500** or 506/636-5064; www.cbsa.gc.ca).

What You Can Take Home from Canada

U.S. Citizens: For specifics on what you can bring back and the corresponding fees,

download the invaluable free pamphlet *Know Before You Go* online at **www.cbp. gov.** (Click on "Travel," and then click on "Know Before You Go.") Or contact the **U.S. Customs & Border Protection (CBP),** 1300 Pennsylvania Ave. NW, Washington, DC 20229 (© **877/287-8667**) and request the pamphlet.

U.K. Citizens: For information, contact **HM Customs & Excise** at © **0845/ 010-9000** (from outside the U.K., 020/ 8929-0152), or consult their website at **www.hmce.gov.uk.**

Australian Citizens: A helpful brochure available from Australian consulates or Customs offices is *Know Before You Go.* For more information, call the **Australian Customs Service** at © **1300/363-263,** or log on to **www.customs.gov.au.**

New Zealand Citizens: Most questions are answered in a free pamphlet available at New Zealand consulates and Customs offices: *New Zealand Customs Guide for Travellers, Notice no. 4.* For more information, contact **New Zealand Customs,** The Customhouse, 17–21 Whitmore St., Box 2218, Wellington (© **04/473-6099** or 0800/ 428-786; **www.customs.govt.nz**).

---

3 WHEN TO GO

THE CLIMATE

Toronto is truly sublime in the fall. It's my favorite time of year for a number of reasons: The climate is brisk but temperate, the skies are sunny, the city parks are a riot of color, and the cultural scene is in full swing. Another great time to see the city—if you don't mind a dusting of snow—is December, with its holiday festivities. I can also make strong arguments for visiting in spring or summer, when the city's many gardens are blooming and the calendar is full of festivals. However, I feel it's my duty to warn you away in January: The temperature can be unbearably cold, and there's less to do.

Never mind what the calendar says; these are Toronto's true seasons: **Spring** runs from late March to mid-May (though occasionally there's snow in mid-Apr); **summer,** mid-May to mid-September; **fall,** mid-September to mid-November; and **winter,** mid-November to late March. The highest recorded temperature is 105°F (41°C); the lowest, –27°F (–33°C). The average date of first frost is October 29; the average date of last frost is April 20. The windblasts from Lake Ontario can be fierce, even in June. Bring a light jacket or cardigan.

(Tips) Don't Forget the Sunscreen

Because of Canada's image of a land of harsh winters, many travelers don't realize that summer can be scorching. "The UV index goes quite high, between 7 and 10, in Toronto," says Dr. Patricia Agin of the Coppertone Solar Research Center in Memphis. A UV index reading of 7 can mean sunburn, so don't forget to pack your sunscreen and a hat, especially if you're planning to enjoy Toronto's many parks and outdoor attractions.

Toronto's Average Temperatures °F (°C)

	Jan	Feb	Mar	Apr	May	June	July	Aug	Sept	Oct	Nov	Dec
High	30 (1)	31 (1)	39 (4)	53 (12)	64 (18)	75 (24)	80 (27)	79 (26)	71 (22)	59 (15)	46 (8)	34 (1)
Low	18 (8)	19 (7)	27 (3)	38 (3)	48 (9)	57 (14)	62 (17)	61 (16)	54 (12)	45 (7)	35 (2)	23 (5)

HOLIDAYS

Toronto celebrates the following holidays: New Year's Day (Jan 1), Good Friday and Easter Monday (Mar or Apr), Victoria Day (Mon following the third weekend in May), Canada Day (July 1), Simcoe Day (first Mon in Aug), Labour Day (first Mon in Sept), Thanksgiving (second Mon in Oct), Remembrance Day (Nov 11), Christmas Day (Dec 25), and Boxing Day (Dec 26).

On Good Friday and Easter Monday, schools and government offices close; most corporations close on one or the other, and a few close on both. Only banks and government offices close on Remembrance Day (Nov 11).

CALENDAR OF EVENTS

January, February, March, and April are dominated by trade shows, such as the International Boat and Automobile shows, Metro Home Show, Outdoor Adventure Sport Show, and more. For information, call **Tourism Toronto** (© 800/499-2514 or 416/203-2600; www.torontotourism.com).

For an exhaustive list of events beyond those listed here, check http://events.frommers.com, where you'll find a searchable, up-to-the-minute roster of what's happening in cities all over the world.

JANUARY

Chinese New Year Celebrations, downtown. 2009 is the Year of the Ox. Festivities include traditional and contemporary performances of Chinese opera, dancing, music, and more. For **Harbourfront** celebration information, call © **416/973-4000** or visit www.

harbourfrontcentre.com; for the **Rogers Centre,** call © **877/666-3838** or check **www.rogerscentre.com**. The New Year starts on January 26.

Toronto WinterCity Festival, citywide. Formerly known as WinterFest, this 2-week celebration blankets the city with fun, mostly outdoor, events. It features ice-skating shows, snow play, performances, art shows, and more. For information, visit **www.toronto.ca**. Late January through early February.

Winterlicious, citywide. Baby, it's cold outside, but Toronto's restaurants really know how to heat things up. Roughly 130 of the city's finest eateries offer prix-fixe lunch menus for C$20 (£10) and dinner menus for C$35 (£17.50). See **www.toronto.ca/special_events** for a complete listing. Late January through early February.

FEBRUARY

International Readings at Harbourfront, Harbourfront. This weekly series invites authors from around the globe to read from their most recent works. Participants have included David Sedaris, Pico Iyer, and Jhumpa Lahiri. For information, call Harbourfront at ℂ **416/973-4000** or go to **www.readings.org**. February through June.

ALOUD: A Celebration for Young Readers, Harbourfront. A 3-day literary fun fest for kids. For information, call Harbourfront at ℂ **416/973-4000** or go to **www.readings.org**. Mid-February.

MARCH

Canada Blooms, Metro Toronto Convention Centre. At this time of year, any glimpse of greenery is welcome. Canada Blooms treats visitors to 2.5 hectares (6 acres) of indoor garden and flower displays, seminars with green-thumb experts, and competitions. For information, call ℂ **416/593-0223** or visit **www.canadablooms.com**. Second or third week of March.

St. Patrick's Day Parade, downtown. Toronto's own version of the classic Irish celebration. For information, call ℂ **416/487-1566.** March 17.

One-of-a-Kind Craft Show & Sale, Exhibition Place. More than 400 crafts artists from across Canada display their unique wares at this 4-day show. For information, visit **www.oneofakindshow.com**. Late March.

Toronto Festival of Storytelling, Harbourfront. Now in its 31st year, this event celebrates international folklore, with storytellers imparting legends and fables from around the world. For information, call ℂ **416/973-4000** or check **www.torontofestivalofstorytelling.ca**. Late March to early April.

APRIL

Santé: Toronto International Wine Festival, Yorkville. Newly renamed and expanded, Santé now celebrates international wines as well as Ontario vintages. For information, call ℂ **416/928-3553.** Events scattered through month of April.

Blue Jays Season Opener, Rogers Centre. Turn out to root for your home-away-from-home team. For tickets, call ℂ **888-OK-GO-JAY** or 416/341-1234, or visit **http://toronto.bluejays.mlb.com**. Mid-April.

The Shaw Festival, Niagara-on-the-Lake, Ontario. This festival presents the plays of George Bernard Shaw and his contemporaries, as well as modern works. Call ℂ **800/511-7429** or 905/468-2172, or visit **www.shawfest.com**. Mid-April through first weekend of November.

Sprockets Toronto International Film Festival for Children, citywide. 2009 marks the 12th anniversary of this movie event, which screens more than 100 movies from 29 countries. Call ℂ **416/968-FILM,** or visit **http://sprockets.ca** for details. Mid-April.

Total Health Show, Metro Convention Centre. Founded in 1975, this 3-day event organizes panels and events with medical professionals, authors, alternative practitioners, organic farmers, and local chefs to talk about public and personal health issues. For information, call ℂ **416/924-9800** or visit **www.totalhealthshow.com**. Mid-April.

MAY

CONTACT Toronto Photography Festival, citywide. This annual month-long event shows the work of more than 500 Canadian and international photographers. For information, call ℂ **416/539-9595** or visit **www.contactphoto.com**. May 1 to 31.

The Stratford Festival, Stratford, Ontario. Featuring a wide range of contemporary and classic plays, this festival always includes several works by Shakespeare. Call ✆ **800/567-1600** or check out **www.stratfordfestival.ca**. Early May through mid-November.

Doors Open Toronto, citywide. This weekend event invites city residents and visitors alike to tour some of Toronto's architectural marvels. Some of the more than 150 participating buildings aren't normally open to the public, and all are free of charge. Visit **www.toronto.ca/doorsopen**. Late May.

Inside Out Lesbian and Gay Film Festival, citywide. Toronto has no shortage of film festivals, but Inside Out, now in its 19th year, is unique. This 11-day event has nurtured plenty of new talent and supported many established artists. Call ✆ **416/977-6847** or check out **www.insideout.on.ca**. Late May.

JUNE

Luminato, citywide. First launched in 2007, this 9-day festival of "arts + creativity" has quickly become a highlight of the city's calendar. Featuring music, dance, theater, art, and educational programs, it really does offer something for the whole family. For information, visit **www.luminato.com**. Early to mid June.

North by Northeast Festival, citywide. Known in the music biz as NXNE, the 3-day event features rock and indie bands at 28 venues. For information, visit **www.nxne.com**. Mid-June.

Waterfront Blues, Woodbine Park in the Beaches. This used to be the Distillery District's blues fest. Toronto shows that it's got soul in this 3-day festival of Canada's best blues musicians. The event is free; no tickets are required. For information, visit **www.distilleryblues. com**. First or second weekend in June.

Canada Dry Festival of Fire, Ontario Place. Formerly known as the Symphony of Fire, this fireworks extravaganza lights up Toronto's waterfront, with the pyrotechnics synchronized to music. For information, call ✆ **416/314-9900**. Or visit www.ontarioplace. com. Late June-early July.

Taste of Little Italy, College Street between Euclid and Shaw streets. Restaurants, craftspeople, musicians, and other performers put on displays during this 3-day festival for the entire family. For information, visit **www.tasteoflittle italy.ca**. Mid-June.

Telus Toronto International Dragon Boat Festival, Centre Island. More than 160 teams of dragon-boaters compete in the 2-day event, which commemorates the death of the Chinese philosopher and poet Qu Yuan. For information, visit **www.dragonboats. com**. Third weekend in June.

Pride Week & Pride Parade, citywide. Celebrating Toronto's gay and lesbian community, Pride Week features events, performances, symposiums, and parties. It culminates in an extravagant Sunday parade, one of the biggest in North America. For information, call ✆ **416/92-PRIDE** or 416/927-7433, or visit **www.pridetoronto.com**. Late June.

TD Canada Trust Toronto Jazz Festival, citywide. This 10-day festival showcases international artists playing every jazz style—blues, gospel, Latin, African, traditional—at 49 venues. For information, call ✆ **416/928-2033** or check out **www.tojazz.com**. Late June.

JULY

Canada Day Celebrations, citywide. July 1, 2009, marks the nation's 142nd birthday. Street parties, fireworks, and other special events commemorate the day. For information, contact **Tourism**

Toronto (© 800/363-1990 or 416/203-2600; www.torontotourism.com). Weekend of July 1.

Summerlicious, citywide. It's just like January's Winterlicious event, except that you can dine alfresco. The prix-fixe menus (C$20/£10 lunch; C$35/£17.50 dinner) are the best deal around. See **www.toronto.ca/special_events** for a complete list. First two weeks of July.

The Fringe—Toronto's Theatre Festival, citywide. More than 90 troupes participate in this 10-day festival of contemporary and experimental theater. Shows last no more than an hour. For information, call © **416/966-1062** or visit **www.fringetoronto.com**. First week of July.

Grand Prix of Toronto, the Exhibition Place Street circuit. Unexpectedly suspended in 2008, the Grand Prix is expected to return in 2009. Still known by its original name, the Molson Indy, this is one of Canada's major races on the IndyCar circuit. Away from the track, you'll find live music and beer gardens. For information, call © **416/922-7477** or visit **www.grandprix toronto.com**. Third weekend in July.

RBC Canadian Open, Glen Abbey Golf Club, Oakville. Formerly called the PGA Tour Canadian Open, Canada's national golf tournament has featured the likes of Greg Norman and Tiger Woods in recent years. Visit **www. rbccanadianopen.com** for more information. Mid- to late July.

Beaches International Jazz Festival, Queen Street East between Woodbine and Beech avenues. Both local and international jazz artists turn out for this annual festival, which plays out over 9 days. All of the performances are free. For information, visit **www. beachesjazz.com**. Late July.

Caribana, citywide. Toronto's version of Carnival transforms the city. It's complete with traditional foods from the Caribbean and Latin America, ferry cruises, picnics, children's events, concerts, and arts-and-crafts exhibits. Visit **www.caribana.com**. Late July through early August.

AUGUST

Beerlicious, Fort York. More than 70 major Ontario breweries and microbreweries turn out for this celebration of suds. There's also a wide selection of food from local restaurants, as well as live blues, swing, and jazz music. *Take note:* Fort York is normally a great spot for kids, but no one under 19 is allowed at this event. For info, call © **416/698-7206** or visit **www.beerfestival.ca**. First weekend in August.

Canadian National Exhibition, Exhibition Place. One of the world's largest exhibitions, this 18-day extravaganza features midway rides, display buildings, free shows, and grandstand performers. The 3-day Canadian International Air Show (first staged in 1878) is a bonus. Call © **416/393-6300** for information, or visit **www.theex.com**. Mid-August through Labour Day.

Rogers Cup, Rexall Centre at York University. This international tennis championship is an important stop on the pro tennis tour. In 2009, the men play in Montréal and the women in Toronto. In 2010, they'll swap. For information, call © **877/283-6647** or visit **www.tenniscanada.com**. Mid- to late August.

SEPTEMBER

Toronto International Film Festival, citywide. The stars come out for the second-largest film festival in the world. More than 250 films from 70 countries are shown over 10 days. For information, call © **416/968-FILM** or log on to **www.torontointernationalfilm festival.ca**. Early September.

Word on the Street, Queen's Park. This open-air event celebrates the written word with readings, discounted books and magazines, and children's events. Other major Canadian cities hold similar events on the same weekend. For information, call ✆ **416/504-7241** or visit **www.thewordonthestreet.ca**. Last weekend in September.

Muskoka Autumn Studio Tour, Muskoka region, Ontario. This 2-day arts festival invites travelers to visit the studios of local artists and craftspeople. For information, check out **www. muskoka.com/tour**. Late September.

The Clothing Show, Exhibition Place. More than 300 booths, featuring everything from indie design to vintage couture, all under one roof. For information, call ✆ **416/516-9859** or visit www.theclothingshow.com. Last weekend of September.

OCTOBER

Oktoberfest, Kitchener–Waterloo, about 1 hour from Toronto. This famed 9-day drinkfest features cultural events, plus a pageant and parade. For information, call ✆ **888/294-4267** or 519/570-4267 or visit **www.oktoberfest.ca**. Mid-October.

International Festival of Authors, Harbourfront. Founded in 1980, this renowned 10-day literary festival is the most prestigious in Canada. It draws more than 100 authors from 25 countries to perform readings and on-stage interviews. Among the literary luminaries who have appeared are Salman Rushdie, Margaret Drabble, Thomas Kenneally, Joyce Carol Oates, A. S. Byatt, and Margaret Atwood. For information, call Harbourfront at ✆ **416/973-4000** or visit **www.readings.org**. October 21 to 31, 2009.

Toronto Maple Leafs Opening Night, Air Canada Centre. Torontonians love their hockey team, and opening night is always a big event. For tickets, call

✆ **416/872-5000** or visit **http:// mapleleafs.nhl.com**. October.

NOVEMBER

Royal Agricultural Winter Fair and Royal Horse Show, Exhibition Place. The 12-day show is the largest indoor agricultural and equestrian competition in the world. Displays include vegetables and fruits, crafts, farm machinery, livestock, and more. A member of the British royal family traditionally attends the horse show. Call ✆ **416/263-3400,** or check **www.royalfair.org** for information. Mid-November.

Santa Claus Parade, downtown. A favorite with kids since 1905, it features marching bands, floats, clowns, and jolly St. Nick. American visitors are usually surprised that the parade's in November, but it's better than watching Santa try to slide through slush. For information, contact **Tourism Toronto** (✆ **800/363-1990** or 416/203-2600; or visit www.thesantaclausparade.com). Third Sunday of November.

Cavalcade of Lights, Nathan Phillips Square. During this holiday celebration, lights decorate trees in and around Nathan Phillips Square, parties and performances take over the skating rink, and ice sculptures decorate the square. There are also Saturday-night fireworks. Visit **www.toronto.ca** for more information. Late November through late December.

Canadian Aboriginal Festival, Rogers Centre. More than 1,500 Native American dancers, drummers, and singers attend this weekend celebration. There are literary readings, an arts-and-crafts market, lacrosse-playing, and traditional foods. Call ✆ **519/751-0040,** or visit **www.canab.com**. Last weekend in November.

DECEMBER

First Night Toronto and New Year's Eve at City Hall. First Night is an

> **(Moments) Jump Up!**
>
> One of the undisputed highlights of summer in Toronto is the annual Caribana festival. Created in 1967 as a community heritage celebration to tie in with Canada's centennial, Caribana has become North America's largest street festival, drawing more than a million visitors from North America, Britain, and the Caribbean each year. Originally based on Trinidad's Carnival, the festival now draws on numerous cultures—Jamaican, Guyanese, Brazilian, and Bahamian, to name a few—for its music, food, and events.
>
> During the 2 weeks that it runs, you will see the influence of Caribana around the city. It starts with a bang (literally, as there are steel drums involved) at Nathan Phillips Square in front of Toronto city hall, with a free concert that features calypso, salsa, and soca music. In the days that follow, there are boat cruises, dances, and concerts; the King and Queen Extravaganza, which showcases some of the most amazing costumes you could hope to see; and an arts festival. The highlight is the Caribana Parade, which brings together masquerade and steel-drum bands, dancers, and floats in a memorable feast for all the senses. This is one party you just can't miss.

alcohol-free family New Year's Eve celebration. There are a variety of musical, theatrical, and dance performances at downtown venues. In Nathan Phillips Square and in Mel Lastman Square in North York, concerts begin at around 10pm to usher in the countdown to the New Year. Visit **www.toronto.ca** for more information. December 31.

4 GETTING THERE & GETTING AROUND

GETTING TO TORONTO
By Plane

FROM THE U.S. Canada's only national airline, **Air Canada** (✆ 888/247-2262; www.aircanada.ca), operates direct flights to Toronto from most major American cities and many smaller ones. It also flies from major cities around the world and operates connecting flights from other U.S. cities.

One new option is **Porter Airlines** (✆ 888/619-8622 or 416/619-8622; www.flyporter.com), which flies to Toronto's Island Airport from New York City, Halifax, Montréal, Québec City, and Ottawa. At press time, Porter's only U.S. flights were from the Big Apple, but the company plans to expand into other U.S. cities.

One more Canadian-based option is **WestJet** (✆ 888/WEST-JET; www.westjet. com), which has service between Toronto and San Francisco, Los Angeles, and Phoenix. It flies out of Terminal 3 at Pearson.

Among U.S. airlines, **American, United, US Airways, Northwest,** and **Delta** all fly to Toronto's Pearson International Airport. For the airlines' toll-free numbers, see p. 262.

FROM ABROAD There's frequent service (direct and indirect) to Toronto from around the world.

Several airlines operate from the United Kingdom. **British Airways** and **Air Canada** fly direct from London's Heathrow airport. Air Canada also flies direct from Glasgow and Manchester. In 2007, **flyglobespan** (© 08712/710-415; www.flyglobespan.com) began service to Hamilton, Ontario, a city that is a 45-minute drive from Toronto. Hamilton is now connected to 13 U.K. destinations.

In Australia, **Air Canada** has an agreement with **Qantas** and flies from Sydney to Toronto, stopping in Honolulu. From New Zealand, **Air Canada** cooperates with **Air New Zealand,** scheduling on average three flights a week from Auckland to Toronto via Honolulu, Fiji, or both.

From Cape Town, South Africa, **Delta** operates via New York; **Air Canada** via Frankfurt; and **South African Airways,** via Miami or New York. Several airlines fly from Johannesburg, including **British Airways** via Heathrow and **South African Airways** via Miami or New York.

Most flights arrive at **Pearson International Airport,** in the northwest corner of metro Toronto, approximately 30 minutes from downtown. The trip usually takes 10 to 15 minutes longer during the weekday morning rush (7–9am) and evening rush (4–7pm). A few (mostly commuter) flights land at the **Toronto Island Airport,** a short ferry ride from downtown.

Pearson serves more than 50 airlines. In 2004, its long-awaited new terminal, officially named **Terminal 1,** opened to international traffic; however, it didn't open to U.S. flights until 2007. The other passenger terminal is the **Trillium Terminal 3.** Both terminals are airy and modern, with moving walkways, huge food courts, and many retail stores. For general airport information, including the Lost & Found department, call the **Greater Toronto Airport Authority** at © 416/776-3000 (www.gtaa.com).

Arriving at the Airport

Pearson International Airport is the busiest in Canada, and its terminals are massive (particularly Terminal 1). Expect a long walk to the Immigration and Customs area, which you will have to clear in Toronto even if you're flying on to another Canadian destination. (There are maps of both terminals online at www.gtaa.com). There are tourism information booths at both terminals.

Getting into Town from the Airport

To get from the airport to downtown, take Highway 427 south to the Gardiner Expressway East. A **taxi** costs about C$50 (£25). A slightly sleeker way to go is by flat-rate **limousine,** which starts at C$50 (£25). Note that at press time, taxi fares within Toronto jumped because of fuel prices; however the fare from the airport hasn't changed—yet. Two reliable limo services are **Aaroport** (© 416/745-1555) and **Air-Line** (© 905/676-3210). You don't need a reservation. Most first-class hotels run their own **hotel limousine** services; check when you make your reservation.

The convenient **Airport Express bus** (© 905/564-6333 or www.torontoairportexpress.com) travels between the airport, the bus terminal, and major downtown hotels—the Westin Harbour Castle, Fairmont Royal York, The Sheraton Centre Toronto, and the Delta Chelsea—every 20 to 30 minutes, from 4:55am to 12:55am. The fare is C$18.50 (£9.25) one-way, C$30 (£15) round-trip.

The cheapest way to go is by **bus and subway,** which takes about an hour. During the day, you have three options: the no. 192 "Airport Rocket" bus to Kipling station, the no. 58A bus to Lawrence West station, or the no. 307 bus to Eglinton West station. In the middle of the night, you can take the no. 300A bus to Yonge and Bloor. The fare of C$2.75 (£1.35) includes free transfer to the subway (which is available till 1:30am). All buses make stops at both terminals 1 and 3. It doesn't matter which bus you use; they all take roughly the same amount of time. (The Airport Rocket reaches the subway fastest,

(Tips) Getting Through the Airport

- Arrive at Pearson International Airport at least 60 minutes before a domestic flight, 90 minutes before a flight to the U.S., and 120 minutes before an international flight (some international airlines require passengers to arrive 3 hours in advance; check with your airline about its policies). You can check the average wait times at your airport by going to the TSA **Security Checkpoint Wait Times** site (http://waittime.tsa.dhs.gov).
- Know what you can carry on and what you can't. For the latest updates on items you are prohibited to bring in carryon luggage, go to **www.tsa. gov/travelers/airtravel**.
- Unlike the U.S., where you must use a TSA-approved lock for your checked luggage or else leave it unlocked, you can lock your luggage when flying in Canada.
- Beat the ticket-counter lines by using the self-service electronic ticket kiosks at the airport or even printing out your boarding pass at home from the airline website. Using curbside check-in is also a smart way to avoid lines.
- Help speed up security before you're screened. Remove jackets, shoes, belt buckles, heavy jewelry, and watches and place them either in your carry-on luggage or the security bins provided. Place keys, coins, cellphones, and pagers in a security bin. If you have metallic body parts, carry a note from your doctor. When possible, keep packing liquids in checked baggage.

---

but the subway ride to downtown is twice as long as from the other stations.) For more information, call the **Toronto Transit Commission,** or TTC (© **416/393-4636;** www.toronto.ca/ttc).

Long-Haul Flights: How to Stay Comfortable

- Your choice of airline and airplane will definitely affect your leg room. Find more details about U.S. airlines at **www.seatguru.com**. For international airlines, the research firm Skytrax has posted a list of average seat pitches at **www.airlinequality.com**.
- Emergency exit seats and bulkhead seats typically have the most legroom. Emergency exit seats are usually left unassigned until the day of a flight (to ensure that someone able-bodied fills the seats); it's worth checking in online at home (if the airline offers that option)

or getting to the ticket counter early to snag one of these spots for a long flight. Many passengers find that bulkhead seating offers more legroom, but keep in mind that bulkhead seats have no storage space on the floor in front of you.

- To have two seats for yourself in a three-seat row, try for an aisle seat in a center section toward the back of coach. If you're traveling with a companion, book an aisle and a window seat. Middle seats are usually booked last, so chances are good you'll end up with three seats to yourselves. And in the event that a third passenger is assigned the middle seat, he or she will probably be more than happy to trade for a window or an aisle.
- To sleep, avoid the last row of any section or the row in front of an emergency

> ## (Tips) Don't Stow It—Ship It
>
> Though pricey, it's sometimes worthwhile to travel luggage-free, particularly if you're toting sports equipment, meetings materials, or baby equipment. Specialists in door-to-door luggage delivery include **SkyCap International** (www.sky capinternational.com) and **Sports Express** (www.sportsexpress.com).

exit, as these seats are the least likely to recline. Avoid seats near highly trafficked toilet areas. Avoid seats in the back of many jets—these can be narrower than those in the rest of coach. Or reserve a window seat so you can rest your head and avoid being bumped in the aisle.

- Get up, walk around, and stretch every 60 to 90 minutes to keep your blood flowing. This helps avoid **deep vein thrombosis,** or "economy-class syndrome." See the box "Avoiding 'Economy-Class Syndrome,'" p. 45.
- Drink water before, during, and after your flight to combat the lack of humidity in airplane cabins. Avoid alcohol, which will dehydrate you.

By Car

Crossing the border by car gives you a lot of options—the U.S. highway system leads directly into Canada at 13 points. If you're driving from Michigan, you'll enter at Detroit-Windsor (I-75 and the Ambassador Bridge) or Port Huron–Sarnia (I-94 and the Bluewater Bridge). If you're coming from New York, you have more options. On I-190, you can enter at Buffalo–Fort Erie; Niagara Falls, New York–Niagara Falls, Ontario; or Niagara Falls, New York–Lewiston. On I-81, you'll cross the Canadian border at Hill Island; on Route 37, you'll enter at either Ogdensburg-Johnstown or Rooseveltown-Cornwall.

From the United States you are most likely to enter Toronto from the west on Highway 401 or Highway 2 and the Queen Elizabeth Way. If you come from the east via Montréal, you'll also use 401 and 2.

Here are approximate driving distances to Toronto: from Boston, 911km (565 miles); Buffalo, 155km (96 miles); Chicago, 859km (533 miles); Cincinnati, 806km (500 miles); Detroit, 379km (235 miles); Minneapolis, 1,564km (970 miles); Montréal, 545km (338 miles); New York, 797km (494 miles); Ottawa, 453km (281 miles); and Québec City, 790km (491 miles).

Be sure you have your driver's license and car registration if you plan to drive your own vehicle into Canada. It isn't a bad idea to carry proof of automobile liability insurance, too.

If you are a member of the American Automobile Association (AAA), the **Canadian Automobile Association (CAA)** Central Ontario Branch in Toronto (© **416/ 221-4300;** www.caa.ca) provides emergency road service.

I don't recommend driving in Toronto, but if you're planning to make side trips outside of the city, you may wish to rent a car in Toronto or at Pearson International Airport. If you pay with credit card, you might get automatic coverage (check with your credit card issuer before you go). Be sure to read the fine print of the rental agreement—some companies add conditions that will boost your bill if you don't fulfill certain obligations, such as filling the gas tank before returning the car. For listings of the major car rental agencies in Toronto, please see "Car Rental Agencies" in the appendix (p. 264).

By Train

Amtrak's "Maple Leaf" service links New York City and Toronto via Albany, Buffalo, and Niagara Falls. It departs daily

(Tips) Coping with Jet Lag

Jetlag is a pitfall of traveling across time zones. If you're flying north–south and you feel sluggish when you touch down, your symptoms will be the result of dehydration and the general stress of air travel. When you travel east–west or vice-versa, your body becomes confused about what time it is, and everything from your digestive system to your brain is knocked for a loop. Traveling east is more difficult on your internal clock than traveling west because most peoples' bodies are more inclined to stay up late than to fall asleep early.

Here are some tips for combating jet lag:

- **Reset your watch** to your destination time before you board the plane.
- **Drink lots of water** before, during, and after your flight. Avoid alcohol.
- **Exercise and sleep well** for a few days before your trip.
- If you have trouble sleeping on planes, **fly eastward on morning flights.**
- **Daylight** is the key to resetting your body clock. At the website for **Outside In** (www.bodyclock.com), you can get a customized plan of when to seek and avoid light.

from Penn Station. The journey takes 12¹/₂ hours. Note that the lengthy schedule allows for extended stops at Customs and Immigration checkpoints at the border. Both trains arrive in Toronto at Union Station on Front Street, 1 block west of Yonge Street, opposite the Fairmont Royal York Hotel. The station has direct access to the subway. Call **Amtrak** at ⓒ **800/ USA-RAIL** or 800/872-7245, or visit **www. amtrak.com.**

By Bus

Greyhound (ⓒ **800/231-2222;** www. greyhound.com) is the best-known bus company that crosses the U.S. border. You can travel from almost anywhere in the United States. You'll arrive at the Metro Coach Terminal downtown at 610 Bay St., near the corner of Dundas Street. Another option is **Coach Canada** (**www.coach canada.com**), which travels to New York and Quebec.

The bus may be faster and cheaper than the train, and its routes may be more flexible if you want to stop along the way. Bear in mind that it's more cramped, toilet facilities are meager, and meals are taken at somewhat depressing rest stops.

Depending on where you are coming from, check into Greyhound's special unlimited-travel passes and discount fares. It's hard to provide sample fares because bus companies, like airlines, are adopting yield-management strategies, causing prices to change from day to day.

GETTING AROUND
By Public Transportation
The **Toronto Transit Commission,** or TTC (ⓒ **416/393-4636** for 24-hr. information; recordings available in 18 languages; www.toronto.ca/ttc), operates the subway, bus, streetcar, and light rapid transit (LRT) system.

Fares, including transfers to buses or streetcars, are C$2.75 (£1.38) or 10 tokens for C$22.50 (£11.25) for adults. Students, ages 13 to 19, with valid ID and seniors pay C$1.85 (93p), or 10 tickets for C$15 (£7.50); children 12 and under pay C70¢ (35p), or 10 tickets for C$5 (£2.50). You can buy a special day pass for C$9 (£4.50) that's good for unlimited travel for one person after 9:30am on weekdays and all day on weekends (there has been talk of removing the weekday rush-hour restriction, but that hasn't happened yet).

Flying with Film & Video

Never pack film—exposed or unexposed—in checked bags, because the new, more powerful scanners in U.S. airports can fog film. The film you carry with you can be damaged by scanners as well. X-ray damage is cumulative; the faster the film, and the more times you put it through a scanner, the more likely the damage. Film under 800 ASA is usually safe for up to five scans. If you're taking your film through additional scans, U.S. regulations permit you to demand hand inspections. In international airports, you're at the mercy of airport officials. On international flights, store your film in transparent baggies, so you can remove it easily before you go through scanners. Keep in mind that airports are not the only places where your camera may be scanned: High-traffic attractions are X-raying visitors' bags with increasing frequency.

Most photo supply stores sell protective pouches designed to block damaging X-rays. The pouches fit both film and loaded cameras. They should protect your film in checked baggage, but they also may raise alarms and result in a hand inspection.

You'll have little to worry about if you are traveling with **digital cameras.** Unlike film, which is sensitive to light, the digital camera and storage cards are not affected by airport X-rays, according to Nikon. Carry-on scanners will not damage **videotape** in video cameras, but the magnetic fields emitted by the walk-through security gateways and handheld inspection wands will. Always place your loaded camcorder on the screening conveyor belt or have it hand-inspected. Be sure your batteries are charged; you may be required to turn the device on to ensure that it's what it appears to be.

For surface transportation, you need a token, a ticket, or exact change. You can buy tokens and tickets at subway entrances and at authorized stores that display the sign TTC TICKETS MAY BE PURCHASED HERE. Bus drivers do not sell tickets, nor will they make change. Always obtain a free transfer where you board the train or bus, in case you need it. In the subways, use the push-button machine just inside the entrance. On streetcars and buses, ask the driver for a transfer.

THE SUBWAY It's fast (especially compared with snarled surface traffic), clean, and very simple to use. There are two major lines—Bloor–Danforth and Yonge–University–Spadina—and one smaller line, Sheppard, in the northern part of the city. The Bloor Street east–west line runs from Kipling Avenue in the west to Kennedy Road in the east (where it connects with Scarborough Rapid Transit to Scarborough Centre and McCowan Rd.). The Yonge Street north–south line runs from Finch Avenue in the north to Union Station (Front St.) in the south. From there, it loops north along University Avenue and connects with the Bloor line at the St. George station. A Spadina extension runs north from St. George to Downsview station at Sheppard Avenue. The Sheppard line connects only with the Yonge line at Sheppard Station and runs east through north Toronto for just 6km (3³/₄ miles).

The LRT system connects downtown to Harbourfront. The fare is one ticket or token. It runs from Union Station along Queens Quay to Spadina, with stops at

Queens Quay ferry docks, York Street, Simcoe Street, and Rees Street; then it continues up Spadina to the Spadina subway station. The transfer from the subway to the LRT (and vice versa) at Union Station is free.

The subway operates Monday to Saturday from 6am to 1:30am and Sunday from 9am to 1:30am. From 1am to 5:30am, the Blue Night Network operates on basic surface routes. It runs about every 30 minutes. For route information, pick up a "Ride Guide" at subway entrances or call © **416/393-4636.** Multilingual information is available.

BUSES & STREETCARS Where the subway leaves off, buses and streetcars take over. They run east–west and north–south along the city's arteries. When you pay your fare (on bus, streetcar, or subway), always pick up a transfer so that you won't have to pay again if you want to transfer to another mode of transportation.

TAXIS In many cities this is an expensive mode of transportation, but this is especially true of Toronto. In June 2008, rates were raised (again) because of the high cost of fuel. It's C$4 (£2) the minute you step in and 25 cents (13p) for each additional 155 meters. Fares can quickly mount up. You can hail a cab on the street, find one in line in front of a big hotel, or call one of the major companies—**Diamond** (© **416/366-6868**), **Royal** (© **416/777-9222**), or **Metro** (© **416/504-8294**). If you experience problems with cab service, call the **Metro Licensing Commission** (© **416/392-3082**).

FERRY SERVICE Toronto Parks and Recreation operates ferries that travel to the Toronto Islands. Call © **416/392-8193** for schedules and information. Round-trip fares are C$6.50 (£3.25) adults, C$4 (£2) seniors and children 15–19, C$3 (£1.50) children 3–14, free for children 2 and under.

By Car

Toronto is a rambling city, but that doesn't mean that a car is the best way to get around. Toronto has the dubious distinction of being recognized as the worst city in Canada in which to drive. It has gotten so bad that the government has started monitoring certain intersections with cameras, some especially designed to catch cars running red lights, which have been sarcastically dubbed "red-light districts."

Humor aside, driving can be a frustrating experience because of the high volume of traffic, drivers' disregard for red lights, and meager but pricey parking options. This is particularly true downtown, where traffic inches along and parking lots are scarce. I strongly recommend that you avoid driving in the city.

RENTAL CARS If you decide to rent a car, try to make arrangements in advance. Companies with outlets at Pearson International Airport include **Thrifty, Budget, Avis, Hertz, National,** and **Enterprise** (see "Fast Facts: Toronto," p. 256, for toll-free phone numbers.). The rental fee depends on the type of vehicle, but keep in mind that the quoted price does not including the 13% in sales taxes. It also does not include insurance; if you pay with a particular credit card, you might get automatic coverage (check with your credit card issuer before you go). Be sure to read the fine print of the rental agreement— some companies add conditions that will boost your bill if you don't fulfill certain obligations, like filling the gas tank before returning the car. *Note:* If you're under 25, check with the company—many will rent on a cash-only basis, some only with a credit card, and others will not rent to you at all.

Car-rental insurance probably does not cover liability if you cause an accident. Check your own auto insurance policy, the rental company policy, and your credit card coverage for the extent of coverage: Is your destination covered? Are other drivers

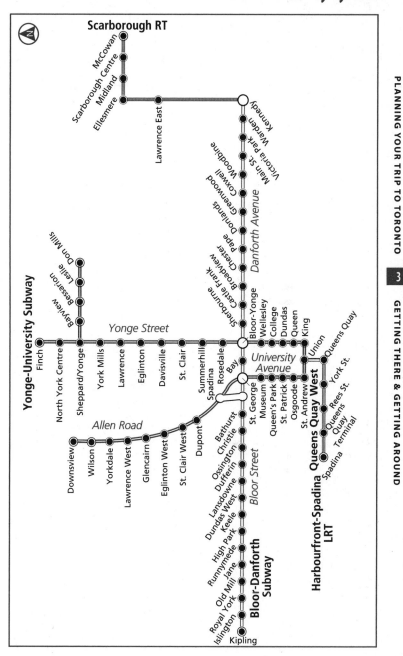

covered? How much liability is covered if a passenger is injured? (If you rely on your credit card for coverage, you may want to bring a second credit card with you, as damages may be charged to your card and you may find yourself stranded with no money.)

PARKING It's not fun finding parking in downtown Toronto, and parking lots have a wide range of fees. Generally speaking, the city-owned lots, marked with a big green "P," are the most affordable. They charge about C$2 (£1) per half-hour. After 6pm and on Sunday, there is usually a maximum rate of C$12 (£6). Observe the parking restrictions—otherwise, the city will tow your car away, and it'll cost more than C$100 (£50) to get it back.

DRIVING RULES A right turn at a red light is permitted after coming to a full stop, unless posted otherwise. The driver and front-seat passengers must wear seat belts; if you're caught not wearing one, you'll incur a substantial fine. The speed limit in the city is 50kmph (30 mph). You must stop at pedestrian crosswalks. If you are following a streetcar and it stops, you must stop well back from the rear doors so passengers can exit easily and safely. (Where there are concrete safety islands in the middle of the street for streetcar stops, this rule does not apply, but exercise care nonetheless.) Radar detectors are illegal.

5 MONEY & COSTS

Toronto is the most expensive city in Canada, but to visitors from places such as New York, London, and Tokyo, it will seem surprisingly affordable. However, the cost of taxis will raise New Yorkers' eyebrows, in part because the rates are higher and in part because Toronto is a sprawling city. Museum admission prices are another high-priced item; Londoners who are familiar with the free-admission policy at the British Museum may be shocked that it costs C$20 (£ 10) to get into the Royal Ontario Museum.

CURRENCY

Canadians use **dollars** and **cents:** Paper currency comes in C$5, C$10, C$20, C$50, and C$100 denominations. Coins come in 1-, 5-, 10-, and 25-cent, and 1- and 2-dollar denominations. The gold-colored C$1 coin is a "loonie"—it sports a loon on its "tails" side—and the large gold-and-silver-colored C$2 coin is a "toonie." If you find these names somewhat . . . ah, colorful, just remember that there's no swifter way to reveal that you're a tourist than to say "one-dollar coin."

Ideally, you should exchange enough petty cash to cover airport incidentals, tipping, and transportation to your hotel before you leave home; however, it's very easy to withdraw money upon arrival at an ATM at Pearson airport. Check with your local American Express or Thomas Cook office or with your bank. American Express cardholders can order foreign currency over the phone at ✆ **800/807-6233.**

It's best to exchange currency or traveler's checks at a bank, not a currency exchange, hotel, or shop. Get up-to-the-minute exchange rates online before you go at **www.xe.com/ucc**.

ATMS

The easiest and best way to get cash away from home is from an ATM (automated teller machine), sometimes referred to as a "cash machine," or a "cashpoint." The **Cirrus** (✆ **800/424-7787;** www.mastercard.com) and **PLUS** (✆ **800/843-7587;** www.visa.com) networks span the globe. Go to your bank card's website to find ATM locations at your destination. Be sure you know your daily withdrawal limit before

The Canadian Dollar & U.S. Dollar/U.K. Pound

In 2008, for the first time in over 30 years, the Canadian dollar and the U.S. dollar traded at parity. For that reason, we've eliminated listing the U.S. equivalents of Canadian prices in this guide. The prices cited are given in Canadian dollars (C$) and U.K. pounds sterling (£ or p for pence), with all amounts over C$10 rounded to the nearest dollar. In this guide, C$1 is equal to US$1/50p. The actual exchange rate will fluctuate by a few pennies.

Here's a table of equivalents:

C$	US$	UK£	US$	C$	UK£
1.00	1.00	0.50	1.00	1.00	0.50
5.00	5.00	2.50	5.00	5.00	2.50
10.00	10.00	5.00	10.00	10.00	5.00
20.00	20.00	10.00	20.00	20.00	10.00
50.00	50.00	25.00	50.00	50.00	25.00
80.00	80.00	40.00	80.00	80.00	40.00
100.00	100.00	50.00	100.00	100.00	50.00

you depart. *Note:* Many banks impose a fee every time you use a card at another bank's ATM, and that fee can be higher for international transactions than for domestic ones. In addition, the bank from which you withdraw cash may charge its own fee. For international withdrawal fees, ask your bank.

Note: Banks that are members of the **Global ATM Alliance** charge no transaction fees for cash withdrawals at other Alliance member ATMs; these include Bank of America, Scotiabank (Canada, Caribbean, and Mexico), Barclays (U.K. and parts of Africa), Deutsche Bank (Germany, Poland, Spain, and Italy), and BNP Paribas (France).

CREDIT CARDS

MasterCard and Visa are almost universally accepted in Toronto; American Express has become more common, but many independent boutiques and small restaurants still don't accept it. Overall, credit cards are a smart way to "carry" money. They also provide a convenient record of all your expenses, and they generally offer relatively good exchange rates.

You can withdraw cash advances from your credit cards at banks or ATMs, but high fees make credit card cash advances a pricey way to get cash. Keep in mind that you'll pay interest from the moment of your withdrawal, even if you pay your monthly bills on time. Also, note that many banks now assess a 1% to 3% "transaction fee" on *all* charges you incur abroad (whether you're using the local currency or your native currency).

TRAVELER'S CHECKS

Traveler's checks are something of an anachronism in Toronto, since ATMs have made getting cash accessible at any time. However, traveler's checks are still widely accepted—and unlike cash, can be replaced if lost or stolen.

You can buy traveler's checks at most banks. They are offered in denominations of $20, $50, $100, $500, and sometimes $1,000. Generally, you'll pay a service charge ranging from 1% to 4%.

The most popular traveler's checks are offered by **American Express** (© 800/ **807-6233** or © **800/221-7282** for card holders—this number accepts collect calls,

What Things Cost in Toronto	C$	UK£
Taxi from the airport to downtown	50.00	25.00
Subway/bus from the airport to downtown	2.75	1.38
Local telephone call	0.25	0.13
Double at the SoHo Metropolitan (very expensive)	310.00	155.00
Double at the Gladstone Hotel (moderate)	185.00	92.50
Double at Victoria University (inexpensive)	80.00	40.00
Three-course lunch for one at Le Sélect (moderate)*	35.00	17.50
Lunch combo for one at Asia Republik (inexpensive)*	5.95	2.99
Three tapas plates at Jamie Kennedy Wine Bar (moderate)*	23.00	11.50
Three-course dinner for one at North 44 (very expensive)*	220.00	110.00
Pint of beer at Mill Street Brew Pub	7.00	3.50
Coca-Cola (355-ml/12-oz. can)	1.00	0.50
Cup of coffee (black, not latte)	2.00	1.00
Admission to the Royal Ontario Museum	20.00	10.00
Movie ticket	12.00	6.00
Ticket for the National Ballet of Canada	45.00	22.50
375-ml (12.7-oz.) bottle of Inniskillin Vidal Icewine (LCBO)	60.00	30.00

*Includes tax and tip but not wine.

offers service in several foreign languages, and exempts Amex gold and platinum cardholders from the 1% fee.); **Visa** (© 800/732-1322); and **MasterCard** (© 800/223-9920).

Be sure to keep a record of the traveler's checks serial numbers separate from your checks, in the event that they are stolen or lost. You'll get a refund faster if you know the numbers.

American Express, Thomas Cook, Visa, and **MasterCard** offer **foreign currency traveler's checks,** useful if you're traveling to one country or to the euro zone; they're accepted at locations where dollar checks may not be.

Another option is the new prepaid traveler's check cards, reloadable cards that work much like debit cards but aren't linked to your checking account. The **American Express Travelers Cheque Card,** for example, requires a minimum deposit, sets a maximum balance, and has a one-time issuance fee of $15. You can withdraw money from an ATM (for a fee of $2.50 per transaction, not including bank fees), and the funds can be purchased in dollars, euros, or pounds. If you lose the card, your available funds will be refunded within 24 hours.

6 HEALTH

STAYING HEALTHY

While Toronto has excellent doctors and fine hospitals, it's common sense to prepare for the trip as you would for any other. The SARS outbreak here in 2003 was huge news at the time, but there has not been a subsequent outbreak.

General Availability of Health Care

Toronto has excellent hospitals and doctors—though hopefully you won't have any occasion to discover this personally. Bring any prescriptions you might require with you. Decongestants, cough and cold remedies, and allergy medications are available without prescription in pharmacies. One big chain is **Pharma Plus,** which has a store at 63 Wellesley St., at Church Street (© **416/924-7760**). It's open daily from 8am to midnight. Other Pharma Plus branches are in College Park, Manulife Centre, Commerce Court, and First Canadian Place. The only 24-hour drugstore near downtown is **Shopper's Drug Mart** at 700 Bay St., at Gerrard Street West (© **416/979-2424**).

WHAT TO DO IF YOU GET SICK AWAY FROM HOME

In downtown Toronto, the **University Health Network** manages three hospitals: **Toronto General** at 200 Elizabeth St., **Princess Margaret** at 610 University Ave., and **Toronto Western** at 399 Bathurst St. The UHN has a central switchboard for all three (© **416/340-3111**).

The staff or concierge at your hotel should be able to help you locate a doctor. You can also call the **College of Physicians and Surgeons of Ontario,** 80 College St. (© **416/967-2626**), for a referral from 8am to 5pm Monday through Friday.

For emergency dental services from 8am till midnight, call the **Dental Emergency Service** (© **416/485-7121**). After midnight, your best bet is the **University Health Network,** which manages three downtown hospitals (© **416/340-3111**). Otherwise, ask the front-desk staff or concierge at your hotel.

We list **additional emergency numbers** in the "Fast Facts" appendix, p. 256.

Avoiding "Economy-Class Syndrome"

Deep vein thrombosis, or as it's know in the world of flying, "economy-class syndrome," is a blood clot that develops in a deep vein. It's a potentially deadly condition that can be caused by sitting in cramped conditions—such as an airplane cabin—for too long. During a flight (especially a long-haul flight), get up, walk around, and stretch your legs every 60 to 90 minutes to keep your blood flowing. Other preventative measures include frequent flexing of the legs while sitting, drinking lots of water, and avoiding alcohol and sleeping pills. If you have a history of deep vein thrombosis, heart disease, or another condition that puts you at high risk, some experts recommend wearing compression stockings or taking anticoagulants when you fly; always ask your physician about the best course for you. Symptoms of deep vein thrombosis include leg pain or swelling, or even shortness of breath.

Healthy Travels to You

The following government websites offer up-to-date health-related travel advice.
- **Australia:** www.smartraveller.gov.au
- **Canada:** www.hc-sc.gc.ca/index_e.html
- **U.K.:** www.dh.gov.uk
- **U.S.:** www.cdc.gov/travel

7 SAFETY

Toronto enjoys an unusually safe reputation as far as big cities go. But keep in mind that it is a big city, with all of the difficulties that implies. While parks such as Allan Gardens and Trinity Bellwoods have been cleaned up in recent years, they are still not places you should venture into at night. During the day, keep your valuables close and your eyes peeled for pickpockets. This is important to keep in mind when you're at a major tourist attraction and when you're on the subway.

Speaking of Toronto's public transit system, there are a couple of things to keep in mind. If it's late and you're alone on an almost-empty platform, wait for the train by the big "DWA" sign (it stands for **"Designated Waiting Area,"** and it has an intercom and a closed-circuit TV camera trained on it). There is a DWA area at every TTC station. If you are traveling by bus, there is a **"Request Stop"** program in effect between 9pm and 5am, in which female passengers can disembark at streets in between regular TTC bus stops. For information about these safety features, visit **www.toronto.ca/ttc/safety.htm**.

8 SPECIALIZED TRAVEL RESOURCES

TRAVELERS WITH DISABILITIES

Most disabilities shouldn't stop anyone from traveling. There are more options and resources out there than ever before.

Toronto is a very accessible city. Curb cuts are well made and common throughout the downtown area; special parking privileges are extended to people with disabilities who have special plates or a pass that allows parking in no-parking zones. The subway and trolleys are not accessible, but the city operates **Wheel-Trans**, a special service for those with disabilities. Visitors can register for this service. For information, call ✆ **416/393-4111** or visit **www.toronto.ca/ttc/special.htm**.

Community Information Toronto, 425 Adelaide St. W., at Spadina Avenue, (✆ **416/397-4636**), may be able to provide limited information and assistance about social-service organizations in the city. It does not have specific accessibility information on tourism or hotels, though. It's available daily from 8am to 10pm.

Organizations that offer a vast range of resources and assistance to travelers with disabilities include **MossRehab** (✆ **800/CALL-MOSS;** www.mossresourcenet.org); the **American Foundation for the Blind (AFB;** ✆ **800/232-5463;** www.afb.org); and **SATH** (Society for Accessible Travel & Hospitality; ✆ **212/447-7284;** www.sath.org). **AirAmbulanceCard.com** is now partnered with SATH and allows you to

Wedded Bliss for Gay & Lesbian Couples

Niagara Falls used to be one of the most popular places to honeymoon, but Toronto today is one of the most in-demand wedding destinations. After same-sex marriage became legal in Ontario in 2003, gay and lesbian couples flocked to the city to marry. (In July 2006, the Civil Marriage Act legalized same-sex marriage across Canada. The new law will apply to civil ceremonies—religious institutions will not be bound by it.)

If you want to get married in Toronto, it's pretty simple: Go with your partner to the Registrar General's office at 900 Bay St. (at Wellesley), bring ID (including your passport and birth certificate), pay a small fee, and the marriage license will be yours; there's no residency requirement. See **www.toronto.ca** for details and an application form that you can download. For help organizing a wedding beyond the confines of city hall, check out the wedding-planner pages at **www.toronto.com**. One company that specializes in planning same-sex weddings is **I Do in Toronto** (© **888/418-1188**; www.idointoronto.com). While many wedding ceremonies are being conducted at the **Toronto Civic Wedding Chambers,** 100 Queen St. W. (© **416/363-0316**), couples are increasingly choosing to wed elsewhere. One popular place is the **Metropolitan Community Church of Toronto** (© **416/406-6228**; www.mcctoronto.com), which has been very active in the battle for same-sex marriage rights.

preselect top-notch hospitals in case of an emergency. **Flying with Disability** (www.flying-with-disability.org) is a comprehensive information source on airplane travel.

For more on organizations that offer resources to travelers, go to frommers.com.

GAY & LESBIAN TRAVELERS

Toronto is a member of the Big Four, the term for the North American cities with the largest gay communities (the others are San Francisco, New York, and Chicago). For the city's large gay population, estimated at about 250,000, community life is centered north and south of the intersection of Church and Wellesley streets, an area known as the Gay Village, but gay-friendly establishments aren't limited to one neighborhood. One of Toronto's most celebrated events is Pride Week in June (see "Calendar of Events," p. 29). Also,

Toronto has become a popular spot for gay and lesbian couples to marry; see "Wedded Bliss for Gay & Lesbian Couples," above, for details.

Gay and lesbian travelers can pick up a copy of the free biweekly *Xtra!* at many bookstores, including the **Glad Day Bookshop,** 598A Yonge St., second floor (© **416/961-4161**). To read *Xtra!* before you get to town, log in to **www.xtra.ca**. You can also sign up for its Toronto e-mail list, with information about local events and breaking news.

Another resource is **Gay Toronto** (www.gaytoronto.com), which lists gay-friendly restaurants, bars, nightclubs, guesthouses, travel agencies, and other businesses and organizations. The **Gay Toronto Tourism Guild** has a website with event links at **www.gaytorontotourism.com**. The daily news website **www.365gay.com** features Toronto travel information.

The International Gay and Lesbian Travel Association (IGLTA; ☏ 800/448-8550 or 954/776-2626; www.iglta.org) is the trade association for the gay and lesbian travel industry, and offers an online directory of gay- and lesbian-friendly travel businesses and tour operators.

Gay.com Travel (☏ 800/929-2268 or 415/644-8044; www.gay.com/travel or www.outandabout.com) is an excellent online successor to the popular *Out & About* print magazine. It provides regularly updated information about gay-owned, gay-oriented, and gay-friendly lodging, dining, sightseeing, nightlife, and shopping establishments in every important destination worldwide. British travelers should click on the "Travel" link at www.uk.gay.com for advice and gay-friendly trip ideas.

The Canadian website GayTraveler (www.gaytraveler.ca) offers ideas and advice for gay travel all over the world.

For more gay and lesbian travel resources visit frommers.com.

SENIOR TRAVEL

When in Toronto, seniors can expect to receive discounts on the TTC (subway and bus), and on many (but not all) admissions to attractions. Keep in mind that it is usually necessary to show photo identification when purchasing discounted tickets or admissions. Members of CARP (Canadian Association of Retired Persons; ☏ 416/363-8748; www.carp.ca) or AARP (the American analog; ☏ 888/687-2277; www.aarp.org), can get discounts on hotels, airfares, and car rentals. Anyone over 50 can join.

Frommers.com offers more information and resources on travel for seniors.

FAMILY TRAVEL

The family vacation is a rite of passage for many households, one that in a split second can devolve into a *National Lampoon* farce. But in Toronto, a city that boasts a plethora of family-friendly sites, such as the Ontario Science Centre, Paramount Canada's Wonderland, Harbourfront, and the Toronto Zoo, you'll find that a family trip really can offer something for everyone.

For more suggestions on family and kid-oriented entertainment in Toronto, see "Especially for Kids," in chapter 7. If you're already in town, pick up a copy of *Toronto Families,* a free magazine produced by the publishers of *Today's Parent* (an award-winning national magazine). You can also check it out online at www.torontofamilies.ca.

Helpful features in this guide include "Family-Friendly Hotels" (p. 82) and "Family-Friendly Restaurants" (p. 105). To locate those accommodations, restaurants, and attractions that are particularly kid friendly, refer to the "Kids" icon throughout this guide.

Recommended family travel websites include Family Travel Forum (www.familytravelforum.com), a comprehensive site that offers customized trip planning; Family Travel Network (www.familytravelnetwork.com), an online magazine providing travel tips; TravelWithYourKids.com, a comprehensive site written by parents for parents offering sound advice for long-distance and international travel with children.

For a list of more family-friendly travel resources, turn to the experts at frommers.com.

WOMEN TRAVELERS

Toronto is an easy place to be for solo travelers, male or female. At night, take note of the TTC's "Request Stop" program for women traveling on buses (see p. 46). Check out the award-winning website Journeywoman (www.journeywoman.com), a "real-life" women's travel-information network where you can sign up for a free e-mail newsletter and get advice on everything from etiquette and dress to safety. The travel guide *Safety and Security for Women Who Travel, 2nd edition,* by Sheila Swan and

Peter Laufer (Travelers' Tales Guides), offers common-sense tips on safe travel. For general travel resources for women, go to frommers.com.

VEGETARIAN TRAVEL

Before you arrive in Toronto, check out the **Toronto Vegetarian Association** (www.veg.ca). Its long list of resources includes a vegetarian directory to the city. **Happy Cow's Vegetarian Guide to Restaurants & Health Food Stores** (www.happycow.

net) has a restaurant guide with more than 6,000 restaurants in 100 countries. **VegDining.com** also lists vegetarian restaurants (with profiles) around the world **Vegetarian Vacations** (www.vegetarianvacations.com) offers vegetarian tours and itineraries.

There are many vegetarian restaurants (or restaurants with impressive vegetarian options) listed in chapter 6. These include **Camros Organic Eatery, Kalendar, the Queen Mother Café,** and **Rice Bar.**

9 SUSTAINABLE TOURISM/ECOTOURISM

Sustainable tourism is conscientious travel. It means being careful with the environments you explore, and respecting the communities you visit. Two overlapping components of sustainable travel are **ecotourism** and **ethical tourism. The International Ecotourism Society (TIES)** defines ecotourism as responsible travel to natural areas that conserves the environment and improves the well-being of local people. TIES suggests that ecotourists follow these principles:

* Minimize environmental impact.
* Build environmental and cultural awareness and respect.
* Provide positive experiences for both visitors and hosts.
* Provide direct financial benefits for conservation and for local people.
* Raise sensitivity to host countries' political, environmental, and social climates.
* Support international human rights and labor agreements.

You can find some eco-friendly travel tips and statistics, as well as touring companies and associations—listed by destination under "Travel Choice"—at the **TIES** website, www.ecotourism.org. Also check out **Ecotravel.com**, which lets you search for sustainable touring companies in several categories (water-based, land-based, spiritually oriented, and so on).

While much of the focus of eco-tourism is about reducing impacts on the natural environment, ethical tourism concentrates on ways to preserve and enhance local economies and communities, regardless of location. You can embrace ethical tourism by staying at a locally owned hotel or shopping at a store that employs local workers and sells locally produced goods.

Responsible Travel (www.responsibletravel.com) is a great source of sustainable travel ideas; the site is run by a spokesperson for ethical tourism in the travel industry. **Sustainable Travel International** (www.sustainabletravelinternational.org) promotes ethical tourism practices and manages an extensive directory of sustainable properties and tour operators around the world.

In the U.K., **Tourism Concern** (www.tourismconcern.org.uk) works to reduce social and environmental problems connected to tourism. The **Association of Independent Tour Operators** (AITO; www.aito.co.uk) is a group of specialist operators leading the field in making holidays sustainable.

Volunteer travel has become increasingly popular among those who want to venture beyond the standard group-tour experience to learn languages, interact with locals, and make a positive difference while on vacation. Volunteer travel usually doesn't

(Tips) It's Easy Being Green

We can all help conserve fuel and energy when we travel. Here are a few simple ways you can help preserve your favorite destinations:

- Each time you take a flight or drive a car greenhouse gases release into the atmosphere. You can help neutralize this danger to the planet through "carbon offsetting"—paying someone to invest your money in programs that reduce your greenhouse gas emissions by the same amount you've added. Before buying carbon offset credits, just make sure that you're using a reputable company, one with a proven program that invests in renewable energy. Reliable carbon offset companies include **Carbonfund** (www.carbonfund.org), **Terra-Pass** (www.terrapass.org), and **Carbon Neutral** (www.carbonneutral.org). **Air Canada** has partnered with **Zerofootprint,** a not-for-profit organization, to offer the option of purchasing a carbon offset for your flight when you book it on **www.aircanada.com.**

- Whenever possible, choose nonstop flights; they generally require less fuel than indirect flights that stop and take off again. Try to fly during the day—some scientists estimate that nighttime flights are twice as harmful to the environment. And pack light—each 15 pounds of luggage on a 5,000-mile flight adds up to 50 pounds of carbon dioxide emitted.

- Call the **Green Tourism Association of Toronto** for inspiration and advice about eco-friendly travel (© **416/392-1288**).

- Rely on public transportation to get around Toronto: The **TTC** is safe and clean, and it makes it easy to get to downtown, midtown, and uptown sights.

require special skills—just a willingness to work hard—and programs vary in length from a few days to a number of weeks. Some programs provide free housing and food, but many require volunteers to pay for travel expenses, which can add up quickly.

For general info on volunteer travel, visit **www.volunteerabroad.org** and **www. idealist.org**.

10 PACKAGES FOR THE INDEPENDENT TRAVELER

Do you really need a package tour to visit Toronto? Generally speaking, no—it's easy to arrange accommodations and show tickets yourself. However, if you're determined to see a particular show (or the Canadian Opera Company, whose performances are at 99% capacity on average), a package could be a good idea. Package tours are simply a way to buy the airfare, accommodations, and other elements of your trip (such as car rentals, airport transfers, and sometimes even activities) at the same time and often at discounted prices.

One good source of package deals is **Tourism Toronto** itself, which lists deals on its website (www.seetorontonow.com).

- If renting a car is necessary to take a side trip (such as Niagara-on-the-Lake), ask the rental agent for a hybrid, or rent the most fuel-efficient car available. You'll use less gas and save money at the tank.
- Take a look at **"The City of Toronto Green Guide"** online at **www.toronto. ca/greenguide/index.htm**.
- Where you stay during your travels can have a major environmental impact. To determine the green credentials of a property, ask about trash disposal and recycling, water conservation, and energy use; also question if sustainable materials were used in the construction of the property. The website **www.greenhotels.com** recommends green-rated member hotels around the world that fulfill the company's stringent environmental requirements. Also consult **www.environmentallyfriendlyhotels.com** for more green accommodation ratings.
- At hotels, request that your sheets and towels not be changed daily. (Many hotels already have programs like this in place.) Turn off the lights and air-conditioner (or heater) when you leave your room.
- Eat at locally owned and operated restaurants that use produce grown in the area. This contributes to the local economy and cuts down on greenhouse gas emissions by supporting restaurants where the food is not flown or trucked in across long distances. Visit **Sustain Lane** (www.sustainlane. org) to find sustainable eating and drinking choices around the U.S.; also check out **www.eatwellguide.org** for tips on eating sustainably in the U.S. and Canada.

Several of Toronto's hotels (including the **Park Hyatt, the Fairmont Royal York,** and the **Delta Chelsea**) offer special packages; see chapter 5. Several big **online travel agencies**—Expedia.com, Travelocity, Orbitz, Site59, and Lastminute.com—also do a brisk business in packages.

Maxxim Vacations (© 800/567-6666; www.maxximvacations.com) is a Canadian company that has a long track record with Toronto package tours. One advantage with their packages is that you can guarantee

you'd get to see the show (or shows) you have your heart set on while in town.

Travel packages are also listed in the travel section of your local Sunday newspaper. Or check ads in national travel magazines such as *Arthur Frommer's Budget Travel Magazine, Travel + Leisure, National Geographic Traveler,* and *Condé Nast Traveler.*

For more information on Package Tours and for tips on booking your trip, see frommers.com.

11 ESCORTED GENERAL-INTEREST TOURS

Escorted tours are structured group tours, with a group leader. The price usually includes everything from airfare to hotels,

meals, tours, admission costs, and local transportation.

Frommers.com: The Complete Travel Resource

Planning a trip or just returned? Head to **Frommers.com,** voted Best Travel Site by *PC Magazine*. We think you'll find our site indispensable before, during and after your travels—with expert advice and tips; independent reviews of hotels, restaurants, attractions, and preferred shopping and nightlife venues; vacation giveaways; and an online booking tool. We publish the complete contents of over 135 travel guides in our **Destinations** section, covering over 4,000 places worldwide. Each weekday, we publish original articles that report on **Deals and News** via our free **Frommers.com Newsletters.** What's more, **Arthur Frommer** himself blogs 5 days a week, with cutting opinions about the state of travel in the modern world. We're betting you'll find our **Events** listings an invaluable resource; it's an up-to-the-minute roster of what's happening in cities everywhere—including concerts, festivals, lectures, and more. We've also added weekly **podcasts, interactive maps,** and hundreds of new images across the site. Finally, don't forget to visit our **Message Boards,** where you can join in conversations with thousands of fellow Frommer's travelers and post your trip report once you return.

There are some great special-interest tours you can take part in while you're in town (see below), and the city is easy to navigate and explore without a group. However, if you do want an escorted tour, there are several options, including **Great Adventure Tours** (© **800/638-3945;** www.greatadventuretours.com), which explores Toronto and Niagara, and **SWT Tours** (© **212/988-1359;** www.poshnosh.com), which specializes in theater tours.

Despite the fact that escorted tours require big deposits and predetermine hotels, restaurants, and itineraries, many people derive security and peace of mind from the structure they offer. Escorted tours—whether they're navigated by bus, motorcoach, train, or boat—let travelers sit back and enjoy the

trip without having to drive or worry about details. They take you to the maximum number of sights in the minimum amount of time with the least amount of hassle. They're particularly convenient for people with limited mobility, and they can be a great way to make new friends.

On the downside, you'll have little opportunity for serendipitous interactions with locals. The tours can be jam-packed with activities, leaving little room for individual sightseeing, whim, or adventure—plus they often focus on the heavily touristed sites, so you miss out on many a lesser known gem.

For more information on Escorted General-Interest Tours, including questions to ask before booking your trip, see frommers.com.

12 SPECIAL-INTEREST TRIPS

ARCHITECTURAL & CULTURAL TOURS

Toronto is a city made for walking, and there's no shortage of options for those

willing to pound the pavement. The **Royal Ontario Museum** has a **ROMwalks** program (© **416/586-5513**) throughout the summer that offers guided tours of architectural highlights and neighborhoods from the Entertainment District to the Danforth. During the summer, **Heritage Toronto** (© **416/338-0684;** www. heritagetoronto.org) offers walking tours of several neighborhoods, including Cabbagetown and Rosedale.

BIKE TOURS

Year-round, **A Taste of the World Neighbourhood Bicycle Tours and Walks** ★ (© **416/923-6813;** www.torontowalks bikes.com) leads visitors through the nooks and crannies of such places as Chinatown, Yorkville, and Rosedale. It's particularly well known for its "haunted" tours, including one about the ghosts of Yorkville (remember, that chic neighborhood stands atop a former cemetery).

Another option is the **Toronto Bicycling Network** (© **416/766-1985;** www. tbn.ca). The association organizes tours and provides information about routes you can explore in and around the city.

CHEFS & GOURMETS

Bonnie Stern is a local legend, and the **Bonnie Stern Cooking School** is a wonderful place to pick up some of her culinary secrets (she teaches many of the classes herself). The school is located at 6 Erskine Ave. (3 blocks north of the Eglinton subway station); call © **416/484-4810** for information, or visit **www. bonniestern.com**. The school offers classes in everything from challah baking to Moroccan cooking.

The Metropolitan hotels in Toronto are renowned for their restaurants, so perhaps it's no surprise that the company has created **Insider Gourmet Tours** (www. metropolitan.com/packages). It includes a visit to the St. Lawrence Market, trips into the kitchens of some of the best restaurants in the city, and a winery tour in the Niagara Region.

ECOLOGY & WILDLIFE

If you're interested in exploring the Toronto region's natural wonders, contact **Toronto and Region Conservation** at © **416/661-6600,** or visit **www.trca parks.ca**. The organization offers tours that include bird-watching and wildlife viewing.

(Tips) **Ask Before You Go**

Before you invest in a package deal or an escorted tour:

- Always ask about the **cancellation policy.** Can you get your money back? Is there a deposit required?
- Ask about the **accommodations choices and prices** for each. Then look up the hotels' reviews in a Frommer's guide and check their rates online for your specific dates of travel. Also find out what types of rooms are offered.
- Request a complete **schedule** (escorted tours only).
- Ask about the **size** and demographics of the group (escorted tours only).
- Discuss what is included in the **price**—transportation, meals, tips, airport transfers, and so on (escorted tours only).
- Finally, look for **hidden expenses.** Ask whether airport departure fees and taxes, for example, are included in the total cost—they rarely are.

PLANNING YOUR TRIP TO TORONTO

3

STAYING CONNECTED

HARBOR TOURS

Mariposa Cruise Line (© **800/976-2442** or 416/203-0178; www.mariposacruises. com) operates 1-hour narrated tours of the waterfront and the Toronto Islands from mid-May to September. Tours leave from the Queen's Quay Terminal at 207 Queens Quay W.

For a real thrill, board the *Kajama,* a three-masted, 50m (164-ft.) schooner, for a 90-minute cruise. The schedule varies, but through July and August three tours a day take place on weekdays and weekends. For more information, call the **Great Lakes Schooner Company,** 249 Queens Quay W., Suite 111 (© **800/267-3866** or 416/260-6355; www.greatlakesschooner. com).

13 STAYING CONNECTED

TELEPHONES

To call Toronto from the U.S.:

Canada and the U.S. use the same area-code system. Simply dial 1, the Toronto area code (416 or 647), and the number.

To call Toronto from other countries:
1. Dial the international access code: 00 from the U.K., Ireland, or New Zealand; or 0011 from Australia.
2. Dial the country code 1.
3. Dial the city code 416 or 647 and then the number.

To make international calls: To make international calls from Toronto, first dial 00 and then the country code (U.K. 44, Ireland 353, Australia 61, New Zealand 64). Next dial the area code and number. However, if you are calling the U.S. from Toronto, you need only to dial 1 and then the area code and phone number.

For directory assistance: Dial 411 if you're looking for a phone number; online, visit **www.canada411.com**.

For operator assistance: If you need operator assistance in making a call, dial 0.

Toll-free numbers: Numbers beginning with 800 or 866 are toll-free within Canada and the U.S. However, calling an 800 number from other countries is not toll-free. In fact, it costs the same as an overseas call.

CELLPHONES

The three letters that define much of the world's wireless capabilities are **GSM** (Global System for Mobile Communications), a big, seamless network that makes for easy cross-border cellphone use throughout Europe and dozens of other countries worldwide. In the U.S., T-Mobile and AT&T Wireless use this quasi-universal system; in Canada, Microcell and some Rogers customers are GSM, and all Europeans and most Australians use GSM. GSM phones function with a removable plastic SIM card, encoded with your phone number and account information. If your cellphone is on a GSM system, and you have a world-capable multiband phone such as many Sony Ericsson, Motorola, or Samsung models, you can make and receive calls across civilized areas around much of the globe. Just call your wireless operator and ask for "international roaming" to be activated on your account. Unfortunately, per-minute charges can be high—usually $1 to $1.50 in Western Europe and up to $5 in places like Russia and Indonesia.

For many, **renting** a phone is a good idea. While you can rent a phone from any number of overseas sites, including kiosks at airports and at car-rental agencies, we suggest renting the phone before you leave home. North Americans can rent one before leaving home from **InTouch USA** (© **800/872-7626;** www.intouchglobal. com) or **RoadPost** (© **888/290-1606** or 905/272-5665; www.roadpost.com). InTouch will also, for free, advise you on

> **(Tips) Hey, Google, did you get my text message?**
>
> It's bound to happen: The day you leave this guidebook back at the hotel for an unencumbered stroll through Leslieville, you'll forget the address of the lunch spot you had earmarked. If you're traveling with a mobile device, send a text message to ℂ **46645 (GOOGL)** for a lightning-fast response. For instance, type "edward levesques kitchen toronto" and within 10 seconds you'll receive a text message with the address and phone number. This nifty trick works in a range of search categories: Look up weather ("weather toronto"), language translations ("translate goodbye in chinese"), currency conversions ("10 pounds in csd"), movie times ("harry potter 60605"), and more. If your search results are off, be more specific ("sailor gay bar church street"). For more tips and search options, see www.google.com/sms. Regular text message charges apply.

whether your existing phone will work overseas; simply call ℂ **703/222-7161** between 9am and 4pm EST, or go to http://intouchglobal.com/travel.htm.

Most U.S. cellphone carriers have roaming agreements with Canadian cellphone carriers. Before leaving home, check with your carrier for rates and availability. You can rent a cellphone in Toronto from **Hello Anywhere** (ℂ **888/729-4355** or 416/367-4355; www.helloanywhere.com). Also, cellphone rentals are available through many of Toronto's more upscale hotels, including the **Park Hyatt Toronto,** the **Metropolitan Hotel,** and the **Sutton Place Hotel.**

VOICE-OVER INTERNET PROTOCOL (VOIP)

If you have Web access while traveling, you might consider a broadband-based telephone service (in technical terms, **Voice-over Internet Protocol,** or **VoIP**) such as Skype (www.skype.com) or Vonage (www.vonage.com), which allows you to make free international calls if you use their services from your laptop or in a cybercafe. The people you're calling must also use the service for it to work; check the sites for details.

INTERNET/E-MAIL
With Your Own Computer

Wireless fidelity (Wi-Fi) internet access is becoming more common in Toronto. One not-for-profit group, **Wireless Toronto** (**www.wirelesstoronto.ca**), is dedicated to bringing no-fee access to places across the city. You'll need to create an account to use the group's website (it's free of charge), but it's worth it to get the latest information.

Increasing numbers of hotels and cafes are offering Wi-Fi. To find public Wi-Fi hotspots at your destination, go to **www.jiwire.com**; its Hotspot Finder holds one of the world's largest directories of public wireless hotspots.

Without Your Own Computer

Most major airports have **Internet kiosks** that provide basic Web access for a per-minute fee that's usually higher than cybercafe prices. Check out copy shops like **Kinko's** (FedEx Kinkos), which offers computer stations with fully loaded software (as well as Wi-Fi).

For help locating cybercafes and other establishments where you can go for internet access, please see "Internet Access" in the appendix (p. 258).

Online Traveler's Toolbox

Veteran travelers usually carry some essential items to make their trips easier. Following is a selection of handy online tools to bookmark and use.

- **Airplane Food** (www.airlinemeals.net)
- **Airplane Seating** (www.seatguru.com and www.airlinequality.com)
- **City of Toronto** (www.toronto.ca) is the official municipal guide to Toronto, a straightforward source of practical information peppered with profiles of fun places to visit and announcements of festivals, free concerts, kids' events, and more.
- **Girl Talk Toronto: A Mini City Guide** (www.journeywoman.com/girltalk/toronto.html) runs the gamut from the serious (transit safety) to the frivolously fun (the best places to shop for shoes). This user-friendly site also highlights arty spots, off-the-beaten-path attractions, and the best places for brunch, all from a female perspective.
- *Globe and Mail* (www.globeandmail.com)
- **Green Tourism Association of Toronto** (www.tourgreen.ca) is an excellent resource for eco-friendly travelers. There's information about car-free transportation, outdoor activities and sports, and healthy dining.
- **Help! We've Got Kids** (www.helpwevegotkids.com) is just what parents of young children need: comprehensive listings of special events, attractions, and services that work for the small fry.
- **Maps** (www.mapquest.com)
- **Subway Navigator** (www.subwaynavigator.com)
- **Ticketmaster** (www.ticketmaster.ca)
- **Time and Date** (www.timeanddate.com)
- **Toronto.com** (www.toronto.com) boasts articles on arts and culture, as well as a hotel directory, restaurant reviews, community news, and events listings. One of its best features is its extensive use of photographs.
- **Toronto Arts & Culture** (www.livewithculture.ca) is a new initiative from local government to have all of the cultural events, festivals, and concerts that happen in Toronto listed in one place.
- *Toronto Life* (www.torontolife.com) has extensive restaurant listings, as well as links for events, activities, and nightlife.
- *Toronto Star* (www.thestar.com) includes everything from theater and concert reviews to local news and weather conditions.
- **Toronto Transit Commission** (www.ttc.ca)
- **Toronto Vegetarian Association** (www.veg.ca)
- **Travel Warnings** (http://travel.state.gov, www.fco.gov.uk/travel, www.voyage.gc.ca, or www.dfat.gov.au/consular/advice)
- **Universal Currency Converter** (www.xe.com/ucc)
- **Visa ATM Locator** (www.visa.com); **MasterCard ATM Locator** (www.mastercard.com)
- **Weather** (www.intellicast.com and www.weather.com)

House-Swapping

House-swapping is becoming a more popular and viable means of travel; you stay in their place, they stay in yours, and you both get an authentic and personal view of the area, the opposite of the escapist retreat that many hotels offer. Try **HomeLink International** (Homelink.org), the largest and oldest home-swapping organization, founded in 1952, with over 11,000 listings worldwide ($75 for a yearly membership). **HomeExchange.com** ($49.95 for 6,000 listings) and **Inter-Vac.com** ($68.88 for over 10,000 listings) are also reliable. Many travelers find great housing swaps on **Craigslist** (www.craigslist.org), too, though the offerings cannot be vetted or vouched for. Swap at your own risk.

14 TIPS ON ACCOMMODATIONS

Whether you're seeking a historic hotel with old-world elegance or looking for all the conveniences of the office in your "home" away from home, you'll find a perfect place to stay in Toronto. The city's accommodations run the gamut from intimate boutique inns to large, comfortable convention hotels. Proximity to major attractions (such as the CN Tower, Harbourfront, the Rogers Centre, and the Eaton Centre) can cost a bundle. Even budget hotels charge more than C$150 (£75) a night in the high season, which runs from April to October. And remember to factor the 5% accommodations tax and the 5% GST into what you spend. Before you make a reservation, it's important to have some sense of what you'd like to see and do in town. Toronto is a sprawling metropolis, with attractions, dining districts, and ethnic communities scattered throughout. Keep in mind that you want to be as close as possible to the sights that interest you most.

For tips on surfing for hotel deals online, visit frommers.com.

Suggested Toronto Itineraries

Toronto is a wonderful city in which to get lost. Start anywhere in the downtown core, and walk in any direction for no more than 15 minutes. You'll see eclectic modern buildings side by side with neo-Gothic and Art Deco architecture, catch a fair glimpse of the city's ethnic spectrum, and walk right into a pleasing patch of greenery.

This is a happy coincidence because the layout and organization of the city mean you *will* almost certainly get lost at least once during your stay. Streets have names, not numbers, and they have a crazy-making habit of changing their monikers as they go along. In Midtown, the must-see Avenue Road, for example, turns into Queen's Park Crescent, then into University Avenue as you head south, and into Oriole Parkway if you go north. My best advice: Relax and enjoy the ride.

1 ORIENTATION

CITY LAYOUT

Toronto is laid out in a grid . . . with a few interesting exceptions. **Yonge Street** (pronounced *young*) is the main north–south artery, stretching from Lake Ontario in the south well beyond Highway 401 in the north. Yonge Street divides western cross streets from eastern cross streets. The main east–west artery is **Bloor Street,** which cuts through the heart of downtown.

"Downtown" usually refers to the area from Eglinton Avenue south to the lake, between Spadina Avenue in the west and Jarvis Street in the east. Because this is such a large area, I have divided it into five sections. **Downtown West** runs from the lake north to College Street; the eastern boundary is Yonge Street. **Downtown East** goes from the lake north to Carlton Street (once College St. reaches Yonge, it becomes Carlton St.); the western boundary is Yonge Street. **Midtown** extends from College Street north to Davenport Road; the eastern boundary is Jarvis Street. **The Danforth/The East End** runs east to Danforth Avenue; the western boundary is Broadview Avenue. **Uptown** is the area north of Davenport Road.

In Downtown West, you'll find many of the lakeshore attractions: Harbourfront, Ontario Place, Fort York, Exhibition Place, and the Toronto Islands. It also boasts the CN Tower, city hall, the Four Seasons Centre for the Performing Arts, the Rogers Centre (formerly known as SkyDome), Chinatown, the Art Gallery of Ontario, and the Eaton Centre. Downtown East includes the Distillery District, the St. Lawrence Market, the Sony Centre (formerly the Hummingbird Centre), the St. Lawrence Centre for the Arts, and St. James's Cathedral. Midtown contains the Royal Ontario Museum; the Gardiner Museum; the University of Toronto; Markham Village; and chic Yorkville, a prime area for shopping and dining. The Danforth/The East End features Riverdale Farm, the historic Necropolis, and Greektown. Uptown has traditionally been a residential area, but

> ⓘ **Tips**   **TAP into TO, the Toronto Ambassador Program**
>
> Following the lead of such cities as New York and Sydney, Toronto is training some of its citizens to act as tour guides in popular neighborhoods. Tours take an hour or more, and they're free of charge. Call ☏ **416/338-2786** or click on to **www.toronto.ca/tapto** for more information. Every effort is made to match visitors and greeters by interest, so if you are particularly curious about architecture, history, food, or culture, make sure to mention that when you book your tour.

it's now a fast-growing entertainment area, too. Its attractions include the Sunnybrook park system and the Ontario Science Centre.

North Toronto is another developing area, with theaters such as the Toronto Centre for the Arts, galleries, and some excellent dining. It's not yet a prime tourist destination, but it gets a few mentions throughout this guide.

Toronto sprawls so widely that quite a few of its primary attractions lie outside the downtown core. These include the Toronto Zoo, Paramount Canada's Wonderland, and the McMichael Canadian Art Collection.

FINDING AN ADDRESS   This isn't as easy as it should be. Your best bet is to call ahead and ask for directions, including landmarks and subway stations. Even the locals need to do this.

THE NEIGHBORHOODS IN BRIEF

Downtown West

The Toronto Islands These three islands in Lake Ontario—Ward's, Algonquin, and Centre—are home to a handful of residents and no cars. They're a spring and summer haven where Torontonians go to in-line skate, bicycle, boat, and picnic. Centre Island, the most visited, holds the children's theme park Centreville. Catch the ferry at the foot of Bay Street by Queens Quay.

Harbourfront/Lakefront The landfill where the railroad yards and dock facilities once stood is now a glorious playground opening onto the lake. This is home to the Harbourfront Centre, one of the most important literary, artistic, and cultural venues in Canada.

Financial District Toronto's major banks and insurance companies have their headquarters here, from Front Street north to Queen Street, between Yonge and York streets. Toronto's first skyscrapers rose here; fortunately, some of the older structures have been preserved. Ultramodern BCE Place incorporated the facade of a historic bank building into its design.

Entertainment District Also known as the Theatre District, it's an area of dense cultural development stretching from Front Street north to Queen Street and from Bay Street west to Bathurst Street. King Street West is home to most of the important venues, including the Royal Alexandra Theatre, the Princess of Wales Theatre, and Roy Thomson Hall. Just north is the Four Seasons Centre for the Performing Arts (the new home of the Canadian Opera Company and the National Ballet of Canada), and south are the Convention Centre, the CN Tower, and the Rogers Centre.

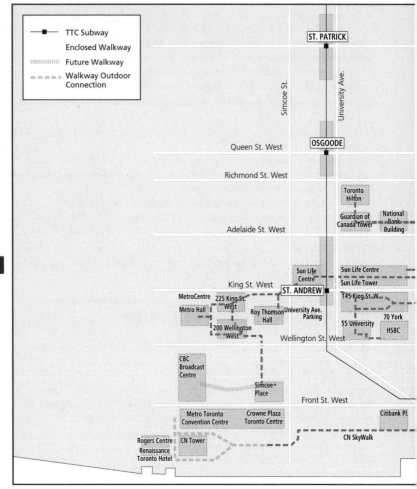

Chinatown Dundas Street West from University Avenue to Spadina Avenue and north to College Street are the boundaries of Chinatown. As the Chinese community has grown, it has extended along Dundas Street and north along Spadina Avenue. Here, you'll see a fascinating mixture of old and new. Hole-in-the-wall restaurants share the sidewalks with glitzy shopping centers built with Hong Kong money.

Kensington Market Just west of Spadina Avenue and north of Dundas Street West is one of Toronto's most colorful neighborhoods. Successive waves of immigration—Eastern European Jews, Portuguese, West Indian— have left their mark. Filled with tiny but wonderful food shops, restaurants, and vintage clothing stores, it's easy to while away an afternoon here (especially on the car-free summer Sundays,

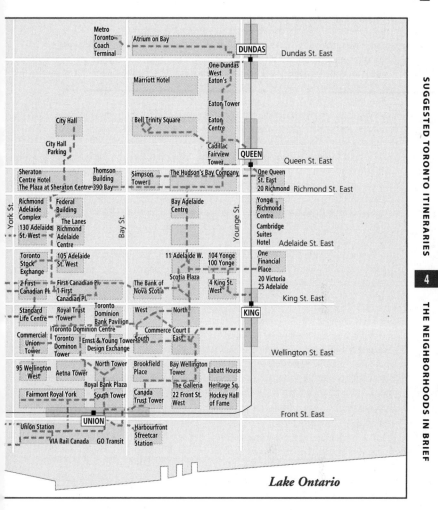

Lake Ontario

when the area becomes a pedestrian-only zone).

Queen Street West This stretch from University Avenue to Bathurst Street offers an eclectic mix—popular mainstream shops, funky boutiques, second-hand bookshops, and vintage-clothing emporiums. It's also home to Toronto's gourmet ghetto, with bistro after trattoria after cafe lining the street. Unfortunately,

the excellent food along this strip is frequently served with heaps of attitude. Despite the intrusion of mega-retailers, many independently owned boutiques flourish.

Art & Design District In the past, Queen Street West (see above) was considered edgy. Now that description is more accurately applied to West Queen West, which starts at Bathurst Avenue

Underground Toronto

As if it weren't enough to know Toronto's streets, you also need an understanding of the labyrinthine walkways beneath the pavement. This wide-ranging network is an excellent way to get around the downtown core when the weather is grim. You can eat, sleep, dance, shop, and go to the theater without even donning a coat.

You can walk from the Dundas subway station south through the Eaton Centre until you hit Queen Street; turn west to the Sheraton Centre and then head south. You'll pass through the Richmond-Adelaide Centre, First Canadian Place, and Toronto Dominion Centre, and go all the way (through the dramatic Royal Bank Plaza) to Union Station. En route, branches lead off to the stock exchange, Sun Life Centre, and Metro Hall. Additional walkways link Simcoe Plaza to 200 Wellington West and to the CBC Broadcast Centre. Other walkways run around Bloor Street and Yonge Street and elsewhere in the city. Check the "Underground Toronto" map on p. 60, or look for the large, clear underground PATH maps throughout the concourse.

This underground city even has its own attractions. First Canadian Place in particular is known for free lunch-hour lectures, opera and dance performances, and art exhibits.

and runs west to Gladstone Avenue. This neighborhood is one of the coolest in the city, full of art galleries; one-of-a-kind boutiques selling clothing, housewares, and antiques; and up-and-coming restaurants.

Little Italy This thriving, lively area, filled with open-air cafes, trattorias, and shops, serves the Italian community along College Street between Euclid and Shaw. The trendies can't seem to stay away, which has driven up prices in what was once an inexpensive neighborhood.

DOWNTOWN EAST

Old Town/St. Lawrence Market During the 19th century, this area, east of Yonge Street between the Esplanade and Adelaide Street, was the focal point of the community. Today, the market's still going strong, and attractions such as the glorious St. James Cathedral draw visitors.

The Beaches Communal, youthful, safe, and comfortable—these adjectives describe this neighborhood that's just 15 minutes from downtown at the end of the Queen Street East streetcar line. A summer resort in the mid-1800s, The Beaches' boardwalk and beach ensure that it remains casual and family-oriented. In 2006, there was a local poll to rename this area "The Beach" (a term preferred by many residents), but The Beaches is still the way the neighborhood is known to just about everyone.

Leslieville When I moved away from Toronto 5 years ago, this was a down-on-its-luck stretch of Queen Street East between Carlaw and Leslie Street. Once an industrial area, it was basically the place you passed through on your way to The Beaches. Now, it's on the fast track to gentrification, with a slew of upstart boutiques, vintage and antique stores, and excellent bistros. Its borders are expanding too—you'll see "Leslieville" signs after you cross Broadview Avenue.

Little India Gerrard Street East between Greenwood Avenue and Main Street is well known for its festival-like atmosphere. It's partly because of the multicolored lights that light up the street at night, but the vibrant streetlife is visible at any time of day. The blocks are filled with Indian restaurants, grocers, and shops that specialize in saris or that sell beautiful textiles.

MIDTOWN

Queen's Park and the University Home to the Ontario Legislature and many of the colleges and buildings that make up the University of Toronto, this neighborhood extends from College Street to Bloor Street between Spadina Avenue and Bay Street.

Yorkville Originally a village outside the city, this area north and west of Bloor and Yonge streets became Toronto's Haight-Ashbury in the 1960s. Now it's a haute district filled with designer boutiques, galleries, cafes, and restaurants.

The Annex This area fell into neglect for many years, but since the early 1980s, much of it has been lovingly restored. It stretches from Bedford Road to Bathurst Street and from Harbord Street to Dupont Avenue. Many of the tremendous turn-of-the-20th-century homes are still single-family dwellings, though as you walk west it segues into the U of T student ghetto. Revered urban-planning guru Jane Jacobs has long called this area home.

Koreatown The bustling blocks along Bloor Street West between Bathurst and Christie streets are filled with Korean restaurants; alternative-medicine practitioners such as herbalists and acupuncturists; and shops filled with made-in-Korea merchandise. One of the first Korean settlements in Toronto, it is now primarily a business district.

Rosedale Meandering tree-lined streets with elegant homes and manicured lawns are the hallmarks of this residential community, from Yonge and Bloor streets northeast to Castle Frank and the Moore Park Ravine. Named after the residence of Sheriff William Jarvis (the man who is largely credited with putting down the 1837 Upper Canada Rebellion), its name is synonymous with Toronto's wealthy elite.

Church Street/The Gay Village Between Gerrard Street and Bloor Street East, along Church Street, lies the heart of Toronto's gay and lesbian community. Restaurants, cafes, and bars fill this relaxed, casual neighborhood. Church Street is where 19th-century Toronto's grandest churches were built.

Cabbagetown Once described by writer Hugh Garner as the largest Anglo-Saxon slum in North America, this gentrified neighborhood of Victorian and Edwardian homes stretches east of Parliament Street to the Don Valley between Gerrard Street and Bloor Street. The sought-after residential district got its name because the front lawns of the homes, occupied by Irish immigrants (who settled here in the late 1800s), were, it is said, covered with row upon row of cabbages. Riverdale, Toronto's only inner-city farm, is at the eastern edge of this district.

Greektown Across the Don Valley Viaduct, Bloor Street becomes the Danforth, which marks the beginning of Greektown. It's lined with old-style Greek tavernas and hip Mediterranean bars and restaurants that are crowded from early evening until early morning. The densest wining-and-dining area starts at Broadview Avenue and runs 6 blocks east.

Forest Hill Second to Rosedale as the city's prime residential area, Forest Hill is home to Upper Canada College and Bishop Strachan School for girls. It stretches west of Avenue Road between St. Clair Avenue and Eglinton Avenue.

Eglinton Avenue The neighborhood surrounding the intersection of Yonge Street and Eglinton Avenue is jokingly known as "Young and Eligible." It's a bustling area filled with restaurants— including some of the town's top rated—and nightclubs. To the east, it intersects with the 243-hectare (600-acre) Sunnybrook park system and with the Ontario Science Centre.

2 THE BEST OF TORONTO IN 1 DAY

You'd better put on your comfiest walking shoes, because seeing the best of Toronto in a day means covering a lot of territory. This itinerary explores the city's most famous attractions, including the ones everyone back home will ask you about (hello, CN Tower). It's a downtown walk that will take you from the city's highest point to its waterfront, from its commercial core to its lofty public buildings—but my favorite part is the refreshing green space along the way. ***Start:*** *Union Station and walk west to the CN Tower.*

❶ CN Tower ★

Today you're starting at the top, baby. Even if the famous tower isn't the tallest in the world anymore, you can't overlook Toronto's most celebrated icon (plus, the new glass elevator makes the ride up even more of a thrill). Beginning your tour here will give you a perspective not so much on Toronto as on the city's position in this corner of North America. If it's a clear day, you'll be able to see all the way to Niagara Falls. But even if it isn't clear out, you can check out my favorite section, the amazing glass floor. I haven't gotten up the nerve to jump up and down on it yet, but just standing on it and looking all the way down to the ground is scarier than any thrill-park ride I've ever experienced. See p. 132.

❷ Rogers Centre ★

This is the domed stadium formerly known as SkyDome. I don't recommend taking the time to do the formal tour, but you've got to appreciate the massive statues of cheering (and jeering) spectators on its facade. And if you want to see the Toronto Blue Jays play ball (or the Toronto Argonauts play

football, Canadian-style), come back here later in the day. See p. 150.

❸ Toronto Music Garden ★★★

I know that getting to the waterfront is no joy, but it's entirely worth it when you reach the tranquil Toronto Music Garden. This is one of my favorite green spaces in the city. The Music Garden was designed by world-renowned cellist Yo-Yo Ma and landscape architect Julie Moir Messervy to invoke Bach's First Suite for Unaccompanied Cello. It may sound like a weird concept, but when you're wandering around the grounds, it's simply serene. See p. 151.

❹ Harbourfront Centre ★★

This is the kind of place where you could easily spend a day, so you may need to tear yourself away to stay on track. I love to watch the glassblowers, potters, jewelry makers, and other artisans at work in the Craft Studio; the Artists' Gardens, a series of diverse landscapes created by local talent, are another highlight. Depending on how active you feel, this is also your chance to get out on the water: The Harbourfront Canoe and Kayak School will let you rent a boat and can offer instruction. See p. 125.

See p. 125.

> **5** **TAKE A BREAK**
> If you want to sit outside and watch the lakefront traffic—boat and human—go for a light meal or a drink at the casual **BoatHouse Grill** (✆ **416/203-6300**), on the ground floor of the Queen's Quay building. A more upscale restaurant is **Pearl Harbourfront Chinese Cuisine** (✆ **416/203-1233**). The Queen's Quay complex also has a variety of cafes and food vendors just outside, if you want just a quick bite. See p. 125.

6 Air Canada Centre ★
One nice thing about walking back to the downtown core this way is that you can cross through the Air Canada Centre, which is a lot more pleasant than the other options. This sports complex is home to both the Raptors basketball team and the Maple Leafs hockey team, but it also hosts blockbuster music concerts; you'll see photographs of some of the acts as you walk through the passageway. See p. 149.

7 Union Station ★
This is one of the city's underappreciated wonders. Toronto's temple to trains is a Beaux Arts beauty, and I never pass up the excuse to walk through its main hall when I'm in the area. Pop in to admire the tile ceiling designed by architect Rafael Gaustavino. Until the age of mass air travel, Union Station was the first place new immigrants saw when they arrived in Toronto.

8 Hockey Hall of Fame ★★
Whatever the NHL is doing, hockey-loving Torontonians come here to get a fix of the sport, and so can you. My favorite thing about this complex is its interactive nature: Sure, you can admire the trophies and memorabilia, but nothing beats whacking away at virtual targets (no! no! the other players!). See p. 149.

9 The Eaton Centre
I prefer local boutiques to mass-market chain stores, but the call of this particular mall is impossible to resist. Shopwise, you won't find many surprises here (Roots, Banana Republic, Club Monaco, Indigo Books Music & More, H&M, the Apple Store, Williams-Sonoma, Gap . . .) but the triple-decker balconies make for great people-watching. Also, check out Michael Snow's installation of soaring Canada geese under the skylight. See p. 144.

> **10** **TAKE A BREAK**
> The Eaton Centre has a food court on its lower level that offers some surprisingly good options, such as the **Made in Japan** teriyaki outlet and the **Richtree** cafeteria-style restaurant (good salads). Another good choice is the **City Grill** restaurant, on the upper level. This affordable spot has many picks under C$15 (£7.50), including great salads (try the Niagara Picnic Salad with blue cheese, pecans, and grilled chicken), grilled fish, burgers, and pasta.

11 Yonge-Dundas Square ★
If you want to catch a show in the Theatre District tonight, swing by the **T.O. Tix booth** here for half-price tickets. At this time of day, there won't be much going on here, though it's a great place to rest and people-watch. See p. 210.

12 Old City Hall ★
This building project was *way* over budget when it opened in 1899. Looking at it today, it's not hard to see why; for starters, it uses red stone from the Credit Valley west of Toronto, brown stone shipped up from New Brunswick, and gray stone from north of Toronto. Massive gargoyles crouch near the top; the smaller ones that you have to get up close to see are said to be caricatures of 19th-century politicians. Stop inside to see the stained-glass windows while you're here.

THE BEST OF TORONTO IN 1 DAY   SUGGESTED TORONTO ITINERARIES

4

DAY ONE
1. CN Tower
2. Rogers Centre
3. Toronto Music Garden
4. Harbourfront Centre
5. Queen's Quay
6. Air Canada Centre
7. Union Station
8. Hockey Hall of Fame
9. The Eaton Centre
10. Eaton Centre Dining
11. Yonge-Dundas Square
12. Old City Hall
13. New City Hall
14. Royal Alexandra Theatre

DAY TWO
1. Yorkville
2. Royal Ontario Museum
3. Food Studio at ROM
4. George R. Gardiner Museum of Ceramic Art
5. Victoria College
6. Queen's Park and the Ontario Legislature
7. Allan Gardens
8. Cabbagetown
9. Riverdale Farm
10. Necropolis
11. Daniel et Daniel
12. Distillery Historic District

DAY THREE
1. Casa Loma
2. Kensington Market
3. Chocolate Addict
4. Chinatown
5. Art Gallery of Ontario
6. Sharp Centre for Design
7. Queen Street West
8. Tortilla Flats
9. The Art & Design District
10. Museum of Contemporary Canadian Art
11. Little Italy

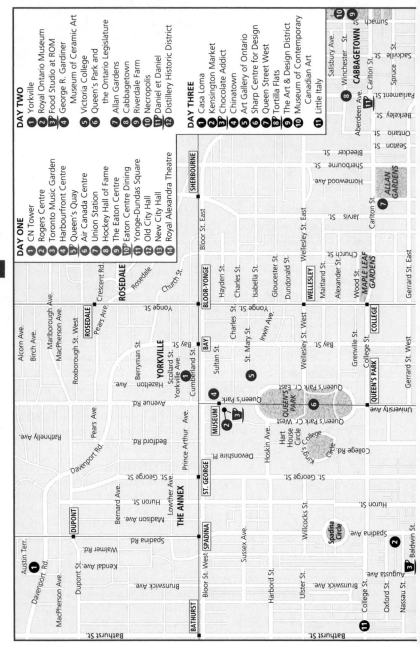

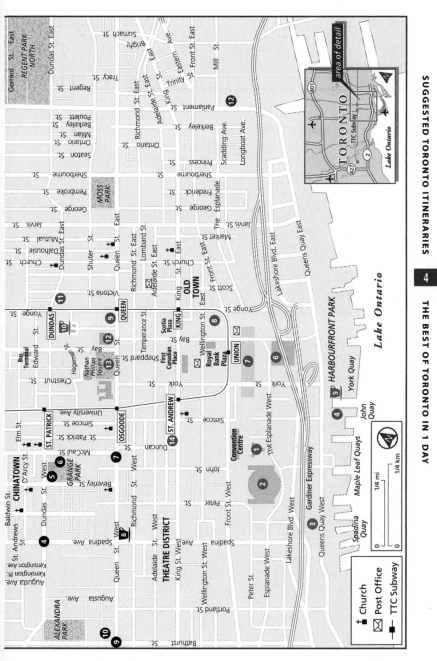

⑬ New City Hall ★

I love this spot at any time of year. In summer, you get the Reflecting Pool and fountains, and in winter, there's the skating rink. In the background, there's the modernist masterpiece city hall building itself; walk up toward it, and you'll see the Henry Moore sculpture *The Archer*. See p. 144.

⑭ Royal Alexandra Theatre ★★

If you picked up tickets earlier at the T.O. Tix booth, you can go inside this glamour puss of Toronto's Theatre District. You're right by the Princess of Wales Theatre (p. 208), too. Walking between the two puts you on Canada's Walk of Fame, where you'll see many names you know (Mike Myers, Jim Carrey, John Candy . . .). See p. 208.

3 THE BEST OF TORONTO IN 2 DAYS

After you've taken in Toronto's best-known landmarks by following the tour above, it's time to get to know the city's heart a little better. When I was growing up here in the 1970s and '80s, city planners were busy ripping down old buildings and slapping up shiny new ones, but fortunately some of the city's historic gems were preserved. In the past 5 years, Toronto has embarked on some pretty ambitious projects with the goal of restoring and expanding upon what's already here—and the results are wonderful, as you'll see for yourself. *Start: Bay Station.*

① Yorkville ★

To me, this is the funniest neighborhood in Toronto. Today, it's filled with chic boutiques and elegant galleries (and high-priced condo developments, some of which are currently under construction); back in the 1960s, it was home to the city's hippies; a century before that, it was a cemetery. Progress? See p. 142.

② Royal Ontario Museum ★★★

This excellent museum embarked upon a Daniel Libeskind–designed renovation a few years ago. Ambitiously titled Renaissance ROM, it was intended to expand the viewing area, largely through the addition of six crystal galleries that jut out over Bloor Street West. Where you spend your time here will depend on whether you have kids in tow: the small fry will insist on the dinosaurs and the Bat Cave. My favorite section is the Chinese galleries, which include a Ming tomb. See p. 134.

☕ TAKE A BREAK

The Royal Ontario Museum has a wonderful—but very expensive—restaurant in C5 (but be warned, it's often closed because of private events). A great bet for lunch or a snack is the ROM's **Food Studio** (🕾 **416/586-7926**). This cafeteria-style eatery serves fresh salads, pizza, and pasta, as well as more exotic fare.

④ George R. Gardiner Museum of Ceramic Art ★★

Face-lifts are a common preoccupation among Toronto museums. Just across the street from the ROM, the Gardiner revealed its new visage in 2006. I normally wouldn't recommend seeing one museum right after the other, but the ROM and the Gardiner are so different that it's manageable (plus you've just had a snack, right?). See p. 133.

⑤ Victoria College ★

This historic college is federated with the University of Toronto but maintains its own digs just east of the rest of the campus.

It has a pretty college quad, bordered by imposing Romanesque architecture (there's some blocky 1960s stuff, too, but try to ignore that). See p. 170.

❻ Queen's Park & the Ontario Legislature ★

This sweeping midtown park is also home to Ontario's legislative building. It's possible to do a tour on most days, though I'm partial to sitting on one of the many benches, admiring the building's pink-stone facade and the flower gardens in front. See p. 145.

❼ Allan Gardens ★

This was Toronto's first civic park, and the Edwardian Palm House conservatory is still a glamorous relic of the past. But it was only recently, when the University of Toronto's old greenhouses were relocated here and reborn as a conservatory for children, that Allan Gardens became a fun place to hang out again. See p. 151.

❽ Cabbagetown ★★

I simply love this neighborhood. You can't walk these residential streets without getting a powerful sense of Toronto's history. Once considered a slum, Cabbagetown is now filled with beautifully restored Victorian and Queen Anne–style houses. Even the first housing project in Canada, Spruce Court (at the intersection of Sumach and Spruce), looks like a charming collection of cottages. For a complete tour, see p. 175.

❾ Riverdale Farm ★★

For a lot of people, this farm is almost a sacred space. Whenever you visit, you'll find kids here, many of whom live in inner-city apartment blocks. But at Riverdale, you'll find them learning about farm life, playing with lambs, and cuddling bunnies. Sound bucolic? It is quite possibly the most serene spot in Toronto (well, if you can ignore those bleating goats). See p. 155.

❿ Necropolis ★

This Victorian cemetery is not only picturesque, but also filled with monuments to famous people who played key roles in Toronto's history. And the Gothic Revival chapel, tiny though it is, is considered one of the most perfect examples of this style anywhere. See p. 152.

> ⑪ **TAKE A BREAK**
> If you go to an event in Toronto and discover that **Daniel et Daniel** is catering it, you know that you're in excellent hands. At the shop, in addition to the divine pastries and chocolates, you can order salads and prepared meals for takeout. 248 Carlton St. ✆ **416/968-9275.** See p. 175.

⑫ Distillery District ★★★

This is the perfect place to finish your tour. Once the home of the largest distillery in Canada, today it's a multifaceted complex that has something for everyone. The red-brick architecture is a Victorian wonder, but the art galleries, restaurants, and boutiques are all completely modern. You might want to stay well into the evening: Performing-arts troupes are based here, and if you're visiting in clement weather, there's probably an open-air art fair or festival going on. See p. 132.

4 THE BEST OF TORONTO IN 3 DAYS

Spend your first 2 days following the earlier tours, and top it off with this exploration of Toronto's cultural mosaic and its art scene. At its core, Toronto is a patchwork of distinctive neighborhoods. This tour will take you through some of the oldest, which have evolved over the years. *Start: Dupont Station and walk 2 blocks north.*

❶ Casa Loma ★★★

I believe in starting your day on a high note, literally and figuratively. Casa Loma really is a castle, and it's on a hill that gives you an inspiring view of the sweep of the city (you'll see a lot more of Toronto than you did from the CN Tower the day before yesterday). But while you can admire the view for free, I strongly encourage you to visit the castle, too. The elegant rooms and period furniture are appropriately grand, though my favorite moments come when you get to climb the towers (one Norman, one Scottish, both great). See p. 143.

❷ Kensington Market ★★

You couldn't get further from the Old Money refinement of Casa Loma. Kensington Market is a multiethnic mélange with strong smells (fish markets) and strong sounds (stores with pumping stereos, conversations in a dozen different languages on any street you cross). This was a Jewish neighborhood long ago, but successive waves of immigration have added Portuguese and West Indian flavors. If you want to bring home some great finds, do some shopping in this area (check out Tom's Place, Fresh Baked Goods, and Courage My Love, all in chapter 9). See p. 150.

---

❸ TAKE A BREAK

It's not a cafe, so there's no place to sit down. But **Chocolate Addict** ★ is the perfect spot to get some ice cream or chocolate truffles to fuel your adventures (that's what keeps me going, anyway). 185 Baldwin St. ℂ **416/979-5809.** See p. 166.

---

❹ Chinatown ★★

Toronto has a large Chinese population dispersed throughout the city, but this is the historic home of the Chinese community. It's changed since its early days, particularly because of the infusion of Hong Kong money. It's such a large and significant area that it's a shame no official entryway exists.

The recent addition of gilded statues of dragons and the like on poles in the middle of Spadina Avenue is a nice touch, however. See p. 141.

❺ Art Gallery of Ontario ★

At press time the renovation is in full frenzy, and the gallery is closed. It's slated to reopen in November 2008, and the newly expanded space will be a must-see. The AGO has the best collection of Henry Moore sculpture in the world, as well as European masters, Canadian painters and sculptors, and African and Australian aboriginal art. See p. 131.

❻ Sharp Centre for Design

It amuses me that Toronto had such a reputation for being straitlaced in the past. It's always seemed to me that when people do wacky things here, hardly anyone raises an eyebrow. Take Casa Loma. Or this relatively new addition to the city's architectural landscape. Don't bother going inside (you can't get in unless you're a student of the Ontario College of Art & Design); all the drama is right in front of you. See p. 145.

❼ Queen Street West ★

Until recently, this would have been the Wild West of the downtown core. Now it's mainly a space for some very cool boutiques (Price Roman, Fashion Crimes, Peach Berserk, and the like; see chapter 9). It's also got a reputation as Toronto's Gourmet Ghetto—innovative yet well-priced menus abound in these parts. See chapter 6.

---

❽ TAKE A BREAK

You've earned a hearty meal, and you can have a proper one here at **Tortilla Flats.** I'm pretty much obsessed with the potato skins (cheese, bacon, and sour cream—who wouldn't be?), but there's plenty to choose from on the menu. Just try to resist the margaritas . . . or not. 458 Queen St. W. ℂ **416/203-0088.**

❾ The Art & Design District ★★★

This is one of Toronto's most exciting neighborhoods. Until relatively recently it was divey and derelict and, quite honestly, a depressing place to be. Now it's filled with art galleries and independent boutiques run by local designers. Mid- to late afternoon is the perfect time to check it out, because everything is open (some of the shops are closed all morning) and the street is full of life. See p. 141.

❿ Museum of Contemporary Canadian Art ★★

You've already seen the iconic art of the AGO; now's your chance to see what happening in today's art scene. MOCCA is a gallery that is getting a reputation for its (sometimes freaky) temporary exhibits. Hey, tattoos and body piercings are art, too. See p. 140.

⓫ Little Italy ★★

For years, Little Italy was written up as the coolest neighborhood in the city, the country, even North America. Then other areas, like the Art & Design District and the Distillery historic district (which you visited yesterday) started hogging the limelight. Truthfully, Little Italy is still fabulous, and the best time to see it is at night. Stop at a sexy bar like **Sutra** (p. 220) for drinks; enjoy dinner at a trattoria such as **Veni Vidi Vici** (p. 107); and dance the night away at **El Convento Rico** (p. 222). See p. 141.

Where to Stay

Choosing a hotel is always a careful balancing of cost, location, and amenities, but this equation is especially complex in Toronto. The city is expansive—attractions, restaurants, and shops are scattered within broad borders—so it can be tricky to decide where to base yourself. And accommodations are expensive. While bargains can be had, even downtown, proximity to central attractions such as the CN Tower, Harbourfront, the Rogers Centre, and the Eaton Centre, drives up the cost of a stay (though you'll read about some great budget-priced downtown options in this chapter).

To help you find lodgings near the destinations that interest you most, I have grouped them by both price and location. Most are in the neighborhoods defined in chapter 4 as Downtown West, Downtown East, and Midtown. I've also included a few hotels close to Pearson International Airport.

If you're having trouble finding a hotel, call **Tourism Toronto** (© **800/499-2514** or 416/203-2600) or visit the website at **www.seetorontonow.com** for advice. Keep in mind that some special deals are available only through a hotel's website. The **Fairmont Royal York** (p. 74) almost always has an online deal; the **Park Hyatt Toronto** (p. 85) often does too.

---

1 BEST HOTEL BETS

- **Best Historic Hotel:** The (gloved) hands-down winner is **Le Meridien King Edward,** 37 King St. E. (© **800/543-4300**), which was built in 1903 and is a sterling example of Edwardian architecture and opulence (thanks to a major renovation and several face-lifts). Over the years, the crème de la crème of society has trotted through the lobby, with its pink-marble columns and ornate frescoes. In the 1960s, the Beatles holed up in the King Eddy while 3,000 fans stormed the lobby. See p. 82.
- **Best for Business Travelers:** The **Metropolitan Hotel,** 108 Chestnut St. (© **800/668-6600**), is just a few minutes from the Financial District, and its amenities are competitive with those of its pricier competitors. Features include a 24-hour business center and in-room amenities such as fax/modem hookups, large work desks, and cordless two-line phones. The restaurants, Hemispheres and Lai Wah Heen, are favorite sites for business lunches. See p. 73.
- **Best Budget Hotel:** Given the location and amenities, it's hard to beat the **Hotel Victoria,** 56 Yonge St. (© **800/363-8228**), for price. The hotel is close to the Eaton Centre, Chinatown, and the Financial District, and its double rooms start at C$120 (£60) per night. See p. 80.
- **Best Hotel Dining:** The prize goes to **Senses,** 318 Wellington St. W. (© **416/961-0055**), at the **SoHo Metropolitan** for its divine combination of delicious fare, sensuous setting, and impeccable service. Close runners-up are the Hilton Toronto's very grand dining room, **Tundra** (© **416/860-6800**); the Fairmont Royal York's new offering, **Epic** (© **416/860-6949**); and the Park Hyatt's restaurant, **Annona** (© **416/924-5471**). See p. 101, 101, 74, and 112.

- **Best for a Stylish Stay:** The **Hôtel Le Germain,** 30 Mercer St. (© **866/345-9501**), one of Toronto's boutique hotels, is a stunner, with its dramatic design and lots of artwork in public and private spaces alike (even the elevators). See p. 76.
- **Best Gay-Friendly Hotel:** Everyone comes to the **Clarion Hotel & Suites Selby,** 592 Sherbourne St. (© **800/4-CHOICE**). In a Victorian building in a predominantly gay neighborhood, this Belle Epoque hotel draws gay, lesbian, and straight travelers. See p. 88.
- **Best for Travelers with Disabilities:** The **Fairmont Royal York,** 100 Front St. W. (© **800/441-1414**), pays a lot of attention to accessibility. The adaptations accommodate wheelchair users, the visually impaired, and the hearing impaired. See p. 74.

2 DOWNTOWN WEST

VERY EXPENSIVE

Hilton Toronto ★★   The Hilton Toronto isn't what it used to be—and that's a good thing. A few years ago the company splurged on a C$25-million face-lift, and suddenly the Hilton was one of the most attractive large hotels in the city. On the western edge of the Financial District—and right across the street from the Four Seasons Centre for the Performing Arts—the 32-story Hilton boasts generously sized rooms decorated with streamlined luxury in mind. Because of the hotel's excellent location overlooking the wide boulevard of University Avenue, many rooms (and the glass elevators) have superb vistas. Because of its proximity to the Financial District, the Hilton is a favorite among business travelers; the closeness to the Four Seasons Centre will undoubtedly appeal to opera buffs, too. Executive rooms include perks such as ultraplush terry bathrobes, trouser presses, and access to a private lounge that serves complimentary breakfast and evening snacks. The hotel is also home to the magnificent **Tundra** (p. 101), which serves top-notch Canadian cuisine.

145 Richmond St. W., Toronto, ON M5H 2L2. © **800/445-8667** or 416/869-3456. Fax 416/869-1478. www. toronto.hilton.com. 601 units. From C$319 (£160) double. Children 18 and under stay free in parent's room. Weekend packages available. AE, DC, MC, V. Subway: Osgoode. **Amenities:** 3 restaurants; bar; indoor and outdoor lap pools; health club; Jacuzzi; sauna; children's programs; concierge; business center; room service; massage; babysitting; same-day laundry service/dry cleaning. *In room:* A/C, TV, Wi-Fi, minibar, coffeemaker, hair dryer, iron.

The Metropolitan Hotel ★★   Off Dundas Street West, the hotel is a 5-minute stroll north of the business district and about 2 minutes west of the Eaton Centre. But why walk when you can take advantage of the complimentary limo service to any downtown core address? That perk is just one of the ways in which the Metropolitan attempts to compete with its pricier competitors. Rooms are spacious and designed with comfort in mind, featuring Italian linens, down duvets, and individual climate control. My favorite detail is that you can open the windows if you like, which makes this hotel a rarity in Toronto. The two restaurants are huge draws. **Lai Wah Heen** (p. 103), which serves classic Cantonese cuisine, is a top choice for business entertaining among natives as well as visitors. The modern-style ground-floor **Hemispheres** restaurant offers a Continental menu. Also, the Metropolitan has a partnership with the Toronto Symphony Orchestra, which offers guests special packages.

108 Chestnut St., Toronto, ON M5G 1R3. © **800/668-6600** or 416/977-5000. Fax 416/977-9513. www. metropolitan.com. 427 units. From C$320 (£160) double. Children 17 and under stay free in parent's

room. AE, DC, DISC, MC, V. Parking C$28 (£14). Subway: St. Patrick. **Amenities:** 2 restaurants; bar; indoor pool; health club; Jacuzzi; sauna; concierge; courtesy limo; 24-hr. business center (w/PCs and Macs); Wi-Fi; room service; massage; babysitting; same-day laundry service/dry cleaning. *In room:* A/C, TV, minibar, coffeemaker, hair dryer, iron, safe.

SoHo Metropolitan Hotel ★★★ This boutique hotel personifies grown-up elegance. The guest rooms are beautiful—done in a serene palette of neutral tones and blond wood—and they make better use of technology than any other Toronto hotel. Switches adjacent to the headboard control all of the lights in the room. Curtains open and close at the flick of a switch. Another control lowers a privacy screen that lets light in but shields you from view. The marble bathroom floor heats up at your command. The in-room safe is big enough for a laptop and has an outlet inside to charge your computer battery. There are no tatty DO NOT DISTURB signs; instead, another control panel lets you indicate your desire to be left alone or request housekeeping as need be. Of course, the telephones are cordless. The SoHo Met is also home to one of Toronto's best restaurants, **Senses** (p. 101).

318 Wellington St. W., Toronto, ON M5V 3T4. © **800/668-6600** or 416/599-8800. Fax 416/599-8801. www.metropolitan.com/soho. 93 units. From C$310 (£155) double. AE, DC, MC, V. Parking C$30 (£15). Subway: St. Andrew. **Amenities:** Restaurant; bar; health club; concierge; business center; room service; laundry service; dry cleaning. *In room:* A/C, TV, Wi-Fi, minibar, coffeemaker, hair dryer, iron, safe.

EXPENSIVE

Fairmont Royal York ★★ Built by the Canadian-Pacific Railroad in 1929, this massive hotel has 1,365 guest rooms and suites, and 35 meeting and banquet rooms. The old-fashioned lobby is magnificent; just sitting on a plush couch and watching the crowd is an event. Still, you have to decide whether you want to stay under the same roof with countless business travelers, shoppers, tour groups, and conventioneers. Service is remarkably efficient but necessarily impersonal; the downtown location, across from Union Station and just steps from the Theater District and the Hummingbird Centre, is excellent. The hotel pays particular attention to accessibility, making adaptations to some guest rooms so that they are specially designed for wheelchair users, the hearing impaired, and the visually impaired. Every public area in the hotel is wheelchair accessible. Other special features include the Elizabeth Milan Day Spa, Epic restaurant, and the Library Bar, which serves the best martinis in the city.

100 Front St. W., Toronto, ON M5J 1E3. © **800/441-1414.** Fax 416/368-9040. www.fairmont.com/royal york. 1,365 units. From C$225 (£113) double. Packages available. AE, DC, DISC, MC, V. Parking C$30 (£15). Subway: Union. Pets accepted. **Amenities:** 5 restaurants; 2 bars/lounges; skylit indoor pool; health club; spa (w/special packages for guests); Jacuzzi; sauna; concierge; business center; Wi-Fi; shopping arcade;

(**Finds**) **Hidden Gallery**

Even if you're not a guest at the **Fairmont Royal York,** take time to stop by the hotel. It's loaded with Art Deco charms, and it's got some tempting watering holes and places to dine. It also has its own gallery of photographs, which is located on the mezzanine level, just above the lobby. The black-and-white prints reveal a great deal of Toronto history, which, of course, is intimately tied to the hotel's history. There are also candid portraits of some of the hotel's more famous guests, including one of a young Queen Elizabeth II.

Delta Chelsea **1**
The Drake Hotel **6**
Fairmont Royal York **12**
The Gladstone Hotel **6**
Hilton Toronto **5**
Holiday Inn on King **7**
Hôtel Le Germain **8**
Hotel Victoria **13**
The Metropolitan Hotel **3**
Renaissance Toronto Hotel **10**
Sheraton Centre Toronto Hotel **4**
SoHo Metropolitan Hotel **9**
The Strathcona **11**
Toronto Marriott Eaton Centre **2**
Westin Harbour Castle **14**

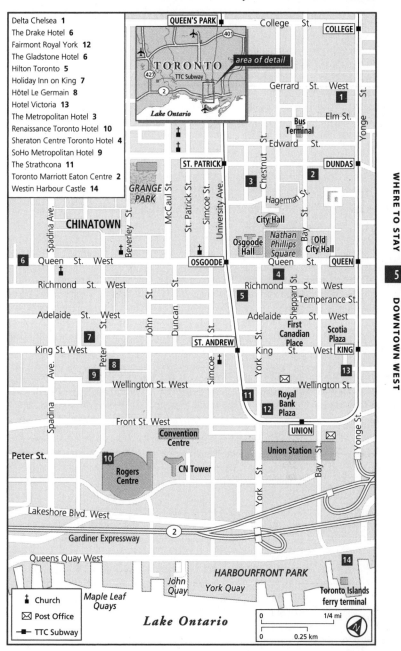

WHERE TO STAY

5

DOWNTOWN WEST

salon; room service; babysitting; same-day laundry service/dry cleaning. *In room:* A/C, TV, minibar, coffeemaker, hair dryer, iron.

Holiday Inn on King

The blinding-white facade of this building suggests that some architect mistook Toronto for the Tropics. No matter—its location is hot, with the Theater District, gourmet ghetto, Chinatown, and the Rogers Centre nearby. It's also close to the Financial District, which explains the mix of business travelers and vacationers. Half the floors are office space; guest rooms start at the ninth floor and go up to the 20th. The good-size guestrooms were completely renovated in 2007, and the results are very attractive. Each one has a two-line cordless phone, double-glazed windows and individually controlled air-conditioning. While the amenities have improved, the price of the average room has increased, too, making this a far cry from a traditional Holiday Inn.

370 King St. W. (at Peter St.), Toronto, ON M5V 1J9. (*C*) **800/263-6364** or 416/599-4000. Fax 416/599-7394. www.hiok.com. 435 units. From C$230 (£115) double. Extra person C$20 (£10). AE, DISC, MC, V. Parking C$18 (£9). Subway: St. Andrew. Pets accepted. **Amenities:** Restaurant; bar; small outdoor pool; health club; Jacuzzi; sauna; room service; massage. *In room:* A/C, TV, Wi-Fi, coffeemaker, hair dryer.

Hôtel Le Germain ★★

Located in Toronto's Theater District, this hotel offers edgy elegance. Elevators are "wrapped" in words of English and French poetry. The vast lobby manages to be at once intimate and grand. The library lounge area boasts a fireplace, an espresso maker, a wall of objets d'art, and cozy white couches. The breakfast "room" on the second floor is like an expansive landing and the tables are all communal. The guest rooms are beautifully designed: The ceilings are high, the desk can be moved around to your liking (it's attached to the wall on one side), and the linens and robes are by Frette. My favorite feature, though, is the glass wall in every bathroom, which allows light in from the main room and makes everything feel more spacious (there are blinds for those who want their privacy). All guests have access to the exercise room on the 11th floor, which has floor-to-ceiling windows and an open-air terrace.

30 Mercer St., Toronto, ON M5V 1H3. (*C*) **866/345-9501** or 416/345-9500. Fax 416/345-9501. www. germaintoronto.com. 122 units. From C$275 (£138) double. AE, DC, MC, V. Parking C$30 (£15). Subway: St. Andrew. **Amenities:** Restaurant; bar; health club; concierge; business center; room service; babysitting; laundry service; dry cleaning. *In room:* A/C, TV, Wi-Fi, minibar, coffeemaker, hair dryer, iron, safe.

Renaissance Toronto Hotel Downtown

If you're a diehard baseball fan, this Marriott hotel is a dream come true—70 rooms overlook the verdant Astroturf of the Rogers Centre, home of the Toronto Blue Jays. The field-view rooms are amazing if you remember one thing: The view goes both ways. Soon after it opened, the hotel became notorious when the amorous antics of a pair of guests showed up on the JumboTron, the giant screen that's supposed to be showing the on-field action. The incident is now a minor local legend. The lesson: All rooms have shades; remember to use them! The guest rooms are all a good size, but there's a definite pecking order: Rooms that face the city are the least expensive, with uninspiring views. Still, this is a strong contender as a tourist hotel—it's in a great location for theater, dining, and sights.

1 Blue Jays Way, Toronto, ON M5V 1J4. (*C*) **800/237-1512** or 416/341-7100. Fax 416/341-5091. www. renaissancehotels.com/yyzbr. 348 units. From C$239 (£120) double. AE, DC, DISC, MC, V. Parking C$30 (£15). Subway: Union. **Amenities:** Restaurant; bar; indoor pool; squash courts; health club; sauna; concierge; business center; Wi-Fi; room service; same-day laundry service/dry cleaning. *In room:* A/C, TV, coffeemaker, hair dryer, iron.

Westin Harbour Castle ★

This convention hotel is on the lakefront, just across from the Toronto Islands ferry docks. Not surprisingly, the views are among the best in

ⓘ Tips   No Smoking, Please

It seemed like a novelty just a few years ago, when the **Westin Harbour Castle** Hotel designated all of its guest rooms non-smoking (part of a larger initiative of the Westin chain in North America). Now, it's almost commonplace. Several Toronto hotels, including the **Hotel le Germain, the Drake Hotel, the Renaissance Toronto Hotel Downtown, the Toronto Marriott Downtown Eaton Centre, the Courtyard Toronto Downtown, the Hotel Victoria,** and the new **Hazelton Hotel,** are entirely non-smoking.

the city. The trade-off is that it is somewhat out of the way. It's a 5-minute walk to Union Station, but to get there you have to cross under the Gardiner Expressway, one of Toronto's ugliest and most desolate patches. The hotel tries to compensate with shuttle bus service; you'll also find a public-transit stop and a queue of cabs at the hotel. Regardless, it's unlikely you'll want to go for an evening stroll around the neighborhood. Recognizing the lack of things to do in the vicinity, management has wisely populated the hotel with attractions. The dining options are excellent: Toula attracts Toronto residents as well as visitors in droves. There are also terrific sports facilities, giving this monolithic hotel the feel of a resort.

1 Harbour Sq., Toronto, ON M5J 1A6. ⓒ **800/WESTIN-1** or 416/869-1600. Fax 416/361-7448. www.westin. com/harbourcastle. 977 units. From C$209 (£105) double. Extra person C$30 (£15). Children stay free in parent's room. Weekend packages available. AE, DC, MC, V. Parking C$28 (£14). Subway: Union and then LRT to Queens Quay. **Amenities:** 2 restaurants; 2 bars; indoor pool; 2 tennis courts; 2 squash courts; excellent health club; spa; Jacuzzi; sauna; children's center; concierge; business center; Wi-Fi; salon; room service; laundry service; dry cleaning. *In room:* A/C, TV, minibar, coffeemaker, hair dryer, iron.

MODERATE

Delta Chelsea ★★ ⓚ Kids ⓥ Value   It's impossible for a hotel to be all things to all people, but the Delta Chelsea comes pretty close. Luxury seekers should look elsewhere, and backpackers won't be able to afford it, but the Delta Chelsea meets the needs of many of those in between. This is a particularly good bet for young families. Guest rooms are bright and cheery; a few have kitchenettes. On the Signature Club floor for business travelers, rooms have cordless speakerphones, faxes, well-stocked desks, and ergonomic chairs. The hotel boasts a four-story indoor waterslide, plus grown-up amenities such as Deck 27, a lounge with a panoramic view of Toronto. The hotel has partnerships with CanStage, Soulpepper, the CN Tower, and Paramount Canada's Wonderland, and guests enjoy access to tickets for everything from blockbuster shows to special events (some tickets may be included in the price of a weekend package).

33 Gerrard St. W., Toronto, ON M5G 1Z4. ⓒ **800/243-5732** or 416/595-1975. Fax 416/585-4362. www. deltahotels.com. 1,590 units. From C$179 (£90) double. Extra person C$20 (£10). Children 17 and under stay free in parent's room. Weekend packages available. AE, DC, DISC, MC, V. Parking C$29 (£15). Subway: College. **Amenities:** 3 restaurants; 3 bars; 2 pools (1 for adults only); health club; Jacuzzi; sauna; children's center; billiards room; concierge; tour desk; business center; Wi-Fi; salon; babysitting; laundry service; dry cleaning. *In room:* A/C, TV, coffeemaker, hair dryer, iron.

The Drake Hotel ★★ ⓕ Finds   The Drake opened in February 2004 to universal acclaim. Part of the appeal is its rags-to-riches pedigree: The Drake was rescued by owner Jeff Stober, who injected C$6 million into the property, creating a boutique hotel. The

Flophouse Chic

Once a leafy suburb of Toronto (and, for a short time in the late 19th century, a city in its own right), **Parkdale** had become a grim and depressing place by the 1980s and '90s. Named for its proximity to High Park, it was better known for its drug treatment centers, rundown buildings, and homeless population. No street represented this better than Parkdale's southern artery, Queen Street West, between Roncesvalles and Bathurst. But in the past few years, things have changed. Artists, designers, and young entrepreneurs flocked to Parkdale for cheap rent and accessibility to the downtown core. West Queen West, as the stretch west of Bathurst is known, was christened **The Art & Design District,** home of the Museum of Contemporary Canadian Art (p. 140) relocated there.

The march of gentrification continues, with boutiques and bistros spreading ever westward—and hotels opening their doors to tourists. Both the **Drake** and the **Gladstone** spent several years as notorious flophouses, but their completely renovated interiors are now reserved for chic visitors who want to be at Toronto's cutting edge. Their small rooms and relative distance from the usual tourist attractions means that they won't appeal to everyone. Also, while Parkdale is much safer than it used to be, the Centre for Mental Health and Addiction is still located at no. 1001, and as you walk west you will see pawnshops and other reminders of the gritty old neighborhood.

renovation is gorgeous. While the 19 guest rooms are mostly on the tiny side—ranging from 14 to 36 sq. m (150–385 sq. ft.)—they're cleverly designed and have good amenities (CD/DVD players and lovely linens, for example). The Drake's strength is in its public spaces, and for a property this small, it has lots of them: a restaurant and bar, a rooftop lounge, and a cafe; an exercise studio for yoga classes; and a performance venue, the Underground, that features live music. There are also works of art throughout the hotel. The Drake has been warmly welcomed by Toronto's arts community, and this is the one hotel in town where you're far more likely to meet city residents than visitors.

1150 Queen St. W., Toronto, ON M6J 1J3. (C) **416/531-5042.** Fax 416/531-9493. www.thedrakehotel.ca. 19 units. From C$189 (£95) double. AE, MC, V. Subway: Osgoode and then streetcar west to Beaconsfield. **Amenities:** 2 restaurants; cafe; 2 bars; yoga studio; massage room. *In room:* A/C, TV, Wi-Fi; hair dryer, iron.

The Gladstone Hotel ★★ (Finds This lovely Victorian red-brick hotel first opened its doors in 1889 and has housed guests continuously since then. After a massive renovation, the hotel relaunched itself as a chic place to stay in December 2005. Each guest room was created by different Canadian artists. They range from the film-noir setting of the "Parlour of Twilight," which channels the spirit of Raymond Chandler, to the riotous "Red Room," a sumptuous confection of color, pattern, and texture. If you're a light sleeper, this may not be the place for you. The hotel has retained its original windows—which open to let air in—but they have single-pane glass. Earplugs are provided on the nightstand, but given that the Gladstone is situated near railway tracks, this may not afford enough peace and quiet for everyone's liking. The hotel uses its public spaces as a rotating art gallery, and its Melody Bar is widely regarded as the best place in Toronto for karaoke.

1214 Queen St. W., Toronto, ON M6J 1J6. ☎ **416/531-4635.** Fax 416/539-0953. www.gladstonehotel. com. 51 units. From C$185 (£93) double. AE, MC, V. Subway: Osgoode and then streetcar west to Gladstone. **Amenities:** Restaurant; cafe; bar. *In room:* A/C, TV, Wi-Fi; hair dryer, iron, safe.

Sheraton Centre Toronto Hotel ★★ (Kids)

It's entirely possible to stay at this hotel and never venture outside—the Sheraton complex includes restaurants, bars, and a cinema, and the building connects to Toronto's underground city. If you long for a patch of green, the hotel provides that, too: The south side of the lobby contains a manicured garden with a waterfall. Am I making the place sound like a monolith? Well, it is. But it's an excellent home base for families because of its location and extensive list of child-friendly features, including a children's center and a huge pool.

Most of the guest rooms in this skyscraper-heavy neighborhood lack a serious view, though as you near the top of the 46-story complex, the sights are inspiring indeed. Designed for business travelers, the Club Level rooms contain mini-business centers with a fax/printer/copier and two-line speakerphone.

123 Queen St. W., Toronto, ON M5H 2M9. ☎ **800/325-3535** or 416/361-1000. Fax 416/947-4854. www. sheratontoronto.com. 1,377 units. From C$145 (£73) double. Extra person C$20 (£10). 2 children 17 and under stay free in parent's room. Packages available. AE, DC, MC, V. Parking C$33 (£17). Subway: Osgoode. **Amenities:** 2 restaurants; bar; gigantic heated indoor/outdoor pool; health club; spa; Jacuzzi; sauna; children's center; concierge; tour desk; business center; Wi-Fi; shopping arcade; room service; babysitting; laundry service; dry cleaning. *In room:* A/C, TV, coffeemaker, hair dryer, iron.

The Strathcona ★ (Value)

If you want to be in the Financial District but don't want to pay a bundle, this is a great option. For years, The Strathcona has been one of the best buys in the city, and a recent renovation has made it more attractive. It sits in the shadow of the Fairmont Royal York, a short walk from all major downtown attractions. The trade-offs aren't as extensive as you might think. The Strathcona's rooms are on the small side but are no less comfortable for their compact design.

60 York St., Toronto, ON M5J 1S8. ☎ **800/268-8304** or 416/363-3321. Fax 416/363-4679. www.the strathconahotel.com. 194 units. From C$175 (£88) double. AE, DC, MC, V. Subway: Union. **Amenities:** Cafe; bar; access to nearby health club; bike rental; children's center; concierge; tour desk; car-rental desk; room service; babysitting; laundry service; dry cleaning. *In room:* A/C, TV, Wi-Fi; hair dryer, iron.

Toronto Marriott Downtown Eaton Centre

Attention, shoppers: Want proximity to Toronto's central shrine to commerce? Consider the Marriott, which is connected to the Eaton Centre. This hotel caters to the tourist crowd: While a good concierge at any hotel can point you in the direction of, say, a hot restaurant, the Marriott has desks set up to facilitate day-trip planning and other activities. Because of its location, this is a fine choice for determined sightseers. One caveat is that the area immediately surrounding the Eaton Centre is pickpocket heaven. On the positive side, it's always busy in this neighborhood; in summer the Yonge-Dundas Square (p. 210) offers open-air concerts and films.

Most of the Marriott's guest rooms are well sized, and all of them now have 32-inch flatscreen TVs. Because you'll find office towers in all directions, blocking many of the views, a pleasant surprise is the view of the beautiful 19th-century Holy Trinity Church from the Parkside restaurant.

525 Bay St. (at Dundas St.), Toronto, ON M5G 2L2. ☎ **800/905-0667** or 416/597-9200. Fax 416/597-9211. www.marriotteatoncentre.com. 459 units. From C$175 (£88) double. AE, DC, DISC, MC, V. Parking C$27

ⓘ Tips   **For Travelers in Need**

ⓘ Tips   **For Travelers in Need**

If you should suddenly find yourself without a place to stay in Toronto, call the **Travellers' Aid Society of Toronto** (☎ **416/366-7788;** www.travellersaid.ca). The organization will find you last-minute accommodations, and they can also assist in crisis situations. They maintain booths at the airport, as well as Union Station.

(£14). Subway: Dundas. **Amenities:** 3 restaurants; bar; indoor rooftop pool; health club; Jacuzzi; sauna; concierge; tour desk; car-rental desk; business center; Wi-Fi; room service; massage; same-day laundry service/dry cleaning. *In room:* A/C, TV, coffeemaker, hair dryer, iron.

INEXPENSIVE

Hotel Victoria ★★ ⓥValue   In a landmark downtown building near the Hummingbird Centre and the Hockey Hall of Fame, the Victoria retains the glamorous touches of an earlier age, such as crown moldings and marble columns in the lobby. It's Toronto's second-oldest hotel (built in 1909), but the facilities are upgraded annually. Because of its size, the 56-room hotel offers an unusually high level of personal service and attention, which you normally wouldn't expect in budget accommodations. Standard rooms are on the small side but are nicely put together; deluxe rooms are larger and have coffeemakers and minifridges. Another nice touch: complimentary wireless Internet access throughout the hotel.

56 Yonge St. (at Wellington St.), Toronto, ON M5E 1G5. ☎ **800/363-8228** or 416/363-1666. Fax 416/363-7327. www.hotelvictoria-toronto.com. 56 units. From C$120 (£60) double. Extra person C$20 (£10). Rates include continental breakfast. AE, DC, MC, V. Subway: King. **Amenities:** Restaurant; access to nearby health club; Wi-Fi; babysitting; laundry service; dry cleaning. *In room:* A/C, TV, hair dryer, iron.

3 DOWNTOWN EAST

EXPENSIVE

Cambridge Suites Hotel ★★ ⓥValue   The Cambridge sits on the edge of the Financial District, catering to a corporate crowd that never wants to be more than a few steps from the office. The emphasis is on comfortable luxury, starting with the fact that all units are suites. The smallest start at a generous 51 sq. m (550 sq. ft.) and move up to deluxe duplexes. (In fact, the Jacuzzi-outfitted penthouse suites have come to the attention of celebrities tired of Toronto's tried-and-true star-catering hotels; the views are breathtaking.) The amenities for business travelers are solid. If you can drag yourself away from the cozy desk area, which has two two-line telephones and a fax, you can enjoy some of the comforts of home: fridge, microwave, and dining ware, plus coffee, tea, and snacks. And if you hand over your shopping list, the staff will stock the fridge, too.

15 Richmond St. E. (near Yonge St.), Toronto, ON M5C 1N2. ☎ **800/463-1990** or 416/368-1990. Fax 416/601-3751. www.cambridgesuitestoronto.com. 229 units. From C$225 (£113). Rates include continental breakfast. AE, DC, DISC, MC, V. Parking C$18 (£9). Subway: Queen. **Amenities:** Restaurant; bar; small health club (and access to much larger health club nearby); spa; Jacuzzi; sauna; concierge; business center; room service; babysitting; laundry service; dry cleaning. *In room:* A/C, TV, Wi-Fi, fax, minibar, fridge, coffeemaker, hair dryer, iron.

College St.

COLLEGE `1`

`2`

Carlton St.

ALLAN GARDENS

TORONTO

area of detail

TTC Subway

Lake Ontario

`3`

Gerrard St. East

Elm St.

Bus Terminal

Edward St.

Chestnut St.

Yonge St.

Church St.

Jarvis St.

Sherbourne St.

DUNDAS

Dundas St. East

Hagerman St.

Eaton Centre

City Hall

Bay St.

Nathan Phillips Square

Old City Hall

Queen St.

QUEEN

Victoria St.

`4`

`5`

Shuter St.

MOSS PARK

Queen St. East

Sheppard St.

Temperance St.

Richmond St. East

`6`

✉ Lombard St.

`7`

Adelaide St. East

First Canadian Place

Scotia Plaza

OLD TOWN

King St. West

KING

King St. East

`8`

Church St.

Market St.

Jarvis St.

Sherbourne St.

✉ Wellington St. East

Royal Bank Plaza

Bay St.

Scott St.

Front St. East

The Esplanade

UNION ✉

Union Station

Yonge St.

Sony Centre

✝ Church

✉ Post Office

■— TTC Subway

0   1/4 mi

0   0.25 km

Lakeshore Blvd. East

Bond Place Hotel **4**
Cambridge Suites Hotel **6**
Courtyard Toronto Downtown **1**
Days Inn & Conference Centre **2**
Holiday Inn Express Toronto Downtown **7**
Le Meridien King Edward **8**
Neill-Wycik College Hotel **3**
Pantages Suites Hotel and Spa **5**

WHERE TO STAY

5

DOWNTOWN EAST

(Kids) Family-Friendly Hotels

Delta Chelsea (p. 77)   This perennial family favorite has a Family Fun Zone, a multiroom play area with live bunnies and fish, a video arcade, and the only indoor waterslide in downtown Toronto (it's open year-round, too). You can play together in the family pool here or drop off the tykes for babysitting. Kids will enjoy the in-room family movies, Super Nintendo, cookie jar (replenished daily), and nightly turndown gift. Some of the Delta Chelsea's restaurants have half-price kids' menus, further reducing the strain on the family purse.

Four Seasons Hotel Toronto (p. 84)   A hop and a skip from the newly renovated Royal Ontario Museum, this hotel has its own attractions. Guests can borrow free bicycles and video games, and use the indoor pool. Upon arrival, room service brings the kids complimentary cookies and milk. The concierge and housekeeping staff can arrange excellent babysitting services.

Sheraton Centre Toronto Hotel (p. 79)   The endless attractions of this complex—including restaurants with special menus for tykes and a cinema—mean there's a lot to keep the little ones entertained. There's a supervised play center, as well as on-call babysitting services. Kids also enjoy in-room video games and a welcome gift. A limited number of Family Guest Rooms boast a toy chest, some kid-size furniture, a fridge, and a microwave.

Le Meridien King Edward ★★   At one time, the King Eddie was the only place in Toronto where Hollywood royalty, such as Liz Taylor and Richard Burton, would stay. In the 1980s, after years of neglect, some local investors spent C$40 million to rescue it. The result recalls its former glory, with rosy marble columns and a glass-domed rotunda dominating the lobby. Although the guest rooms aren't what I'd call spacious—28 to 33 sq. m (300–350 sq. ft.) is standard—their uniformly high ceilings give them a sweeping grandeur that is unusual. Unlike the standard-issue rooms in many competing hotels, these guest rooms have been decorated with a personal touch. The bathrooms are particularly nice, with large marble tubs.

Afternoon tea is an institution at the King Eddie (it's served in the mirrored lounge just off the lobby). The wood-paneled Consort Bar is perfect for people-watching while sipping a champagne cocktail.

37 King St. E., Toronto, ON M5C 2E9. ℂ **800/543-4300** or 416/863-9700. Fax 416/863-4102. www. starwoodhotels.com. 298 units. From C$249 (£125) double. AE, DC, MC, V. Parking C$30 (£15). Subway: King. Pets accepted. **Amenities:** 2 restaurants; bar; health club; Jacuzzi; sauna; concierge; Wi-Fi; room service; babysitting; laundry service; dry cleaning. *In room:* A/C, TV, fax, minibar, hair dryer, iron.

Pantages Suites Hotel and Spa   This hotel is in a prime location just a block away from the Eaton Centre. But Victoria Street is so quiet, you'd never guess that you're downtown and a short walk from most of Toronto's big attractions. The Pantages plays up the fact that it's an oasis of serenity in the middle of the city. Guest rooms are decked out in a soothing palette of neutrals, and they all have cushy duvets and 400-thread-count linens. Better yet, many rooms have a Jacuzzi tub. The hotel also pays careful attention to security (important, because the Eaton Centre area has long been a favorite with petty thieves), with features such as room-key-only access to the elevator.

200 Victoria St. (at Shuter St.), Toronto, ON M5B 1V8. ✆ **866/852-1777** or 416/362-1777. Fax 416/214-5618. www.pantageshotel.com. 157 units. From C$229 (£115) double. Rates include continental breakfast. AE, DC, MC, V. Parking C$28 (£14). Subway: Queen. **Amenities:** Restaurant; bar; spa; Jacuzzi; sauna; concierge; business center; room service; laundry service; dry cleaning. *In room:* A/C, TV, Wi-Fi, fax, minibar, coffeemaker, hair dryer, iron.

MODERATE

Courtyard Toronto Downtown ★
Anyone who knows the Marriott chain of hotels knows that its Courtyard hotels are usually out of the city center. This bright and shiny property near Yonge and College is an exception, convenient both to the Financial District downtown and to the chic cafes and shops of Midtown—a claim few other hotels in the city can make.

The lobby, with its double-sided fireplace, has a surprisingly intimate feel given the size of the hotel (truth be told, it's due to the fact that tour groups have a separate reception area). The guest rooms don't tend to be big, but they do have a lot of comforts, including windows that open, high-speed Internet access ports, and a second sink outside the bathroom. Ongoing refurbishments keep guest rooms looking fresh rather than lived in. While Courtyards are generally regarded as business hotels, this one has family-friendly facilities such as a children's wading pool.

475 Yonge St. (1 block north of College St.), Toronto, ON M4Y 1X7. ✆ **800/847-5075** or 416/924-0611. Fax 416/924-8692. www.courtyard.com/yyzcy. 575 units. From C$139 (£70) double. AE, DC, MC, V. Parking C$30 (£15). Subway: College. **Amenities:** 2 restaurants; bar; health club; tour desk; business center; room service; laundry service; dry cleaning. *In room:* A/C, TV, Wi-Fi, minibar, coffeemaker, hair dryer, iron, safe.

INEXPENSIVE

Bond Place Hotel ★
The location is right—a block from the Eaton Centre, around the corner from the Canon and Elgin theaters—and so is the price. Perhaps that's why this hotel tends to be popular with tour groups. (The fact that the staff speaks several European and Asian languages doesn't hurt either.) The rooms are on the small side. Book as far in advance as you can; the hotel is usually packed, especially in summer.

65 Dundas St. E., Toronto, ON M5B 2G8. ✆ **800/268-9390** or 416/362-6061. Fax 416/360-6406. www.bondplacehoteltoronto.com. 287 units. From C$100 (£50) double. Extra person C$20 (£10). Weekend packages available. AE, DC, DISC, MC, V. Parking C$15 (£7.50). Subway: Dundas. **Amenities:** Restaurant; bar; concierge; tour desk; car-rental desk; room service; laundry service; dry cleaning. *In room:* A/C, TV, coffeemaker, hair dryer, iron.

Days Inn & Conference Centre Toronto Downtown
Now that Maple Leaf Gardens is retired (hockey has moved to the Air Canada Centre, and at the time of this writing, there's talk of tearing it down to make way for a supermarket), the Days Inn's location isn't what it used to be. Still, this hotel isn't far from the downtown core, and its reasonable rates continue to draw business, particularly with those traveling for leisure (and on a budget). Extensive renovations have spruced up both the public areas and the guest rooms.

30 Carlton St., Toronto, ON M5B 2E9. ✆ **800/329-7466** or 416/977-6655. Fax 416/977-0502. www.dayshoteltoronto.ca. 538 units. From C$125 (£63) double. Extra person C$20 (£10). Children 17 and under stay free in parent's room. Summer discounts available. AE, DISC, MC, V. Parking C$18 (£9). Subway: College. **Amenities:** Restaurant; cafe; bar; indoor pool; sauna; concierge; tour desk; car-rental desk; laundry service; dry cleaning. *In room:* A/C, TV, fridge, coffeemaker, hair dryer, iron.

ⓥalue   Summer-Only Stays

From September to early May, the dorms at the University of Toronto and at Ryerson Polytechnic University are full of students. But in summer, many of these rooms are rented out to budget-minded travelers. If you don't mind your in-room amenities on the spartan side, you can save a lot of money this way—and get a great downtown or midtown location, too.

Neill-Wycik College Hotel   During the school year, this is a Ryerson residence. Some students work here in the summer, when the Neill-Wycik morphs into a guesthouse. Rooms have beds, chairs, desks, and phones but no air-conditioning or TVs (although there is a TV lounge). Groups of five bedrooms share two bathrooms and one kitchen with a refrigerator and stove. The hotel has two roof decks, on the 5th and 23rd floors. It's less than a 5-minute walk to the Eaton Centre. 96 Gerrard St. E. (between Church and Jarvis sts.), Toronto, ON M5B 1G7. ⓒ **800/268-4358** or 416/977-2320. Fax 416/977-2809. www. neill-wycik.com. 300 units, none w/private bathroom. C$64 (£32) double; C$94 (£47) family (2 adults, plus children). MC, V. Subway: College. **Amenities:** Cafe; sauna; 24-hr. coin-op laundry.

Victoria University at the University of Toronto   This is a steal for this very expensive neighborhood (just a 2-minute walk from tony Yorkville). Victoria University offers simple rooms with plain furnishings (a bed, desk, and chair are standard), but the surroundings are splendid. Many of the rooms are in Burwash Hall, a 19th-century building that overlooks a peaceful, leafy quad. All rooms are down the street from the Royal Ontario Museum and up the street from Queen's Park. Guests are provided with linens, towels, and soap. 140 Charles St. W., Toronto, ON M5S 1K9. ⓒ **416/585-4524.** Fax 416/585-4530. www.vicu.utoronto.ca. 700 units, none w/private bathroom. C$60 (£30) single; C$80 (£40) double (2 twin beds). Rates include breakfast. MC, V. Subway: Museum. **Amenities:** Access to health club w/Olympic-size pool; tennis courts; laundry room. *In room:* No phone.

Holiday Inn Express Toronto Downtown   The main selling point of this no-frills hotel is its location, close to the Financial District and the Eaton Centre. It often offers special promotions, so be sure to ask. Rooms tend to be small, with standard amenities.

111 Lombard St. (between Adelaide and Richmond sts.), Toronto, ON M5C 2T9. ⓒ **800/228-5151** or 416/367-5555. Fax 416/367-3470. www.ichotelsgroup.com. 196 units. From C$125 (£63) double. Rates include continental breakfast. AE, DC, DISC, MC, V. Parking C$20 (£10). Subway: King or Queen. **Amenities:** Laundry service; dry cleaning. *In room:* A/C, TV, Wi-Fi, coffeemaker, hair dryer, iron.

4 MIDTOWN

VERY EXPENSIVE

Four Seasons Hotel Toronto ★★ ⓚids   The Rolling Stones call the Four Seasons home in Toronto, and during the Toronto International Film Festival, you can't get in for love or money. The hotel, in the ritzy Yorkville district, has earned a reputation for offering fine service and complete comfort. The public areas are decorated like a French parlor, with marble floors and dramatic floral arrangements. Rooms tend to be on the small side (a standard model is only about 30 sq. m/323 sq. ft.), but they're well designed and easy on the eye. Corner rooms have charming balconies affording great views of the street scene below. The formal dining room, Truffles, is a Toronto institution. The second-floor Studio Cafe is a favorite among the business crowd; its menu features many health-conscious, low-fat dishes. The Avenue bar is a perfect perch for people-watching.

21 Avenue Rd., Toronto, ON M5R 2G1. ℂ **800/268-6282** or 416/964-0411. Fax 416/964-2301. www. fourseasons.com/toronto. 380 units. From C$340 (£170) double. Weekend discounts and packages available. AE, DC, DISC, MC, V. Parking C$30 (£15). Subway: Bay. **Amenities:** 2 restaurants; 2 bars/lounges; indoor/outdoor pool; health club; Jacuzzi; bike rental; concierge; weekday courtesy limo to downtown; business center; room service; massage; babysitting; same-day laundry service/dry cleaning. *In room:* A/C, TV, Wi-Fi, minibar, hair dryer, iron, safe.

The Hazelton Hotel ★ The Hazelton opened in August 2007, declaring itself Toronto's first five-star hotel. So what if no organization actually awarded its stars? (The Hazelton's claim is that it was built to five-star specifications.) It is undeniably beautiful, with an understated masculine glamour obvious in both public spaces and guestrooms (designed by Yabu Pushelberg). Rooms are spacious, and the bathrooms are particularly delightful, with heated marble floors and a small TV screen in the wall above the sink. The hotel also boasts an excellent Mark McEwan restaurant and a screening room that seats 25. The downside? Yorkville Avenue is currently under so much construction that you may want a hardhat just to walk down the street. And the Hazelton is just a little *too* starstruck, dubbing one dining room the "Neil Young Room," though the Canadian musician has no connection with the hotel.

118 Yorkville Ave., Toronto, ON M5R 1C2. ℂ **866/473-6301** or 416/964-6300. Fax 416/963-6399. www. thehazeltonhotel.com. 77 units. From C$450 (£225) double. AE, DC, DISC, MC, V. Parking C$30 (£15). Subway: Bay. **Amenities:** Restaurant; indoor lap pool; health club; spa; concierge; weekday courtesy limo to downtown; business center; room service; massage; babysitting; same-day laundry service/dry cleaning. *In room:* A/C, TV, Wi-Fi, minibar, hair dryer, iron, safe.

Park Hyatt Toronto ★★★ The Park Hyatt is upgrading this property again, less than a decade after a C$60-million renovation in 2003, cementing its reputation as the last word in luxe. The guest rooms in the North Tower are among the most generously proportioned in town—the *smallest* is 46 sq. m (495 sq. ft.). A glamorous lobby dotted with Eastern-inspired objets d'art links the North and South towers. The ground-floor restaurant **Annona** (p. 112) is a treat for gourmets. Mordecai Richler famously called the 18th-floor Roof Lounge the only civilized place in Toronto. But his comment predated the opening of the Stillwater Spa. It features the Couples Sanctuary, which has a whirlpool tub, fireplace, and side-by-side massage tables—perfect for inseparable romantics. This hotel's convenient location across the street from the Royal Ontario Museum affords all the advantages of Yorkville, as well as a reprieve from the construction-laden mess that Yorkville Avenue has become.

4 Avenue Rd., Toronto, ON M5R 2E8. ℂ **800/233-1234** or 416/925-1234. Fax 416/924-6693. www.park toronto.hyatt.com. 346 units. From C$325 (£163) double. Weekend packages available. AE, DC, DISC, MC, V. Parking C$30 (£15). Subway: Museum or Bay. Pets accepted. **Amenities:** Restaurant; 2 bars; health club; spa; Jacuzzi; sauna; concierge; business center; Wi-Fi; room service; babysitting; laundry service; dry cleaning. *In room:* A/C, TV, fax, minibar, coffeemaker, hair dryer, iron, safe.

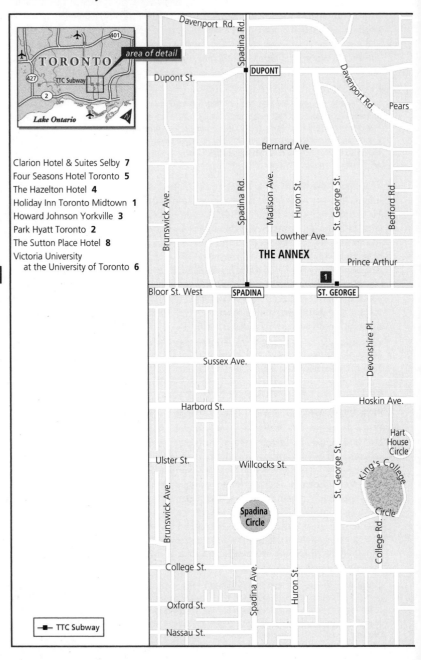

Clarion Hotel & Suites Selby **7**
Four Seasons Hotel Toronto **5**
The Hazelton Hotel **4**
Holiday Inn Toronto Midtown **1**
Howard Johnson Yorkville **3**
Park Hyatt Toronto **2**
The Sutton Place Hotel **8**
Victoria University
   at the University of Toronto **6**

5

WHERE TO STAY

MIDTOWN

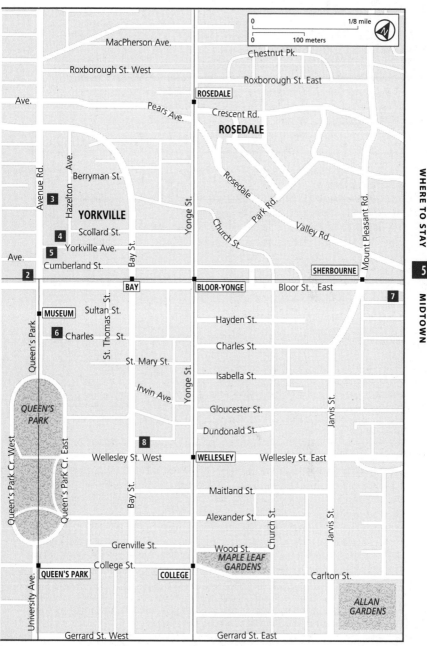

(Tips) **Bed & Breakfasts in Toronto**

A B&B can be an excellent alternative to standard hotel accommodations. **Toronto Bed & Breakfast Reservation Service** (© 877/922-6522; www.toronto bandb.com) has a short but wide-ranging list of accommodations in the city. Downtown doubles start at C$125 (£63). The organization will make your reservation and send you a confirmation. The **Downtown Toronto Association of Bed and Breakfast Guest Houses** (© 416/410-3938; www.bnbinfo.com) has listings for most of metro Toronto, not just downtown. **Bed and Breakfast Canada** (© 800/239-1141 or 905/524-5855; www.bbcanada.com) has a very long list of independent B&B operators. Doubles start at C$85 (£43).

EXPENSIVE

The Sutton Place Hotel ★   Although it towers over the intersection of Bay and Wellesley, The Sutton Place boasts the advantages of a small hotel—particularly detail-oriented, personalized service. In addition to hosting a galaxy of stars, the hotel draws sophisticated business and leisure travelers in search of serious pampering. Famous guests expect to be left alone here, and management protects their privacy. In other words, autograph seekers should go elsewhere.

The spacious guest rooms are decorated in a similar, though scaled-down, style. A few suites have full kitchens. Not that you'd want to cook while you're here—the lovely ground-floor Accents restaurant serves Continental fare, and across the street, the star-studded Bistro 990 produces impeccable French cuisine. One downside is that The Sutton Place stands alone in its neighborhood. It's about a 10- to 15-minute walk to attractions such as the Royal Ontario Museum and the Yorkville shopping district.

955 Bay St., Toronto, ON M5S 2A2. © **800/268-3790** or 416/924-9221. Fax 416/924-1778. www.toronto. suttonplace.com. 294 units. From C$185 (£93) double. Extra person C$20 (£10). Children 17 and under stay free in parent's room. AE, DC, MC, V. Parking C$28 (£14). Subway: Wellesley. Pets accepted. **Amenities:** Restaurant; bar; indoor pool; health club; sauna; concierge; business center; salon; room service; massage; babysitting; laundry service; dry cleaning. *In room:* A/C, TV, Wi-Fi, minibar, coffeemaker, hair dryer, iron, safe.

MODERATE

Clarion Hotel & Suites Selby ★ (Finds)   Ornate chandeliers, stucco moldings, and high ceilings make this 1890s Victorian building an absolute stunner. In a predominantly gay neighborhood, the Selby attracts gay and straight couples, as well as seniors (the latter group gets special discounts). All of the rooms now have private bathrooms, but only a few have an old-fashioned claw-foot tub. While there' no concierge, the staff is very friendly and will provide plenty of recommendations for what to see and do. History buffs will love the fact that Ernest Hemingway lived here for a couple of years while he was on staff at the *Toronto Star* newspaper (and yes, there is a Hemingway suite).

592 Sherbourne St., Toronto, ON M4X 1L4. © **800/4-CHOICE** or 416/921-3142. Fax 416/923-3177. www. choicehotels.ca/hotels/hotel?hotel=CN534. 82 units. From C$149 (£75) double. Rates include continental breakfast. AE, DISC, MC, V. Parking C$20 (£10). Subway: Sherbourne. **Amenities:** Access to nearby health club; laundry room. *In room:* A/C, TV, Wi-Fi, coffeemaker, hair dryer, iron.

Holiday Inn Toronto Midtown (Value)   Considering this hotel's tony location—steps from Yorkville and several museums, including the Royal Ontario Museum—the price is hard to beat. The rooms are small but comfortable and outfitted with well-lit worktables. All rooms have free high-speed Internet access, but there aren't many other amenities or services. This is a good home base for a leisure traveler who prizes location over other considerations. If you're not planning to hang out a lot in your hotel room, it's a small trade-off to make for the price.

280 Bloor St. W. (at St. George St.), Toronto, ON M5S 1V8. ☎ **888/HOLIDAY** or 416/968-0010. Fax 416/968-7765. ww.ichotelsgroup.com. 209 units. From C$150 (£75) double. Weekend and other packages available. AE, DC, DISC, MC, V. Parking C$22 (£11). Subway: St. George. **Amenities:** Restaurant; coffee shop; health club; room service; babysitting; laundry service; dry cleaning. *In room:* A/C, TV, Wi-Fi, coffeemaker, hair dryer, iron.

Howard Johnson Yorkville   Formerly the Venture Inn, this hotel is a bargain in a very expensive neighborhood. It's a little pricier than it used to be, but it also has a few more amenities. The Yorkville location is excellent, which compensates for small rooms (you're probably not going to want to spend much time there, as is the case with many value-priced hotels).

89 Avenue Rd., Toronto, ON M5R 2G3. ☎ **800/446-4656** or 416/964-1220. Fax 416/964-8692. www. hojoyorkville.com. 69 units. From C$120 (£60) double. Rates include continental breakfast. AE, DC, MC, V. Parking C$22 (£11). Subway: Bay or Museum. Pets accepted. **Amenities:** Concierge; Wi-Fi; laundry service; dry cleaning. *In room:* A/C, TV, hair dryer, iron.

5 AT THE AIRPORT

EXPENSIVE

Hilton Toronto Airport ★   I'm not enthusiastic about staying out by Pearson International Airport, but rooms do tend to be larger, as exemplified by this Hilton. One of the property's main attractions is its 152 mini-suites—which have a king-size bed in the bedroom, a sofa bed in the living room, a color TV in both rooms, and three phones. Another lure is the chain's well-regarded array of business-oriented amenities.

5875 Airport Rd., Mississauga, ON L4V 1N1. ☎ **866/565-4555** or 905/677-9900. Fax 905/677-7782. www. hilton.com. 419 units. From C$199 (£100) double. Extra person C$25 (£13). Children stay free in parent's room. Weekend packages available. AE, DC, DISC, MC, V. Parking C$15 (£7.50). **Amenities:** Restaurant; bar; indoor pool; nearby golf course; health club; spa; sauna; children's center; concierge; car-rental desk; business center; Wi-Fi; room service; same-day laundry service/dry cleaning. *In room:* A/C, TV, fax, minibar, coffeemaker, hair dryer, iron.

Sheraton Gateway Hotel in Toronto International Airport ★   Talk about convenience. You don't even need to go outdoors to get here—just take the skywalk from Terminal 3 (or a free shuttle from the other terminals). If you're planning a very short trip that requires flying out of the city almost as soon as you fly in, this hotel makes an awful lot of sense. Rooms are comfortable, spacious, and, most importantly, fully soundproof (remember, you're still at the airport!). Club rooms have extra perks, such as ergonomic chairs, a fax/printer/copier, and access to a private lounge that serves complimentary breakfast and snacks.

Toronto AMF, Box 3000, Toronto, ON L5P 1C4. ☎ **800/325-3535** or 905/672-7000. Fax 905/672-7100. www.sheraton.com. 474 units. From C$179 (£90) double. AE, DC, DISC, MC, V. Parking C$20 (£10). Pets accepted. **Amenities:** Restaurant; bar; indoor pool; health club; Jacuzzi; sauna; concierge; business center; Wi-Fi; room service; massage; babysitting; laundry service; dry cleaning. *In room:* A/C, TV, dataport, coffeemaker, hair dryer, iron, safe.

Toronto Marriott Airport Hotel   While the Marriott is popular with business travelers, it is also trying to attract leisure travelers with weekend discounts of up to 50%. Rooms are comfortable and spacious, with standard amenities and no surprises. Of the two restaurants off the lobby, I recommend the Mikado, a Japanese restaurant where your meal can be cooked right at your table (think food as performance art).

901 Dixon Rd., Toronto, ON M9W 1J5. 🄲 **800/905-2811** or 416/674-9400. Fax 416/674-8292. www. marriott.com. 424 units. From C$135 (£68) double. Extra person C$20 (£10). Weekend packages available. AE, DC, DISC, MC, V. Parking C$18 (£9). **Amenities:** 2 restaurants; cafe; bar; skylit indoor pool; nearby golf course; health club; Jacuzzi; sauna; concierge; car-rental desk; business center; Wi-Fi; room service; babysitting; same-day laundry service/dry cleaning. *In room:* A/C, TV, minibar, coffeemaker, hair dryer, iron.

Where to Dine

Toronto's dining scene is as vibrant and multifaceted as the city itself. There is something for every palate here, in every price range. If you're craving the cuisine of a particular nation, you'll find it within the city's borders. Toronto's dining scene is a highlight for any visitor. This chapter details my favorite spots, and while there are some spectacular break-the-bank places listed (when traveling, you've got to splurge a little, right?), the focus is on affordable spots that serve unforgettable meals.

DINING NOTES Dining out in Toronto does not have to be an expensive venture, but the tax level is high. Meals are subject to the 8% provincial sales tax and to the 5% GST. In other words, tax and tip together can add 28% or more to your bill. Restaurants normally leave tipping to the diner's discretion unless there are six or more people at the table. The usual amount for good service is 15%, jumping to 20% at the pricier establishments. The price of a bottle of wine is generally quite high because of the tax on imports; get around it by ordering an Ontario vintage—local wines enjoy a rising international reputation. Remember that there is a 10% tax on alcohol. Keep in mind that many restaurants change their menus and policies at a moment's notice. If a listing says a restaurant doesn't accept reservations, but you have your heart set on eating there, it doesn't hurt to call and ask if a reservation (or an exception) could be made.

1 BEST DINING BETS

- **Best Alfresco Dining:** The lovely patio at **Amuse-Bouche,** 96 Tecumseth St. (© 416/ 913-5830), is perfect. Tecumseth is a quiet, mostly residential street, so you can talk without shouting over traffic noise—and away from exhaust fumes. See p. 102.
- **Best for a Romantic Dinner:** I'm the first to admit that I'm biased, but the **Rosewater Supper Club,** 19 Toronto St. (© 416/214-5888), is my idea of perfect romance (it's where my husband proposed). Relax and let the pampering begin. See p. 110.
- **Best Healthy Fare:** I'm *not* into health food, but I can't resist the delicious but calorie- and health-conscious fare at **Four,** 187 Bay St. (© 416/368-1444). See p. 104.
- **Best Bistro:** Bistros often do well with comfort foods, but **Edward Levesque's Kitchen,** 1290 Queen St. E. (© 416/465-3600), takes it up a notch with farm-fresh ingredients, sophisticated pairings, and smooth service. See p. 110.
- **Best Tapas:** The cooking at **Torito Tapas Bar,** 276 Augusta Ave. (© 647/436-5874), is delicious, and it's served with a sense of humor. See p. 109.
- **Best Cheap Lunch:** It's impossible to beat the deal at **Crystal Rolls,** 372 Bloor St. W. (© 416/921-6787), with its Zen-like setting, friendly service, and C$5.95 (£2.98) lunch combo. See p. 116.
- **Best Greek:** The cooking at **Pan on the Danforth,** 516 Danforth Ave. (© 416/466-8158), will convince you that Pan was actually the god of food, not forests. This is Greek cuisine updated with panache. See p. 119.

WHERE TO DINE

6

BEST DINING BETS

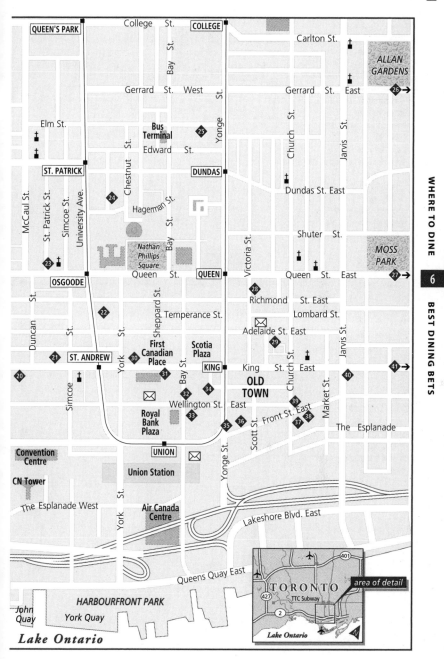

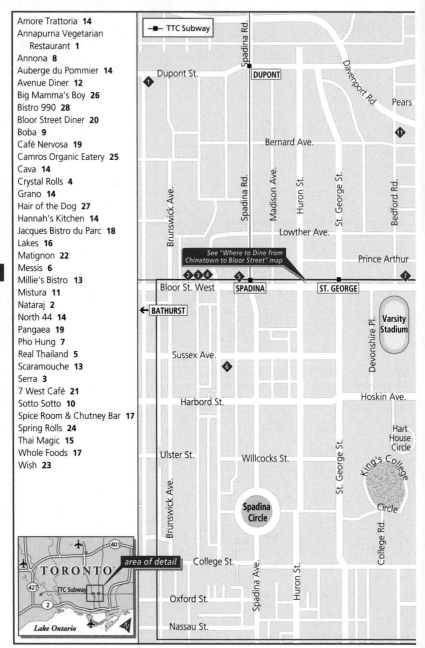

Amore Trattoria **14**
Annapurna Vegetarian
   Restaurant **1**
Annona **8**
Auberge du Pommier **14**
Avenue Diner **12**
Big Mamma's Boy **26**
Bistro 990 **28**
Bloor Street Diner **20**
Boba **9**
Café Nervosa **19**
Camros Organic Eatery **25**
Cava **14**
Crystal Rolls **4**
Grano **14**
Hair of the Dog **27**
Hannah's Kitchen **14**
Jacques Bistro du Parc **18**
Lakes **16**
Matignon **22**
Messis **6**
Millie's Bistro **13**
Mistura **11**
Nataraj **2**
North 44 **14**
Pangaea **19**
Pho Hung **7**
Real Thailand **5**
Scaramouche **13**
Serra **3**
7 West Café **21**
Sotto Sotto **10**
Spice Room & Chutney Bar **17**
Spring Rolls **24**
Thai Magic **15**
Whole Foods **17**
Wish **23**

TTC Subway

Spadina Rd.

Davenport Rd.

Dupont St.

DUPONT

Pears

Bernard Ave.

Brunswick Ave.

Spadina Rd.

Madison Ave.

Huron St.

St. George St.

Bedford Rd.

Lowther Ave.

See "Where to Dine from
Chinatown to Bloor Street" map

Prince Arthur

Bloor St. West

SPADINA

ST. GEORGE

← **BATHURST**

Devonshire Pl.

**Varsity
Stadium**

Sussex Ave.

Harbord St.

Hoskin Ave.

Hart
House
Circle

St. George St.

King's College

Ulster St.

Willcocks St.

Spadina
Circle

Circle

Brunswick Ave.

College Rd.

TORONTO

401

427

2

Lake Ontario

TTC Subway

area of detail

College St.

Spadina Ave.

Huron St.

Oxford St.

Nassau St.

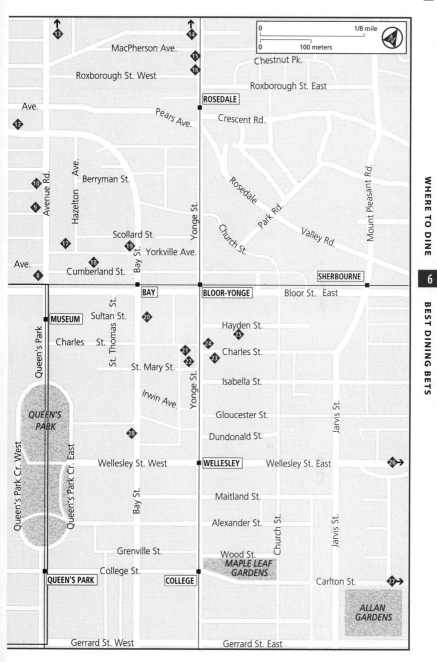

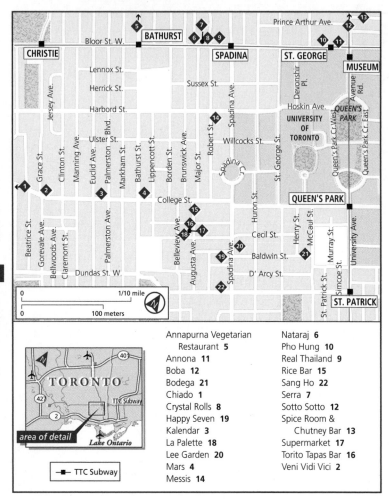

Annapurna Vegetarian
  Restaurant **5**
Annona **11**
Boba **12**
Bodega **21**
Chiado **1**
Crystal Rolls **8**
Happy Seven **19**
Kalendar **3**
La Palette **18**
Lee Garden **20**
Mars **4**
Messis **14**

Nataraj **6**
Pho Hung **10**
Real Thailand **9**
Rice Bar **15**
Sang Ho **22**
Serra **7**
Sotto Sotto **12**
Spice Room &
  Chutney Bar **13**
Supermarket **17**
Torito Tapas Bar **16**
Veni Vidi Vici **2**

- **Best Out-of-Towner:** Talk about catching on like wildfire—the **Elements Restaurant, Culinary Theatre & Lounge,** at Taboo Resort in the Muskoka region (© 705/687-2233), is a work of art. Give yourself over to the genius chef by having one of the three-, five-, or seven-course tasting menus. See p. 250.
- **Best for Families: Grano,** 2035 Yonge St. (© 416/440-1986), is an Italian restaurant that knows how to treat the *ragazzini.* A more casual choice is deli-style **Shopsy's,** 33 Yonge St. (© 416/365-3333). See p. 122 and 112.
- **Best for a Red-Meat Fix: Barberian's,** 7 Elm St. (© 416/597-0335), has boosted the level of protein in Torontonians' diets since 1959. It also serves great martinis and desserts, but everyone comes here for the meat. See p. 100.

- **Best Pizza:** A small local chain, **Terroni,** 106 Victoria St. (© **416/955-0258**), makes even the simplest margherita pizza a delight. See p. 112.
- **Best for a Celebration:** The atmosphere at **Blowfish,** 668 King St. W. (© **416/860-0606**), is lively every night of the week. See p. 102.
- **Best Sushi: Hiro Sushi,** 171 King St. E. (© **416/304-0550**), has Chef Hiro Yoshida offering up classically prepared sushi as well as a few unique specialties. But there is competition from **Blowfish Restaurant & Sake Bar,** 668 King St. W. (© **416/860-0606**). See p. 110 and 102.
- **Best Afternoon Tea:** While I enjoy a traditional English tea, I'm fascinated by the Chinese-themed afternoon tea at **Annona** at the Park Hyatt, 4 Avenue Rd. (© **416/924-5471**). See p. 112.
- **Best Desserts:** It's a tie. Dufflet Rosenberg bakes up a storm at **Dufflet Pastries,** 787 Queen St. W. (© **416/504-2870**). You'll find her name on the dessert list at some of the city's top restaurants. And then there's the **Senses Bakery,** 2 Queen St. E. (© **416/364-7303**). Resistance is futile. See "Sweet Treats: Toronto's Dessert Cafes," on p. 123.

---

2 RESTAURANTS BY CUISINE

American
Far Niente ★★ (Downtown West, $$$, p. 102)
Four ★★★ (Downtown West, $$, p. 104)
Jump Cafe & Bar ★★ (Downtown West, $$$, p. 103)

Asian
Crystal Rolls ★★ (Midtown, $, p. 116)
Queen Mother Cafe ★ (Downtown West, $, p. 108)
Rice Bar (Downtown West, $, p. 108)
Spring Rolls (Midtown, $, p. 118)

Bistro
Biff's Bistro & Wine Bar ★★ (Downtown East, $$$, p. 109)
Bloor Street Diner (Midtown, $$, p. 114)
Brassaii ★ (Downtown West, $$$, p. 102)
Edward Levesque's Kitchen ★★★ (Downtown East, $$$, p. 110)
Lakes ★ (Uptown, $$$, p. 121)
La Palette ★ (Downtown West, $$, p. 105)

Le Sélect Bistro ★ (Downtown West, $$, p. 105)
Thuet ★★ (Downtown West, $$$$, p. 101)
Wish ★ (Downtown East, $$$, p. 110)

Canadian
Canoe Restaurant & Bar ★ (Downtown West, $$$$, p. 100)
Tundra ★★ (Downtown West, $$$$, p. 101)

Chinese
Happy Seven (Downtown West, $, p. 108)
Lai Wah Heen ★★★ (Downtown West, $$$, p. 103)
Lee Garden (Downtown West, $$, p. 105)
Sang Ho ★ (Downtown West, $$, p. 107)

Comfort Food
Big Mamma's Boy ★ (Downtown East, $$, p. 111)

WHERE TO DINE

6

RESTAURANTS BY CUISINE

Key to Abbreviations: $$$$ = Very Expensive $$$ = Expensive $$ = Moderate $ = Inexpensive

Continental

HotHouse Cafe (Downtown East, $$, p. 111)

Deli

Shopsy's (Downtown East, $, p. 112)

Eclectic

Cava ★★★ (Uptown, $$, p. 122)

Lolita's Lust & The Chinchilla Lounge ★ (The East End, $$$, p. 118)

Messis ★ (Midtown, $$, p. 116)

Perigee ★★★ (Downtown East, $$$$, p. 109)

Swan (Downtown West, $$, p. 107)

Taro Grill ★ (Downtown West, $$, p. 107)

French

Auberge du Pommier ★★ (Uptown, $$$$, p. 120)

Bistro 990 ★★★ (Midtown, $$$$, p. 113)

Bodega (Downtown West, $$, p. 104)

Jacques Bistro du Parc (Midtown, $$, p. 115)

Matignon (Midtown, $$$, p. 113)

Fusion

Boba ★ (Midtown, $$$, p. 113)

Pangaea ★ (Midtown, $$$, p. 114)

The Rivoli ★★ (Downtown West, $$, p. 106)

Spice Room & Chutney Bar ★★ (Midtown, $$$$, p. 113)

Supermarket ★ (Downtown West, $, p. 109)

Greek

Astoria Shish Kebob House (The East End, $, p. 120)

Avli ★ (The East End, $$, p. 119)

Mezes (The East End, $, p. 120)

Myth ★★ (The East End, $$$, p. 118)

Pan on the Danforth ★ (The East End, $$, p. 119)

Penelope (Downtown West, $$, p. 106)

Health-Conscious

Annapurna Vegetarian Restaurant (Midtown West, $, p. 116)

Camros Organic Eatery ★ (Midtown, $, p. 116)

Four ★★★ (Downtown West, $$, p. 104)

Indian

Annapurna Vegetarian Restaurant (Midtown West, $, p. 116)

Nataraj ★ (Midtown, $, p. 117)

Skylark ★ (Downtown East, $, p. 112)

International

Annona ★ (Midtown, $$$, p. 112)

Brassaii ★ (Downtown West, $$$, p. 102)

North 44 ★★★ (Uptown, $$$$, p. 120)

Richtree Market Restaurant (Downtown West, $$, p. 106)

Rosewater Supper Club ★ (Downtown East, $$$, p. 110)

Scaramouche ★ (Uptown, $$$$, p. 121)

Senses ★★★ (Downtown West, $$$$, p. 101)

Italian

Amore Trattoria ★★ (Uptown, $$, p. 122)

Café Nervosa (Midtown, $$, p. 114)

Dante's ★★ (North of the City, $$, p. 124)

Grano ★ (Uptown, $$, p. 122)

Il Fornello ★ (Downtown West, $$, p. 104)

Mistura ★ (Midtown, $$$, p. 114)

Serra ★★ (Midtown, $$, p. 116)

Sotto Sotto ★★ (Midtown, $$$, p. 114)

Terroni (Downtown East, $, p. 112)

Veni Vidi Vici ★★ (Downtown West, $$, p. 107)

Japanese/Sushi

Blowfish Restaurant & Sake Bar ★★ (Downtown West, $$$, p. 102)

Hiro Sushi ★ (Downtown East, $$$, p. 110)

Light Fare

Big Mamma's Boy ★ (Downtown East, $$, p. 111)

Bloor Street Diner (Midtown, $$, p. 114)

Camros Organic Eatery ★ (Midtown, $, p. 116)

Hannah's Kitchen (Uptown, $, p. 122)

HotHouse Cafe (Downtown East, $$, p. 111)

Jamie Kennedy Wine Bar ★★★ (Downtown East, $$, p. 111)

Kalendar ★★ (Downtown West, $, p. 108)

Peter Pan (Downtown West, $$, p. 106)

Terroni (Downtown East, $, p. 112)

Mediterranean

Millie's Bistro ★★ (Uptown, $$$, p. 121)

Myth ★★ (The East End, $$$, p. 118)

Vertical ★ (Downtown West, $$$, p. 103)

Persian

Camros Organic Eatery ★ (Midtown, $, p. 116)

Pizza

Amore Trattoria ★★ (Uptown, $$, p. 122)

Big Mamma's Boy ★ (Downtown East, $$, p. 111)

Il Fornello ★ (Downtown West, $$, p. 104)

Serra ★★ (Midtown, $$, p. 116)

Terroni (Downtown East, $, p. 112)

Veni Vidi Vici ★★ (Downtown West, $$, p. 107)

Portuguese

Chiado ★★ (Downtown West, $$$$, p. 100)

Quebecois

Le Papillon (Downtown East, $$, p. 111)

Seafood

Chiado ★★ (Downtown West, $$$$, p. 100)

Rodney's Oyster House ★ (Downtown West, $$, p. 106)

Sang Ho ★ (Downtown West, $$, p. 107)

Spanish

Torito Tapas Bar ★★★ (Downtown West, $, p. 109)

Steak

Barberian's ★ (Downtown West, $$$$, p. 100)

Tapas

Cava ★★★ (Uptown, $$, p. 122)

Chiado ★★ (Downtown West, $$$$, p. 100)

Jamie Kennedy Wine Bar ★★★ (Downtown East, $$, p. 111)

Torito Tapas Bar ★★★ (Downtown West, $, p. 109)

Thai

Real Thailand ★★ (Midtown, $, p. 118)

Thai Magic ★ (Uptown, $$$, p. 122)

Vegetarian

Annapurna Vegetarian Restaurant (Midtown West, $, p. 116)

Crystal Rolls ★★ (Midtown, $, p. 116)

Camros Organic Eatery ★ (Midtown, $, p. 116)

Kalendar ★★ (Downtown West, $, p. 108)

Millie's Bistro ★★ (Uptown, $$$, p. 121)

Queen Mother Cafe ★ (Downtown West, $, p. 108)

Rice Bar (Downtown West, $, p. 108)

Vietnamese

Pho Hung (Midtown, $, p. 117)

This is where you will find Toronto's highest concentration of great restaurants. **Little Italy,** which runs along College Street, and **Chinatown,** which radiates from Spadina Avenue, have more restaurants than any other parts of the city.

VERY EXPENSIVE

Barberian's ★ STEAK   Not getting enough protein? Get thee to Harry Barberian's upscale steakhouse, which has been going strong since 1959 (his son, Arron, has since taken over). The room is cozy in a clubby way, with dark woods and framed newspapers. The menu rarely changes, but you won't hear any grousing—the crowd is too busy sipping martinis. The highlights are the eight steaks, from 9-ounce sirloin to 23-ounce porterhouse, all served with rice and spuds. The less traditional can partake of dishes like cheese or beef fondue for two, which is on the late-night menu (10pm–midnight). For all intents and purposes, there is only one dessert: Grand Marnier soufflé for two. The wine list is about 800 bottles strong, so bring your reading specs. Celebrity sightings aren't uncommon, but autograph seeking is frowned upon.

7 Elm St. ℂ **416/597-0335.** www.barberians.com. Reservations required. Main courses C$29–C$55 £15–£28). AE, DC, MC, V. Mon–Fri noon–2:30pm; daily 5pm–midnight. Subway: Dundas.

Canoe Restaurant & Bar ★ CANADIAN   The inspiring view makes this the place to see Toronto lit up at night. The interior isn't so shabby, either, with polished wooden floors and furnishings. Corporate types predominate, not only because Canoe is in the Financial District, but also because the prices best suit expense accounts. The meat-heavy menu showcases modern Canadian cuisine. Grilled veal tenderloin served with acorn squash and warm sage-infused goat cheese vies for attention with maritime sea scallops served with a tartlet of caramelized potatoes and double-smoked bacon. A few "spa-inspired" dishes are lower in fat. The wine list only scratches the surface of the bottles in stock; if you're craving a certain vintage, be sure to ask.

54th floor, Toronto Dominion Tower, 66 Wellington St. W. ℂ **416/364-0054.** www.canoerestaurant.com. Reservations required. Main courses C$39–C$45 (£20–£23). AE, DC, MC, V. Mon–Fri 11:45am–2:30pm and 5–10:30pm. Subway: King.

Chiado ★★ PORTUGUESE/SEAFOOD/TAPAS   What could be more luxurious than having fresh fish flown in from Portugal each day? (Though with fuel prices rising I wonder how much longer this will be possible.) Chiado is one of the most elegantly formal dining rooms in the city. The opulent main room has marble floors, oil paintings,

---

> ## ⓘ Tips   A Note on Smoking
>
> A provincial law came into effect in June 2006 that made it all but impossible to smoke at Ontario restaurants: no more indoor smoking at restaurants (even in separately ventilated dining rooms), and patios that have any sort of covering have also had to go smoke-free. This has made for a great deal of confusion, since tableside umbrellas that are close-set apparently count as covering, according to the law. You can still smoke on uncovered patios—for now.

and fresh orchids, and draws a sophisticated crowd. Servers are models of professional-ism, attentive without hovering. The menu favors seafood, from starters like grilled squid with roasted peppers to entrees such as poached or grilled salted cod. The wine list features a long list of rich and complex wines, with rich prices to match. If you're determined to dine here without breaking the bank, let me recommend the tapas menu, which is mostly priced at C$10 (£5) and below.

864 College St. (at Concorde Ave.). ℭ **416/538-1910.** www.chiadorestaurant.ca. Reservations required. Main courses C$30–C$48 (£15–£24). AE, DC, MC, V. Mon–Fri noon–2:30pm, Mon–Sun 5–10pm. Subway: Queen's Park and then any streetcar west to Ossington.

Senses ★★★ INTERNATIONAL   Harry Wu, who already has two excellent restaurants—Lai Wah Heen (p. 103) and Hemispheres—is the man behind this venture at his SoHo Metropolitan Hotel (p. 74). The Senses brand now encompasses a bakery, cafes, and a gourmet food emporium (p. 198), but this is the granddaddy of them all. Dining here is an experience for—what else?—all the senses. The serene sandy tones are serious eye candy, the background music soothes, and velvety banquettes rub you the right way. Get revved up for starters like the salad of seared tuna, cucumber, nashi pear, and avocado, or the lobster and scallops layered with Osetra caviar and spicy mayonnaise. The main-dish triple-seared beef tenderloin with Stilton-and-miso tart and foie gras sauce is beautifully executed. The apple crumble with cardamom ice cream is a fantastic finish. Service is extremely well informed and professional.

At the SoHo Metropolitan, 318 Wellington St. W. ℭ **416/961-0055.** www.senses.ca. Reservations strongly recommended. Main courses C$29–C$45 (£15–£23). AE, DC, MC, V. Tues–Sun 6–10pm; bar and bistro daily 4pm–1am. Subway: St. Andrew.

Thuet ★★ BISTRO   If you visited Centro uptown on a previous visit, you may already have sampled some of Chef Marc Thuet's excellent cooking. His new spot is both a bistro and a bakery, and it allows the fourth-generation chef from Alsace to make use of some of his family secrets (some of the artisan bread-making recipes come from his ancestor Marcel Thuet, who was whipping up breads with a starter instead of yeast 200 years ago). The bistro's menu is hearty and rich, with entrees like a mille-feuille of yellowfin tuna, ocean trout and foie gras, and an aged beef tenderloin with a ravioli of braised tripe. Don't be surprised if you're tempted to return to the bakery after you've eaten here.

609 King St. W. ℭ **416/603-2777.** www.thuet.ca. Reservations required. Main courses C$26–C$37 (£13–£19). AE, DC, MC, V. Thurs–Sat 6–10:30pm. Subway: St. Andrew and then a streetcar west to Portland St.

Tundra ★★ CANADIAN   Sophisticated and opulent, Tundra is designed to evoke elements of the Canadian landscape. How does one suggest the majesty of, say, a giant redwood? With columns wrapped in semitransparent fabric and lit from within, of course! (The stunning result is like a gargantuan Noguchi lamp.) Every detail, from the one-armed wing chairs to the Frette linens, is beautifully executed. The cuisine is just as artful. Arctic char is paired with Malpeque oysters and fried leeks; Nova Scotia lobster mates with tomato-avocado-bean salad and Yukon Gold potatoes. The results are elegantly complex. The wine list is exhaustive, so don't hesitate to ask for recommendations—service is well informed and helpful.

Hilton Toronto, 145 Richmond St. W. ℭ **416/860-6800.** www.toronto.hilton.com. Reservations strongly recommended. Main courses C$25–C$39 (£13–£20). AE, DC, MC, V. Daily 6:30am–10pm. Subway: Osgoode.

WHERE TO DINE

6

DOWNTOWN WEST

Amuse-Bouche ★★★ BISTRO/ECLECTIC/VEGETARIAN This is one of Toronto's most exceptional dining experiences. Tucked away on a quiet street, Amuse-Bouche is a cozy spot in winter (when you dine inside the red-walled main room), and an airy one in summer (when you can take a seat on the patio out front). Technically speaking, an *amuse bouche* is a little dish served at the beginning of a meal, something small yet interesting enough to tantalize your mouth and make you curious about what will follow. Amuse-Bouche achieves this feat with each plate, making the complex and the complicated seem natural. Somehow black cod ceviche with pink grapefruit is enhanced by the pineapple caipirinha sorbet on the same plate, just as the salmon and grilled shrimp are set off perfectly by fennel salad and miso-mustard jus. It's interesting to have so many strong flavors on a plate at once, but to have them come together in such harmony is a great achievement.

96 Tecumseth St. ✆ **416/913-5830.** www.amusebboucherestaurant.com. Reservations strongly recommended. Main courses C$23–C$30 (£12–£15). Five-course prix fix menu C$70 (£35). AE, MC, V. Tues–Sat 6pm–10:30pm. Subway: St Andrew, then a streetcar west to Tecumseth St., and walk 1 block north.

Blowfish Restaurant & Sake Bar ★★ JAPANESE/SUSHI Taking its name from a high-risk Japanese delicacy, the blowfish (which is not on the menu here), this restaurant is a rare pleasure. Tucked inside a former bank building, the soaring ceilings lend the room true grandeur. Eateries in trendy areas come and go, but Blowfish's impressive attention to detail makes me hope that this one will be around for a while.

The menu features the expected sushi and sashimi, and the quality and presentation are uniformly excellent. But there are lots of other options, from the starters (barbecued salmon skin and green salad make a stellar pair in peppery dressing) to the mains (sea bass or black cod in a sweet miso marinade). Even the free bowls of warm and salty edamame are delicious, and the service is friendly and helpful. My one caveat to diners is to eat here on the early side, because the restaurant transforms into a lounge at 11pm.

668 King St. W. ✆ **416/860-0606.** www.blowfishrestaurant.com. Reservations strongly recommended. Main courses C$19–C$38 (£9.50–£19). AE, MC, V. Mon–Sat 5pm–2am. Subway: St Andrew and then a streetcar west to Bathurst.

Brassaii ★ BISTRO/INTERNATIONAL Named for the 1920s French photographer whose prints adorn the walls, Brassaii offers a picture-perfect setting. The cavernous dining room is decorated in dusky gray and black, and tall vases stand in the windows, each holding a single long-stemmed calla lily. While the menu frequently changes, it might include entrees such as braised duck atop lentils and spinach, or shoulder of lamb with chickpeas and tomato. The desserts are not to be missed, particularly the elegant apple crumble with berries and caramel ice cream. The wine list is substantial, and there are some very good vintages available by the glass. Still, my favorite drink here is the Brassaii martini, which blends a couple of types of fruit juice with 7-Up and vodka. I know it sounds bizarre, but it's a deliciously sweet drink. On weekdays, Brassaii is open for breakfast, lunch, and dinner.

461 King St. W. ✆ **416/598-4730.** www.brassaii.com. Reservations recommended. Main courses C$18–C$39 (£9–£20). AE, MC, V. Mon–Fri 7:30–11am and 11:30am–midnight; Sat 10am–2:30pm and 5:30pm–midnight; Sun 10am–3pm. Subway: St. Andrew and then a streetcar west to Spadina Ave.

Far Niente ★★ AMERICAN This longtime favorite of the suited Financial District set has been thoroughly renovated and relaunched. Gone is the casual Californian earth-tone palette, mounds of greenery, wine racks, and simple wooden tables and chairs. This incarnation of Far Niente is all about sleekness, from its leather banquettes to its soft lighting. The good news is that the menu is just as strong as ever. Starters run the gamut from tiger shrimp in a yellow curry broth to Malpeque oysters served with horseradish and shallots. Main courses are even more inventive, with such dishes as lobster potpie (a half-pound of lobster in a tarragon cream sauce in a puff pastry crust). The main-course menu also covers the basics, with simply grilled steak and seafood plates.

187 Bay St. (at Wellington St.). ℂ **416/214-9922**. www.farnientegrill.com. Reservations recommended. Main courses C$18–C$38 (£9–£19). AE, DC, MC, V. Mon–Fri 11:30am–11pm; Sat–Sun 5–11pm. Subway: King.

Jump Cafe & Bar ★★ AMERICAN   Jump is such a see-and-be-seen spot that you might suspect it's all show and no substance. Actually, the food is anything but an after-thought. To start, consider steamed mussels in ginger-and-coconut-milk broth or grilled tiger shrimps on Thai mango-peanut salad. The menu features dishes such as grilled 10-ounce New York Black Angus steak with Yukon Gold fries, salsa, and mushroom gravy. The more adventurous have other choices, such as *osso buco* with spinach-and-lemon risotto. The wine list favors the New World, and there are a fair number of selections by the glass. Service is smooth, and the only complaint I could possibly make is that Jump never seems to settle down.

   A sprawling space in Commerce Court, it can be tricky to find. Just follow the buzz—as the decibel level rises, you'll know you're on the right track.

1 Wellington St. W. ℂ **416/363-3400**. www.jumpcafe.com. Reservations required. Main courses C$17–C$44 (£8.50–£22). AE, DC, MC, V. Mon–Fri 11:45am–midnight; Sat 5pm–midnight. Subway: King.

Lai Wah Heen ★★★ CHINESE   This is one hotel dining room where you'll find more locals than visitors. The interior is vintage Art Deco; spare pictograms dominate the walls of the two-level space. A suited-up crowd dominates at lunch; at dinner, a few dolled-up couples manage to sneak in. The massive menu is mainly Cantonese, with some Szechuan specialties. It offers abalone shredded and stir-fried with bean sprouts or braised with fresh vegetables and oyster sauce. Those with tamer tastes (or restricted budgets) can choose among meat or noodle dishes; the dim sum list alone goes on for several pages. There are several lunch and dinner prix-fixe specials, combining five or six dishes for C$36 (£18) and up.

In the Metropolitan Hotel, 110 Chestnut St. ℂ **416/977-9899**. www.metropolitan.com/lwh. Reservations recommended. Main courses C$18–C$44 (£9–£22). AE, DC, MC, V. Daily 11:30am–3pm; Sun–Thurs 5:30–10:30pm; Fri–Sat 5:30–11pm. Subway: St. Patrick.

Vertical ★ MEDITERRANEAN   When you dine in the heart of Toronto's Financial District, you run the risk of stumbling into a watering hole for heavily imbibing suits. Play it safe and head for Vertical, a restaurant whose prime location in First Canadian Place is secondary to the cooking. The high-ceilinged dining room has a swanky setting, but the real draw is the menu: ravioli stuffed with crab-and-asparagus, pappardelle with wild-boar bolognese, and a beet salad with pine nuts and ricotta. Vertical's greatest strength, though, is its fresh seafood; since the offerings change daily it's hard to predict the specials, but pan-seared ocean trout and grilled branzino are regularly featured. Desserts are easier to predict—I recommend the rhubarb-and-strawberry crostata or the dark chocolate tart. Service is seamlessly smooth.

In First Canadian Place, 100 King St. W. ℂ **416/214-2252**. www.verticalrestaurant.ca. Reservations recommended. Main courses C$21–C$45 (£11–£23). AE, DC, MC, V. Mon–Fri 11:30am–midnight. Subway: King.

Tips **Online Reservations**

One of my favorite dining websites is **OpenTable.com.** While it doesn't have a long track record in Toronto, its reservation system is reliable and its restaurant roster is growing (at press time there are 69 eateries on the list). The good news is that the list includes gems such as Canoe, Cava, North 44, Vertical, and Perigee. But be careful when you're making a reservation, because the list also features restaurants in Ottawa (a 5-hr. drive from Toronto) and Windsor (a mere 4-hr. drive).

MODERATE

Bodega FRENCH   A quiet spot infused with Gallic charm, Bodega is a short walk from the Art Gallery of Ontario. The two dining rooms have fireplaces, picturesque tapestries, and gilt-framed mirrors lining the walls. The menu is traditional French, with a focus on meats. Grilled beef tenderloin soaks up cognac sauce, and duck breast mixes well with wild blueberries. The wine list boasts some Bordeaux grandes dames as well as a nice mix of Ontario vintages.

30 Baldwin St. *©* **416/977-1287.** www.bodegarestaurant.com. Reservations recommended. Main courses C$19–C$31 (£9.50–£16). AE, DC, MC, V. Daily 11:30am–2:30pm and 5–11pm. Subway: St. Patrick.

Four ★★★ **Finds** AMERICAN/HEALTH-CONSCIOUS   I've been a longtime fan of Far Niente (p. 102), so I was curious when this restaurant opened in the restaurant's basement. The space used to be a bar, and I wondered how a windowless subterranean restaurant would survive. It turns out that the food here is so incredible—and moderately priced—that I forgot about the lack of a view. Four advertises itself as having a "balanced approach to guilt-free dining," and it turns out that good-for-you can mean delicious. Every dish on the menu is under 650 calories, from the ocean trout with beluga lentils and sherry-mustard-dressed salad to the beef tenderloin with roasted root vegetables (those are both main courses, by the way). Service is friendly and thoughtful. My only caveat is not to go too early: before 7pm, the bar area is packed with noisy Financial District types who are used to thinking of the spot as a watering hole. (In fairness, the cocktails are hard to resist, particularly the pernod-chambord-raspberry one.)

187 Bay St. (at Wellington St.). *©* **416/368-1444.** www.fourtoronto.com. Reservations recommended. Main courses C$12–C$26 (£6–£13). AE, DC, MC, V. Mon–Fri 11:30am–3:30pm and 4:30–10pm. Subway: King.

Il Fornello ★ ITALIAN/PIZZA   Toronto has a wealth of Italian restaurants, but small local chain Il Fornello has become something of an institution. Its hallmark is flexibility. Salads, such as the Caesar and the excellent Roma (a mix of greens, goat cheese, walnuts, and roasted peppers), are available in half- and full-size portions. Pastas range from traditional fettuccine Alfredo to a lighter linguine with chicken, pesto, plum tomatoes, and pine nuts. In most cases, you can substitute rice pasta for wheat, a thoughtful option that makes Il Fornello a great option for anyone with a wheat allergy or celiac disease. The long list of pizzas includes combinations like braised onion with Gorgonzola and fresh rosemary (pizzas can be made with wheat-free dough, too).

The King Street West location is right across the street from Roy Thomson Hall and down the block from the Royal Alexandra and Princess of Wales theaters (servers know to pick up the pace when you're watching the clock before a performance). Other branches are at Queen's Quay Terminal (*©* **416/861-1028**), 576 Danforth Ave. (*©* **416/466-2931**),

Bayview Village (© **416/227-1271**), and 1560 Yonge St., just north of St. Clair Avenue **105**
(© **416/920-7347**).

214 King St. W. © **416/977-2855**. www.ilfornello.com. Reservations recommended for pre-theater din-ners. Main courses C$10–C$24 (£5–£12). AE, DC, MC, V. Mon–Thurs 11:30am–10pm; Fri 11:30am–11pm; Sat 4:30–11pm. Subway: St Andrew.

La Palette ★ BISTRO   This is a terrific addition to the Kensington Market neighbor-hood. The 30-seat dining room is cozy and informal, with considerate, low-key service. The menu is classic, from ballantine of chicken stuffed with peppers and rice to lamb chops with a crusty coating of mustard and rosemary. Save room for the irresistible citron tart and dark-chocolate cake.

256 Augusta Ave. © **416/929-4900**. Reservations recommended. Main courses C$12–C$19 (£6–£9.50). AE, MC, V. Sun–Thurs 5:30–11pm; Fri–Sat noon–midnight. Subway: St. Patrick and then a streetcar west to Augusta Ave.

Le Sélect Bistro ★ BISTRO   Le Sélect has a longstanding reputation as Toronto's favorite Parisian-style bistro, and its location on Wellington Street West (a few blocks from its previous home) is outstanding. The change in venue isn't the only improvement: Le Sélect went through an agonizing bureaucratic nightmare over its esteemed wine cellar, in which the restaurant was forced to prove that its vintages were purchased from wineries and not homemade hooch (if you're interested in the full story, visit the restaurant's website). The good news is that the bottles are out of bondage and available for quaffing. The menu emphasizes traditional rib-sticking fare such as steak frites and cassoulet, all nicely done. There are a few vegetarian options too, such as mushroom risotto.

432 Wellington St. W. © **416/596-6405**. www.leselect.com. Reservations recommended. Main courses C$22–C$30 (£11–£15); 3-course prix-fixe menu C$35 (£18). AE, DC, MC, V. Sun–Thurs 11:30am–11:30pm; Fri–Sat 11:30am–midnight. Subway: Osgoode.

Lee Garden CHINESE   If lines are a measure of the success of a restaurant, Lee Garden is the hands-down Toronto champ. The draw is a Cantonese menu weighted heavily toward seafood such as shrimp, lobster, and cod. The signature dish is fork-tender grandfather smoked chicken with honey and sesame seeds. The kitchen also works won-ders with tofu.

WHERE TO DINE

6

DOWNTOWN WEST

(Kids) **Family-Friendly Restaurants**

Grano (p. 122)   Don't worry that a noisy babe-in-arms might disrupt diners—this lively, slightly chaotic eatery welcomes families. The owners have four kids, and they love to fuss over the *bambini*.

Millie's Bistro (p. 121)   This is a perennially popular spot with families. Tykes have a special menu, and most of the Mediterranean food can be eaten without cutlery.

Shopsy's (p. 112)   When the kids are sick of eating out and craving comfort food, this is where to take them. Home-style chili and macaroni and cheese hit the spot, and ice cream dominates an entire section of the menu.

331 Spadina Ave. ℂ **416/593-9524.** Reservations not accepted. Main courses C$12–C$22 (£6–£11). AE, MC, V. Daily 4pm–midnight. Subway: Spadina and then LRT south to Baldwin St.

Penelope GREEK   If you're in a rush to see a show at the Royal Alex, the Princess of Wales, or Roy Thomson Hall, come here for hearty food in a hurry. (And if you're seeing a show at the Hummingbird Centre, check out the Penelope outpost across from it at 6 Front St. E.; ℂ **416/947-1159.**) Give the friendly staff an hour or less, and they will stuff you with spanakopita, moussaka, or souvlaki.

225 King St. W. ℂ **416/351-9393.** www.peneloperestaurant.com. Reservations recommended for pre-theater dinner. Main courses C$11–C$25 (£5.50–£13). AE, DC, MC, V. Mon–Wed 11:30am–10pm; Thurs–Fri 11:30am–11:30pm; Sat 4:30–11:30pm. Subway: St. Andrew.

Peter Pan LIGHT FARE   When I was in high school, Peter Pan was the classy restaurant you went to for pre-prom dinner or a big date. The crowd at this fun, relaxed place is forever young, easily pleased by the old-fashioned bar, ever-changing art exhibits, and friendly service. The menu is awash in Eurasian food-speak; simpler dishes are best. The Peter Pan burger is always a top choice.

373 Queen St. W. ℂ **416/593-0917.** www.peterpanbistro.com. Reservations recommended. Main courses C$12–C$21 (£6–£11). AE, MC, V. Mon–Wed noon–midnight; Thurs–Sat noon–1am; Sun noon–11pm. Subway: Osgoode.

Richtree Market Restaurant INTERNATIONAL   On the first floor of beautiful Brookfield Place, this isn't so much a restaurant as a cafeteria. The gimmick: Diners roam from food station to food station, waiting in line at each, in order to pick up their appetizer, main course, bread, and beverage (each is in a separate place). The upside: fresh food, often prepared while you wait. The catch: Diners are automatically charged a 15% gratuity for "service." The common complaint: Diners who leave their partially eaten meal to go get something else find that their food has been cleared away when they return. Offerings include sushi, *rösti* (Swiss-style shredded potatoes pan-fried in sweet butter), thin-crust pizzas, and pastas. At the grilling station, the choices might include a rotisserie Cornish hen and an 8-ounce New York strip. The Richtree is best visited with a group—that way, you can minimize the time you spend waiting in line, and someone can guard your tray when you leave the table.

In Brookfield Place, 42 Yonge St. ℂ **416/366-8986.** www.richtree.ca. Reservations recommended for groups. Main courses C$12–C$23 (£6–£12). AE, MC, V. Daily 7:30am–midnight (2am on Fri–Sat). Subway: Union.

The Rivoli ★★ FUSION   The Riv is better known as a club than a restaurant—the back room plays host to live music, stand-up comics, and poetry readings. What most people don't know is that the kitchen is just as creative. Chicken marinated in jerk spices comes with sautéed spinach and plantain chips; mussels are steamed in green curry jazzed up with coconut and lime. The less adventurous can partake of the spinach-and-pear salad or the house burger. The low prices draw a mixed crowd of starving artists, budget-conscious boomers, and Gen-Xers. *Caveat:* If you're planning to talk over dinner, get there before the back room starts filling up.

332–334 Queen St. W. ℂ **416/597-0794.** www.rivoli.ca. Reservations accepted only for groups of 6 or more. Main courses C$11–C$21 (£5.50–£11). AE, MC, V. Daily 11:30am–2am. Subway: Osgoode.

Rodney's Oyster House ★ SEAFOOD   Rodney has been providing Torontonians with fresh oysters for the past 2 decades. A favorite with the Financial District set, the restaurant is lively at all times of day (particularly the patio in good weather). The setting is as unpretentious as you could find. The main draw is the incredibly fresh oysters, and the lobster and salmon dishes are worth more than a look. While you're visiting, check out the "Wall of Fame."

469 King St. W. ℂ **416/363-8105.** www.rodneysoysterhouse.com. Reservations recommended (reservations cannot be made for the patio except for groups of 10 or more). Main courses C$10–C$23 (£5–£12). AE, DC, MC, V. Mon–Sat 11am–1am. Subway: St. Andrew.

Sang Ho ★ CHINESE/SEAFOOD   There's no end of eateries in the eastern end of Chinatown, but Sang Ho is the one with the longest queue out front. The restaurant boasts not only a top-notch kitchen, but also a lovely dining room with several teeming aquariums. The regular menu never changes, but wall-mounted boards list many daily specials. Seafood is the obvious choice. Service is speedy and responsive. Try to go on a weeknight, when the waits are short.

536 Dundas St. W. ℂ **416/596-1685.** Reservations not accepted. Main courses C$11–C$19 (£5.50–£9.50). MC, V. Sun–Thurs noon–10pm; Fri–Sat noon–11pm. Subway: St. Patrick.

Swan ECLECTIC   The room recalls a retro soda fountain, with a counter and swirly stools on one side and booths with Formica tables on the other. Just don't expect to find a strawberry-banana float on the menu. The youngish hipsters who congregate here slurp up martinis and oysters. The menu avoids the trendy trap, managing both roasted capon with bourbon gravy and braised beef short ribs marinated in beer and marmalade. There's a nice selection of wines, almost all available by the glass. The popular weekend brunch features the usual eggy plates as well as some surprises: Spicy Moroccan olives or smoked arctic char salad, anyone?

892 Queen St. W. ℂ **416/532-0452.** Reservations recommended. Main courses C$17–C$26 (£8.50–£13). AE, DC, MC, V. Mon–Fri noon–10pm; Sat–Sun 10am–10pm. Subway: Osgoode and then any streetcar west to Euclid Ave.

Taro Grill ★ ECLECTIC   Hip Taro Grill has something that most trendy spots can't claim—staying power. Its secret? A mix of clever cooking, helpful service, and a glamorous high-ceilinged space. The menu refuses to be easily characterized. Just when you think you've pegged the Cal-Ital pizza-pasta-salad triad, out of the blue come tempura veggies or Asian-influenced New Zealand lamb. Affordable bottles, mainly from Australia and South Africa, fill the wine list.

492 Queen St. W. ℂ **416/504-1320.** Reservations recommended. Main courses C$14–C$22 (£7–£11). AE, MC, V. Daily noon–4pm and 6–10pm. Subway: Osgoode and then any streetcar west to Bathurst St.

Veni Vidi Vici ★★ ITALIAN/PIZZA   This is a Little Italy gem that serves delicious food in a swanky setting. The menu roams all over Italy, offering up pasta dishes such as linguine with mixed seafood, risotto with portobello, cremini, and porcini mushrooms, and thin-crust pizzas (there are plenty of meat dishes for the carnivorous, too). Desserts return to the classics, such as crème brûlée with fresh berries. The wine list is particularly strong in Italian reds. This is also a great spot for a Sunday brunch—the menu is incredibly diverse, ranging from crepes filled with strawberries and caramelized apples to a breakfast pizza of eggs, smoked sausage, pancetta, red peppers, and mushrooms.

650 College St. (at Grace St.). ℂ **416/536-8550.** http://venividivici.sites.toronto.com. Reservations recommended. Main courses C$14–C$25 (£7–£12.50). AE, MC, V. Tues–Sat 5pm–2am, Sun noon–midnight. Subway: Queen's Park and then a streetcar west to Grace St.

(Tips)   **The Hot Dog Monopoly**

While you're exploring Toronto's downtown core, you may find yourself wondering why there are so many hot dog carts—and why there aren't any other kinds of treats available. Believe it or not, a local law prohibits the sale of food on the street except for precooked meat products in the form of wieners served on a bun (though veggie dogs are also available). At press time, there's talk of changing this law. Hot dog!

INEXPENSIVE

Happy Seven CANTONESE/CHINESE/SZECHUAN   This eatery boasts kitschy touches like plastic Buddhas and a tank full of fish and crawly critters. They may not be everybody's cup of (green) tea, but the kitchen is widely acknowledged as one of the best in Chinatown. Seafood dishes are a favorite, though there are many plates for vegetarians. Portions are extremely generous.

358 Spadina Ave. ✆ **416/971-9820.** Reservations not accepted. Main courses C$9–C$15 (£4.50–£7.50). MC, V. Daily 4pm–5am. Subway: Spadina and then LRT south to Baldwin St.

Kalendar ★★ LIGHT FARE/VEGETARIAN   This has been a gem for years, serving sandwiches stuffed with portobello mushrooms, havarti, and roasted red peppers, and five "scrolls"—phyllo pastries filled with delights like artichoke hearts, eggplant, and hummus. The "nannettes" (pizzas) are baked nan breads topped with such ingredients as smoked salmon, capers, and red onions. The ambience recalls a French bistro. In summer, the sidewalk patio is just the place to sit and watch the world.

546 College St. (just west of Bathurst St.). ✆ **416/923-4138.** www.kalendar.com. Main courses C$8–C$15 (£4–£7.50). MC, V. Mon–Fri 11am–midnight; Sat–Sun 11am–3pm. Subway: Queen's Park and then any streetcar west to Bathurst St.

Queen Mother Cafe ★ ASIAN/VEGETARIAN   Beloved by vegetarians, trend-hoppers, and reformed hippies, the Queen Mum is a Queen Street West institution with old-fashioned wooden furnishings and an underlit interior. The menu's lengthy descriptions are required reading. Ping Gai turns out to be chicken breast marinated in garlic, coriander, and peppercorns, served with lime sauce atop steamed rice. Bah Me Hang is egg noodles and stir-fried veggies in a spicy lime-coriander sauce. In good weather, make for the garden patio at the back of the building.

208 Queen St. W. ✆ **416/598-4719.** www.queenmothercafe.ca. Reservations accepted only for groups of 6 or more. Main courses C$13–C$20 (£6.50–£10). AE, MC, V. Mon–Sat 11:30am–1am; Sun noon–midnight. Subway: Osgoode.

Rice Bar (Value) ASIAN/VEGETARIAN   Kensington Market has long been known as a place to buy food, thanks to its fresh produce stalls and small groceries, but in the past year it's become a dining destination, too. Rice Bar is easy to miss from the street, and inside the decor is strictly utilitarian (except for the floral pillowcases against the wall). The menu is designed around the notion of building your own meal in a bowl. You start with a selection of rice (basmati, jasmine, or wild) and add your choice of ingredients (all organic and additive-free). Service is on the slow side, but pleasant. The rice bowls come in several sizes, including the gargantuan Hungry Hungry Human. There are several house-designed bowls, too, including the much-loved Dragon Boat (rice noodles in a cilantro broth with tofu and kimchee).

319 Augusta Ave. ✆ **416/922-7423.** Rice bowls C$6–C$14 (£3–£7). MC, V. Tues–Sun 11am–10pm. Subway: Spadina and then a streetcar south to College St.

Supermarket ★ FUSION   This restaurant offers up a fusion menu that is innovative, delicious, and affordable. The plates are tapaslike, but are called "izakaya," and they allow you to sample a wide range of flavors (try the steamed PEI mussels in a green Thai curry). Later in the evening, Supermarket shifts gears to become a live music venue, featuring jazz, funk, soul, and reggae (p. 217).

268 Augusta Ave. ✆ **647/840-0501.** www.supermarkettoronto.com. Reservations strongly recommended on weekends. Tapas plates C$5–C$15 (£2.50–£7). MC, V. Kitchen: Mon–Thurs 5:30–11pm; Fri–Sun 5:30–10pm. Subway: Spadina and then a streetcar south to College St.

Torito Tapas Bar ★★★ Finds   SPANISH/TAPAS   Kensington Market—and Augusta Avenue in particular—is filled with excellent restaurants, but this one is my very favorite. Torito is a little gem that has made a big splash since it opened. You could put it down to the delicious dishes they serve (roasted quail with a pomegranate glaze, smoked trout with potato salad). But I think that it's also partly to do with the place's sense of humor. How can you not love a restaurant that offers "tongue in cheek"? (They mean it literally: braised tongue beside seared-and-braised cheek in a red-wine sauce. Honest, it's good!) The list of drinks is long, interesting and well-priced. I've never developed a taste for sherry, but there are plenty of options for those who have. I'll stick with the cava (sparkling Spanish wine) and sangria.

276 Augusta Ave. ✆ **647/436-5874.** www.toritotapasbar.com. Reservations not accepted. Tapas plates C$5–C$11 (£2.50–£5.50). Daily 5:30–11pm. MC, V. Subway: Spadina and then a streetcar south to College St.

---

4 DOWNTOWN EAST

VERY EXPENSIVE
Perigee ★★★ Finds   ECLECTIC   Perigee can be tough to find, especially when it's dark out (the restaurant is located in a back alley at the southern end of the Distillery historic district, and up one flight of stairs). The good news is that once you have found it, you can relax in the capable hands of the well-trained and thoughtful staff. Perigee's kitchen is located at the center of the dining room, so you can watch the chefs at work, laboring over the grilled yellowfin tuna with diver scallops in a curry sauce, or the roasted Ontario lamb atop brioche with melted Laguiole cheese. Try to save room for the chocolate soft cake, and incredible confection with salted caramel sauce and passion fruit sorbet. The truly adventuresome can try the nine-course Omakase (tasting) menu—but the catch is that the whole table has to order it.

In the Distillery District, 55 Mill St. (at Parliament St.). ✆ **416/364-1397.** www.perigeerestaurant.com. Reservations strongly recommended. Main courses C$36–C$52 (£18–£26); 9-course prix-fixe menu C$120 (£60). AE, DC, MC, V. Tues–Thurs 5:30–9:30pm, Fri–Sat 5:30–10:30pm. Subway: King and then a streetcar east to Parliament St.

EXPENSIVE
Biff's Bistro & Wine Bar ★★ BISTRO   The same team that created a trio of excellent eateries (Jump, Canoe, and Auberge du Pommier) has come up with a classic bistro,

with dishes priced somewhat lower than at the other establishments. The setting hits the right notes, with wood paneling and potted palms among the cozy-but-chic touches. The menu is equally fine, with pan-fried halibut covered with a second skin of thinly sliced potatoes, and traditional roast leg of lamb. The prime downtown location is a boon for Financial District types at lunch and theater-goers in the evening.

4 Front St. E. (at Yonge St.). © **416/860-0086.** www.biffsrestaurant.com. Reservations strongly recommended. Main courses C$21–C$34 (£11–£17). AE, DC, MC, V. Mon–Fri noon–2:30pm; Mon–Sat 5–10pm. Subway: Union or King.

Edward Levesque's Kitchen ★★★ BISTRO   Leslieville, once a no-man's land between Riverdale and The Beaches, is Toronto's hottest neighborhood (sorry, West Queen West), and Edward Levesque's Kitchen is one important reason. This small, unpretentious bistro offers cooking so sophisticated and service so smooth that it caught the attention of the *New York Times*. The cooking is sublime, and while the menu changes constantly, you're in safe hands whether you choose grilled leg of Ontario lamb rubbed with cumin and garlic, or an asparagus, chive and lemon risotto paired up with Atlantic salmon. This is an extremely popular place for brunch, and it's no mystery why when you try the frittata made with goat cheese and fresh rosemary (the restaurant won't take reservations for anything but dinner, so go early!).

1290 Queen St. E. © **416/465-3600.** www.edwardlevesque.ca. Reservations accepted only for dinner. Main courses C$16–C$24 (£8–£12). AE, MC, V. Thurs–Fri 11:30am–2:30pm; Tues–Sat 5:30–10pm; Sat–Sun 9am–3pm; Sun 5:30–9pm. Subway: Queen and then a streetcar east to Leslie St.

Hiro Sushi ★ JAPANESE/SUSHI   Widely regarded as the best sushi chef in the city, Hiro Yoshida draws a horde of Financial District types at lunch and couples at dinner. The monochromatic setting is comfortably minimalist, and diners are encouraged to relax and leave their meal in Hiro's capable hands in true *omakase* style. The sushi varieties range from the expected to the inventive; you can also choose sashimi, tempura, and bento box combinations.

171 King St. E. © **416/304-0550.** Reservations recommended. Main courses C$22–C$35 (£11–£18). AE, DC, MC, V. Tues–Fri noon–2:30pm; Tues–Sat 5:30–10:30pm. Subway: King.

Rosewater Supper Club ★ INTERNATIONAL   This triple-decked pleasure dome is packed almost every night with dressed-up diners who pass the time checking each other out. Personally, I'm still caught up in the scenery: Marble, moldings, and a waterfall make quite an impression. So does the menu, with appetizers like carpaccio of seared caribou with a citrus-gin relish. Main courses include roast sirloin of lamb with parsnip gratin and hazelnut sauce, and coq au vin with butternut squash. Don't miss the rhubarb apple crisp with a vanilla-plum sorbet for dessert. The wine list focuses on France and California, with some excellent Ontario vintages.

19 Toronto St. (at Adelaide). © **416/214-5888.** www.libertygroup.com/rosewater/rosewater.html. Reservations required. Main courses C$26–C$39 (£13–£20). AE, DC, MC, V. Mon–Fri 11:30am–2:30pm, Mon–Sat 5:30–10pm. Subway: King.

Wish ★ (Finds) BISTRO   Hidden behind a simple whitewashed facade, Wish is a charmer that offers cozy ambience, excellent cooking, and friendly service (a rare combination in this neighborhood). In summer, the vibrant patio might draw you to it, but during the rest of the year you have to wait till you're through the front door before you're seduced by the setting, which is very shabby-chic. The menu is just as elegant, with starters such as Pernod-glazed calamari. Mains run the gamut from braised lamb shank to portobello mushroom risotto. The dessert selection is limited, as is the wine list—but there's an impressive martini menu.

3 Charles St. E. ☎ **416/935-0240.** Reservations recommended. Main courses C$18–C$34 (£9–£17). AE, MC, V. Mon–Fri 10am–10pm, Sat–Sun 5pm–midnight. Subway: Yonge/Bloor.

MODERATE

Big Mamma's Boy ★ (**Value**) COMFORT FOOD/LIGHT FARE/PIZZA I don't know Big Mamma, but I can tell you that her boy can cook. This Cabbagetown find is located in a restored 19th-century manor house, but while the interior rooms are stately (sweeping ceilings, Corinthian columns, and grand archways), the atmosphere is relaxed and welcoming. There's also a patio for fair-weather dining. Best of all there's a long menu with something for everyone. Big Mamma's Boy is justly famous for its pizzas (I love the Acropolis, with its goat cheese, garlic, kalamata olive, and hot capicolla), and they're available on gluten-free pies, which is one reason why the restaurant is beloved by people with celiac disease or wheat allergies.

554 Parliament St. ☎ **416/927-1593.** www.bigmammasboy.ca. Main courses C$12–C$20 (£6–£10). AE, MC, V. Mon–Sat 4:30–11pm; Sun 11am–11pm. Subway: Wellesley then bus east to Parliament.

HotHouse Cafe CONTINENTAL/LIGHT FARE When restaurants make the claim of having "something for everyone," I usually run the other way. But the HotHouse Cafe is an exception. The exhaustive menu ranges from salads to pizzas, omelets to pastas, and burgers to vegetarian mains, and they do a nice job with it all. (Don't expect complicated fare here, though; the HotHouse keeps things simple.) The restaurant is famous for its Sunday buffet brunch, which, at C$18 (£9) per person, is a good value if you're in the mood to indulge. There are made-to-order omelet stations, lots of options, and live jazz music.

35 Church St. ☎ **416/366-7800.** www.hothousecafe.com. Reservations strongly recommended, particularly for Sun brunch. Main courses C$13–C$28 (£6.50–£14). AE, DC, MC, V. Mon–Thurs 11am–midnight; Fri–Sat 11am–1am; Sun 9:30am–11pm. Subway: King or Union.

Jamie Kennedy Wine Bar ★★★ (**Value**) LIGHT FARE/TAPAS My favorite wine bar is still one of the best bets in Toronto. Jamie Kennedy is a local legend, and his commitment to locally sourced, organic produce makes eating even the simplest dish here a joy. The chef's innovative take on bistro cuisine is reminiscent of a tapas bar: All of the plates are small (with prices to match), and dishes include crisp Yukon Gold frites, asparagus with poached egg and pine nuts, and tender duck confit with polenta. The staff is helpful and knowledgeable; ask about the difference between a glass of Ontario Riesling and a French sauvignon blanc, and you're likely to get a taste of each as well as an explanation. The only caveat is that reservations aren't accepted, so show up early, and be willing to take a seat at the bar since tables are in short supply.

9 Church St. ☎ **416/362-1957.** www.jkkitchens.com. Reservations not accepted. Small courses C$5–C$14 (£2.50–£7). AE, MC, V. Mon–Sat 11:30am–11pm; Sun 11am–11pm. Subway: King or Union.

Le Papillon QUEBECOIS The Québécois butterfly has migrated to new digs, but they're just steps away from the old location on Church Street. If you think crepes are simply for breakfast, stop by Le Papillon and think again. While you'll find many fruit-filled numbers, the best are savory crepes, which combine, for example, bacon, apples, and cheddar. Created from a mixture of white and buckwheat flour, the crepes make a satisfying lunch. For dinner, add some onion soup and a green salad, or go for *tourtière,* a traditional Québécois pie that includes beef, veal, *and* pork. Note that by the time this

111

WHERE TO DINE

6

DOWNTOWN EAST

book is in your hands, Le Papillon will have a second location in the Beaches at 1001 Eastern Avenue (see the website for details).

69 Front St. E. ℭ **416/367-0303.** www.lepapillon.ca. Reservations recommended. Crepes and main courses C$16–C$24 (£8–£12). AE, DC, MC, V. Tues–Fri noon–2:30pm; Tues–Wed 5–10pm; Thurs 5–11pm; Fri 5pm–midnight; Sat 11am–midnight; Sun 11am–10pm. Subway: Union.

INEXPENSIVE

Shopsy's Kids DELI   This Toronto institution has been in business for over 75 years. Its large patio, festooned with giant yellow umbrellas, draws crowds for breakfast, lunch, dinner, and in between. This is where you go for heaping corned beef or smoked-meat sandwiches served on fresh rye, or for comfort foods like macaroni and cheese and chicken pot pie. Shopsy's also boasts one of the largest walk-in humidors in the city (which is not subject to the smoking crackdown).

33 Yonge St. ℭ **416/365-3333.** www.shopsys.ca. Reservations accepted only for groups of 6 or more. Main courses C$9–C$16 (£4.50–£8). AE, MC, V. Mon–Wed 6:30am–11pm; Thurs–Fri 6:30am–midnight; Sat 8am–midnight; Sun 8am–10pm. Subway: Union or King.

Skylark ★ Finds INDIAN   Restaurant reviewers aim to sound impartial, but we all have our biases. One of mine is that I avoid buffets. While I know that plenty of people appreciate them, I don't gravitate to rapidly cooling food. So it's really saying something for me to admit that Skylark has an outstanding buffet. Not only do they get such dishes as the spicy beef masala and the smooth butter chicken right, but they're also served at the right temperature (and frequently restocked), making for a delightful feast. Vegetarians have plenty of options here, too. This restaurant is out of the way for travelers who want to stick close to the downtown core, but it's an exceptional deal for those who don't mind going a bit off the beaten path.

1433 Gerrard St. E. (at Coxwell). ℭ **416/469-1500.** Dinner buffet C$11 (£5.50); main courses C$8–C$12 (£4–£6). MC, V. Daily noon–10pm (till 11pm Fri–Sat). Subway: Coxwell and then a bus to Gerrard St. E.

Terroni ITALIAN/LIGHT FARE/PIZZA   From its humble beginnings on Queen Street West, Terroni has grown into a local minichain. The setting is informal, with kitchen-style tables and chairs and a wall-mounted chalkboard with daily specials. The antipasti, salads, and pizzas, are uniformly delightful. They range from the simplest margherita pizza to a gourmet salad of cooked oyster mushrooms drizzled with balsamic vinegar and served atop a bed of arugula. Other locations are at 720 Queen St. W. (ℭ **416/504-0320**) and 1 Balmoral Ave. (ℭ **416/925-4020**).

106 Victoria St. ℭ **416/955-0258.** Main courses C$10–C$18 (£5–£9). MC, V. Mon–Sat 9am–10pm. Subway: Queen.

5 MIDTOWN

VERY EXPENSIVE

Annona ★ INTERNATIONAL   This Park Hyatt Toronto's street-level dining room is an exercise in elegance, with floor-to-ceiling windows (all the better to people-watch). It draws a business crowd, Yorkville shoppers, and hotel guests, serving scrambled eggs with smoked salmon and capers for breakfast, seafood risotto with morel mushrooms and asparagus at lunch, and pan-seared black Angus medallions in red-wine sauce for dinner. The desserts are to die for, especially the caramelized pineapple tart with rum ice cream.

Park Hyatt Toronto, 4 Avenue Rd. ℂ **416/924-5471.** www.parktoronto.hyatt.com. Reservations recommended for dinner. Main courses C$22–C$40 (£11–£20). AE, DC, MC, V. Mon–Fri 6:30am–11pm; Sat–Sun 7am–11pm. Subway: Museum or Bay.

Bistro 990 ★★★ FRENCH   Because Hollywood types frequent Toronto, it's no surprise to see the stars out for a night on the town. Bistro 990 is just across the street from the tony Sutton Place Hotel, so it attracts more than its fair share of big names. The Gallic dining room is charming, and the service is all-around attentive. The menu offers updated hors d'oeuvres, such as octopus and veggies in citrus marinade. Main dishes stick to *grand-mère*'s recipes, such as the satisfying roasted half chicken with garlicky mashed potatoes, and calf's liver in white-wine sauce. Sweets, such as the pineapple tarte tatin, are made daily.

990 Bay St. (at St. Joseph). ℂ **416/921-9990.** www.bistro990.ca. Reservations required. Main courses C$26–C$42 (£13–£21). AE, DC, MC, V. Mon–Fri noon–3pm; Mon–Sat 5–11pm (Sun 10pm). Subway: Wellesley.

Spice Room & Chutney Bar ★★ FUSION   I know, I can't believe I'm advising you to eat in a mall. But honestly, this stunning restaurant at Hazelton Lanes is definitely worth a visit. Surrounded by heavy drapes and textiles to block out the mall world beyond, the scene is one of exotic luxury, and the attentive service is in keeping with the elegant atmosphere. Greg Couillard, one of Toronto's most famous chefs, blends flavors from Asia, Africa, India, the Middle East, and the Caribbean, and the results are seductive (and often quite spicy). Try the Afro Samurai (seared Saku tuna with a fiery spice rub) and the beef tenderloin flavored with Madagascan peppers and ginger.

At Hazelton Lanes, 55 Avenue Rd. ℂ **416/935-000.** www.spiceroommanyata.com. Reservations required. Main courses C$33–C$45 (£17–£23). AE, DC, MC, V. Tues–Sat 5:30–11pm. Subway: Bay.

EXPENSIVE

Boba ★ FUSION   Stunning turn-of-the-20th-century houses abound in this part of town, and Boba is in one of the most charming. Set back from the street, it has a front patio for summer dining. Inside, the pastel-hued walls and tasseled lampshades exude a warm Provençal style. Boba is a scene every night, with a mix of dressed-up and dressed-down professionals table-hopping with abandon. What draws them is the inventive cuisine, which has turned co-chefs Barbara Gordon and Bob Bermann into local celebrities. One highlight is Gordon's wonderful Muscovy duck two ways, with the breast cooked rare and the leg braised. Grilled salmon is also just so, nicely mated with curried vegetable risotto. Desserts are overwhelming, particularly the Valrhona chocolate triangle with crème fraîche ice cream, raspberries, and berry coulis.

90 Avenue Rd. ℂ **416/961-2622.** www.boba.ca. Reservations recommended. Main courses C$21–C$32 (£11–£16). AE, DC, MC, V. Mon–Sat 5:45–10pm. Subway: Bay.

Matignon (Finds) FRENCH   A bit off the beaten track, this small restaurant has intimate rooms festooned with all things French. The crowd includes many regulars, and the ambience is that of a low-key bistro. The short menu is filled with classics from the old country, including Angus steak rolled in crushed pepper and flambéed with cognac, and rack of lamb with mustard and herbs of Provence.

51 St. Nicholas St. ℂ **416/921-9226.** www.matignon.ca. Reservations recommended. Main courses C$23–C$32 (£12–£16). AE, MC, V. Mon–Fri 11:30am–2:30pm; Mon–Thurs 5–10pm; Fri–Sat 5–11pm. Subway: Wellesley.

Mistura ★ ITALIAN   The modern Italian menu here draws well-dressed 20- and 30-somethings. The food is satisfying without being overly heavy—think spinach and ricotta gnocchi with light but creamy Gorgonzola sauce and toasted walnuts. The meaty entrees might include a tender veal chop with rosemary roasted potatoes and portobello mushrooms, or sweetbreads with chickpea polenta and caramelized root veggies. The well-organized wine list is heavy with Italian and California vintages.

265 Davenport Rd. ℭ 416/515-0009. www.mistura.ca. Reservations recommended. Main courses C$20–C$42 (£10–£21). AE, DC, MC, V. Mon–Wed 5:30–10pm; Thurs–Sat 5:30–11pm. Subway: Bay.

Pangaea ★ FUSION   The dramatic, massive dining room comes complete with an undulating aluminum ceiling and coral walls. Perhaps to compete with the surroundings, the chic crowd likes to dress up. The menu changes every month. Appetizers such as white asparagus soup with roasted shallots and morel mushrooms are classically French. Main dishes strike boldly in different directions: glazed salmon with bok choy, water chestnuts, and ginger, for example, or rack of lamb roasted in sunflower seeds and honey and served with whiskey sauce. The professional staff knows its way around the wine list, which favors the Western Hemisphere.

1221 Bay St. ℭ **416/920-2323.** www.pangaearestaurant.com. Reservations recommended. Main courses C$25–C$45 (£13–£23). AE, DC, MC, V. Mon–Sat 11:30am–11:30pm. Subway: Bay.

Sotto Sotto ★★ ITALIAN   Imagine the Bat Cave decorated by a Florentine, with aged frescoes, wall-mounted stonework, and wax-dripping candelabra. Tables are close together, but the jovial suits and couples don't seem to mind. Efficient service lacks warmth, though the kitchen makes up for it. The menu leans to the lightweight, with a few irresistible creamy-sauced pastas. Main courses of meat or fish, such as Cornish hen and swordfish, are nicely grilled. The risotto is lovely—just be warned that at least two people at the table must order it to have it served. There's a nice wine list, with many selections available by the glass.

116A Avenue Rd. (north of Bloor St.). ℭ **416/962-0011.** www.sottosotto.ca. Reservations required. Main courses C$17–C$42 (£8.50–£21). AE, DC, MC, V. Sun–Thurs 5:30–11pm; Fri–Sat 5pm–midnight. Subway: Bay or Museum.

MODERATE

Bloor Street Diner BISTRO/LIGHT FARE   If you've shopped until you've dropped along Bloor Street West, this is just the place to grab a bite to eat and let your feet and your credit card recover. It's two restaurants in one: Le Café/Terrasse is an informal bistro that serves decent soups, salads, and sandwiches all day; La Rotisserie is a slightly more upscale dining room with heartier Provençal-style fare. Basics are what they do best. Try to snag a seat on the patio overlooking Bay Street.

In the Manulife Centre, 55 Bloor St. W. ℭ **416/928-3105.** www.bloorstreetdiner.com. Main courses C$12–C$27 (£6–£14). AE, DC, MC, V. Daily 7am–1am. Subway: Bay or Yonge/Bloor.

Café Nervosa ITALIAN   Reed-thin models playing with their food at the next table, leopard skin decking the room, and limos parked out front—you must be at Café Nervosa, a casually hip Yorkville hangout. The name is borrowed from the coffee shop on TV's *Frasier,* with a wacky ambience all its own. The menu boasts nicely constructed panini, pizzas, and salads, and the portions tend to be generous.

75 Yorkville Ave. ℭ 416/961-4642. www.cafenervosa.ca. Reservations only for groups of 6 or more. Main courses C$10–C$28 (£5–£14). AE, DC, MC, V. Sun–Thurs 11am–10pm (to 11pm in summer); Fri–Sat 11am–11pm. Subway: Bay.

Allergy Awareness

Dining out when you have a food allergy or intolerance can be a risky proposition, and that's doubly true when you're traveling. But many Toronto restaurants (and some shops) are becoming increasingly aware of the issue and are able to make accommodations. Before you travel, check out websites such as **Toronto Celiac** (torontoceliac.blogspot.com) and **Gluten-Free Guidebook** (www.glutenfreeguidebook.com); there are also tips about dining out with food allergies at **frommers.com**. Here are some spots to check out.

- **Amuse-Bouche** (p. 102): Whether you dine a la carte or order the tasting menu, the staff is well versed in food allergies, so say the word and dine comfortably. They have been known to bake gluten-free bread when informed in advance that a gluten-intolerant diner will be eating there.

- **Big Mamma's Boy** (p. 111): You don't need to ask if this restaurant is safe for the gluten-intolerant: A huge sign hangs at the front advertising its gluten-free menu, which includes pizzas, pastas, and traditional comfort-food dishes.

- **Camros Organic Eatery** (p. 116): This takeout spot at Yonge and Bloor offers vegetarian Persian-inspired cooking. The lentil-rich dishes are gluten-free, and the restaurant lists all ingredients in every dish.

- **Il Fornello** (p. 104): People with wheat allergy or celiac disease don't usually hang out at pasta restaurants, but this one is the exception. Il Fornello's alternative menu—available at all of its Toronto locations—offers rice pasta and gluten-free pizza crusts.

- **Jamie Kennedy Wine Bar** (p. 111): The staff is impressively informed about food allergies and very helpful. All of the dishes are made from scratch, so the staff knows all of the ingredients, but they are also aware of the possibility of cross-contamination and can advise you about potential issues.

- **Swiss Chalet:** Who says that fast food can't be healthy? This allergy-aware Canadian chain can provide complete nutritional information as well as precise details about allergens from peanuts to sulfites. 362 Yonge St. at Gerrard. ✆ **416/597-0101.** www.swisschalet.com.

- **Whole Foods:** Located in Yorkville's Hazelton Lanes, this upscale grocery store is the place to shop if you suffer from a food allergy. Clear labeling and a wide range of allergen-free options make for a nice change. In Hazelton Lanes, 87 Avenue Rd. ✆ **416/944-0500.** www.wholefoodsmarket.com.

Jacques Bistro du Parc FRENCH The ratio of ladies- to lads-who-lunch is about three to one at Jacques Bistro du Parc around noontime, but in the evening, the ratio evens out. The menu is that of a genuine French brasserie, with omelets, quiches, and niçoise salads, plus meatier main courses like green-peppercorn steak and Dijon-coated rack of lamb. Many wines are available by the glass, and bottles tend to be reasonably priced. Service can be considered relaxed or slow, depending on your mood.

126A Cumberland St. ℭ **416/961-1893.** Reservations recommended on weekends. Main courses C$16–C$32 (£8–£16). AE, MC, V. Mon–Sat 11:30am–3pm and 5–10:30pm. Subway: Bay.

Messis ★ (Value) ECLECTIC   This is one of Toronto's prime training grounds for up-and-coming young chefs. The food is for gourmets, though the prices are comparatively low. The menu changes frequently, keeping as its mainstays Italian pastas and Mediterranean meat dishes, and ranging into Asia, too. For a starter, the herbed goat cheese and cumin phyllo pastry is a delicious choice. Main courses include oven-roasted Atlantic salmon with jasmine rice and sun-dried fruit. Service is well intentioned, though occasionally clunky. The California-dominated wine list is as reasonably priced as the food.

97 Harbord St. ℭ **416/920-2186.** www.messis.ca. Reservations accepted. Main courses C$13–C$24 (£6.50–£12). AE, MC, V. Sun–Thurs 5:30–10pm; Fri–Sat 5:30–11pm. Subway: Spadina and then the LRT south to Harbord St.

Serra ★★ (Finds) ITALIAN/PIZZA   I've been dining at Serra since my student days at the University of Toronto. Back then, I loved it for its excellent food, friendly service, and reasonable prices. Guess what? It hasn't changed. This is an upscale-looking spot: The diners are casually chic, and Serra's look is sleek, with a wood-paneled bar in one corner and mahogany tables for two. The trattoria-worthy fare includes thin-crust pizza topped with olives, prosciutto, and goat cheese; light-sauced pasta dishes teeming with shrimp; and grilled focaccia sandwiches.

378 Bloor St. W. ℭ **416/922-6999.** www.serrarestaurant.com. Main courses C$12–C$25 (£6–£13). AE, DC, MC, V. Daily noon–11pm (no lunch on summer weekends). Subway: Spadina.

INEXPENSIVE

Annapurna Vegetarian Restaurant ★ HEALTH-CONSCIOUS/INDIAN/ VEGE-TARIAN   This was one of the first vegetarian restaurants in Toronto, and it's still going strong after more than 25 years. I'm always suspicious of food that's billed as healthy—I'd rather have stuff that tastes good—but Annapurna's southern Indian satisfies on both fronts.

1085 Bathurst St. ℭ **416/537-8513.** Reservations not accepted. Main courses C$8–C$14 (£4–£7). MC, V. Mon–Tues and Thurs–Sat 11:30am–9pm; Wed 11:30am–6pm. Subway: Bathurst.

Camros Organic Eatery ★ (Finds) HEALTH-CONSCIOUS/LIGHT FARE/PER-SIAN/VEGETARIAN   Yonge and Bloor is a tough place to find a non-fast-food lunch. But this terrific little place is merely a block away. Try the Adas Polo, a traditional rice dish with cinnamon and raisins, or the Gheymeh, a satisfying lentil stew. There's more to love about this place, including comprehensive ingredient lists, to help people with food allergies, and takeout containers that are 100% biodegradable.

25 Hayden St. ℭ **416/960-0723.** www.camroseatery.com. Reservations not accepted. 2-item combo C$7.50 (£3.75). MC, V. Mon–Fri 11:30am–7:30pm. Subway: Yonge/Bloor.

Crystal Rolls ★ (Value) ASIAN/VEGETARIAN   The menu roams around Asia, offering up excellent renderings of Pad Thai, Malaysian noodles, and Szechwan classics. There are some more creative entrees too, like the soft-shell crab curry with ginger sticky rice, and the Vietnamese pork chop rubbed with lemon grass and spices. There's also a menu for vegetarians. If you're on a budget, try Crystal Rolls's combo lunch: a salad, spring roll, rice, and entree for C$5.95 (£3).

Great Greasy Spoons

While Toronto's top-notch dining spots can be enchanting, I just can't resist the lure of the greasy spoon. You know the kind of place I mean: fluorescent lighting, a bottle of ketchup on every Formica tabletop, vinyl-upholstered booths, and aromas of strong coffee and frying bacon. Some suggestions:

Perhaps Toronto's best-known greasy spoon is **Mars,** 432 College St. at Bathurst Street (✆ **416/921-6332**); it sports a neon sign that claims the diner is "Just out of this world." In addition to the all-day breakfast menu, it boasts cheese blintzes, grilled burgers, and a great turkey club. Another location at 2363 Yonge St., just north of Eglinton Avenue (✆ **416/322-7111**), has kitschy mock-diner decor that doesn't hold a candle to the real McCoy.

Avenue Diner, 222 Davenport Rd. at Avenue Road (✆ **416/924-5191**), is just up the street from the Park Hyatt and the Four Seasons hotels, which explains the frequent celebrity sightings (signed and framed photos stand as a permanent record of stars' visits). In business since 1946, the Avenue serves a steady supply of omelets, French toast, and hamburgers.

The first **Sunset Grill** opened in Toronto in 1985, and outposts have recently started popping up around the city. For three-egg omelets, pancakes, and bottomless cups of coffee, check out its central downtown location at 1 Richmond St. W. (✆ **416/861-0514**).

The Goof, 2379 Queen St. E. (✆ **416/694-3605**), is officially named the Garden Gate Restaurant. But certain letters burned out of the neon "Good Food" sign, giving this Beaches neighborhood mainstay its name. In addition to the usual diner grub, this spot has star power, as evidenced by Jennifer Lopez sightings.

Finally, there's **Fran's,** which has locations at 20 College St. (✆ **416/923-9867**) and at the Pantages Hotel (200 Victoria St.; ✆ **416/304-0085**). Fran's is something of a Toronto institution—and it's the perfect place to have breakfast 24 hours a day.

372 Bloor St. W. ✆ **416/921-6787.** www.crystalrolls.com. Main courses C$8–C$14 (£4–£7). AE, MC, V. Mon–Thurs 11:30am–10pm; Fri 11:30am–11pm; Sat 1–11pm; Sun 1–10pm. Subway: Spadina.

Nataraj ★ INDIAN   There's usually a bit of a wait for a table—Nataraj's cuisine is popular with Annex residents, and its prices are affordable to U of T students. But the service is swift, so tables open up rather quickly. The cooking is from the northern part of the subcontinent, so expect lots of seafood. A number of plates will appeal to vegetarians. The tandoor baked breads are simply sublime.

394 Bloor St. W. ✆ **416/928-2925.** www.nataraj.ca. Reservations not accepted. Main courses C$9–C$13 (£5.50–£6.50). AE, DC, MC, V. Lunch buffet Mon–Fri noon–2:30pm, dinner daily 5–10:30pm. Subway: Spadina.

Pho Hung VIETNAMESE   Pho usually translates as "soup," but that's a bit misleading—it's more like a meal in a bowl. There are 15 good choices here, and the lemon grass–or coriander-scented broths are chock-full of meat, noodles, and vegetables. The menu also features a range of chicken, pork, and seafood dishes, and a tangy beef fondue.

The clientele includes both suits and students, and the wine list is longer and better than you might expect.

200 Bloor St. W. © **416/963-5080.** Reservations recommended for groups of 4 or more. Main courses C$8–C$15 (£4–£7.50). V. Mon–Sat 11am–10pm. Subway: St. George or Museum.

Real Thailand ★★ THAI   Even in this neighborhood, known for its moderate-to-low-priced restaurants that serve excellent food, Real Thailand stands out. Its food is simply outstanding, and it serves the best green curry chicken I've tasted outside of Thailand. The menu favors spicy tastes, but accommodating staff will get the kitchen to turn down the heat if that's your preference. There aren't a lot of choices for vegetarians here, but if you love seafood you're in luck.

350 Bloor St. W. © **416/924-7444.** Main courses C$7–C$14 (£3.50–£7). MC, V. Daily 11:30am–10:30pm. Subway: Spadina.

Spring Rolls ASIAN   What to have for dinner tonight: Chinese, Vietnamese, Thai, or Singaporean? If you can't decide, your best bet is Spring Rolls. The name may make you think its offerings are meager, but the multi-page menu will set you straight. Tenderly executed barbecued pork and fried shrimp dishes abound. Vegetarians don't have as many choices as you might expect, though there are a few top-notch vermicelli-and-veggie plates.

693 Yonge St. © **416/972-6623.** www.springrolls.ca. Reservations recommended. Main courses C$10–C$15 (£5–£7.50). MC, V. Sun–Thurs 11am–11pm; Fri–Sat 11am–midnight. Subway: Yonge/Bloor.

---

6 THE DANFORTH/THE EAST END

Just about everything *will* be Greek to you in the East End along Danforth Avenue. Known appropriately enough as Greektown, this is where to come for low-cost, hearty meals—though some of the restaurants have become quite trendy in recent years.

EXPENSIVE

Lolita's Lust & The Chinchilla Lounge ★ ⓕ Finds ECLECTIC   Lolita's is a bit of a tease. The Danforth is famous for its bustling Greek tavernas, but this bohemian spot feels removed from that scene. The decor is eclectic, just like the menu itself. Baked halibut pairs up nicely with a cilantro-apricot sauce, and lemon-scented crepes are filled with feta and spinach. Desserts include a to-die-for bread pudding with maple sugar caramel and a chocolate sauce.

513 Danforth Ave. © **416/465-1751.** www.lolitaslust.ca. Reservations recommended. Main courses C$15–$28 (£7.50–£14). AE, MC, V. Daily 5pm–2am. Subway: Chester.

Myth ★★ GREEK/MEDITERRANEAN   Part trendy bar, part restaurant, this generous space is large enough to encompass both. The ambience is classical Greece meets MTV. Ornate oversize shields share space with a series of TVs running an endless loop of mythic movies. Starters, ranging from traditional spanakopita to tuna tartare with beet and taro-root chips, are impossible to ignore. Main courses, such as rabbit braised in port and cinnamon, or pizza topped with spiced lamb, zucchini, and onion purée, are just as demanding. As the night goes on, the crowd gathers at the bar, where a DJ starts spinning music at 11pm.

417 Danforth Ave. (between Logan and Chester). © **416/461-8383.** http://myth.to. Reservations recommended. Main courses C$11–C$29 (£5.50–£15). AE, MC, V. Mon–Wed 5–11pm; Thurs–Sun noon–11pm (bar open till 2am nightly). Subway: Chester.

Sleepless in Toronto: What to Do When the Midnight Munchies Attack

We've all heard of cities that never sleep. Well, Toronto isn't one of them. The city's restaurant scene starts to doze off around 10pm, even on weekends. Sure, there are 24-hour doughnut shops, but if you're looking for something more substantial, try one of the following late-night options.

- **Hair of the Dog** sounds like a bar, but it's a low-key restaurant in Toronto's Gay Village that's open every night till 2am. The eclectic menu includes plenty of seafood and Asian-inspired dishes. 425 Church St. ℂ 416/964-2708. Subway: College.
- **Happy Seven** (p. 108) serves Chinese food in a kitschy setting until 5am.
- **Rodney's Oyster House** (p. 106) is open till 1am 6 nights a week, with the city's freshest oysters served in a relaxed, informal restaurant (just remember the patio closes before the rest of the restaurant does).
- **7 West Café** is open 24 hours a day. Delish sandwiches and pasta platters hit the spot. Those with serious sugar cravings can indulge in cakes and pies from several of the city's best bakers. 7 Charles St. W. ℂ 416/928-9041. Subway: Yonge/Bloor.
- If you're on the Danforth, you're in luck: Many of the terrific Greek tavernas and restaurants there, like **Myth** (p. 118), stay open until the wee hours, even on weeknights.

MODERATE

Avli ★ GREEK   A white stucco archway contributes to the cavelike feel of the narrow street-level room, though the recent expansion to the second floor has created an airier place to dine. Always noisy, occasionally raucous, this taverna serves up some of the best food on the Danforth—nongreasy, thoughtfully prepared, and carefully seasoned. Meze starters are standard: *kopanisti* (spicy feta with peppers) and hummus, for those who want cold food; grilled octopus and steamed mussels, for those who like it hot. Main courses are standouts. The half chicken stuffed with cashews, dates, apples, and rice is exquisite, and the meat moussaka is the best around.

401 Danforth Ave. ℂ 416/461-9577. www.avlirestaurant.com. Reservations recommended. Main courses C$12–C$22 (£6–£11). AE, DC, MC, V. Daily noon–midnight. Subway: Chester.

Pan on the Danforth ★ GREEK   This long-established eatery updates classic Greek dishes with panache. Salmon is stuffed with mushrooms and spinach and wrapped in phyllo pastry, and a smoked baked pork chop comes with feta-scalloped potatoes and zucchini relish. The well-chosen wine list favors the New World. The crowd is fairly sophisticated, which may explain the cryptic message over the bar: YOU'VE DONE IT ALREADY.

516 Danforth Ave. ℂ 416/466-8158. www.panonthedanforth.com. Reservations accepted only for parties of 3 or more. Main courses C$16–C$25 (£8–£13). AE, MC, V. Sun–Thurs noon–11pm; Fri–Sat noon–midnight. Subway: Chester or Pape.

Astoria Shish Kebob House GREEK This restaurant is more upscale and has a wider range of offerings than you might expect from the name. Whatever the protein, it seems to respond well to broiling—beef, lamb, chicken, and seafood all get similar treatment. Vegetarians can try the souvlaki or moussaka, among others. Expect a wait if you arrive after 8:30pm or so on weekends.

390 Danforth Ave. C **416/463-2838.** www.astoriashishkebobhouse.com. Reservations recommended; accepted on weekdays only. Main courses C$10–C$16 (£5–£8). AE, MC, V. Mon–Wed and Fri–Sat 11am–1am; Thurs and Sun 11am–midnight. Subway: Chester.

Mezes GREEK This sophisticated space doles out exactly what it promises. *Mezes* are light snacks meant to keep you going until you have a real dinner in front of you. Still, it's worth spoiling your appetite to indulge in these appetizers. Choices range from grilled calamari and octopus to spicy eggplant dip and leek pie. Do try to save room for the honey-sweet baklava. (Note that there are a few main-course-size dishes, but keep in mind that chicken souvlaki is available everywhere on the Danforth, so stick with the delicious mezes here.)

456 Danforth Ave. C **416/778-5150.** www.mezes.ca. Reservations accepted till 7:30pm (only walk-ins available for later time slots). Appetizers C$5–C$10 (£2.50–£5). AE, MC, V. Mon–Thurs 11am–midnight; Fri–Sat 11am–1am; Sun noon–midnight. Subway: Chester.

7 UPTOWN

This area is too large to be considered a neighborhood, stretching as it does from north of Davenport Road to Steeles Avenue. While it doesn't have the concentration of restaurants that the downtown area enjoys, a number of stellar options make the trip north worthwhile.

VERY EXPENSIVE

Auberge du Pommier ★★ FRENCH Don't have time to drop by your French country house this weekend? To the rescue comes Auberge du Pommier, a cozy château that exudes Provençal-style charm. Diners outfitted in business casual relax in the care of expert servers. The menu doesn't offer many surprises, but what it does, it does well. Appetizers set a high standard, with dishes like creamy lobster and white-bean soup, and baked artichokes stuffed with French goat cheese. Entrees, such as pan-seared scallops with braised oxtail in a cabernet *jus,* keep up the pace.

4150 Yonge St. C **416/222-2220.** www.aubergedupommier.com. Reservations recommended. Main courses C$39–C$46 (£20–£23). AE, DC, DISC, MC, V. Mon–Fri 11:45am–2:30pm; Mon–Thurs 5–9pm; Fri–Sat 5:30–9:30pm. Subway: York Mills.

North 44 ★★★ INTERNATIONAL This is the one restaurant that even people who've never set foot in Toronto have heard about. It's profiled extensively in food and travel magazines, but can it possibly live up to its reputation? In a word, yes. The spare Art Deco decor recently got a face-lift, and the results are stunning. The soft lighting and strategically situated mirrors wrap the dining room—and its occupants—in a lovely glow. The menu, which changes with the seasons, borrows from Mediterranean, American, and Asian sources. The results are inspiring to the palate and the eye. On the list of main courses, you might find grilled veal tenderloin with orange peppercorns, toasted barley,

and root veggies, or roasted Muscovy duck breast with orange-soy marinade and foie
gras. There are always a few pasta and pizza choices, such as caramelized squash ravioli
with black truffle essence. It's impossible to come here without being seduced into a
three-course meal. The desserts, such as lemon meringue *mille-feuille,* are among the best
in the city and are accompanied by a wide range of icewines (a sweet dessert wine). The
wine list is comprehensive, though most of the prices veer off into the stratosphere. What
really sets North 44 apart is its seamless service. Those who don't like to be pampered
should stay away.

2537 Yonge St. ℂ **416/487-4897.** www.north44restaurant.com. Reservations required. Main courses
C$39–C$55 (£20–£28). AE, DC, MC, V. Mon–Sat 5–11pm. Subway: Eglinton.

Scaramouche ★ INTERNATIONAL   Tucked into an upscale apartment building,
Scaramouche isn't easy to find. But it's blessed with one of the most romantic settings in
the city: Floor-to-ceiling windows afford a panoramic view of the downtown skyline
(securing a window seat is no mean feat, but fortunately, most tables have decent sightlines). The unobtrusive servers pay attention to the details. The menu is laden with
caviar, foie gras, truffles, and oysters; main dishes include the likes of venison loin
wrapped in smoked bacon in a red-wine glaze. The wine list has a broad reach, and there's
a nice selection of cognacs.

1 Benvenuto Place (off Avenue Rd.). ℂ **416/961-8011.** www.scaramoucherestaurant.com. Reservations
required. Main courses C$38–C$46 (£19–£23). AE, DC, MC, V. Dining room Mon–Sat 5:30–10pm; pasta bar
Mon–Fri 5:30–10:30pm, Sat 5:30–11pm. Subway: St. Clair, then a streetcar west to Avenue Rd., and walk
4 blocks south to Edmund Ave.; Benvenuto is the 1st street on the left.

EXPENSIVE

Lakes ★ BISTRO   Plush banquettes and close-set tables heighten the sense of intimacy in the narrow dining room. A casually well-dressed crowd drops by during the
week; on Saturday, couples spend candlelit quality time. The menu changes every few
months, with jazzed-up bistro classics such as duck confit with cranberry-shallot glaze
and garlic mashed potatoes, grilled Provimi veal liver, and Gruyère-and-Emmenthal
fondue for two making frequent appearances. The banana crème brûlée is a perennial
favorite dessert.

1112 Yonge St. ℂ **416/966-0185.** Reservations strongly recommended. Main courses C$20–C$28
(£10–£14). AE, DC, MC, V. Mon–Fri noon–3pm and 5:30–11pm; Sat 6–11pm. Subway: Rosedale.

Millie's Bistro ★★ (Kids MEDITERRANEAN/VEGETARIAN   Subtle as its signage
is, Millie's is hard to miss. The sole gastronomic draw in this neighborhood, it lures even
jaded downtown dwellers, attracting an unusual mix of young-to-middle-age courting
couples, families with tiny tykes (who appreciate the kids' menu), and groups gearing up
for a night on the town. The sprawling menu includes dishes from Spain, southern
France, Italy, Turkey, and Morocco. Start with tapas—perhaps Catalan-style goat cheese
with basil and olive oil; Turkish flatbread with a topping of lamb, yogurt, and mint; or a
b'stilla (aromatic chicken wrapped in herbed semolina). Better still, sample them all—the
cheery staff will arrange them on platters for sharing. Main dishes include paella with
saffron, shrimp, clams, quail, and chorizo sausage. On the wide-ranging wine list, Spanish selections are a particularly good value.

1980 Avenue Rd. (south of York Mills). ℂ **416/481-1247.** Reservations recommended. Main courses
C$16–C$28 (£8–£14). AE, DC, MC, V. Daily 11:30am–11pm. Subway: York Mills and then walk (10–15 min.)
west or take a taxi (about C$5/£2.25).

Thai Magic ★ THAI   Arrangements of orchids, cascading vines, and Thai statuary grace the enchanting entry. The serene staff handles frenetic crowds with ease; this spot is filled with locals, especially on Thursday and Friday nights. The meal is served Western-style, rather than in the Thai fashion of bringing all courses to the table at once. Delicate appetizers like chicken-filled golden baskets vie for attention with not-too-spicy soups. Entrees range from chicken with cashews and whole dried chiles to a coriander-infused lobster in the shell.

1118 Yonge St. 🕐 **416/968-7366.** Reservations recommended. Main courses C$15–C$21 (£7.50–£11). AE, MC, V. Mon–Sat 5–11pm. Subway: Summerhill.

MODERATE

Amore Trattoria ★★ ITALIAN/PIZZA   This double-decker restaurant is a neighborhood favorite with groups and families alike. Pandemonium reigns on the first floor; upstairs, the cognoscenti can gaze over a balcony at the tumult below. The cheerful staff takes it all in stride. With 22 pastas, 21 pizzas, 6 meat dishes, and daily specials, the menu can be an intimidating experience for the indecisive. Fortunately, the kitchen consistently produces top-notch dishes, from simple salads of mesclun and goat cheese to spaghetti in brandy-tomato sauce with sweet Bermuda onion. Wine is served in tumblers in classic rustic-Italian style.

2425 Yonge St. 🕐 **416/322-6184.** Reservations accepted only for groups of 6 or more. Main courses C$12–C$20 (£6–£10). AE, MC, V. Mon–Thurs 11:30am–10:30pm; Fri 11:30am–11pm; Sat 10:30am–11pm; Sun 10:30am–10pm. Subway: Eglinton.

Cava ★★★ ECLECTIC/TAPAS   While I was sad to see Avalon close its doors in 2006 after an 11-year run, Chef Chris McDonald has opened an extraordinary restaurant uptown. This jewel of a dining room is hidden in an alleyway, so the trick is finding it. But the effort is worth it since Cava offers exquisite tapaslike plates and sparking wines at prices that won't break your budget. The menu does have its pricey side (a flute of Nicolas Feuillatte champagne is C$20/£10), but if you stick with salt cod cake with chipotle cream, four oysters on the half-shell with tomatillo salsa, or 3-minute flank steak with chimichurri, you can't go wrong.

1560 Yonge St. 🕐 **416/979-9918.** www.cavarestaurant.ca. Reservations strongly recommended. Tapas plates C$6–C$17 (£3–£8.50). AE, DC, MC, V. Daily 5–10pm. Subway: St. Clair.

Grano ★ **Kids** ITALIAN   While Toronto has no shortage of Italian eateries, few spots have as much ambience as Grano. The old-fashioned trattoria contains several dining areas, and the small courtyard at the back is heaven on sunny days. This is a high-energy spot that attracts celebratory groups (one clever friend of mine had her wedding-rehearsal dinner here); it's also welcoming to families accompanied by *bambini*. The cooking is hearty, from tender *osso buco* to ricotta gnocchi paired with shrimp in white-wine sauce. The desserts are a serious draw—you must try the white chocolate and raspberry tart at least once.

2035 Yonge St. 🕐 **416/440-1986.** www.grano.ca. Reservations recommended. Main courses C$12–C$25 (£6–£13). AE, DC, MC, V. Mon–Fri 9:30am–11pm; Sat 9am–11pm. Subway: Davisville or Eglinton.

INEXPENSIVE

Hannah's Kitchen LIGHT FARE   National magazines and newspapers have published several of its recipes, but this cubbyhole-like eatery remains defiantly low-key. Diners seat themselves at wooden banquettes or tiny tables. The menu includes many

Sweet Treats: Toronto's Dessert Cafes

I've got a serious sweet tooth, and to my mind dessert should be its own food group. Here are some of the city's most delicious places to satisfy a sugar craving and do some people-watching at the same time.

Caffe Demetre ★   In the heart of Greektown on the Danforth, Demetre is known for its old-world ambience as well as such treats as Belgian waffles, oversize sundaes, cakes, tortes, and baklava. It's popular at all hours of the evening with a casual crowd, and on weekends it draws families. Closing time is midnight Sunday through Thursday, and 3am Friday and Saturday. 400 Danforth Ave. ✆ **416/778-6654.** Subway: Broadview.

Desserts by Phipps   The cafe serves salads and sandwiches, but the decadent desserts draw the crowds. Cappuccino chiffon cake is a direct hit, as are the moist, but not gooey, apple confections. 420 Eglinton Ave. W. ✆ **416/481-9111.** Subway: Eglinton.

Dufflet Pastries ★   On menus around town, you'll sometimes see mention of "desserts by Dufflet." *Divine* is the word that best describes these confections. Owner Dufflet Rosenberg bakes some of the most delectable tortes, tarts, and pastries in the city. The problem is deciding where to start. The cafe also serves light fare. 787 Queen St. W. ✆ **416/504-2870.** www.dufflet.com. Subway: Osgoode and then any streetcar west to Euclid Ave.

Greg's Ice Cream ★★ (Finds)   One taste of Greg's homemade ice cream and you'll be an addict. (I should know—I've been one since high school!) Different flavors are available each day, and the staff is generous with samples. It's hard to pick a favorite flavor, but the roasted marshmallow would definitely be up there. 750 Spadina Ave. ✆ **416/962-4734.** Subway: Spadina.

Just Desserts   This cafe stays open practically around the clock on weekends for those in need of a sugar fix. Around 40 desserts are available—as many as 12 different cheesecakes, 10 or so pies, plus an array of gateaux, tortes, and meringues. 555 Yonge St. (at Wellesley). ✆ **416/963-8089.** Subway: Wellesley.

Senses Bakery ★★ (Finds)   It's always seemed strange to me that the Eaton Centre lacked a good cafe—but there's one across the street. The menu has some light, lunch-appropriate food here too, but the real draw is the divine collection of pastry confections and chocolates. 2 Queen St. E. ✆ **416/364-7303.** Subway: Queen.

Sicilian Ice Cream Company (Finds)   This old-fashioned ice-cream parlor is Toronto's top purveyor of Italian gelato. 712 College St. ✆ **416/531-7716.** Subway: Queen's Park and then a streetcar west.

SOMA Chocolatemaker ★★ (Finds)   The devotion to chocolate at this Distillery District shop and cafe can be described as religious zeal. I'm enamored of both the gourmet truffles and the addictive ice creams, so I guess that makes me a cult member. In the Distillery District, 55 Mill St. ✆ **416/815-7662.** Subway: King and then a streetcar east to Parliament St.

pasta dishes, both cold (pesto radiatore salad with chicken and pine nuts is the top pick) and hot (the penne arrabiata is the spiciest in town), with three or four daily specials. Occasional forays into the exotic include a few Indonesian rice dishes and the ever-popular pad Thai. Desserts are a must, so check out the selection behind the counter on your way in.

2221 Yonge St. ℂ **416/481-0185.** Reservations not accepted. Main courses C$7–C$14 (£3.50–£7). MC, V. Mon–Fri 10am–10pm. Subway: Eglinton.

8 NORTH OF THE CITY

Toronto is a sprawling city, and as it has expanded, restaurants have cropped up in formerly out-of-the-way regions. This area is beyond the reach of the Toronto subway system. If you've rented a car to go to the McMichael Canadian Art Collection in Kleinburg or to the Canada's Wonderland theme park, you might want to stop on the way back downtown.

MODERATE

Dante's ★★ ITALIAN   Predating the current boom in the area, Dante's has been the favorite local spot for down-home cooking since 1976. It's not hard to figure out why. The menu has something for everyone, the food is consistently good, and the prices are reasonable. Don't expect to find exotic risottos—stick to heaping plates of pasta like rigatoni with black and green olives, or homemade cannelloni. One serving of chicken parmigiano can feed two adults.

267 Baythorn Dr. (just off Yonge St.), Thornhill. ℂ **905/881-1070.** Main courses C$16–C$22 (£8–£11). AE, MC, V. Mon–Thurs noon–10pm; Fri–Sat noon–midnight.

What to See & Do

First, the good news: Toronto has amazing sights that appeal to travelers of all stripes. The bad news? No matter how long your stay, you won't be able to fit everything in. Toronto is a sprawling city, and while downtown and midtown boast most of the best attractions, some wonderful sights are in less accessible areas. Travelers in 2009 will be able to enjoy the newly renovated and expanded Art Gallery of Ontario. Other prime Toronto Attractions, such as the Royal Ontario Museum, the Gardiner Museum, and the Ontario Science Centre have already completed their renovations and are completely open to visitors again.

Keep in mind that many Toronto attractions could take up an entire day. The Ontario Science Centre, Harbourfront, and Paramount Canada's Wonderland all come to mind. That's not even mentioning the parks, the arts scene, or the shopping possibilities. My best advice is to relax and bring a good pair of walking shoes. The best way to appreciate Toronto is on foot.

1 THE TOP ATTRACTIONS

ON THE LAKEFRONT

Harbourfront Centre ★★ **(Kids)**   Back in 1972, the federal government took over a 38-hectare (94-acre) strip of waterfront land to preserve the vista. It wasn't exactly prime real estate at the time, but that has changed in decades since. The abandoned warehouses and crumbling factories have yielded to a stunning urban playground that stretches over the old piers. Today, Harbourfront is one of the most popular destinations for locals and visitors alike—a great place to spend time strolling, picnicking, gallery hopping, biking, shopping, and sailing.

Queen's Quay, at the foot of York Street, is the first stop you'll encounter on the LRT line from Union Station (you can also get there in 5 min. on foot walking south from Front Street, but that requires you to go under the Gardiner Expwy., which I personally hate). From here, boats depart for harbor tours, and ferries leave for the Toronto Islands. In this renovated warehouse, you'll find the Premiere Dance Theatre and two floors of shops. To get something to eat, you can stay at Queen's Quay's casual BoatHouse Grill or walk west to **York Quay**'s Lakeside Terrace restaurant. York Quay also boasts an art gallery and ever-changing art installations, and an information booth where you can pick up information on Harbourfront events.

Harbourfront has several venues devoted to the arts. The **Power Plant** is a contemporary art gallery; behind it is the **Du Maurier Theatre Centre.** At the **Craft Studio** you can watch artisans blow glass, throw pots, and make silk-screen prints. You can buy their works at **Bounty Contemporary Canadian Craft Shop.** The **Artists' Gardens** currently includes mature and new outdoor gardens created by landscape architects, designers, and other artists.

More than 4,000 events take place annually at Harbourfront, including the **Harbourfront Reading Series** in June and the **International Festival of Authors** in October (see

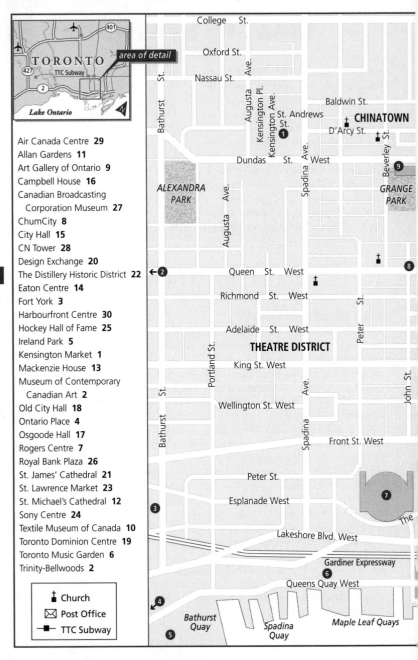

Air Canada Centre **29**
Allan Gardens **11**
Art Gallery of Ontario **9**
Campbell House **16**
Canadian Broadcasting
  Corporation Museum **27**
ChumCity **8**
City Hall **15**
CN Tower **28**
Design Exchange **20**
The Distillery Historic District **22**
Eaton Centre **14**
Fort York **3**
Harbourfront Centre **30**
Hockey Hall of Fame **25**
Ireland Park **5**
Kensington Market **1**
Mackenzie House **13**
Museum of Contemporary
  Canadian Art **2**
Old City Hall **18**
Ontario Place **4**
Osgoode Hall **17**
Rogers Centre **7**
Royal Bank Plaza **26**
St. James' Cathedral **21**
St. Lawrence Market **23**
St. Michael's Cathedral **12**
Sony Centre **24**
Textile Museum of Canada **10**
Toronto Dominion Centre **19**
Toronto Music Garden **6**
Trinity-Bellwoods **2**

✝ Church
✉ Post Office
━■━ TTC Subway

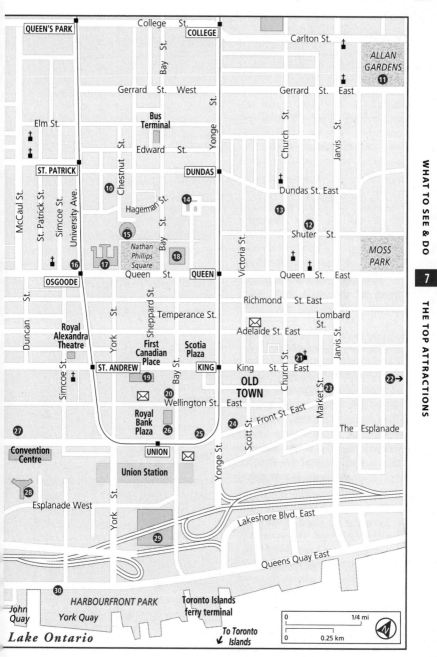

QUEEN'S PARK

College St.

COLLEGE

Carlton St.

ALLAN GARDENS 11

Bay St.

Gerrard St. West

Gerrard St. East

Elm St.

Bus Terminal

Edward St.

Church St.

Jarvis St.

ST. PATRICK

Chestnut St.

DUNDAS

Dundas St. East

10

Hageman St.

14

13

12

McCaul St.

St. Patrick St.

Simcoe St.

University Ave.

15

Nathan Phillips Square

18

Shuter St.

MOSS PARK

16

17

Queen St.

QUEEN

Queen St. East

OSGOODE

Victoria St.

Duncan St.

Sheppard St.

Temperance St.

Richmond St. East

Lombard St.

Adelaide St. East

Royal Alexandra Theatre

York St.

First Canadian Place

Scotia Plaza

Jarvis St.

Simcoe St.

ST. ANDREW

Bay St.

KING

King St. East

OLD TOWN

21

22 →

23

19

20

Wellington St. East

Church St.

Market St.

7

WHAT TO SEE & DO

THE TOP ATTRACTIONS

27

Royal Bank Plaza

26

25

24

Scott St.

Front St. East

The Esplanade

Convention Centre

UNION

Yonge St.

28

Union Station

York St.

Esplanade West

Lakeshore Blvd. East

29

Queens Quay East

30

HARBOURFRONT PARK

Toronto Islands ferry terminal

0   1/4 mi

John Quay

York Quay

Lake Ontario

To Toronto Islands

0   0.25 km

WHAT TO SEE & DO

THE TOP ATTRACTIONS

7

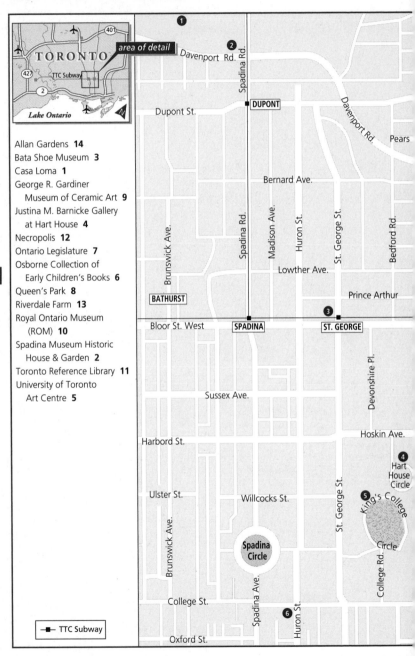

Allan Gardens **14**
Bata Shoe Museum **3**
Casa Loma **1**
George R. Gardiner
  Museum of Ceramic Art **9**
Justina M. Barnicke Gallery
  at Hart House **4**
Necropolis **12**
Ontario Legislature **7**
Osborne Collection of
  Early Children's Books **6**
Queen's Park **8**
Riverdale Farm **13**
Royal Ontario Museum
  (ROM) **10**
Spadina Museum Historic
  House & Garden **2**
Toronto Reference Library **11**
University of Toronto
  Art Centre **5**

TORONTO
area of detail
TTC Subway
Lake Ontario

— TTC Subway

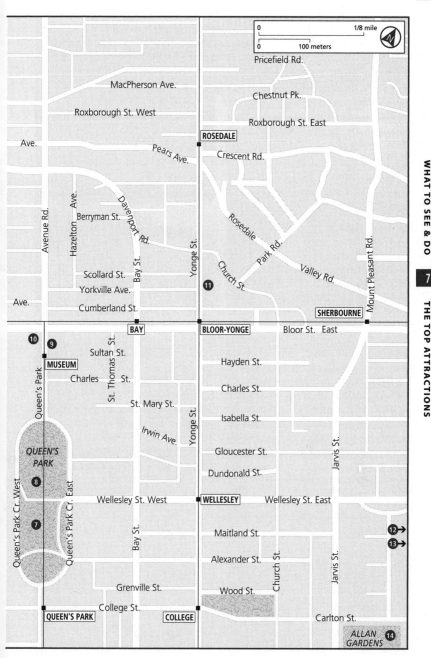

0   1/8 mile
0   100 meters

Pricefield Rd.

MacPherson Ave.

Chestnut Pk.

Roxborough St. West

Roxborough St. East

ROSEDALE

Ave.

Pears Ave.

Crescent Rd.

Rosedale

Davenport Rd.

Berryman St.

Hazelton Ave.

Avenue Rd.

Park Rd.

Valley Rd.

Mount Pleasant Rd.

Bay St.

Yonge St.

Church St.

Scollard St.

Yorkville Ave.

11

Cumberland St.

Ave.

SHERBOURNE

BAY

BLOOR-YONGE

Bloor St. East

10   **9**

Sultan St.

Hayden St.

MUSEUM

Charles   St.

St. Thomas St.

Queen's Park

Charles St.

St. Mary St.

Isabella St.

Yonge St.

Irwin Ave.

QUEEN'S PARK

Gloucester St.

Jarvis St.

Dundonald St.

8

Wellesley St. West

WELLESLEY

Wellesley St. East

Queen's Park Cr. West

Queen's Park Cr. East

7

12→

Maitland St.

13→

Bay St.

Alexander St.

Church St.

Jarvis St.

Grenville St.

Wood St.

College St.

QUEEN'S PARK

COLLEGE

Carlton St.

ALLAN GARDENS   **14**

Value A Real Deal

You can save a lot of money visiting Toronto's attractions by purchasing a **Toronto CityPass.** See the Royal Ontario Museum, the Hockey Hall of Fame, the Ontario Science Centre, the CN Tower, Casa Loma, and the Toronto Zoo for C$65 (£33) for adults, and C$44 (£22) for kids from 4 to 12. Each booklet of tickets is valid for 9 days from the time the first one is used. You can buy the package at any of the six attractions listed above or online at **www.citypass.com**.

"Calendar of Events" in chapter 3). Other happenings include films, dance, theater, music, children's events, multicultural festivals, and marine events. Harbourfront is best in the summer, but a great destination year-round.

235 Queens Quay W. (*) **416/973-4000.** www.harbourfrontcentre.com. Subway: Union and then LRT to Queen's Quay or York Quay.

Ontario Place ★ **Kids** For all its Space Age looks, this is really just a fun amusement park, much more thrilling than Centreville on Centre Island (see below) but nowhere near as cool as Paramount Canada's Wonderland (p. 136). From a distance, you'll see five steel-and-glass pods suspended on columns 32m (105 ft.) above the lake, three artificial islands, and a huge geodesic dome. The five pods contain a multimedia theater, a children's theater, a high-technology exhibit, and displays that tell the story of Ontario in vivid kaleidoscopic detail. The dome houses Cinesphere, where specially made IMAX movies are shown year-round.

Ontario Place has many attractions targeted at kids, starting with the **H2O Generation Station,** a gigantic "soft play" structure with twisting slides, towers, and walkways. The **Atom Blaster**—which claims to be Canada's largest foam-ball free-for-all—is fun for the whole family. Younger children will enjoy the new **MicroKids** play area with its ball pit, climbing platforms, and other tot-appropriate draws.

At night, the **Molson Amphitheatre** accommodates concert-goers in the reserved seating area under the canopy and on the surrounding grass. For concert information, call (*) **416/260-5600;** for tickets, call **Ticketmaster** ((*) **416/870-8000**).

955 Lakeshore Blvd. W. (*) **416/314-9811,** or 416/314-9900 for recorded info. www.ontarioplace.com. Admission to grounds only C$18 (£9) for ages 6-64, C$12 (£6) for ages 4–5 and seniors, free for children 3 and under; separate fees for rides and events (pricing varies by month). Play All Day pass C$34 (£17) for ages 6-64, C$18 (£9) for ages 4-5 and seniors, free for 3 and under. Mid-May to Labour Day daily 10am-dusk; evening events end and dining spots close later. Closed (except Cinesphere) early Sept–early May. Subway: Bathurst and then Bathurst Street streetcar south.

The Toronto Islands ★ **Kids** In only 7 minutes, an 800-passenger ferry takes you to 245 hectares (605 acres) of island parkland crisscrossed by shaded paths and quiet waterways—a glorious spot to walk, play tennis, bike, feed the ducks, putter around in boats, picnic, or soak up the sun. Of the 14 islands, the two major ones are **Centre Island** and **Ward's Island.** The first is the most popular with tourists; Ward's is more residential (about 600 people live on the islands). Originally, the land was a peninsula, but in the 1800s, storms shattered the finger of land into islands.

On Centre Island, families enjoy **Centreville** ((*) **416/203-0405;** www.centreisland. ca), an old-fashioned amusement park that's been in business since 1966. You won't see the usual neon signs, shrill hawkers, and greasy hot-dog stands. Instead, you'll find a turn-of-the-20th-century village complete with a Main Street; tiny shops; a firehouse; and the Far Enough Farm, where the kids can pet lambs, chicks, and other barnyard animals. The kids will also love trying out the antique cars, fire engines, old-fashioned train, authentic 1890s carousel, flume ride, and aerial cars. An all-day ride pass costs C\$21 (£11) for those 4 feet tall and under, C\$30 (£15) for those over 4 feet; a family pass for four is C\$90 (£45). Centreville is open from 10:30am to 6pm daily from mid-May to Labour Day, and weekends in early May and September.

Lake Ontario. ℰ **416/392-8193** for ferry schedules. Round-trip fare C\$6.50 (£3.25) adults, C\$4 (£2) seniors and children 15–19, C\$3 (£1.50) children 3–14, free for children 2 and under. Ferries leave from docks at the bottom of Bay St. Subway: Union Station and then LRT to Queen's Quay.

DOWNTOWN
Art Gallery of Ontario ★   At press time, the AGO is still closed for renovations. Toronto son Frank Gehry is reinventing the city's best art gallery, and his spectacular design will increase viewing space by 40%. The current claim is that the gallery will reopen in November 2008, but I'm not sure I believe it (the renovation schedule has been somewhat fluid, shall we say). However, it's safe to say that 2009 visitors will be able to see the gallery in its new glory.

The AGO's European collection ranges from the 14th century to the French Impressionists and beyond. Works by Pissarro, Monet, Boudin, Sisley, and Renoir fill an octagonal room. De Kooning's *Two Women on a Wharf* and Karel Appel's *Black Landscape* are just two of the modern pieces. There are several works of particular interest to admirers of the pre-Raphaelite painters, including one by Waterhouse. Among the sculptures, you'll find two beauties—Picasso's *Poupée* and Brancusi's *First Cry.* Even so, its Canadian collection has been the strongest. The paintings by the Group of Seven—which includes Tom Thomson, F. H. Varley, and Lawren Harris—are extraordinary. In addition, other galleries show the genesis of Canadian art from earlier to more modern artists. And don't miss the extensive collection of Inuit art.

Another reason to go: The **Henry Moore Sculpture Centre,** with more than 800 pieces, is the largest public collection of his works. The artist gave them to Toronto because he was so moved by the citizens' enthusiasm for his work—public donations bought his sculpture *The Archer* to decorate Nathan Phillips Square after politicians refused to free up money for it. In one room, under a glass ceiling, 20 or so of his large works stand like silent prehistoric rock formations. Along the walls flanking a ramp are

---

ⓕ Finds   A Tiny Gem of a Gallery

The Ontario College of Art and Design (OCAD), located steps away from the AGO, has its own gallery. Called the **OCAD Professional Gallery,** it was launched in 2007 to explore the connections between art and design. So far the tiny 111-square-meter (1,200-square-foot) space has shown work by Canadian Karim Rashid (famous for his stylish housewares and table accessories) among others. Located at 100 McCaul Street, the gallery is open from Wednesday to Friday 1pm to 7pm, and on weekends from noon to 6pm. There is no admission fee. For more information, call ℰ **416/977-6000** or visit www.ocad.ca.

(Fun Facts) **Tough Enough**

To resist the elements, the CN Tower is built of sturdy stuff—contoured reinforced concrete covered with thick glass-reinforced plastic—and designed to keep ice accumulation to a minimum. The structure can withstand high winds, snow, ice, lightning, and earth tremors.

color photographs showing Moore's major sculptures in their natural locations, which reveal their magnificent dimensions.

The newly opened gallery will include a treasure trove of new pieces, too, including the Thomson family's Canadian collection and European collection (the latter includes Peter Paul Reubens's masterpiece, "The Massacre of the Innocents"). There will also be African and Australian aboriginal art and a photography installation.

317 Dundas St. W. (between McCaul and Beverley sts.). © 416/977-0414. www.ago.net. Museum is closed for renovation; check website for information on its reopening. Subway: St. Patrick.

CN Tower ★★ (Kids) Thanks a lot, Dubai. In 2008, the CN Tower lost its status as the world's tallest freestanding structure in the world to the Bruj Dubai. But in the big picture, who cares? However you approach Toronto, the first thing you see is this slender structure. Glass-walled elevators glide up the 553m (1,815-ft.) tower, first stopping at the 346m-high (1,136-ft.) Look Out level. (The truly fearless can ride up in the incredible new glass-*floored* elevator, which the CN Tower opened in 2008. Take that, Dubai!) You can walk down one level to experience the Glass Floor, my favorite spot at the tower: Through it, you can see all the way down to street level (even as your heart drops into your shoes). As a bonus, if you wait long enough, you'll undoubtedly see some alpha males daring each other to jump on the glass. (They do, and no, it doesn't break—the glass can withstand the weight of 14 adult hippos. Now *that's* a sight I'd like to see.)

Above the Look Out is the world's highest public observation gallery, the Skypod, 447m (1,466 ft.) above the ground. From here, on a clear day you can't quite see forever, but the sweeping vista stretches to Niagara Falls, 161km (100 miles) south, and to Lake Simcoe, 193km (120 miles) north. Unless you're really taken with the tower, I wouldn't recommend it—the view from the Glass Floor is majestic enough for me (for another great—and less expensive—way to view Toronto, see "A Great Toronto Vista," below). Atop the tower sits a 102m (335-ft.) antenna mast erected over 31 weeks with the aid of a giant Sikorsky helicopter. It took 55 lifts (and no hippos) to complete the operation.

The tower attractions are often revamped. Some perennial draws are the IMAX theater and two flight simulators. A series of interactive displays showcases the CN Tower along with such forerunners as the Eiffel Tower and the Empire State Building (and no, I don't think Dubai is mentioned. . .).

301 Front St. W. © 416/868-6937. www.cntower.ca. Admission (Look Out and Glass Floor) C$22 (£11) adults, C$20 (£10) seniors, C$15 (£7.50) children 4–12; Total Tower Experience (Look Out, Glass Floor, Skypod, film, and 2 rides) C$33 (£14) all ages. Daily 9am–11pm (shorter hours in winter). Closed Dec 25. Subway: Union and then walk west on Front St.

The Distillery District ★★★ Although founded in 1832, it wasn't until 2003 that this 45-building complex was reinvented as a historic district. This was once the home of the Gooderham-Worts Distillery, which was Canada's largest distilling company in the

19th century. A miller named James Worts, who emigrated from Scotland in 1831, built the first building on the site: a windmill intended to power a grain mill (the millstone he brought with him is still on display). His brother-in-law, William Gooderham, soon joined him in the business. In 1834, Worts's wife died in childbirth, and in despair, Worts drowned himself in the mill's well. Gooderham took over the business and adopted Worts's son, who eventually joined the business.

The complex is an outstanding example of industrial design from the 19th century. Much of the construction here was done with that Victorian favorite, red brick; you'll see it in everything from the buildings to the streets themselves. One exception is the mill building, which was built out of stone and thus managed to survive an 1869 fire.

The Distillery District has launched an ambitious program of events throughout the year, including a blues festival, a jazz festival, and an outdoor art exhibition; also, a farmers' market takes place on summer Sundays. See chapter 10 for the performing-arts venues and troupes based in the district.

55 Mill St. © **416/367-1800.** www.thedistillerydistrict.com. Free admission. Subway: King, and then streetcar east to Parliament St.

MIDTOWN

George R. Gardiner Museum of Ceramic Art ★★   Across the street from the

ROM is Canada's only specialized ceramics museum. Its ambitious renovation, which was unveiled in June 2006, increased the museum's display space from 1,765 sq. m (19,000 sq. ft.) to 2,694 sq. m (29,000 sq. ft.) and allows far more of the vast—and growing—collection to be on display.

There is plenty here to see. The pre-Columbian department contains fantastic Olmec and Maya figures, and objects from Ecuador, Colombia, and Peru. The majolica collection includes spectacular 16th- and 17th-century salvers and other pieces from Florence, Faenza, and Venice, and a Delftware collection that includes fine 17th-century chargers. The 18th century is heavily represented by Continental and English porcelain: Meissen, Sèvres, Worcester, Chelsea, Derby, and other great names. Among the highlights are objects from the Swan Service—a 2,200-piece set that took 4 years (1737–41) to make—and a collection of commedia dell'arte figures.

One more reason to visit: The Gardiner is home to the latest restaurant by Toronto chef extraordinaire Jamie Kennedy, which is open for lunch and for Friday dinners (see the review of his Wine Bar downtown, p. 111). His Gardiner outpost does get booked

---

(Moments)   A Great Toronto Vista

One of Toronto's best viewing spots is actually free—and it will give you an altogether different picture of the city than you'll get from the CN Tower. The **Bloor Street Viaduct** over the Don Valley connects Bloor Street in midtown Toronto with the East End (where Bloor becomes the Danforth). The pedestrian walkway will afford you what is possibly the most enchanting view of the city. From here, Toronto looks more like a lush forest than a city. There are trees as far as the eye can see, with skyscrapers and towers jutting out here and there. If you don't see it for yourself, you won't believe it. Subway: Castle Frank, and walk east along Bloor to the viaduct.

(Finds) **Serenity Now**

While I'm all for progress, the fact that the ROM's extensive renovations temporarily shut down the **Bishop White Gallery** drove me to distraction. But now the group of serene Southeast Asian Buddhas is back. The wall murals now occupy three walls at one end of the newly unveiled Chinese galleries, with several Buddhas and Bodhisavattas standing (and sitting) in attendance.

up for private events, too, so be sure to call ahead if you want to dine here; the reservation line is ☎ **416/362-1957.**

111 Queen's Park. ☎ **416/586-8080.** www.gardinermuseum.on.ca. Admission C$12 (£6) adults, C$8 (£4) seniors, and C$6 (£3) students with ID, free for children 12 and under. Sat–Thurs 10am–6pm; Fri 10am–9pm. Closed Jan 1, Dec 25. Subway: Museum.

Royal Ontario Museum ★★★ (Kids) This is one of my favorite museums anywhere. The ROM (rhymes with "tom"), as it's affectionately called, is Canada's largest museum, with more than six million objects in its collections. Now that the massive renovation is complete, visitors can appreciate the results. I have to confess to mixed feelings about the space. From Bloor Street the new crystal, which houses six galleries, looks fabulous. Daniel Libeskind's design is an eye-catching übermodern palace of jutting crystal prisms, and you can appreciate it even from blocks away. The interior of the crystal is another story. Much of the glass is blocked or covered (a sensible move, since the light would be blinding on a sunny day), but the result looks like a whitewashed warehouse. Through small openings you can see bits of Bloor Street West, but only a particularly unattractive stretch that is home to fast-food restaurants. The interior, in spite of its high ceilings, lacks the grandeur of the façade.

The collections, on the other hand, are impressively grand. These include the Chinese galleries, which feature an intact Ming tomb as well as the Bishop White Gallery of Chinese Temple Art (my personal favorite—see "Serenity Now," above). There are also wonderful galleries about the ancient world (Egypt, Greece, Cyprus, and Bronze Age Aegean are standouts), the natural world (dinosaurs! Yes, there's also a Bat Cave, and galleries devoted to birds and mammals, but the dinos are impossible to beat), and hands-on galleries that let kids learn while playing (the CIBC Discovery Gallery even has a "dinosaur dig" for would-be paleontologists).

One hint: even if you hate climbing stairs, give the ROM's Stair of Wonders a go. Behind glass panels on the walls are curiosities such as a 20-kilogram hippo jawbone, fossils, antique toy soldiers, and stuffed Birds of Paradise.

100 Queen's Park. ☎ **416/586-8000.** www.rom.on.ca. Admission C$20 (£10) adults, C$17 (£8.50) seniors and students with valid ID, C$14 (£7) children 4–14, free for children 3 and under. Sat–Thurs 10am–6pm; Fri 10am–9:30pm. Closed Jan 1, Dec 25. Subway: Museum.

UPTOWN
Ontario Science Centre ★★★ (Kids) Possibly the best thing about growing up in Toronto was the frequent visits to the OSC. Science was never my favorite subject, but the hands-on approach here was—and is—thrilling. Wherever you look, there are things to touch, push, pull, or crank. Test your reflexes, balance, heart rate, and grip strength; surf the Internet; watch frozen-solid liquid nitrogen shatter into thousands of icy shards;

study slides of butterfly wings, bedbugs, fish scales, or feathers under a microscope; tease your brain with a variety of optical illusions; land a spaceship on the moon; watch bees making honey; see how many lights you can light or how high you can elevate a balloon with your own pedal power. The fun goes on and on through the 10 exhibit halls and more than 800 interactive exhibits.

But that's not all: Small theaters show film and slide shows, and you can see regular 20-minute demonstrations of lasers, metal casting, and high-voltage electricity (which will, literally, make your hair stand on end). Another draw is the IMAX Dome theater, with a 24m (79-ft.) domed screen that creates spectacular effects. There are two eateries on-site: Galileo's Bistro, a buffet-style restaurant that serves alcohol, and Valley Market-place, a cafeteria. The Mastermind shop has a vast collection of educational toys and games. More than a million people visit the OSC every year, so it's best to arrive promptly at 10am to see everything. Make no mistake: The OSC provides a full day's entertainment. Like the ROM, the OSC recently completed a major renovation which added some new hands-on galleries inside and created a new outdoor exhibition space. The highlight is the new KidSpark gallery, designed for kids eight and under.

770 Don Mills Rd. (at Eglinton Ave. E.). © **416/696-3127,** or 416/696-1000 for Omnimax tickets. www.ontariosciencecentre.ca. Admission C$18 (£9) adults, C$14 (£6.75) seniors and children 13–17, C$11 (£5.50) children 4–12, free for children 3 and under. Omnimax admission C$12 (£6) adults, C$9 (£4.50) seniors and children 13–17, C$8 (£4) children 4–12, free for children 3 and under. Combination discounts available. Daily 10am–5pm. Closed Dec 25. Parking C$8 (£4). Subway: Yonge St. line to Eglinton, and then 34 Eglinton bus east to Don Mills Rd. By car: From downtown, take Don Valley Pkwy. to Don Mills Rd. exit and follow signs.

ON THE OUTSKIRTS

The McMichael Canadian Art Collection ★ In Kleinburg, 40km (25 miles) north of the city, the McMichael collection occupies a log-and-stone gallery that sits amid quiet stands of trees on 40 hectares (99 acres) of conservation land. Specially designed for the landscape paintings it houses, the gallery is a work of art. The lobby has a pitched roof that soars 8m (26 ft.) on massive rafters of Douglas fir; throughout the gallery, panoramic windows look south over white pine, cedar, ash, and birch.

Founded by Robert and Signe McMichael, the gallery began in 1965 when they donated their property, home, and collection to the province of Ontario. Today, the collection includes more than 6,000 works, and it highlights Canada's famous circle of landscape painters, the Group of Seven, as well as David Milne, Emily Carr, and their contemporaries. An impressive collection of Inuit and contemporary Native Canadian art and sculpture is also on display. In addition, four galleries contain changing exhibitions of works by contemporary artists.

(Finds) **A Tropical Oasis**

While most of the Ontario Science Centre's offerings are fun for the small fry, one area that adults will appreciate is the re-creation of a rainforest environment. On the bottom level of the building, it's large enough that you can wander a bit and forget the noise and blinking lights just beyond. There are also poison dart frogs and a few other creatures behind glass. *One caveat:* Stay in here for long, and you'll feel as though you've hit a sauna.

(Finds)   Retro Thrills

With the fanfare given to the new rides Paramount Canada's Wonderland introduces each summer, many park-goers overlook the older attractions. The Wild Beast is one of the original roller coasters, and it's still one of the best. The first few times you hurtle along the track, you'll be convinced that the whole rickety structure is about to fall down at any moment. Guess what—it was designed to feel that way! Other tried-and-true favorites include the Minebuster and the Dragon Fire. A bonus: shorter queues!

10365 Islington Ave., Kleinburg. ℂ **888/213-1121** or 905/893-1121. www.mcmichael.com. Admission C$15 (£7.50) adults, C$12 (£6) seniors and students with ID, free for children 5 and under. Daily 10am–4pm (the McMichael advises that you call ahead to confirm hours). Closed Dec 25. Parking C$5 (£2.50). By car: From downtown, take Gardiner Expwy. to Hwy. 427 north, follow it to Hwy. 7, and turn east. Turn left (north) at 1st light onto Hwy. 27. Turn right (east) at Major Mackenzie Dr. and left (north) at 1st set of lights to Islington Ave. and the village of Kleinburg. Or take Hwy. 401 to Hwy. 400 north. At Major Mackenzie Dr., go west to Islington Ave. and turn right. By bus: From Islington station, take bus no. 37 to Steeles Ave., and then take the York Region Transit bus no. 13A to the museum driveway (it's about a 10-min. walk up the driveway from the bus stop); note that separate fares are required for the 2 buses; also, note that the 13A bus does not run on weekends, and offers only morning and evening service on weekdays.

Paramount Canada's Wonderland ★★ (Kids)   Thirty minutes north of Toronto lies Canada's answer to Disney World. The 120-hectare (300-acre) park features more than 200 attractions, including 65 rides, a water park, a play area for tiny tots (KidZville), and live shows.

When I was a teenager, I spent a (fantastic) summer working here, and in some ways, the place hasn't changed much. Because the park relies on a local audience for most of its business, it introduces new attractions every year. 2008 marked the introduction of the Behemoth, Canada's biggest, fastest, and tallest rollercoaster. Other top attractions include The Fly, a roller coaster designed to make every seat feel as though it's in the front car (the faint of heart can't hide at the back of this one!); Sledge Hammer, a "menacing mechanical giant" that stands 24m (80 ft.) tall and hurls riders through accelerated jumps and free-falls; Cliffhanger, a "super swing" that executes 360-degree turns and makes riders feel immune to gravity; and the Xtreme Skyflyer, a hang-gliding and skydiving hybrid that plunges riders 46m (151 ft.) in a free-fall. The roller coasters range from the looping, inverted Top Gun to the track-free suspended Vortex.

The Splash Works water park offers a huge wave pool and water rides spread over 20 acres, from speed slides and tube rides to special scaled-down slides and a kids' play area. You'll also find Hanna-Barbera characters, including Scooby-Doo, strolling around the park (and ready to get their picture taken with the kids). Additional attractions include Wonder Mountain and its high divers (they take the 20m/66-ft. plunge down Victoria Falls to the mountain's base), restaurants, and shops.

9580 Jane St., Vaughan. ℂ **905/832-7000** or 905/832-8131. www.canadas-wonderland.com. Pay-One-Price Passport (includes unlimited rides and shows but not parking, special attractions, or Kingswood Music Theater) C$48 (£24) adults and children over 48 inches tall, C$25 (£12.50) seniors and children aged 3 and up who are under 48 inches tall, free for children 2 and under. June 1–25 Mon–Fri 10am–8pm, Fri–Sat 10am–10pm; June 26 to Labour Day daily 10am–10pm; late May and early Sept–early Oct Sat–Sun 10am–8pm. Closed mid-Oct to mid-May. Parking C$10 (£5). Subway: Yorkdale or York Mills, and then

Where to Eat When You're Going to . . .

In my experience, one of the most difficult things about travel is coordinating where you want to go with where you want to eat. All too often you find yourself at a great museum, only to realize that the great restaurant you wanted to try out is on the other side of town. To make your planning easier, here are some of Toronto's top attractions and the excellent restaurants that are nearby (note that all restaurants mentioned here are reviewed in chapter 6).

- **Art Gallery of Ontario:** Head over to Chinatown for **Sang Ho** (536 Dundas St. W.), **Happy Seven** (358 Spadina Ave.), or **Lee Garden** (331 Spadina Ave.). Or if you want French cuisine, the best nearby is at **Bodega** (30 Baldwin St.).

- **CN Tower** and the **Rogers Centre:** If you're put off by the stratospheric prices at **360,** the CN Tower's restaurant (C\$115/£58 for the steak-and-lobster main course), try walking north a few blocks. Elegant **Brassaii** (461 King St. W.) is expensive but won't break the bank, **Il Fornello** (214 King St. W.) offers moderately priced pizza and pasta, and **Penelope** (225 King St. W.) serves affordable yet yummy Greek cuisine.

- **Four Seasons Centre for the Performing Arts:** Before you take in an opera or a ballet, you can dine at **Tundra,** just across the street in the Toronto Hilton (145 Richmond St. W.). If you're in a bohemian mood, try the **Queen Mother Cafe** (208 Queen St. W.).

- The **Sony Centre** and the **Hockey Hall of Fame:** You're in luck here, because the stellar **Biff's** (4 Front St. E.) is just across the street. You're also right by **Le Papillon** (16 Church St.), **Jamie Kennedy Wine Bar** (9 Church St.), and **Young Thailand** (81 Church St.)—three well-priced places that serve impressive food.

- **Ontario Science Centre:** While people who work at the OSC love to point out that it's in the geographic center of Toronto, it's Nowheresville as far as food is concerned. But if you head west to Yonge Street, you'll be spoiled for choice. If you went to the OSC, presumably you have kids in tow, so **Grano** (2035 Yonge St.) would be an excellent choice. Other good bets include **Hannah's Kitchen** (*©* **416/481-2828;** 2221 Yonge St.; www. hannahskitchen), which is open only on weekdays, or **Amore Trattoria** (2425 Yonge St.), open 7 days a week.

- **Royal Ontario Museum:** The ROM has lost its stellar restaurant to ongoing renovations, but fortunately, the elegant **Annona** (in the Park Hyatt, 4 Avenue Rd.) is just across the street. Nearby Yorkville is full of great spots, including **Jacques Bistro du Parc** (126A Cumberland St.). Head just a few blocks west past Spadina, and you'll find a wide selection of moderately priced spots, such as **Serra** (378 Bloor St. W.) and **Nataraj** (394 Bloor St. W.).

GO Express Bus to Wonderland. By car: From downtown, take Yonge St. north to Hwy. 401 and go west to Hwy. 400. Go north on Hwy. 400 to Rutherford Rd. exit and follow signs. By car from the north, exit at Major Mackenzie.

Toronto Zoo ★★ (Kids)   Covering 284 hectares (701 acres) of parkland, this unique zoological garden contains some 5,000 animals, plus an extensive botanical collection. Pavilions—including Africa, Indo-Malaya, Australasia, and the Americas—and outdoor paddocks house the plants and animals.

One popular zoo attraction is at the **African Savanna** project. It re-creates a market bazaar and safari through Kesho (Swahili for "tomorrow") National Park, past such special features as a bush camp, rhino midden, elephant highway, and several watering holes. It also includes the **Gorilla Rainforest,** one of the most popular sights at the zoo and the largest indoor gorilla exhibit in North America. Another hit is Splash Island, a kids-only water park that includes a replica of a Canadian Coast Guard ship.

Ten kilometers (6 miles) of walkways offer access to all areas of the zoo. During the warmer months, the Zoomobile takes visitors around the major walkways to view the animals in the outdoor paddocks. The zoo has restaurants, a gift shop, first aid, and a family center. Visitors can rent strollers and wagons, and borrow wheelchairs. The African pavilion has an elevator for strollers and wheelchairs. There are ample parking and plenty of picnic areas with tables.

Meadowvale Rd. (north of Hwy. 401 and Sheppard Ave.), Scarborough. ℂ **416/392-5900.** www.toronto zoo.com. Admission C$20 (£10) adults, C$14 (£7) seniors, C$12 (£6) children 4–12, free for children 3 and under. Summer daily 9am–7:30pm; spring and fall daily 9am–6pm; winter daily 9:30am–4:30pm. Last admission 1 hr. before closing. Closed Dec 25. Parking C$8 (£4). Subway: Bloor–Danforth line to Kennedy, and then bus no. 86A north (buses run daily in summer, but on weekdays only during the rest of the year). By car: From downtown, take Don Valley Pkwy. to Hwy. 401 east, exit on Meadowvale Rd., and follow signs.

2 MORE MUSEUMS

Bata Shoe Museum ★★   Imelda Marcos—and anyone else obsessed with shoes (like, say, me!)—would love this museum, which houses the Bata family's 10,000-item collection. The building, designed by Raymond Moriyama, looks like a whimsical shoe-box. The main gallery, "All About Shoes," traces the history of footwear. It begins with a plaster cast of some of the earliest known human footprints, which date to 4 million B.C. You'll come across such specialty shoes as spiked clogs used to crush chestnuts in 17th-century France, Elton John's 12-inch-plus platforms, and Prime Minister Pierre Trudeau's well-worn sandals. One display focuses on Canadian footwear fashioned by the Inuit, while another highlights 19th-century ladies' footwear. The second-story galleries house changing exhibits, which have taken on some serious topics, such as a history of foot binding in China.

327 Bloor St. W. (at St. George St.). ℂ **416/979-7799.** www.batashoemuseum.ca. Admission C$12 (£6) adults, C$10 (£5) seniors, C$6 (£3) students with ID, C$4 (£2) children and youths 5–17, free for children 4 and under. Tues–Wed and Fri–Sat 10am–5pm; Thurs 10am–8pm; Sun noon–5pm. Subway: St. George.

Black Creek Pioneer Village (Kids)   Life here moves at the gentle pace of rural Ontario as it was more than a century ago. The original pioneers on this land were Daniel and Elizabeth Strong, a newlywed couple in 1816 who cleared 40 hectares (100 acres) of wilderness for farming and built a log house in their spare time. Eventually, a village

developed around this site, and many of the existing buildings date from the 1860s. You
can watch the authentically dressed villagers going about their chores—spinning, sewing, rail splitting, sheep shearing, and threshing. Visitors can enjoy the villagers' cooking, wander through the cozily furnished homesteads, visit the working mill, shop at the general store, or rumble past the farm animals in a horse-drawn wagon. The beautifully landscaped village has more than 30 restored buildings to explore. Special events take place throughout the year.

The restaurant is open from 11am to 3pm and features a special children's menu. Light snacks and refreshments are on sale all day at the visitor center.

1000 Murray Ross Pkwy. (at Steeles Ave. and Jane St.), Downsview. © **416/736-1733.** www.blackcreek. ca. Admission C$13 (£6.50) adults, C$12 (£6) seniors and students 15 and up, C$9 (£4.50) children 5–14, free for children 4 and under. May–June Mon–Fri 9:30am–4:30pm, Sat–Sun and holidays 10am–5pm; July–Sept daily 10am–5pm; Oct–Dec Mon–Fri 9:30am–4pm, Sat–Sun and holidays 10am–4:30pm. Closed Jan–Apr, Dec 25. Parking C$6 (£3). Subway: Finch and then bus no. 60 west to Murray Ross Parkway.

Canadian Broadcasting Corporation Museum ★ Kids The CBC has been Canada's national broadcaster since 1936—and its history intersects with the country's own. But this is anything but a time capsule. The museum has interactive exhibits that are fun for kids, and shows film clips that are interesting for all ages. Temporary exhibits explore subjects such as radio sound effects or honor much-loved programs (such as my childhood favorites *The Friendly Giant* and *Mr. Dressup*).

250 Front St. W. © **416/205-5574.** www.cbc.ca/museum. Free admission. Mon–Fri 9am–5pm. Subway: Union.

Design Exchange Located in the old Stock Exchange Building, the Design Exchange—or DX, as it prefers to be known—has become an important Canadian design museum. It features work from disciplines as varied as architecture to fashion, and from landscape design to interactive media design. Note that the Resource Centre has been officially reopened, and its library-like collection of design books, magazines, and other materials can be viewed by appointment (Mon, Wed, and Fri afternoons).

234 Bay St. © **416/363-6121.** www.dx.org. Admission C$5 (£2.50) adults, C$4 (£2) seniors and students with ID, free for children 13 and under. Mon–Fri 10am–5pm; Sat–Sun noon–5pm. Closed Jan 1, Dec 25. Subway: King.

Justina M. Barnicke Gallery at Hart House ★ Finds Hart House is, well, the heart of the University of Toronto community, and the Justina M. Barnicke Gallery is one of its treasures. But don't be taken in by the gallery's small size: Its extensive collection of Group of Seven paintings and other Canadian artworks, both historical and contemporary, is scattered throughout the hallways and rooms of Hart House (it's a public building, so feel free to wander and explore; just remember that the small plaques naming the work and its artist are hidden on the lower-right side of each frame or canvas). The Barnicke is a two-room gallery that features an ever-changing series of monthly exhibits. Occasionally it will show historical works, but its primary focus is on works by contemporary artists working with various media. Some of the shows may shock: *Martyrs Murder,* by Manitoba artist Diana Thorneycroft, was one that got to me. Thorneycroft created dioramas depicting the martyrdom of several Christian saints using children's plastic dolls and photographed the results. It was one of the most memorable exhibits I've ever seen.

At Hart House, 7 Hart House Circle. © **416/978-8398.** www.jmbgallery.ca. Free admission. Mon–Fri 11am–7pm, Sat–Sun 1–4pm. Shorter hours in summer. Closed for summer Sundays and for all statutory holidays. Subway: St. George or Museum.

(Fun Facts) Signs & Whispers

Have you ever wandered around a neighborhood that intrigued you, wishing that you could get some inside information on the place? Now, thanks to **[murmur]**, you can—at least in a few Toronto districts including Kensington Market, the Art & Design District on West Queen West, the Annex around Bloor Street West, and at Fort York. Look for signs that have a green ear logo and a phone number underneath; when you dial that number, you'll hear an interesting tidbit that will deepen your appreciation for what you're seeing. The project was developed as part of the city of Toronto's Culture Capital program, and its creators hope to eventually expand it throughout the city. Visit **www.murmurtoronto.ca** for details.

Museum of Contemporary Canadian Art ★★ MOCCA has relocated to the very hot Art & Design District on Queen Street West. Its growing collection includes works by Stephen Andrews, Genevieve Cadieux, Ivan Eyre, Betty Goodwin, Micah Lexier, Arnaud Maggs, and Roland Poulin, among many others. MOCCA's mandate has been widening in recent years, and that has made this gallery increasingly interesting. Some of the temporary exhibits, such as the 2008 exhibit about tattoo art titled "Art for the Human Canvas," have been real eye-openers. The irreverence and playfulness of this museum makes it a delight to visit.

952 Queen St. W. (✆ **416/395-7430.** www.mocca.toronto.on.ca. Free admission. Tues–Sun 11am–6pm. Closed for all statutory holidays. Subway: Osgoode and then streetcar west to Shaw St.

Textile Museum of Canada ★ This fascinating museum is internationally recognized for its collection of historic and ethnographic textiles and related artifacts. You'll find fine Oriental rugs and tapestries from all over the world. One gallery presents the work of contemporary artists. The museum is small, so only a fraction of the collection is on display, but you'll always find a vibrant, interesting show. Recent exhibits have included "War Rugs" from Afghanistan and military uniform insignia (both displays will still be on in January 2009).

55 Centre Ave. (✆ **416/599-5321.** www.textilemuseum.ca. Admission C$12 (£6) adults; C$8 (£4) seniors; C$6 (£3) students and children 5–14; free for children 4 and under. Daily 11am–5pm (to 8pm Wed). Closed Jan 1, Dec 25. Subway: St. Patrick.

University of Toronto Art Centre ★ (Finds) This is a great find—and one that very few people outside the Toronto university community know about. You enter the center from the University College quad, an Oxford-style cloistered garden that itself is a work of art. Inside, you'll find a gallery housing the Malcove Collection, which consists mainly of Byzantine art dating from the 14th to the 18th centuries. There are early stone reliefs and numerous icons from different periods. One of the Malcove's gems was painted by a German master in 1538: Lucas Cranach the Elder's *Adam and Eve*. The rest of the Art Centre is devoted to temporary exhibitions, which may display University College's collection of Canadian art, or other special exhibits.

15 King's College Circle. (✆ **416/978-1838.** www.utac.utoronto.ca. Free admission. Tues–Fri noon–5pm; Sat noon–4pm. Closed for all statutory holidays. Subway: St. George or Museum.

3 EXPLORING THE NEIGHBORHOODS

Toronto is a patchwork of neighborhoods, and the best way to discover its soul and flavor is to meander along its streets. On foot, you can best appreciate the sights, sounds, and smells that lend each area its particular character. Following are some of the most interesting neighborhoods.

DOWNTOWN WEST

CHINATOWN ★★ Stretching along Dundas Street west from Bay Street to Spadina Avenue and north and south along Spadina Avenue, Chinatown is home to some of Toronto's 350,000 Chinese-Canadian residents. Packed with fascinating shops and restaurants, it even has bilingual street signs.

In **Dragon City,** a large shopping mall at Spadina and Dundas, you'll find all kinds of stores. Some sell Chinese preserves (cuttlefish, lemon ginger, whole mango, ginseng, and antler), and others specialize in Asian books, tapes, records, fashion, and food. A food court features Korean, Indonesian, Chinese, and Japanese cuisine.

As you stroll through Chinatown, stop in at some of the shops and teahouses. A couple of my favorites are **Tap Phong** (p. 185) and **B&J Trading** (p. 199). A walk through Chinatown at night is especially exciting—the sidewalks fill with people, and neon lights shimmer everywhere. You'll pass gleaming noodle houses, windows hung with rows of glossy-brown cooked ducks, record stores selling the top 10 in Chinese, and trading companies filled with Asian produce.

To get to Chinatown, take the subway to St. Patrick and walk west. For more details, see "Walking Tour 1: Chinatown & Kensington Market," in chapter 8.

LITTLE ITALY ★★ Along College Street, between Euclid and Shaw, Little Italy competes with West Queen West to be the hottest spot in the city. The area hums at night, as people crowd the coffee bars, pool lounges, nightclubs, and trattorias. **The Mod Club** (p. 216) is one of the city's best live-music venues. Notable restaurants in the area include **Sottovoce, Chiado** (p. 100), and **Veni Vidi Vici** (p. 107). Great boutiques in the area are **Sim & Jones,** which features chic, smart casual clothing for women, and **Mink** (p. 200), a glittering oasis of faux gemstones. To get there, ride any College Street streetcar west to Euclid Avenue.

QUEEN STREET WEST ★ This street was once considered the heart of Toronto's avant-garde scene. That would be a serious stretch today. Sure, it's home to several clubs—such as the **Rivoli** (p. 217)—where major Canadian artists and singers have launched their careers (see chapter 10), but it's also where you'll find mainstream shops such as Club Monaco, Gap, and Le Chateau. Edgy? Not anymore. (See "Art & Design District," below, if you want a walk on the—somewhat—wilder side.)

Queen Street West officially starts at Yonge Street, but it doesn't really pick up, stylewise, till you cross University Avenue. This is prime shopping territory, with one-of-a-kind clothing boutiques such as **Price Roman** (p. 195) and **Peach Berserk** (p. 194). You'll also find a number of antiquarian bookstores, antiques and/or junk shops, nostalgic record emporiums, kitchen supply stores, and discount fabric houses. To start exploring, take the subway to Osgoode and walk west along Queen Street West.

ART & DESIGN DISTRICT ★★★ Also known as West Queen West. Queen Street west of Bathurst Street used to be a no-man's land—not because it was dangerous, but because little of importance was believed to be that far from the downtown core. How times have changed: This is one of the liveliest 'hoods in the city (one magazine dubbed it the coolest in the country). It's now home to the **Museum of Contemporary Canadian Art** (p. 140), and two of Toronto chicest hotels: the **Drake Hotel** (p. 77) and the **Gladstone Hotel** (p. 78).

West Queen West is all funky fun. It's got great shops for housewares and antiques, such as **Quasi-Modo** (p. 184), and excellent art galleries, such as the **Stephen Bulger** (p. 186). The clothing boutiques are exceptional: glamorous **Cabaret** (p. 196) for vintage, **Girl Friday** (p. 194) for original designs, and **Delphic** (p. 193) for menswear. It's also got some fine-but-affordable dining, such as **Swan** (p. 107). Take the subway to Osgoode and the streetcar over to Bathurst, and start walking west from there.

DOWNTOWN EAST

THE BEACHES This is one of the neighborhoods that makes Toronto a unique city. Here, near the terminus of the Queen Street East streetcar line, you can stroll or cycle along the lakefront boardwalk. Because of its natural assets, it has become a popular residential neighborhood for young boomers and their families, and Queen Street has plenty of browseable stores, such as **Book City** (p. 186). Just beyond Waverley Road, you can turn down through Kew Gardens to the boardwalk and walk all the way past the Olympic Pool to Ashbridge's Bay Park. To get to The Beaches, take the Queen Street East streetcar to Woodbine Avenue.

LESLIEVILLE ★ Queen Street East between Broadview and Leslie Street has become the place to shop for well-priced antique and vintage furniture. Stop in at **Zig Zag** (p. 183), **G.U.F.F.** (p. 182), and **Uppity!** (p. 183). Vintage clothing is another Leslieville specialty: stop in at **Gadabout** (p. 197) or **Thrill of the Find** (p. 197). This is also a great spot for lounges (such as **Barrio,** p. 219) and bistros (such as **Edward Levesque's Kitchen,** p. 110).

MIDTOWN

YORKVILLE ★ This area stretches north of Bloor Street West, between Avenue Road and Bay Street. Since its founding in 1853 as a village outside the city proper, Yorkville has experienced many transformations, and it's going through another right now. In the 1960s, it was Toronto's answer to Haight-Ashbury. In the 1980s, it became the hunting ground of the chic, who spent liberally at **Hermès, Chanel,** and **Cartier.** Today, new condos are going up so quickly that Yorkville feels like one big construction zone. On my last visit I could hardly believe how charmless and bland it had become.

Nevertheless, the area is still a shopper's paradise. **Jeanne Lottie** (p. 194), **Pusateri's** (p. 198), and **Teatro Verde** (p. 199) might bring out my spendthrift side, but they won't break the bank. If you want to be really decadent, visit the **Stillwater Spa** (p. 159) at the Park Hyatt hotel or the **Holt Renfrew Spa** (p. 158). The Aquatic Reiki treatment at the Stillwater—which takes place in a water-filled room—is one of the most memorable massages I've ever tried.

If you're an architecture buff, take a look at the red-brick building on Bloor Street at the end of Yorkville Avenue that houses the **Toronto Reference Library.** Step inside, and you'll find one of Toronto's most serene spots. To reach Yorkville, take the subway to Bay.

MIRVISH VILLAGE One of the city's most illustrious characters is Honest Ed Mirvish, who started his career in the 1950s with a no-frills department store at the corner of Markham and Bloor streets (1 block west of Bathurst). Even from blocks away, neon signs race and advertisements touting bargains hit you from every direction. Among his

other accomplishments, Mirvish saved the Royal Alexandra Theatre on King Street from
demolition; established a row of adjacent restaurants for theater patrons; and developed
this block-long area with art galleries, restaurants, and bookstores. He was responsible for
saving and renovating London's Old Vic, too.

Stop by and browse, and don't forget to step into **Honest Ed's** (see "The Best Bargains" on p. 188). To start your visit, take the subway to Bathurst.

THE EAST END
THE DANFORTH/GREEKTOWN   This eclectic area along Danforth Street east of the
Don River is hot, hot, hot. It swings until the early hours, when the restaurants and bars
are still crowded and frenetic. During the day, visitors can browse the traditional Greek
stores—like **Akropol,** a Greek bakery at no. 458 (✆ **416/465-1232**) that displays stunning multitiered wedding cakes in the window. The neighborhood is becoming more
ethnically diverse, and its new character is reflected by stores like **Blue Moon,** no. 375
(✆ **416/778-6991**), which sells beautiful crafts from the developing world (the store
supports only producers that provide healthy working conditions and fair pay), and **El
Pipil,** no. 267 (✆ **416/465-9625**), which has colorful clothing, knapsacks, and jewelry.
To get to the Danforth, ride the subway to Broadview and walk east.

WHAT TO SEE & DO

4 ARCHITECTURAL HIGHLIGHTS

Toronto is a beautiful city in spite of itself—or, rather, in spite of some of the city planners and developers who have torn down valuable parts of the city's architectural legacy
in the name of progress. Toronto grew by leaps and bounds in the Victorian and Edwardian eras, which is why there are so many stunning buildings from those times (take a walk
around the **University of Toronto campus** for a quick introduction to the different
styles; also, the **Ontario Legislature** and the **old city hall** stand out as particularly striking examples). However, much of the 20th century wasn't as kind: Clumsy planners
plunked the Gardiner Expressway near the waterfront—making what should have been
prime territory into a wasteland—and roughly 28,000 buildings were demolished
between 1955 and 1975. A few of the buildings that went up during that era were stun-
ners, such as Ludwig Mies van der Rohe's black-glass **Toronto-Dominion Centre** and
Viljo Revell's **new city hall.** And although Toronto has its share of forgettable buildings,
enough Gothic-inspired ones survived to allow the city to make a convincing stand-in
for New York on-screen. If you're interested in exploring Toronto's architectural history,
the Royal Ontario Museum's **ROMwalks** programs are an excellent way to go.

Casa Loma ★★★ **Kids**   Every city has its folly, but Toronto has an unusually charming one. It's complete with Elizabethan-style chimneys, Rhineland turrets, secret passageways, an underground tunnel, and a mellifluous name: Casa Loma.

Sir Henry Pellatt, who built it between 1911 and 1914, had a lifelong fascination with
castles. He studied medieval palaces, and gathered materials and furnishings from around
the world, bringing marble, glass, and paneling from Europe; teak from Asia; and oak
and walnut from North America. He imported Scottish stonemasons to build the massive walls that surround the 2.5-hectare (6-acre) site.

Wander through the majestic Great Hall, with its 18m-high (59-ft.) hammer-beam
ceiling; the Oak Room, where three artisans took 3 years to fashion the paneling; and the
Conservatory, with its elegant bronze doors, stained-glass dome, and pink-and-green

(Finds) **Walk This Way**

Several doors on the first story of Casa Loma open to a grand terrace that overlooks the gardens; most visitors step out, look at the gorgeous fountain and flowers below, and then proceed with the castle tour, which is truly a mistake. From the terrace, it's almost impossible to see the entrances to several winding paths that lead around the extensive grounds and command amazing views. Follow the grand staircase down, and enjoy a leisurely ramble.

marble. The castle encompasses battlements and a tower; Peacock Alley, designed after Windsor Castle; and a 1,800-bottle wine cellar. A 244m (800-ft.) tunnel runs to the stables, where Spanish tile and mahogany surrounded the horses.

I find it amusing to compare the Pellatts's private suites. Lady Mary's is overwhelmingly extravagant—you could house a family of four in her bathroom alone. Sir Henry's suite is surprisingly modest: It's relatively tiny, with the greatest extravagance being the bathroom's .5m-diameter (18-inch) showerhead. It makes you wonder which one of them was the *real* driving force behind the building of the castle.

The tour is self-guided; pick up an audiocassette, available in eight languages, upon arrival. From May to October, the gardens are open, too. There's also a Druxy's deli (part of a local chain) on-site, which is good to know, as there aren't many dining options nearby. Casa Loma hosts special events every March, July, and December.

1 Austin Terrace. (©) **416/923-1171.** www.casaloma.org. Admission C$16 (£8) adults, C$10 (£5) seniors and youths 14–17, C$8.75 (£4.38) children 4–13, free for children 3 and under. Daily 9:30am–5pm (last entry at 4pm). Closed Jan 1, Dec 25. Subway: Dupont and then walk 2 blocks north.

City Hall ★ An architectural spectacle, city hall houses the mayor's office and the city's administrative offices. Daringly designed in the late 1950s by Finnish architect Viljo Revell, it consists of a low podium topped by the flying-saucer-shaped Council Chamber, enfolded between two curved towers. Its interior is as dramatic as its exterior. A free brochure detailing a self-guided tour of city hall is available from its information desk; the tour can also be printed from the website below in French, Chinese, German, Italian, Japanese, Korean, Portuguese, and Spanish.

In front stretches **Nathan Phillips Square** (named after the mayor who initiated the project). In summer you can sit and contemplate the flower gardens, fountains, and reflecting pool (which doubles as a skating rink in winter), as well as listen to concerts. Here, you'll find Henry Moore's *The Archer* (formally, *Three-Way Piece No. 2*), purchased through a public subscription fund, and the Peace Garden, which commemorates Toronto's sesquicentennial in 1984. In contrast, to the east stands the **old city hall,** a green-copper-roofed Victorian Romanesque–style building.

100 Queen St. W. (©) **416/338-0338.** www.toronto.ca/city_hall_tour/nps.htm. Free admission. Self-guided tours Mon–Fri 8:30am–4:30pm. Subway: Queen and then walk west to Bay.

Eaton Centre Buttressed at both ends by 30-story skyscrapers, this urban shopping center stretches from Dundas Street south along Yonge Street to Queen Street (557,418 sq. m/6 million sq. ft.). An unusually upscale **Sears** department store anchors the north sections, and more than 285 stores and restaurants and two garages fill the rest. Twenty million people shop here annually.

Inside, the structure opens into the impressive **Galleria,** a 264m-long (866-ft.) glass-domed arcade dotted with benches, orchids, palm trees, and fountains; it's further adorned by Michael Snow's 60 soaring Canada geese, titled *Step Flight*. The birds are made from black-and-white photos mounted on cast fiberglass frames. But let's face it: You're probably here to shop (see chapter 9 for guidance).

Dundas and Yonge sts. ℂ **416/598-8700.** www.torontoeatoncentre.com. Mon–Fri 10am–9pm; Sat 9:30am–7pm; Sun noon–6pm. Subway: Dundas or Queen.

Ontario Legislature ★   At the northern end of University Avenue, with University of Toronto buildings to the east and west, lies Queen's Park. Embedded in its center is the rose-tinted sandstone-and-granite Ontario Legislature, which has stood here since 1893. Its stately domes, arches, and porte cocheres are the work of English architect Richard Waite, who was influenced by the Richardson Romanesque style. Be sure to call ahead before you visit to make sure that the building will be open to the public that day. Try to take the Friday afternoon "Art & Architecture" tour that runs between 2 and 3:30pm (it's free, but advance reservations are required to participate). If you're interested in observing the Ontario Legislature in session, consult its schedule on the website.

111 Wellesley St. W. (at University Ave.). ℂ **416/325-7500.** www.ontla.on.ca. Free admission. Year-round Mon–Fri; Victoria Day–Labour Day Sat–Sun. Call for tour information and reservations. Subway: Queen's Park.

Royal Bank Plaza   Shimmering in the sun, Royal Bank Plaza looks like a pillar of gold, and with good reason. During its construction, 2,500 ounces of gold went into the building's 14,000 windows as a coloring agent. More important, the structure is a masterpiece of architectural design. Two triangular towers of bronze mirror glass flank a 40m-high (130-ft.) glass-walled banking hall. The external walls of the towers are built in a serrated configuration so that they reflect a phenomenal mosaic of color.

In the banking hall, hundreds of aluminum cylinders hang from the ceiling, the work of Venezuelan sculptor Jesús Raphael Soto. Two levels below, a waterfall-and-pine-tree setting is naturally illuminated from the hall above.

Front and Bay sts. Free admission. Subway: Union.

WHAT TO SEE & DO

7

ARCHITECTURAL HIGHLIGHTS

(Tips) **Looking Sharp**

No building in Toronto is more distinctive than the **Sharp Centre for Design.** While it doesn't dominate Toronto's skyline the way that the CN Tower does, it's a work of stark originality. Designed by renowned architect Will Alsop, it opened in 2004 to near-universal shock . . . and acclaim, including a Worldwide Architecture Award from the Royal Institute of British Architects. The upper portion of the structure is referred to as the "table top," and its white-and-black checkerboard body stands 26m (85 ft.) above the street on 12 spindly, colorful legs. It's most dramatic at night, when it's lit by 16 large metal lights with blue bulbs. Sadly, it's only open to students of the Ontario College of Art & Design, not the public. Located on McCaul Street just south of Dundas Street West, you'll see it in the "Chinatown & Kensington Market" tour on p. 162.

(Finds) **A Place in the Sun . . . with Music**

While it's easy to get carried away in the shops of Eaton Centre, don't overlook Trinity Square, on the west side of the building near the Sears department store. The complex surrounds two of Toronto's oldest landmarks: **Church of the Holy Trinity,** dating to 1847, and **Scadding House** (✆ 416/598-4521), home of Trinity's rector. Concerned citizens demanded that the developers not block sunlight from reaching the buildings. They got their way—the sun continues to shine on the church's twin towers.

If you can, drop by on a Monday: Holy Trinity hosts an eclectic concert series called **"Music Mondays"** that features everything from modern jazz to Hindustani classical music (see the church's website at www.holytrinitytoronto.org for the schedule, or call ✆ 416/598-4521, ext. 222). Concerts take place at 12:15pm and there is a requested C$5 (£2.50) donation.

St. James' Cathedral ★★★ This stunning early English Gothic–style Anglican cathedral owes its existence at least in part to a group of American Loyalists. They joined with a group of British immigrants to found a congregation in 1797, and they were given a plot of land, which today is bounded by Church, King, Jarvis, and Adelaide streets. They started building Toronto's first church on this site in 1803. The original frame building was enlarged in 1818 and replaced in 1831—and that burned down in 1839. The first cathedral replaced it, only to be destroyed in the great fire of 1849. The present building was begun in 1850 and completed in 1874. It boasts the tallest steeple in Canada. Inside, there's a Tiffany window in memory of William Jarvis, one of Toronto's founding fathers. All of the stained glass windows are dazzling, but my favorite is the High Altar window—its lower panel bears a distinct resemblance to Leonardo da Vinci's painting of the Last Supper.

In addition to being a great work of architecture, St. James' is a good place to stop and rest for a bit. Unless there's a service going on, it doesn't draw much of a crowd, so it feels like a private oasis in the middle of downtown. St. James' also hosts free concerts every Tuesday at 1pm from September to June.

65 Church St. ✆ 416/364-7865. www.stjamescathedral.on.ca. Free admission. Sun–Fri 7:30am–5:30pm; Sat 9am–3pm. Subway: King.

St. Michael's Cathedral ★★★ The principal seat of the Catholic archdiocese of Toronto, St. Michael's is another 19th-century neo-Gothic structure. Built between 1845 and 1848, it originally had a plain interior design with clear-glass windows and white walls. That changed in 1850, when Armand de Charbonnel became the second Bishop of Toronto. Charbonnel was a Frenchman who lived in Montréal, and at first he was so opposed to his new position that he actually traveled to Rome to beg Pope Pius IX not to make him take it. The pope had other ideas and used Charbonnel's visit to consecrate him in the Sistine Chapel. However, when the new bishop finally arrived in Toronto in September 1850, he threw himself into beautifying St. Michael's. He sold lands that he owned in France and donated the proceeds to the cathedral. He bought dazzling stained-glass windows from France, built interior chapels, and commissioned paintings; he also imported the Stations of the Cross from France (that's why they're in French). While

> **Tips   The Big O**
>
> The University of Toronto has some of the most eclectic architecture in the city. For an introduction, take the walking tour that begins on p. 167. Unfortunately, one of the most talked-about buildings is one that you can't get inside: the **Graduate House,** located at the campus's western edge at 60 Harbord St. (at Spadina Ave.). Designed by architect Thom Mayne, this award-winning building looks not unlike a concrete bunker, and the giant UNIVERSITY OF TORONTO sign only has the last letter visible at most viewing angles, earning the structure the nickname "The Big O."

improvements and additions have been made since Charbonnel's time, no one did more to make St. Michael's the masterpiece it is.

St. Michael's is particularly venerated for its musical tradition. It has its own boys' choir—which has won awards internationally—and of the four Masses they sing weekly, three are on Sunday.

65 Bond St. ☏ **416/364-0234.** www.stmichaelscathedral.com. Free admission. Mon–Sat 6am–6pm; Sun 6am–10pm. Subway: Queen or Dundas.

Toronto Reference Library   Step inside—a pool and a waterfall gently screen out the street noise, and the space opens dramatically to the sky. Light and air flood every corner. This 1977 six-story structure is another masterwork by Toronto architect Raymond Moriyama, who also designed the Bata Shoe Museum.

789 Yonge St. ☏ **416/395-5577.** Free admission. Year-round Mon–Thurs 10am–8pm, Fri–Sat 10am–5pm; Thanksgiving–Apr also Sun 1:30–5pm. Subway: Yonge/Bloor.

5 HISTORIC BUILDINGS

Campbell House   Just across from Osgoode Hall (see below) sits the 1822 mansion of Sir William Campbell, a Loyalist and sixth chief justice of Upper Canada. In 1829, he retired to this mansion, where he lived until his death in 1834. It was moved several blocks from its original location in 1972. The beautifully restored building features a collection of period furniture. Guided tours take about half an hour and provide insight into Toronto's early history.

160 Queen St. W. (at University Ave.). ☏ **416/597-0227.** www.campbellhousemuseum.ca. Admission C$4.50 (£2.25) adults, C$3 (£1.50) seniors and students with ID, C$2.50 (£1.25) children ages 5–12, C$10 (£5) family (2 adults, 2 children). Year-round Mon–Fri 9:30am–4:30pm; May–Oct also Sat–Sun noon–4pm. Closed Dec 25. Subway: Osgoode.

Colborne Lodge   This charming, English-style Regency cottage with a three-sided verandah was built from 1836 to 1837 to take advantage of the view of Lake Ontario and the Humber River. At the time, it was considered way out in the country and a bother to travel to during the harsh winters. In 1873, the owner, a Toronto surveyor and architect named John Howard, donated the house and surrounding land to the city in return for an annual salary. That created High Park (see "Parks, Gardens & Cemeteries," later in this chapter), a great recreational area.

High Park. ℂ **416/392-6916.** Admission C$4.50 (£2.25) adults, C$3 (£1.50) seniors and students 13–18, C$2.50 (£1.25) children 12 and under. Tues–Sun noon–5pm; call ahead as hours vary. Subway: High Park.

Fort York ★ (Kids) This base was established by Lt. Gov. John Graves Simcoe in 1793 to defend "little muddy York," as Toronto was then known. Americans sacked it in April 1813, but the British rebuilt that same summer. Fort York was used by the military until 1880 and was pressed back into service during both world wars.

You can tour the soldiers' and officers' quarters; clamber over the ramparts; and in summer, view demonstrations of drills, music, and cooking. If you can, try to visit on Victoria Day, Canada Day, or Simcoe Day (see "Holidays," p. 29), when plenty of special events take place. These include the ever-popular Kids' Drill, in which kids get to take part in a military exercise.

100 Garrison Rd., off Fleet St., between Bathurst St. and Strachan Ave. ℂ **416/392-6907.** www.fortyork. ca. Admission C$8 (£4) adults, C$4 (£2) seniors and children 13–18, C$3 (£1.50) children 6–12, free for children 5 and under. Free parking. Mid-May to Labour Day daily 10am–5pm; Sept to mid-May Mon–Fri 10am–4pm, Sat–Sun 10am–5pm. Subway: Bathurst and then streetcar no. 911 south.

Mackenzie House This Greek Revival brick row house dates from the mid–19th century. It was once the home of William Lyon Mackenzie, a fiery orator and newspaper editor who had a most unusual career. He became Toronto's first mayor in 1836 . . . and then, in 1837, he led the Upper Canada rebellion against British rule. Mackenzie fled to the United States with a bounty on his head but returned to Toronto after influential friends arranged a pardon. Some of those same friends bought this house for him, and Mackenzie lived here from 1859 until his death in 1861. It's furnished in 1850s style, and in the back is a print shop modeled after Mackenzie's own. Mackenzie was born in Scotland, and celebrations for Hogmanay and Robbie Burns Day are always special here.

82 Bond St. ℂ **416/392-6915.** Admission C$6 (£3) adults, C$4 (£2) seniors and students 13–18, C$3 (£1.50) children 5–12, free for children 4 and under. Higher admission rates are applied on holidays. May–Sept 1 Tues–Sun noon–5pm; Sept 2–Dec Tues–Sun noon–4pm; Jan–Apr Sat–Sun noon–5pm. Subway: Dundas.

Osgoode Hall West of city hall, an impressive, elegant wrought-iron fence extends in front of an equally gracious public building, Osgoode Hall. Legend has it that the fence was built to keep cows from trampling the flowerbeds. Tours of the interior reveal the splendor of the grand staircase, the rotunda, the Great Library, and the fine portrait and sculpture collection. Construction began in 1829, and troops were billeted here after the Rebellion of 1837. It's currently the home of the Law Society of Upper Canada, the headquarters of Ontario's legal profession. The Court of Appeal for Ontario has several magnificent courtrooms here. The courts are open to the public.

130 Queen St. W. ℂ **416/947-3300.** www.osgoodehall.com. Free admission. Mon–Fri 8:30am–5pm. Call for information about tours. Subway: Osgoode.

Spadina Museum Historic House & Garden ★ How do you pronounce "Spadina"? In the case of the avenue, it's Spa-*dye*-na; for this lovely landmark, it's Spa-*dee*-na. Why? Who knows! But if you want to see how the leading lights of the city lived in days gone by, visit the historic home of financier James Austin. The exterior is beautiful; the interior, even more impressive. Spadina House contains a remarkable collection of art, furniture, and decorative objects. The Austin family occupied the house from 1866 to 1980, and successive generations modified and added to the house and its decor.

Spadina House is the next-door neighbor of Casa Loma (p. 143). Between the two is a small but lovely park that is almost hidden by the trees that shade it. Many visitors don't notice it, but locals love it. Grab a bench here if you want to take a breather.

Tours (the only way to see the house) start on the quarter-hour. Be warned that while the guides are excellent, the video that they force you to watch before the tour is bizarre. (The narrator is the "spirit of the house," and his rambling comments—paired with a stagy Irish brogue—will make you wonder if the video is a joke. It isn't!) In summer, you can also tour the gorgeous gardens. *One caveat:* The house has been used for film shoots, for which it suspended its regular admission hours; call ahead to make sure it's open on the day you want to see it.

285 Spadina Rd. ℂ **416/392-6910.** Guided tour C$8 (£4) adults, C$5 (£2.50) seniors and children over 12, C$4 (£2) children 12 and under. Tues–Fri noon–4pm; Sat–Sun noon–5pm. Subway: Dupont.

6 FOR SPORTS FANS

Air Canada Centre ★   This sports and entertainment complex is home to the Maple Leafs (hockey) and the Raptors (basketball). Longtime fans were crushed when the Leafs moved here in 1999 from Maple Leaf Gardens—the arena that had housed the team since 1931—but the Air Canada Centre has quickly become a fan favorite; the center was designed with comfort in mind (the seats are wide and upholstered). Seating is on a steeper-than-usual grade so that even the "nosebleed" sections have decent sightlines.

40 Bay St. (at Lakeshore Blvd.). ℂ **416/815-5500.** www.theaircanadacentre.com. Subway: Union and then LRT to Queen's Quay.

Canada's Sports Hall of Fame   In the center of Exhibition Place, this three-floor space celebrates the country's greatest male and female athletes in all major sports. Complementing the displays are touch-screen computers that tell you everything you could want to know about particular sports personalities and Canada's athletic heritage.

Exhibition Place. ℂ **416/260-6789.** Free admission. Mon–Fri 10am–4:30pm. Subway: Bathurst and then streetcar no. 511 south to end of line.

Hockey Hall of Fame ★★ **Kids**   Ice hockey fans will be thrilled by the artifacts collected here. They include the original Stanley Cup, a replica of the Montréal Canadiens' locker room, Terry Sawchuck's goalie gear, Newsy Lalonde's skates, and the stick Max Bentley used. You'll also see photographs of the personalities and great moments in hockey history. Most fun are the shooting and goalkeeping interactive displays, where you can take a whack at targets with a puck or don goalie gear and face down flying video pucks or sponge pucks.

In Brookfield Place, 30 Yonge St. (at Front St.). ℂ **416/360-7765.** www.hhof.com. Admission C$13 (£6.50) adults, C$9 (£4.50) seniors and children 4–18, free for children 3 and under. Mon–Fri 10am–5pm, Sat 9:30am–6pm, Sun 10:30am–5pm. Closed Jan 1, Dec 25. Subway: Union.

Rogers Centre ★   This is home to the Toronto Blue Jays baseball team and the Toronto Argonauts football team. In 1989, the opening of this stadium, then known as SkyDome, was a gala event. The stadium represents an engineering feat, featuring the world's first fully retractable roof, and a gigantic video scoreboard. It is so large that a 31-story building would fit inside the complex when the roof is closed.

1 Blue Jays Way. ✆ **416/341-2770.** www.rogerscentre.com. Subway: Union and then follow signs and walkway.

---

7 MARKETS

Toronto's markets are an important part of its heritage. The markets have traditionally been surrounded by neighborhoods that have absorbed wave after wave of immigrants into the city's fabric. Make like a local and dive into the fray. In addition to the markets listed below, check out the smaller ones at the **Distillery District** (p. 132) and at **Riverdale Farm** (p. 155).

Kensington Market ★★   This colorful, lively area should not be missed. You'll hear Caribbean, Portuguese, Italian, and other accents as merchants spread out their wares—squid and crabs in pails; chickens, pigeons, bread, cheese, apples, pears, peppers, ginger, and mangoes from the West Indies; salted fish from Portuguese dories; lace, fabrics, and other colorful remnants. There's no market on Sunday. Kensington Avenue itself is a treasure trove of vintage clothing stores. You'll see a lot of junk here, but amazing finds can be had at shops like **Courage My Love** (14 Kensington Ave.; ✆ 416/979-1992). Most of the shops display their wares outdoors in decent weather, adding to the color and charm of the area. Several summer Sundays are car-free in Kensington Market, making for a pedestrian paradise.

Bounded by Dundas St., Spadina Ave., Baldwin St., and Augusta Ave. No central phone. Most stores open Mon–Sat. Subway: St. Patrick and then Dundas St. streetcar west to Kensington.

St. Lawrence Market   This handsome food market is in a vast building constructed around the facade of the second city hall, built in 1850. Vendors sell fresh meat, fish, fruit, vegetables, and dairy products as well as other foodstuffs. The best time to visit is early Saturday morning, shortly after the farmers arrive.

92 Front St. E. ✆ **416/392-7219.** Tues–Thurs 8am–6pm; Fri 8am–7pm; Sat 5am–5pm. Subway: Union.

Ⓕinds   **Say Cheese**

One Kensington Market spot I can't resist is the **Global Cheese Shoppe,** 76 Kensington Ave. (✆ 416/593-9251). It stocks excellent offerings from around the world, and the staff is happy to let you try anything. One irresistible choice is the made-in-Ontario goat cheese. Mmm. . .

WHAT TO SEE & DO

7

MARKETS

8 PARKS, GARDENS & CEMETERIES

DOWNTOWN

Allan Gardens ★ (Kids)   What a difference a few years can make. Allan Gardens used to be down at the heels and seedy, but since the University of Toronto relocated its Botany Greenhouses here in 2004, this park has been infused with new life. This was actually Toronto's first civic park, created on the 4 hectares (10 acres) donated to the city by former mayor George William Allan. Originally called the Horticultural Gardens, the city renamed the park after Allan died in 1901. The stunning glass-domed Palm House conservatory dates back to 1910 and contains six greenhouses. It has been joined by U of T's restored and renovated greenhouses, now called the Allan Gardens Children's Conservatory.

Between Jarvis, Sherbourne, Dundas, and Gerrard sts. ✆ **416/392-1111.** Free admission. Daily dawn–dusk. Subway: Dundas.

Ireland Park ★ (Finds)   In 1847, Toronto was a city of 20,000—until 38,000 Irish immigrants arrived that summer. On June 21, 2007, this memorial to the Irish Famine was opened at Eireann Quay by Mary McAleese, president of Ireland. The park was inspired by Rowan Gillespie's "Departure" series of famine figures, which stand on Dublin's Liffey quayside, depicting Irish emigrants looking out to sea. There are seven figures in Dublin and five in Toronto's new park, which seems appropriate given how many Irish perished on the journey. The figures in Ireland Park were also created by Gillespie, and they are called the "Arrival" series. There is also a memorial in the park to the more than 1,100 who died just after their arrival; their names will be inscribed in a limestone wall.

At Bathurst St. and Queens Quay W., across from Bathurst Quay ✆ **416/601-6906.** www.irelandpark foundation.com. Free admission. Daily dawn–dusk. Subway: Union and then LRT to Spadina and walk west to Bathurst.

Toronto Music Garden ★★★   Toronto is a city of gardens, but this one along Toronto's waterfront is special. Cellist Yo-Yo Ma and landscape designer Julie Moir Messervy created the Toronto Music Garden to invoke Bach's First Suite for Unaccompanied Cello. Between 10am and 8pm, you can rent an audio guide to the music garden complete with commentary from Ma and Messervy, and snippets from the baroque work that inspired them (audio guides are C$5/£2.50 and are available at 539 Queens Quay W.).

475 Queens Quay W. ✆ **416/338-0338.** Free admission. Daily dawn–dusk. Subway: Union and then LRT to Spadina.

Trinity Bellwoods (Finds)   This land was originally part of a military reserve when Toronto was still a small town called York and the British troops were garrisoned at Fort York (p. 148). Eventually parcels were sold to retiring officers, but in 1851, Bishop John Strachan bought up some of the land in order to found a college. Strachan was furious at the University of Toronto's decision to become a secular school, and he founded the Anglican Trinity College in 1852 (of course, Trinity is now part of the university, though it has kept its Anglican traditions). The buildings were torn down, but the beautiful stone and wrought-iron gates that face Queen Street West still remain, and there are Victorian lampposts illuminating the main paths at night. Given the colorful neighborhood it's located in (the Art & Design District), it's no surprise that Trinity Bellwoods has hosted

> **Finds**   **Music Alfresco**
>
> The **Toronto Music Garden** hosts some of the city's best summer concerts. From late June to mid-September, you can count on listening to live music here every Thursday at 7pm and on Sundays at 4pm. Sometimes you'll hear classical music—especially by the baroque composers—but the programs are rather eclectic. Recent offerings have included Spanish flamenco music and traditional Chinese melodies. All performances are free.

some interesting events, including an anarchist book fair and drumming circles. Much of the park is a leash-free zone, so dog owners love it.

Between Dundas St. W., Crawford St., Queen St. W., and Gore Vale Ave. ✆ **416/392-1111.** Free admission. Daily dawn–dusk. Subway: Osgoode and then streetcar west to Bellwoods Ave.

MIDTOWN

High Park ★ Kids   This 161-hectare (398-acre) park in the far west of Midtown was architect John G. Howard's gift to the city. He lived in Colborne Lodge, which still stands in the park (p. 147). The grounds contain a large lake called Grenadier Pond (great for ice skating in wintertime); a small exotic zoo; a swimming pool; tennis courts; sports fields; bowling greens; and vast expanses of green for baseball, jogging, picnicking, bicycling, and more. But my favorite thing is The Dream in High Park, the annual Shakespearean offering, staged every summer (p. 211).

1873 Bloor St. W., stretching south to the Gardiner Expwy. www.toronto.ca/parks. No phone. Free admission. Daily dawn–dusk. Subway: High Park.

Necropolis ★   Located in Midtown East, this is one of the city's oldest cemeteries, dating to 1850. Some of the remains were originally buried in Potters Field, where Yorkville stands today.

Before strolling through the cemetery, pick up a History Tour brochure at the office. You'll find the graves of William Lyon Mackenzie, leader of the 1837 rebellion, as well as those of his followers Samuel Lount and Peter Matthews, who were hanged for their parts in the rebellion. (Mackenzie himself went on to become a member of Parliament. Go figure.) Other notables buried in the 7.2-hectare (18-acre) cemetery include George Brown, one of the fathers of Confederation; Anderson Ruffin Abbot, the first Canadian-born black surgeon; Joseph Tyrrell, who unearthed dinosaurs in Alberta; and world-champion oarsman Ned Hanlan. Henry Langley, who designed the Necropolis' porte cochere and the Gothic Revival chapel—as well as the spires of St. James' and St. Michael's cathedrals (p. 146)—is also buried here.

200 Winchester St. (at Sumach St.). ✆ **416/923-7911.** www.mountpleasantgroupofcemeteries.ca. Free admission. Daily 8am–dusk. Subway: Castle Frank, then bus no. 65 south on Parliament St. to Wellesley, and walk 3 blocks east to Sumach.

UPTOWN & FARTHER AFIELD

Edwards Gardens   This quiet, formal 14-hectare (35-acre) garden is part of a series of parks that stretch over 240 hectares (593 acres) along the Don Valley. Gracious bridges arch over a creek, rock gardens abound, and roses and other seasonal flowers add color and scent. The garden is famous for its rhododendrons. The Civic Garden Centre operates a gift shop and offers free walking tours on Tuesday and Thursday at 11am and 2pm. The Centre also boasts a fine horticultural library.

777 Lawrence Ave. E. (at Leslie St.). ℭ **416/392-8188.** www.toronto.ca/parks. Free admission. Daily dawn–dusk. Subway: Eglinton and then bus no. 51 (Leslie) or 54 (Lawrence).

Mount Pleasant Cemetery ★★ Home to one of the finest tree collections in North America, this cemetery is also the final resting place of many fascinating people, such as Glenn Gould, the celebrated classical pianist; Dr. Frederick Banting and Dr. Charles Best, the Toronto researchers who discovered insulin in 1922; golfer George Knudson; the Massey and Eaton families, whose mausoleums are impressive architectural monuments; Prime Minister William Lyon Mackenzie King; Canada's greatest war hero, Lt. Col. William Barker; and writer and editor Jim Cormier.

375 Mount Pleasant Rd., north of St. Clair Ave. ℭ **416/485-9129.** www.mountpleasantgroupof cemeteries.ca. Free admission. Daily 8am–dusk. Subway: St. Clair.

Scarborough Bluffs ★★ On the eastern edge of Toronto is a natural wonder. The Scarborough Bluffs are unique in North America, and their layers of sand and clay offer a remarkable geological record of the great ice age. Rising up to 105m (350 ft.) above Lake Ontario, they stretch out over 14km ($8^2/_3$ miles). The first 45m (150 ft.) contains fossil plants and animals that were deposited by the advancing Wisconsin Glacier 70,000 years ago. The bluffs were given their name in 1793 by Lady Elizabeth Simcoe, wife of the first Lieutenant Governor of Upper Canada (Ontario); as she sailed to York, as Toronto was then known, she was reminded of the cliffs of Yorkshire.

South of Kingston Rd. www.toronto.ca/parks. No phone. Free admission. Daily dawn–dusk. Subway: Victoria Park, then no. 12 Kingston Rd. bus to Brimley Rd., and then about a 15-min. walk south along Brimley. By car: From downtown, take Don Valley Pkwy. to Hwy. 401 east, exit on Brimley Rd., and drive south.

---

9 ESPECIALLY FOR KIDS

The city puts on a fabulous array of special events for children at **Harbourfront.** In February, there's **ALOUD: A Celebration for Young Readers.** Come April, **Spring Fever** welcomes the season with egg decorating, puppet shows, and more; on Saturday mornings in April, the 5-to-12 set enjoys **cushion concerts.** For information, call ℭ **416/973-4000** or visit **www.harbourfrontcentre.com.**

For more than 30 years, the **Lorraine Kimsa Theatre for Young People,** 165 Front St. E. at Sherbourne Street (ℭ **416/862-2222** for box office, or 416/363-5131 for administration), has been entertaining youngsters. Its season runs from August to May.

The eleventh annual **Sprockets Toronto International Film Festival for Children** screens more than 100 entries from 29 countries in April 2009. Like the Toronto International Film Festival in September, the screenings take place around the city. Call ℭ **416/968-FILM** for details, or visit **http://sprockets.ca.**

Help! We've Got Kids is an all-in-one print and online directory for attractions, events, shops, and services appropriate for kids under 13 in the greater Toronto area. It doesn't provide a lot of detail about most of the entries, but the listings make a great starting point. Visit **www.helpwevegotkids.com.**

Look for the "Kids" icon in the sections above for the following Toronto-area attractions that have major appeal for kids of all ages. The best venues (at least from a kid's point of view) are these:

- **African Lion Safari** (p. 252): Jungle cats. Ring-tailed lemurs. Baby elephants. What kid could ask for anything more?
- **Harbourfront** (p. 125): Kaleidoscope is an ongoing program of creative crafts, active games, and special events on weekends and holidays. There are also a pond, winter ice skating, and a crafts studio.
- **Ontario Place** (p. 130): The Children's Village, water slides, huge Cinesphere, futur-istic pod, and other entertainment are the big hits at this recreational and cultural park. In the Children's Village, kids under 13 can scramble over rope bridges, bounce on an enormous trampoline, or drench one another in the water-play section.
- **Ontario Science Centre** (p. 134): Kids race to be the first at this paradise of hands-on games, experiments, and push-button demonstrations—800 of them.
- **Paramount Canada's Wonderland** (p. 136): The kids can't wait to get on the theme park's roller coasters and daredevil rides. And don't forget to budget for video games.
- **Toronto Zoo** (p. 138): One of the best in the world, modeled after San Diego's—the animals in this 284-hectare (701-acre) park really do live in a natural environment.

For more specialized interests:

- **Allan Gardens Children's Conservatory** (p. 151): For hands-on learning experiences about plants and ecology.
- **Black Creek Pioneer Village** (p. 138): For craft and other demonstrations.
- **Casa Loma** (p. 143): The stables, secret passageway, and fantasy rooms capture chil-dren's imaginations.
- **CN Tower** (p. 132): Especially the simulator games and the glass floor.
- **Fort York** (p. 148): For its reenactments of battle drills, musket and cannon firing, and musical marches with fife and drum.
- **High Park** (p. 152): Wide-open spaces, plus the chance to hang out with llamas.
- **Hockey Hall of Fame** (p. 149): Who wouldn't want the chance to tend goal against Mark Messier and Wayne Gretzky (with a sponge puck), and to practice with the fun and challenging video pucks?
- **Royal Ontario Museum** (p. 134): The top hits are the Ancient Egypt Gallery, the Hands-On Biodiversity Gallery, and the Maiasaur Project.
- **Toronto Islands–Centreville** (p. 130): Riding a ferry to this turn-of-the-20th-century amusement park is part of the fun.

(Finds) A Storybook Sanctuary

The **Osborne Collection of Early Children's Books** is a treasure trove for biblio-philes of all ages. Located at the Lillian H. Smith Branch of the Toronto Public Library (239 College St.; (C) **416/393-7753**), the collection includes a 14th-century manuscript of Aesop's fables, Victorian and Edwardian adventure and fantasy tales, 16th-century schoolbooks, storybooks once owned by British royalty, an array of "penny dreadfuls" (cheap thrillers from the days when a paperback book cost a penny), and Florence Nightingale's childhood library. Special exhibits at the Osborne often feature whimsical subjects. You can visit the library weekdays between 10am and 6pm or Saturdays from 9am to 5pm.

Riverdale Farm ★★ Situated on the edge of the Don Valley Ravine, this working farm located on 3 hectares (7½ acres) right in the city is a favorite with small tots. They enjoy watching the cows, pigs, turkeys, and ducks—and can get close enough to pet many animals, such as the rabbits. Because this really is a farm, you'll see all of the chores of daily life, such as horse grooming, cow and goat milking, egg collecting, and animal feeding. Adults should note that the farm shop has great produce and baked goods, and that there's a farmers' market on-site Tuesdays from May to October.

201 Winchester St. (at Sumach St.). (②) **416/392-6794.** Free admission. Daily 9am–5pm. Subway: Castle Frank, then bus no. 65 south on Parliament St. to Wellesley, and walk 3 blocks east to Sumach.

10 ORGANIZED TOURS

For summer weekends, it's always a good idea to make tour reservations in advance. At slower times, you can usually call the same day or simply show up.

BUS TOURS

If you enjoy bus tours, try the **Hop-On Hop-Off City Tour** offered by **Gray Line,** 184 Front St. E. (② 416/594-3310; www.grayline.ca). It goes to such major sights as the Eaton Centre, city hall, Casa Loma, Yorkville, Chinatown, Harbourfront, the Rogers Centre, and the CN Tower, and a ticket allows you to get on and off the bus over a 2-day period. These narrated tours, which operate daily starting at 10am, cost C$35 (£18) for adults, C$31 (£16) for seniors, and C$18 (£9) for children 4 to 11; free for children 3 and under.

11 OUTDOOR ACTIVITIES

Toronto residents love the great outdoors, whatever the time of year. In summer, you'll see people cycling, boating, and hiking; in winter, they are skating, skiing, and snowboarding.

For additional information on facilities in the parks, golf courses, tennis courts, swimming pools, beaches, and picnic areas, call **Toronto Parks and Recreation** (② **416/392-8186;** www.toronto.ca/parks). Also see "Parks, Gardens & Cemeteries," earlier in this chapter.

BEACHES

The Beaches is the neighborhood along Queen Street East from Coxwell Avenue to Victoria Park. It has a charming boardwalk that connects the beaches, starting at **Ashbridge's Bay Park,** which has a sizable marina. **Woodbine Beach** connects to **Kew Gardens Park** and is a favorite with sunbathers and volleyball players. Woodbine also

---

Ⓣⓘⓟⓢ **Don't Drink the Water!**

Situated on Lake Ontario, Toronto boasts several beaches where you can lap up the sun. Just don't lap up the polluted H_2O, even though you'll see many Torontonians doing just that as they swim through the murky waters. Lake Ontario has high counts of *Escherichia coli,* a very nasty bacteria that can cause ear, nose, and throat infections; skin rashes; and diarrhea—not exactly the kind of souvenir you were looking for. Families will probably want to keep kids out of the water altogether.

boasts the **Donald D. Summerville Olympic Pool.** Snack bars and trinket sellers line the length of the boardwalk.

Personally, I prefer the beaches on the **Toronto Islands.** The ones on **Centre Island,** always the busiest, are favorites with families because of such nearby attractions as **Centreville.** The beaches on **Wards Island** are much more secluded. They're connected by the loveliest boardwalk in the city, with masses of fragrant flowers and raspberry bushes along its edges. **Hanlan's Point,** also in the Islands, is Toronto's only nude beach (I have to confess, I haven't worked up the nerve to sunbathe there . . .).

CANOEING & KAYAKING

The **Harbourfront Canoe and Kayak School,** 283A Queens Quay W. (© **800/960-8886** or 416/203-2277; www.paddletoronto.com), rents canoes and kayaks; call ahead if you are interested in taking private instruction.

You can also rent canoes, rowboats, and pedal boats on the **Toronto Islands** just south of Centreville.

CROSS-COUNTRY SKIING

Just about every park in Toronto becomes potential cross-country skiing territory as soon as snow falls. Best bets are Sunnybrook Park and Ross Lord Park, both in North York. For more information, call **Toronto Parks and Recreation** (© **416/392-8186;** www.toronto.ca/parks). Serious skiers interested in day trips to excellent out-of-town sites like Horseshoe Valley can call **Trakkers Cross Country Ski Club** (© **416/763-0173;** www.trakkers.ca), which also rents equipment.

CYCLING

With biking trails through most of the city's parks and more than 29km (18 miles) of street bike routes, it's not surprising that Toronto has been called one of the best cycling cities in North America. Favorite pathways include the **Martin Goodman Trail** (from The Beaches to the Humber River along the waterfront); the **Lower Don Valley** bike trail (from the east end of the city north to Riverdale Park); **High Park** (with winding trails over 160 hectares/395 acres); and the **Toronto Islands,** where bikers ride without fear of cars. For advice, call the **Ontario Cycling Association** (© **416/426-7416**) or **Toronto Parks and Recreation** (© **416/392-8186;** www.toronto.ca/parks).

Bike lanes are marked on College/Carlton streets, the Bloor Street Viaduct leading to the Danforth, Beverly/St. George streets, and Davenport Road. The Convention and Visitors Association can supply more detailed information.

For a list of bike rental shops, contact the **Toronto Bicycling Network** (© **416/766-1985;** www.tbn.ca). One sure bet is **Wheel Excitement,** 249 Queens Quay W., Unit 110 (© **416/260-9000;** www.wheelexcitement.ca). If you're interested in cycling with a

---

ⓕinds **Walk/Jog/Cycle in Peace**

One of the best places to walk, jog, or cycle in the city is **Mount Pleasant Cemetery** (p. 153). No, I'm not joking! The wide paths of the cemetery are like roads, with lots of space for everyone, from athletic types to parents pushing strollers. Locals love this parklike space, which abounds with trees and statuary, not just tombstones. It's a lively scene and anything but depressing.

group or want information about daily excursions and weekend trips, call the Toronto
Bicycling Network.

FITNESS CENTERS

The **Metro Central YMCA,** 20 Grosvenor St. (© **416/975-9622;** www.ymcatoronto.
org), has excellent facilities, including a 25m (82-ft.) swimming pool, all kinds of cardio-
vascular machines, Nautilus equipment, an indoor track, squash and racquetball courts,
and aerobics classes. The **University of Toronto Athletic Centre,** 55 Harbord St., at
Spadina Avenue (© **416/978-3436;** www.ac-fpeh.com), offers similar facilities.

For yoga aficionados, there's no better place to stretch than **Yoga Plus,** 40 Eglinton
Ave. E., 8th Floor (© **416/322-9936;** www.yogastudio.net). A single class costs C$20
(£10); there's also a pay-what-you-can "Karma" class available. For a listing of all of
Toronto's yoga studios, visit **www.yogatoronto.ca**, which covers the city and the Greater
Toronto Area.

GOLF

Toronto is obsessed with golf, as evidenced by its more than 75 public courses within an
hour's drive of downtown. Here's information on some of the best.

- **Don Valley,** 4200 Yonge St., south of Highway 401 (© **416/392-2465**). Designed by
  Howard Watson, this is a scenic par-71 course with some challenging elevated tees.
  The par-3 13th hole is nicknamed the Hallelujah Corner (it takes a miracle to make
  par). It's considered a good place to start your kids.
- **Humber Valley,** 40 Beattie Ave. at Albion Road (© **416/392-2488**). The relatively
  flat par-70 course is easy to walk, with lots of shade from towering trees. The three
  final holes require major concentration (the 16th and 17th are par 5s).
- The **Glen Abbey Golf Club,** 1333 Dorval Dr., Oakville (© **905/844-1800;** www.
  glenabbey.com). The championship course is one of the most famous in Canada.
  Designed by Jack Nicklaus, the par-73 layout traditionally plays host to the Canadian
  Open.

Travelers who are really into golf might want to consider a side trip to **Muskoka** (see
chapter 11). This area, just 90 minutes north, has some of the best golfing in the country
at courses such as **Taboo** and the **Deerhurst Highlands.**

ICE SKATING & IN-LINE SKATING

Nathan Phillips Square in front of city hall becomes a free ice rink in winter, as does an
area at Harbourfront Centre. Rentals are available on-site. More than 25 parks contain
artificial rinks (also free), including Grenadier Pond in High Park—a romantic spot, with
a bonfire and vendors selling roasted chestnuts. They're open from November to March.

In summer, in-line skaters pack Toronto's streets (and sidewalks). Go with the flow and
rent some blades from **Wheel Excitement** (see "Cycling," above).

JOGGING

Downtown routes might include **Harbourfront** and along the lakefront, or through
Queen's Park and the University. The **Martin Goodman Trail** runs 20km (12 miles)
along the waterfront from The Beaches in the east to the Humber River in the west. It's
ideal for jogging, walking, or cycling. It links to the **Tommy Thompson Trail,** which
travels the parks from the lakefront along the Humber River. Near the Ontario Science
Centre in the Central Don Valley, **Ernest Thompson Seton Park** is also good for jogging. Parking is available at the Thorncliffe Drive and Wilket Creek entrances.

(Moments) **Spas & the City**

Maybe you have a kink in your neck you just can't work out. Maybe you've got a nasty case of jet lag that won't quit. Or perhaps you're just in the mood for some pampering. In Toronto, you won't have to look too far: This city is spa heaven, as far as I'm concerned. The standards are top-notch, the treatments range from the tried and true to the innovative, and the prices tend to be quite reasonable. All of the spas listed here cater to both women and men.

HealthWinds   This is as serene a setting as you'll find anywhere in the city. Standards are extremely high—owner Kailee Kline is a past president of the Spas Ontario association and is its current director of education. Some of the best treatments at HealthWinds take place in the bath—or, more specifically, a hydrotherapy bath with 120 water and air jets, all the better to soothe your aches and pains. While I'm a spa junkie, I've encountered some brilliant techniques at HealthWinds that I haven't encountered elsewhere, such as using hot paraffin on the back to soften up muscles before a massage. 650 Mount Pleasant Rd. (entrance is on Manor Rd.). © **416/488-9545.** www.healthwinds spas.com. Subway: Eglinton, then bus 34 east to Mt. Pleasant, and walk 3 blocks south to Manor Rd.

Holt Renfrew Spa   Located in one of Toronto's most luxurious stores is, appropriately enough, one of the city's most luxurious spas. Decorated in modern-chic blond wood and glass (and with a seemingly endless number of private treatment rooms), the spa provides a full range of services, from manicures to massage. One of the most interesting treatments is the Jet Lag Facial, which rehydrates the skin; during the facial, "lymphatic leg therapy" reduces puffiness and swelling (the new Uplifting Facial has similar results). My personal favorite is the 90-minute Hot Lava Rock Body Massage, which will leave you soothed and happy after a 90-minute deep-tissue massage. Just say aaaaaahhh . . . that *really* hit the spot. Holt Renfrew, 50 Bloor St. W. © **416/ 960-2909.** www.holtrenfrew.com. Subway: Yonge/Bloor.

These areas are generally quite safe, but you should take the same precautions you would in any large city.

ROCK CLIMBING

Toronto has several climbing gyms, including **Joe Rockhead's,** 29 Fraser Ave. (© **416/ 538-7670;** www.joerockheads.com), and the **Toronto Climbing Academy,** 100 Broadview Ave. (© **416/406-5900;** www.climbingacademy.com). You can pick up the finer points of knot tying and belaying. Both gyms also rent equipment.

SNOWBOARDING & SKIING

The snowboard craze shows no sign of abating, at least from January to March (or anytime there's enough snow on the ground). One popular site is the **Earl Bales Park,** 4169 Bathurst Street (just south of Sheppard Ave.), which offers rentals. The park also has an

Stillwater Spa   Water is the theme here, and it undulates in streams under transparent floor panels and courses down walls in miniwaterfalls. Before you even get to the treatment rooms, you'll be dazzled by the changing areas, which include the expected whirlpool and sauna, but also have private cabana-like nooks where you can recline while watching TV with a headset (come in for a spa treatment, and you can spend all day here—seriously). Venture into the main lounge area, and you'll find an aquarium, a fireplace, and a generous supply of biscotti. Many of the treatments are hydrocentric, too, like the delicious-smelling Mandarin Honey Body Glow, which uses a Vichy shower (you lie on the table while warm water cascades over you). My favorite spot is the romantic Couples Sanctuary, which has a whirlpool tub, a fireplace, and two massage tables. Park Hyatt Toronto, 4 Avenue Rd. ℂ **416/924-5471.** www.stillwaterspa.com. Subway: Bay or Museum.

Victoria Spa   I'm a longtime massage fan, and one of the best I've ever had was at the Victoria Spa, which is located on the third floor of the InterContinental Hotel. Decorated in an elaborate style that veers from the classical to the baroque, this spa is wrapped around an indoor pool and lounge. The woman behind the spa is Victoria Sutherland, and you'll find her daily at her pride and joy. The Victoria Spa is famous for its luxurious pedicures, which involve a hot-milk or herbal foot bath, salt scrub, and massage—but in my opinion, all of the treatments, from facials to body therapies, meet the same standard of excellence. The Rose Massage is a sensual treat: Smell the fragrance of roses in the air, lie down on a (massage) bed of velvety rose petals, and get massaged with rose-infused oil. By the time you stroll out it's impossible to look at the world without rose-colored glasses. InterContinental Hotel, 225 Front St. W. ℂ **416/413-9100.** www.victoriaspa.com. Subway: St. Andrew or Union.

alpine ski center, which offers both equipment rentals and coaching. Call (ℂ **416/395-7931**) for more information.

SWIMMING

The municipal parks, including High and Rosedale parks, offer a dozen or so outdoor pools (open June–Sept). Several community recreation centers have indoor pools. For **pool information,** call ℂ **416/338-7665.**

Visitors may buy a day pass to use the pools at the **YMCA,** 20 Grosvenor St. (ℂ **416/975-9622**), and the **University of Toronto Athletic Centre,** 55 Harbord St. at Spadina Avenue (ℂ **416/978-4680**).

TENNIS

There are 200 municipal parks across Toronto with tennis facilities. The most convenient are the courts in High, Rosedale, and Jonathan Ashridge parks. They are open from April

Tips **Skate till You Drop?**

Let's say you'd like to go skating while your traveling companion wants to hit the shops. If you head to **Hazelton Lanes,** you can both get what you want. A central courtyard doubles as a skating rink. Better yet, the shopping center's **Customer Service Centre** (☎ **416/968-8600**) offers complimentary skate rentals. It's hard to beat a deal like that.

to October only. Call **Toronto Parks** (☎ **416/392-1111**) for information. The Toronto Parks website also has a brochure you can download; visit www.toronto.ca/parks.

12 SPECTATOR SPORTS

AUTO RACING   The Grand Prix of Toronto (formerly the Molson Indy; ☎ 416/588-7223; www.grandprixtoronto.com) was cancelled in 2008, much to the shock of fans. The event is supposed to run in July 2009 at the Exhibition Place Street circuit, but check the website for updates.

BASEBALL   **Rogers Centre,** 1 Blue Jays Way, on Front Street beside the CN Tower, is the home of the **Toronto Blue Jays.** For tickets, contact the Toronto Blue Jays, ☎ 888/OK-GO-JAY or 416/341-1234 or http://toronto.bluejays.mlb.com.

BASKETBALL   Toronto's basketball team, the **Raptors,** has its home ground in the **Air Canada Centre,** 40 Bay St. at Lakeshore Boulevard. The NBA schedule runs from October to April. The arena seats 19,500 for basketball. For information, contact the **Raptors Basketball Club,** 40 Bay St. (☎ **416/815-5600;** www.nba.com/raptors). For tickets, call **Ticketmaster** (☎ **416/870-8000**).

FOOTBALL   Remember Kramer on *Seinfeld?* He would watch only Canadian football. Here's your chance to catch a game. **Rogers Centre,** 1 Blue Jays Way, is home to the **Argonauts** of the Canadian Football League. They play between June and November. For information, contact the club at ☎ **416/341-2700** or visit www.argonauts.on.ca. For tickets call **Ticketmaster** (☎ **416/870-8000**).

GOLF TOURNAMENTS   Canada's national golf tournament, the **Bell Canadian Open,** usually takes place at the **Glen Abbey Golf Club** in Oakville, about 40 minutes from the city (☎ **905/844-1800**). Most years, it runs over the Labour Day weekend.

HOCKEY   Hockey isn't Canada's national sport, believe it or not (that's lacrosse), but it's arguably the most popular. The **Air Canada Centre,** 40 Bay St., at Lakeshore Boulevard, is the home of the **Toronto Maple Leafs** (http://mapleleafs.nhl.com). Though the arena seats 18,700 for hockey, tickets are not easy to come by, because many are sold by subscription. The rest are available through **Ticketmaster** (☎ **416/870-8000**).

HORSE RACING   Thoroughbred racing takes place at **Woodbine Racetrack,** Rexdale Boulevard and Highway 427, Etobicoke (☎ **416/675-6110** or 416/675-7223). It's famous for the Queen's Plate (usually contested on the third Sun in June); the Canadian International, a classic turf race (Sept or Oct); and the North America Cup (mid-June). Woodbine also hosts harness racing in spring and fall.

ⓕun Facts **Stephen Colbert vs. the Raptors**

Toronto's basketball team has been on Stephen Colbert's bad side since the very first episode of Comedy Central's *The Colbert Report* on October 17, 2005. At that time, Colbert put the Raptors "On Notice" for losing a game to Maccabi Tel Aviv, the Euroleague champions. Things got worse in early 2007: Because the Raptors' mascot came in ahead of the Saninaw Spirits' Steagle Colbeagle the Eagle in an online poll, Colbert demoted the Raptors to his "Dead to Me" board. Oh, the indignity of being on the same list as bowtie pasta, screw-cap wines, and men with beards!

SOCCER   When I was growing up in Toronto, the soccer team was the Toronto Blizzard (and I have to confess that I didn't notice when the team ceased to exist). Toronto's new soccer club, the **Toronto FC** (http://toronto.fc.mlsnet.com), is getting a lot more attention. It's the first non-U.S. team in Major League Soccer. They play at BMO Field at Exhibition Place; it was built for the FC and it holds 20,195 spectators. For tickets, call **Ticketmaster** (✆ **416/870-8000**).

TENNIS TOURNAMENTS   Canada's international tennis championship, the **Rogers Cup,** takes place in Toronto *and* Montreal every August (the men's and women's championships alternate cities each year). In 2009, the men play in Montréal and the women in Toronto. Expect major names—like Ivanovic, Sharapova, and Williams—to show up. For more information, call ✆ **877/283-6647** or check www.tenniscanada.com.

8

City Strolls

Toronto is one of the best walking cities in the world. I know I'm boasting, but look at the evidence: the patchwork of dynamic ethnic neighborhoods, the impressive architecture, and the many parks. Because the city is such a sprawling place, however, you'll need to pick your route carefully.

The walking tours in this chapter aren't designed to give you an overview. They offer a look at the most colorful and exciting neighborhoods in the city, as well as areas that are packed with sights on almost every corner.

WALKING TOUR 1	CHINATOWN & KENSINGTON MARKET

START:	St. Patrick subway station.
FINISH:	Queen's Park subway station.
TIME:	At least 2 hours. Depending on how long you want to linger at the Art Gallery of Ontario and at various stops, perhaps as long as 8 hours.
BEST TIMES:	Tuesday through Saturday during the day.
WORST TIMES:	Monday, when the Art Gallery is closed.

This walk takes you through the oldest of Toronto's Chinatowns (the city's original Chinatown was on York Street between King and Queen sts., but skyscrapers replaced it long ago). Although at least four Chinatowns exist today, and most Chinese live in the suburbs, the intersection of Dundas Street and Spadina (pronounced spa-*dye*-na) Avenue is still a major shopping and dining area for the Asian community. As a new wave of immigrants has arrived from Southeast Asian countries—Thailand and Vietnam in particular—this old but vibrant Chinatown has taken them in. Today, many businesses here are Vietnamese or Thai.

Successive waves of immigration have also changed the face of the nearby Kensington Market. From the turn of the 20th century until the 1950s, it was the heart of the Jewish community. In the 1950s, Portuguese immigrants arrived to work in the food-processing and meatpacking industries and made it their home. In the '60s, a Caribbean presence arrived. Today, this market retains traces of all these communities.

From the St. Patrick subway station, exit on the northwest corner of Dundas Street and University Avenue, and walk west on Dundas Street. Turn right onto McCaul Street. At no. 131, you'll see:

① St. Patrick's Church
Built in 1861 for Toronto's Irish Catholic community (you could have guessed that from the name, couldn't you?), this church became the base of German-speaking Catholics from 1929 to the late 1960s. Inside, you'll find some of the most beautiful

stained glass in Toronto. The church is also a popular site for concerts.

Go back toward Dundas Street and walk west; looking south on McCaul Street, you'll see:

② Sharp Centre for Design
This building that looks as though it were inspired by a cartoon (it looks like a checkerboard box on stilts) is part of the Ontario College of Art & Design. The Sharp Centre won a Worldwide Award from the

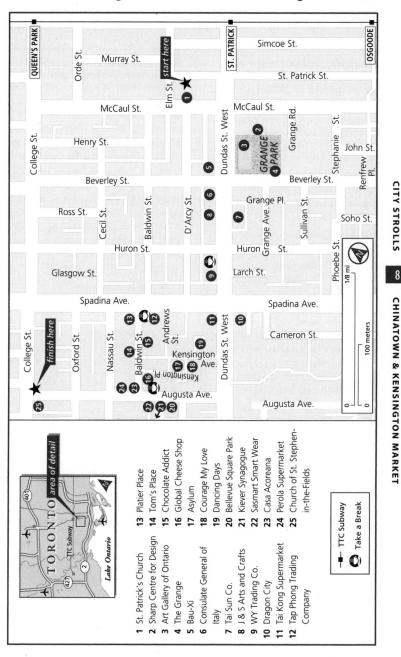

1 St. Patrick's Church
2 Sharp Centre for Design
3 Art Gallery of Ontario
4 The Grange
5 Bau-Xi
6 Consulate General of Italy
7 Tai Sun Co.
8 J & S Arts and Crafts
9 WY Trading Co.
10 Dragon City
11 Tai Kong Supermarket
12 Tap Phong Trading Company
13 Platier Place
14 Tom's Place
15 Chocolate Addict
16 Global Cheese Shop
17 Asylum
18 Courage My Love
19 Dancing Days
20 Bellevue Square Park
21 Kiever Synagogue
22 Sasmart Smart Wear
23 Casa Acoreana
24 Perola Supermarket
25 Church of St. Stephen-in-the-Fields

TTC Subway
Take a Break

Royal Institute of British Architects in 2004; they described it as "courageous, bold, and just a little insane." Admire the insanity from the outside; visitors are not allowed beyond the (unexciting) lobby.

Continue west along Dundas Street. On your left is the:

❸ Art Gallery of Ontario

At press time, architect Frank Gehry's design for a renovated AGO is still a work in progress, and the building is closed. However, the AGO is slated to reopen in November 2008. From prior visits, I can promise that the Canadian and international collections are excellent, and the renovation will increase the number of works on view.

Walk behind the AGO, following Beverley Street south. Behind the AGO, you'll find:

❹ The Grange

Closed for the past 3 years during the AGO's renovation, this historic mansion was the original home of the gallery. Built in 1817, the Georgian mansion is still part of the AGO. The surrounding Grange Park is still a charming spot, in spite of nearby development—Village by the Grange, an apartment and shopping complex is also tucked back here.

Retrace your steps to Dundas Street West and cross so that you're on the north side of the street. On this block, you'll find:

❺ Bau-Xi

This gallery, at 340 Dundas St. W., represents contemporary Canadian artists. It's been in business since 1965 and offers an interesting perspective on the current art scene.

Walk west along Dundas; at the northwest corner of Beverley and Dundas is the:

❻ Consulate General of Italy

It doesn't look like a government building: The rambling late-19th-century mansion, with its sandy brick, quasi-Gothic windows and wrought-iron decoration, is a beauty. Too bad you can't go in.

You're now walking into the heart of Chinatown, with its grocery stores; bakeries; bookstalls; and emporiums selling foods, handcrafts, and other items from Asia.

What follows are some of my favorite stops along the stretch of Dundas Street between Beverley Street and Spadina Avenue. On the south or left side as you go west is:

❼ Tai Sun Co.

At nos. 407–09, the supermarket carries dozens of different mushrooms, all clearly labeled in English, as well as fresh Chinese vegetables, meats, fish, and canned goods. **Melewa Bakery,** no. 433, has a wide selection of pastries, like mung-bean and lotus-paste buns. Outside **Kiu Shun Trading,** no. 441, dried fish are on display; inside, you'll find numerous varieties of ginseng and such miracle remedies as "Stop-Smoking Tea."

On the north side of the street is:

❽ J & S Arts and Crafts

This shop, at no. 430, is a good place to pick up souvenirs, including kimonos and happy coats, kung-fu suits, address books, cushion covers, and all-cotton Chinatown T-shirts. **Kim Moon,** no. 438, is an Asian bakery that features almond cookies, deep-fried taro pastries, and dim sum pork buns.

TAKE A BREAK
Ten Ren Tea, at no. 454 (☏ **416-598-7872**), sells all kinds of tea—black, oolong, green—stored in large canisters at the back of the store. Charming ceramic teapots and cups are on sale here, along with gnarled root ginseng. You can break here for tea—but even if you don't want to sit down, the staff will probably urge you to sample an unfamiliar variety in a tiny cup. Don't worry—it will taste surprisingly good.

At the northwest corner of Huron and Dundas streets is:

❾ WY Trading Co.

At no. 456, **WY Trading Co., Inc.,** has a great selection of records, CDs, and tapes—everything from Chinese folk songs and cantatas to current hit albums from Hong Kong and Taiwan. Even if you don't go in, you'll hear music blaring from inside. At no. 482A, **Po Chi Tong** is a fun store that sells exotic remedies, like deertail extract and liquid-gold ginseng or royal jelly. The best remedy of all time is the "slimming tea." Watch the staff weigh each item out and total the bill with a fast-clicking abacus.

At Spadina Avenue, cross over to the southwest corner to:

❿ Dragon City

The three-level Asian shopping complex at 280 Spadina Ave. is complete with a food court. Here, you'll find books, music, clothing, toys, and homeopathic remedies under one roof.

Spadina Avenue is the widest street in the city because the wealthy Baldwin family had a 40m (131-ft.) swath cut through the forest from Queen Street to Bloor Street so that they could view the lake from their new home on top of Spadina Hill. Later, in the early 20th century, Spadina Avenue became Toronto's garment center and the focal point of the city's Jewish community. Although it's still the garment center, with wholesale and discount fashion houses as well as the fur district (farther south around Adelaide), today it's more Asian than Jewish.

If you enjoy strolling through supermarkets filled with exotic Asian delights, including seasonable fruits such as durian, visit the:

⓫ Tai Kong Supermarket

Look at all the different provisions—chile and fish sauces, fresh meat and fish (including live tilapia in tanks), preserved plums, chrysanthemum tea and other infusions, moon cakes, and large sacks of rice.

> ☕ **TAKE A BREAK**
> For fine, reasonably priced food, a Chinatown favorite is **Happy Seven,** 358 Spadina Ave. (✆ **416/971-9820;** p. 108). If you don't mind lining up, head for the ever-popular **Lee Garden,** 331 Spadina Ave. (✆ **416/593-9524;** p. 105). Continuing north, cross St. Andrews Street.

⓬ Tap Phong Trading Company

This shop, at 360 Spadina Ave., stocks terrific wicker baskets of all shapes and sizes, as well as woks and ceramic cookware, attractive mortars and pestles, and other household items.

Cross Baldwin Street and you'll come to:

⓭ Plaiter Place

At 384 Spadina Ave., Plaiter Place has a huge selection of finely crafted wicker baskets, birdcages, woven blinds, bamboo steamers, hats, and other fun items. **Fortune Housewares,** no. 388, carries kitchen and household items—including brand names—for prices at least 20% lower than elsewhere in the city.

Now double back to Baldwin Street. You're heading into the heart of the **Kensington Market** area, which has always reflected the city's waves of immigration. Once it was primarily a Jewish market; later, it became a Portuguese neighborhood. Today, it is largely Asian and Caribbean, but you can still see many Jewish and Portuguese elements.

Head back to Baldwin Street and walk west, you'll find:

⓮ Tom's Place

This traditional haberdasher—located at 190 Baldwin Street—is a place where you can still haggle for a deal on Italian-made men's shirts. The store also sells women's clothing, but I've had better luck shopping for my husband than for myself here.

Across the street is:

⑮ Chocolate Addict

Located at 185 Baldwin, this tiny temple to chocolate has some truly original offerings (mmm, wasabi truffle…).

At the southwest corner of Baldwin Street and Kensington Avenue is:

⑯ Global Cheese Shoppe

My apologies to the lactose-intolerant, but this store, at 76 Kensington Avenue, is one of my favorites in the neighborhood. The staff will let you have a taste of almost all of the 150 cheeses (well, maybe not all at once).

As you stroll south along Kensington Avenue and pass St. Andrews Street, you will find a series of second-hand- and vintage-clothing stores.

⑰ Asylum

At no. 62 Kensington Ave., on the west side of the street, the store has good jeans, leather jackets, and assorted accessories.

⑱ Courage My Love

The best spot for cheap but chic vintage clothing is at no. 14. It stocks retro gowns and wedding dresses, suits, and accessories, as well as new jewelry and beads for do-it-yourself projects. The $5 rack out front (in nice weather) has some unbelievable deals; if you take some of these exquisite but damaged dresses and coats to a tailor, as I have, you can end up with beautiful, original pieces for a song.

⑲ Dancing Days

At no. 17 (on the east side of the street), you'll find party-ready glad rags that will make you look like an extra in *Grease*.

When you reach Dundas Street, turn right and walk 1 block to Augusta Avenue. Turn right on Augusta Avenue. As you walk north, and cross Wales Avenue, you'll find:

⑳ Bellevue Square Park

On maps this park is often referred to as Denison Square. Either way, it's a lovely spot. While you're checking out the statue of Canadian actor Al Waxman, you may smell marijuana being smoked nearby. Kensington Market is home to some head shops, and smoking cannabis in public—while

illegal—is not uncommon in and around the park.

Stroll through the park; at the corner of Bellevue Avenue and Denison Square, you'll find:

㉑ Kiever Synagogue

This building, at 28 Denison Sq., was completed in 1927. Architect Benjamin Swartz designed it with Byzantine style in mind. The most striking features are the twin domes atop the building (sadly, the building isn't open to the public). The Kiever Synagogue was the first specifically Jewish building designated a historic site by the province of Ontario.

Turn back toward Augusta Avenue, and you'll see:

㉒ Sasmart Smart Wear

This discount store has the strangest assortment of goods you'll find anywhere. OshKosh clothing for kids is on display near antique china; a little farther along is kitchen gear (new and used), luggage, and gadgets. It's a weird, cluttered space, but the prices are unbeatable.

Walk north on Augusta to:

㉓ Casa Acoreana

An old-fashioned store at no. 235, it stocks a full range of fresh coffees, as well as great pecans and filberts.

Just up the street is:

㉔ Perola Supermarket

This store at 247 Augusta Ave. displays cassava and strings of peppers—ancho, arbol, pasilla—hung up to dry and sitting in bins, plus more exotic fruits and herbs.

☕ **TAKE A BREAK**
The **Aspetta Caffe,** 207 Augusta Ave. (✆ **416/916-8275**) is a perfect perch if you want to people-watch while sipping coffee and having a light meal of panini or pasta. If you're in the neighborhood at dinnertime and want a heartier meal, try **La Palette,** 256 Augusta Ave. (✆ **416/929-4900;** p. 105) or **Torito,** 276 Augusta Ave. (✆ **647/436-5874;** p. 109).

Continue north along Augusta Avenue to College Street. Turn west on College and you'll find:

㉕ Church of St. Stephen-in-the-Fields

This small but historically significant church has had to fight hard to ward off the condo developers circling Kensington Market. Ironically, the Anglican Diocesan Council wanted to sell its own church, and the local community—many of whom have no religious connection to the church—came together to save it. The building is a lovely example of Gothic Revival architecture, built in 1858, and contains some splendid stained-glass windows.

On College Street, hop on an eastbound streetcar, which will deliver you to the Queen's Park subway station. The southbound train will take you downtown.

WALKING TOUR 2   UNIVERSITY OF TORONTO

START:	Queen's Park subway station.
FINISH:	The Roof bar at the Park Hyatt Toronto.
TIME:	2 to 4 hours.
BEST TIME:	Weekdays during business hours, or Saturdays.
WORST TIMES:	Sundays, when many buildings are closed or reserved for weddings.

The St. George campus of the University of Toronto is in the heart of the city and is both an essential part of Toronto and a community in and of itself. Its population (roughly 50,000 students, professors, workers, and others are on campus Sept–June) could populate a small city—and if this were a city, it would be one filled with historic buildings, innovative architecture, and gorgeous landscaping. Fortunately, U of T is a public institution, so anyone can enjoy its beauty (few buildings are off limits). Since its founding in 1827, U of T—then called King's College—has been at the forefront of many fields. This was the place where insulin was discovered, where the electronic heart pacemaker was invented, where the first single-lung transplant took place, and where the gene responsible for cystic fibrosis was identified. But U of T is also on the cutting edge of design, and it's currently reinvesting its environment with the Open Space Master Plan (see www.utoronto.ca/openspace for details). The campus is so large that you could spend all day exploring it, but this walking tour will lead you to its highlights. See with your own eyes how a historic university is reshaping itself for the next century.

From the Queen's Park subway station, exit on the northwest corner of College Street and University Avenue. Look north, and you'll see:

❶ Queen's Park

The rose-tinted sandstone-and-granite building that dominates the park is the seat of Ontario's provincial government. It's a stately sight, and the lush park that surrounds it is just as attractive. If the legislature is in session, you can go in to watch it in action.

Walk west along the north side of College Street. Look to your right at:

❷ The Leslie Dan Faculty of Pharmacy

Designed by Lord Norman Foster (the architect who created the Great Court at the British Museum, redeveloped Trafalgar Square, and reconstructed the Reichstag), the building is dramatic. Only the atrium is open to the public, but it is well worth a stop to take in the soaring space that holds two pods (one holds a classroom, the other a lounge).

Continue west on College Street. When you come to King's College Road, you'll see:

❸ The Alumni Gates

Part of U of T's open space initiative is to make the university's entry points more distinctive. The Alumni Gates were a gift to the university from the alumni association in 2003, to mark the association's 100th anniversary. Two columns frame the south entryway and its view of the front of the campus, and a tree-lined boulevard leads north from here.

Turn right, and walk through the Alumni Gates and north up the boulevard. As you walk, you'll see a yellow building, which is the:

❹ Sandford Fleming Building

Named for the man who invented the worldwide system of Standard Time, this Edwardian building was built in 1907 and rebuilt in 1977 after a fire. It's currently home to the Faculty of Applied Science and Engineering.

Next, on your left, is:

❺ Convocation Hall

This hall dates from 1907, just like its neighbor. U of T holds its graduation ceremonies here (it takes a couple of weeks each year to do them all). Archbishop Desmond Tutu has spoken here, as has Vaclav Havel.

In front of you is the green lawn of the front campus circle. Walk to the left around it. On your left will be:

❻ Knox College

This 1915 building has been used in countless movies (*Good Will Hunting* was filmed on U of T's campus, for starters). It's not hard to see why—it's the perfect rendering of a neo-Gothic college. Step inside its sandstone walls to take in its intricate details (don't forget to look up at the ceiling of the Reading Room). Also, step into its quad—the hidden courtyard at its center.

Retrace your steps, turning left as you leave Knox College. Follow the front campus circle as it curves to the right and leads you to:

❼ University College

UC, as it's known, was once an independent university, and it has one of the most fascinating histories in Toronto. Its foundation stone was laid in October 1856—secretly, because the plan to create a nondenominational university had met with such fierce opposition. The tremendous structure was built hastily, and most of the college was completed in 1857 (the 36m/120-ft. tower was finished the following year). UC wasn't just a great achievement in terms of construction, but in purpose as well. Its first president wrote that UC would "enable the sons of the poorest man in the land to compete with the most affluent."

F. W. Cumberland used a combination of styles when designing this building. Take a close look at the columns and the windows, and you'll see that no two are alike. An 1890 fire seriously damaged UC, and substantial segments of it had to be rebuilt. Step inside, turn right, and follow the hallway to its end; turn left, and you'll pass the east staircase with its **coiled dragon** on the newel post (be sure to pet him for luck).

Continue along the corridor until you reach the UC quad, where you'll find:

❽ University Art Centre

This small but stunning gallery contains the **Malcove Collection,** which consists primarily of Byzantine art (p. 140). The gallery also has a substantial Canadian collection, and its temporary gallery hosts various shows.

Walk back through the UC quad and into the building. Follow the corridor back to the east staircase, and walk out the east exit. If it's near lunchtime and your stomach is rumbling, this isn't a bad place to:

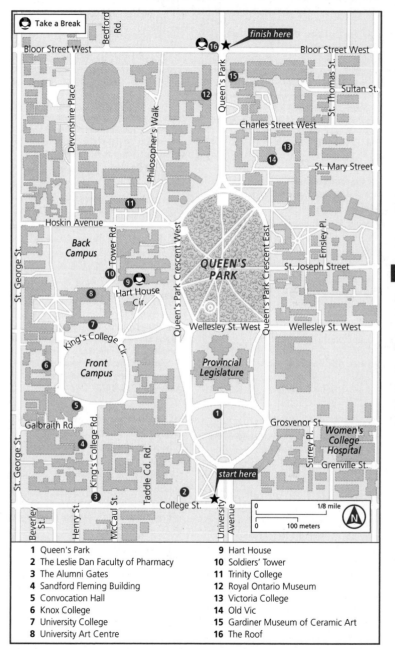

Take a Break

Bloor Street West

Bedford Rd.

finish here

16 ★

Bloor Street West

Queen's Park

15

St. Thomas St.

Sultan St.

Devonshire Place

Philosopher's Walk

12

Charles Street West

13

14

St. Mary Street

11

Hoskin Avenue

St. George St.

Back Campus

Tower Rd.

QUEEN'S PARK

Queen's Park Crescent West

Queen's Park Crescent East

Emsley Pl.

St. Joseph Street

10

9

Hart House Cir.

8

7

King's College Cir.

Front Campus

6

Wellesley St. West

Wellesley St. West

5

Galbraith Rd.

Provincial Legislature

King's College Rd.

Taddle Cd. Rd.

4

1

Grosvenor St.

Women's College Hospital

Surrey Pl.

Grenville St.

3

St. George St.

Beverley St.

Henry St.

McCaul St.

2

College St.

start here ★

University Avenue

0   1/8 mile
0   100 meters

N

1 Queen's Park	**9** Hart House
2 The Leslie Dan Faculty of Pharmacy	**10** Soldiers' Tower
3 The Alumni Gates	**11** Trinity College
4 Sandford Fleming Building	**12** Royal Ontario Museum
5 Convocation Hall	**13** Victoria College
6 Knox College	**14** Old Vic
7 University College	**15** Gardiner Museum of Ceramic Art
8 University Art Centre	**16** The Roof

TAKE A BREAK
Your best bet for a leisurely lunch on campus is right in front of you: Inside Hart House is the **Gallery Grill** (✆ 416/978-2445), a fine restaurant that is open during the school year. Its cooking is innovative, but its gorgeous setting makes it worth a stop just for tea (at last count, there were more than 15 loose-leaf varieties here) or dessert. In summer, you can count on the **Arbor Room**, a casual cafeteria-style restaurant, to be open. It's also in Hart House.

Stepping outside of UC will bring you to Hart House Circle. Walk to the left, and you'll reach the:

9 Hart House

Vincent Massey, grandson of the industrialist Hart Massey, conceived U of T's community center. Vincent was a student at the university at the time, and while it took time for his plans to come to fruition—and 8 years to build—Hart House opened on November 11, 1919. The Gothic Revival building contains reading rooms, a chapel, two dining spots, a billiards room, several club rooms, an interior courtyard, and the **Justina M. Barnicke Gallery** (p. 139). Wander through the building to see the Group of Seven paintings and other works of art.

Exit Hart House on its west side, close to the Justina M. Barnicke Gallery; turn right and walk north. Look back at Hart House to appreciate its:

10 Soldiers' Tower

The tower was added to the west end of Hart House between 1919 and 1924. Its arches are inscribed with the names of U of T alumni who died in both world wars. The tower itself houses a carillon with 51 bells, which are rung to mark special occasions.

Continue walking north till you reach the street. Cross Hoskin Avenue, and you'll be standing in front of:

11 Trinity College

Appearances can be deceiving: The Tudor Gothic Trinity College looks like one of the oldest buildings in the city, but it was built in 1925. It has its own relaxing green quad, as well as an unusually grand **Anglican chapel,** which was designed by Sir Giles Gilbert Scott, who also created Liverpool Cathedral. (If you wish to see the chapel, you'll have to enter through the main entrance of the college; the outside door is locked as a rule.)

If you're facing Trinity College, turn right so that you're walking east along Hoskin. The street curves to the north to join Queen's Park Crescent. Continue walking north. Ahead on your left is the:

12 Royal Ontario Museum

This Toronto treasure has been renovated over the past several years, to the tune of C$200 million. The highlight of the work is the Michael Lee-Chin Crystal, which was designed by Daniel Libeskind and dominates the north side of the museum, which faces onto Bloor Street (you can walk up to Bloor now, or wait to see the crystal till the end of the tour).

Outside the ROM, is a TTC entrance; walk down the stairs, because this is the easiest way to cross Queen's Park (you won't have to pay a fare). Resurface on the other side of Queen's Park. Charles Street is only a few steps north. Turn right on Charles; then turn right again into a laneway that brings you to:

13 Victoria College

Like University College, Victoria College was once a separate university (in some ways, it's still run as if it were; some of U of T's colleges are quite independent). The first thing you will notice is the stunning quad, which some regard as the most beautiful on campus. On your left is the new **Isabel Bader Theatre,** and on your right is **Emmanuel College,** a theological school of the United Church of Canada.

Continue following the laneway to:

14 Old Vic

The red-brick-and-sandstone Victoria College Building—known mainly by its nickname, Old Vic—is a masterpiece of Romanesque Revival architecture. It used to be called New Vic—when it opened in 1892, this was the new home of Victoria

College, which had relocated to Toronto from Cobourg, Ontario. Walk around the entire building to appreciate its intricate architecture. Inside is a bookstore.

Exit Old Vic from its main entrance, which is on its east side. Turn to your left, and you'll find another laneway that leads directly up to Charles Street. Turn left on Charles, and walk west to Queen's Park. Turn right, crossing Charles Street, and continue north on Queen's Park. The ROM is across the street on your left; on your right is the:

⓯ George R. Gardiner Museum of Ceramic Art

Like its neighbor the ROM, the Gardiner has undergone a major renovation. The results are glorious, and the museum's collections of pre-Columbian art, as well as European pieces from the 17th and 18th centuries, are on show again.

Continue walking north; you'll arrive at an intersection with Bloor Street West. If you didn't check out the ROM's crystal earlier, take a look now. Diagonally across from you, on the northwest corner, is the Park Hyatt. Cross to that corner; the entrance to the Park Hyatt is just a few steps north of the intersection.

Turn left to enter the hotel; inside its South Tower, an elevator will take you up to:

⓰ The Roof

This elegant watering hole 18 stories up is one of the best places to get a view of Toronto. If the weather is nice, head out to the balcony, which faces south and provides a spectacular view of the U of T campus.

> **TAKE A BREAK**
> For some light refreshment, stay a while at **The Roof** (p. 220), which mixes some excellent and original cocktails. If you're hungry, there are many restaurants to choose from. **Sotto Sotto,** 116A Avenue Rd. (☏ **416/962-0011;** p. 114), **Boba,** 90 Avenue Rd. (☏ **416/961-2622;** p. 113), and **Jacques Bistro du Parc;** 126A Cumberland St. (☏ **416/961-1893;** p. 115), are all a short walk away. Also nearby, on Bloor Street West, is **Greg's Ice Cream,** 750 Spadina Ave. (☏ **416/962-4734;** p. 123).

WALKING TOUR 3 ST. LAWRENCE & DOWNTOWN EAST

START:	Union Station.
FINISH:	King subway station.
TIME:	2 to 3 hours.
BEST TIME:	Saturday, when the St. Lawrence Market is in full swing.
WORST TIME:	Sunday, when it's closed.

At one time, this area was at the center of city life. Today, it's a little off center, yet it has some historic and modern architectural treasures, and a wealth of history in and around the St. Lawrence Market.

Begin at:
❶ Union Station

Check out the interior of this classical revival beauty, which opened in 1927 as a temple to and for the railroad. The shimmering ceiling, faced with vitrified Guastavino tile, soars 27m (89 ft.) above the 79m-long (260-ft.) hall.

Across the street, at York and Front streets, stands the:

❷ Fairmont Royal York

The venerable railroad hotel is a longtime gathering place for Torontonians. It's the home of the famous Imperial Room cabaret and nightclub, which used to be one of Eartha Kitt's favorite venues. The hotel was once the tallest building in Toronto and the largest hotel in the British Commonwealth. Check out the lobby, with its coffered ceiling and opulent furnishings.

One floor up on the mezzanine is a new **gallery** of black-and-white photographs that cover the hotel's long and illustrious history.

As you leave the hotel, turn left, and walk east on Front Street. At the corner of Bay and Front streets, look up at the stunning:

❸ Royal Bank Plaza

The two triangular gold-sheathed towers rise 41 floors and 26 floors. A 40m-high (131-ft.) atrium joins them, and 150 pounds of gold enhances the mirrored glass. Webb Zerafa Menkes Housden designed the project, which was built between 1973 and 1977.

Cross Bay Street and continue east on Front Street. On the south side of the street is the impressive sweep of **One Front Street,** the main post office building (okay, not an exciting-sounding sight, but an attractive one).

On the north side of the street is:

❹ Brookfield Place

Go inside to view the soaring galleria. Skidmore, Owings, and Merrill, with Bregman & Hamann, designed it in 1993. The twin office towers connect through a huge glass-covered galleria five stories high, spanning the block between Bay and Yonge streets. Designed by artist-architect Santiago Calatrava of Bregman & Hamann, it links the old Midland Bank building to the twin towers.

> **TAKE A BREAK**
> For an unusual dining experience, stop in at **Brookfield Place's Richtree Market** (☏ 416/366-8986; p. 106). Rather than wait for table service, you forage for salads, pastas, and meat dishes at various counters. Or head across the courtyard to **Acqua** (☏ 416/368-7171) for Italian fare. The downstairs food court offers a variety of fast food and casual dining choices. If you prefer a deli sandwich, go to **Shopsy's,** 33 Yonge St. (☏ 416/365-3333; p. 112).

Back out on Front Street, turn left, and continue to the northwest corner of Yonge and Front, stopping to admire the:

❺ Bank of Montreal

The suitably ornate building (1885–86) held the most powerful Canadian bank of the 19th century, a force behind the colonial and federal governments. Inside, the banking hall rises to a beamed coffered ceiling with domed skylights of stained glass. It now houses the Stanley Cup and other hockey trophies, plus the **Hockey Hall of Fame** (p. 149), another example of the city's genius for architectural adaptation. The exterior, embellished with carvings, porthole windows, and a balustrade, is a sight.

From here, you can look ahead along Front Street and see the weird mural by Derek M. Besant that adorns the famous and highly photogenic:

❻ Flatiron or Gooderham Building (1892)

This building was the headquarters of George Gooderham, who expanded his distilling business into railroads, insurance, and philanthropy. At one time, his liquor business was the biggest in the British Empire, and he was also president of the Bank of Toronto. The five-story building occupies a triangular site, with the windows at the western edge beautifully curved and topped with a semicircular tower. The design is by David Roberts.

At the southwest corner of Yonge and Front streets, you can stop in at:

❼ The Sony Centre

The Sony Centre for the Performing Arts sits across Scott Street from the **St. Lawrence Centre.** In 1974, when the Sony was called the O'Keefe Centre, Mikhail Baryshnikov defected from the Soviet Union after performing here.

Continue east along Front Street to the:

❽ Beardmore Building

At 35–39 Front St. E., this and the many other cast-iron buildings lining the street were the heart of the late-19th-century

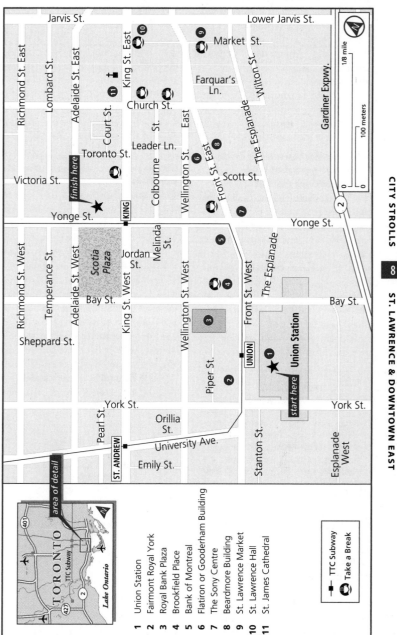

Jarvis St.
Lower Jarvis St.
Richmond St. East
Lombard St.
Adelaide St. East
King St. East
Market St.
Farquar's Ln.
Wilton St.
The Esplanade
Gardiner Expwy.
Court St.
Church St.
King St. East
Leader Ln.
St.
East
Colbourne St.
Wellington St. East
Front St. East
Scott St.
Toronto St.
Victoria St.
finish here
Yonge St.
KING
Yonge St.
Richmond St. West
Temperance St.
Adelaide St. West
Bay St.
King St. West
Scotia Plaza
Jordan St.
Melinda St.
Wellington St. West
The Esplanade
The Esplanade
Bay St.
Sheppard St.
Front St. West
UNION
Union Station
start here
Piper St.
York St.
York St.
Pearl St.
York St.
Orillia St.
University Ave.
ST. ANDREW
Stanton St.
Esplanade West
Emily St.

1/8 mile
100 meters

area of detail

TORONTO
401
427
2
Lake Ontario
TTC Subway

1 Union Station
2 Fairmont Royal York
3 Royal Bank Plaza
4 Brookfield Place
5 Bank of Montreal
6 Flatiron or Gooderham Building
7 The Sony Centre
8 Beardmore Building
9 St. Lawrence Market
10 St. Lawrence Hall
11 St. James Cathedral

TTC Subway
Take a Break

warehouse district, close to the lakefront and railheads. Now they hold stores like **Frida Crafts,** which sells imports from Guatemala, India, and Bangladesh, as well as jewelry, bags, candles, and other knick-knacks; and **Mountain Equipment Co-op,** stocked with durable outdoor-adventure goods. At no. 41–43, note the **Perkins Building,** and at no. 45–49, look for the building with an entirely cast-iron facade. **Nicholas Hoare,** one of the coziest bookstores in the city, is at no. 45.

Continue east along Front Street, crossing Church Street and then Market Street, to the:

❾ St. Lawrence Market

The old market building on the right holds this great market hall, which was constructed around the city's second city hall (1844–45). The elegant pedimented facade that you see as you stand in the center of the hall was originally the center block of the city hall. Today, the market abounds with vendors selling fresh eggs, Mennonite sausage, seafood, meats, cheeses, and baked goods. From Thursday to Saturday, in the north building across the street, a farmers' market starts at 5am.

> ☕ **TAKE A BREAK**
> The most enjoyable places to stop are the stands offering fresh produce in the market itself. Other choices include **Le Papillon,** 16 Church St. ((✆ **416/363-0838;** p. 111), which features a raft of savory dessert crepes, and **HotHouse Cafe,** 35 Church St. ((✆ **416/366-7800;** p. 111).

Exit the market where you came in. Cross Wellington Street, and cut through Market Lane Park and the shops at Market Square, past the north market building. Turn right onto King Street to:

❿ St. Lawrence Hall

This was the focal point of the community in the mid–19th century. This hall was the site of grand city occasions, political rallies, balls, and entertainment. It was here

that Frederick Douglass delivered an anti-slavery lecture; Jenny Lind and Adelina Patti sang in 1851 and 1860, respectively; Gen. Tom Thumb appeared in 1862; and George Brown campaigned for Confederation. William Thomas designed the elegant Palladian-style building, which boasts a domed cupola.

Cross King Street and enter the 19th-century garden. It has a cast-iron drinking fountain for people, horses, and dogs, and flowerbeds filled with seasonal blooms.

If you like, rest on a bench while you admire the handsome proportions of St. Lawrence Hall and listen to the chimes of:

⓫ St. James' Cathedral

Adjacent to the garden on the north side of King Street, this is one of my favorite places in Toronto. The beautiful building and its surrounding park make a serene setting to rest and gather one's thoughts.

From here, you can view one of the early retail buildings, built when King Street was the main commercial street. **Nos. 129–35** was originally an Army and Navy Store; cast iron, plate glass, and arched windows allowed the shopper to see what was available in the store. Also note nos. 111 and 125. The **Toronto Sculpture Garden,** 115 King St. ((✆ **416/485-9658**), is a quiet corner for contemplation.

> ☕ **WINDING DOWN**
> From St. James', the venerable **Le Meridien King Edward,** 37 King St. E. ((✆ **416/863-9700**), is only a block away. You can stop for afternoon tea in the lobby lounge, or light fare or lunch in the **Café Victoria.** Both **La Maquette,** 111 King St. E. ((✆ **416/366-8191**), and **Biagio,** 157 King St. E. ((✆ **416/366-4040**), have appealing courtyards.

From St. James', go south on Church Street for 1 block and turn right into Colbourne Street. From Colbourne, turn left down Leader Lane to Wellington, where you can enjoy a fine view of the mural on the Flatiron Building and of the rhythmic flow of mansard rooflines along the south side of Front Street.

Turn right and proceed to Yonge Street; then turn right and walk to King Street to catch the subway to your next destination.

WALKING TOUR 4   CABBAGETOWN

START:	Allan Gardens.
FINISH:	Sumach and Gerrard (for streetcar to College Station).
TIME:	2 to 3 hours.
BEST TIME:	Tuesdays from May through October, when the Farmers' Market is open in Riverdale Park West.
WORST TIME:	There is no worst time; all of the other attractions on this tour can be seen on weekdays and weekends.

Cabbagetown has experienced more of the vicissitudes of fate than any other neighborhood in Toronto. Built up in the 1840s by Irish immigrants fleeing the Great Famine, the name of the district comes from the cabbage plants they grew in their front yards. It has been both a wealthy enclave and a slum, but today, the residential streets have been gentrified, and the surrounding commercial streets are on an upswing.

Begin at:
❶ Allan Gardens
This was Toronto's first civic park. For many years it ran to the seedy side, but since the University of Toronto took over the care of the greenhouses in 2004, it has become a charming place to visit again. The Children's Conservatory is well worth a look, but the crown jewel of the garden is the Edwardian Palm House.

At the corner of Carlton and Sherbourne, you'll see:
❷ St. Luke's United Church
Known as Sherbourne Street Methodist when the first sermon was preached here in 1887, this is one of Toronto's most beautiful examples of religious architecture. From the outside, the imposing stonework and turrets make it look like a castle. Inside, the sanctuary has been completely refurbished in the past few years. The glorious stained-glass windows are the pièce de résistance (the church once had a wealthy congregation, and you'll see that the windows were all "dedicated" by businessmen trying to outdo one another).

On the north side of Carlton Street is:
❸ St. Peter's Anglican Church
This parish was originally based in a cemetery chapel. In 1866, John Strachan, the Aberdeen-born Bishop of Toronto, opened this church. It's a pretty example of High Victorian Gothic, and later additions are in keeping with its original style.

Walk east along Carlton to:
❹ Daniel et Daniel
This food shop at no. 248 Carlton St. is widely considered one of the best in Toronto. You'll find freshly baked pastries and equally tempting cheeses, pâtés, tarts, cakes, and other treats. My favorite thing is the selection of chocolates (sigh). Resistance is futile.

You're now at the intersection with:
❺ Parliament Street
Parliament Street got its name because the first Upper Canada government buildings in "muddy little York" (as Toronto was then known) were built at its southern end in 1793. Today, it's the main commercial artery of Cabbagetown. This isn't exactly trendy (at press time, Starbucks had yet to set up an outpost on this stretch), but you can make some great finds. At no. 480 is a

branch of **Planet Aid,** the secondhand-clothing store that raises money for projects in the developing world. **Sharon's,** at no. 503, is a small but glamorous boutique with clothing and accessories. **Green's Antiques,** at no. 529, is a true gem, with plenty of great chairs, ottomans, and sofas, many of which have been newly upholstered by the talented staff.

☕ **TAKE A BREAK**
One reliable place to grab a bite is **The Pear Tree,** 507 Parliament St. (📞 **416/962-8190**), which serves hearty salads like the Salmon Caesar or (my pick) the goat cheese and spinach. Another great spot is **Jet Fuel,** 519 Parliament St. (📞 **416/968-9982**), a coffee shop that has become a local landmark (bike couriers love this place). Everything here is made with espresso, so be prepared for a caffeine hit.

Turn right at Winchester Street (at the corner, you'll pass the Laurentian Room—p. 219), and walk east. At the northeast corner of the intersection of Winchester and Metcalfe, you'll see:

⑥ Toronto Dance Theatre

The former St. Enoch's Presbyterian Church was built in 1891 in a Romanesque Revival style. Oddly, the red-brick exterior makes the building (almost) blend in with the rest of the neighborhood (quite a feat, given its size).

Continue east to:

⑦ 94 Winchester Ave.

This was once the home of magician Doug Henning. You can't go inside (it's someone else's home now), but a plaque at the front commemorates his life (1947–2000) and immortalizes him as "magician, teacher, politician." The first two are easy to get, but the last requires some explanation. In 1994, Henning stood for election to Parliament as a member of the Natural Law Party, an organization memorable mainly for its belief in levitation.

Continue walking east on Winchester and turn south onto:

⑧ Sackville Street

This quiet street had some of the loveliest homes in Cabbagetown. While the architecture is an eclectic mix, you'll mostly see variations on Victorian and Queen Anne styles. Walk down to Sackville Place (the street will be only on your left side). Across from it is Pine Terrace, a series of Victorian red-brick town houses built in 1886.

Walk north back to Winchester, and follow it east to Sumach Street, where you'll find:

⑨ Riverdale Park West

This is a lovely park that's a favorite with local families. While you stop to enjoy the scenery, you can learn more about Cabbagetown's history. Look for the large maps and plaques in the park's northwestern corner, and you can learn all about many of the fascinating people who once called the neighborhood theirs. (Hint: Doug Henning fit in very well.) Depending on when you visit, you may find a farmers' market operating in the park, too.

Across from the park, on the north side of Winchester, is the:

⑩ Necropolis

Walk under the Gothic-inspired porte cochere to enter Toronto's city of the dead. This is the prettiest cemetery you could hope to find, and if you stop at the office (on the right side as you step under the archway), you can pick up a free map that will guide you to the final resting places of some of Toronto's famous inhabitants. Check out the imposing stone Celtic cross that marks the grave of William Lyon Mackenzie, the leader of the Upper Canada rebellion who later became the mayor of Toronto (see the entry for **Mackenzie House,** p. 148, for more details).

When you finish here, exit through the porte cochere; on your right is the:

⑪ Necropolis Chapel

This small chapel is a stunning example of High Victorian Gothic style. Architect

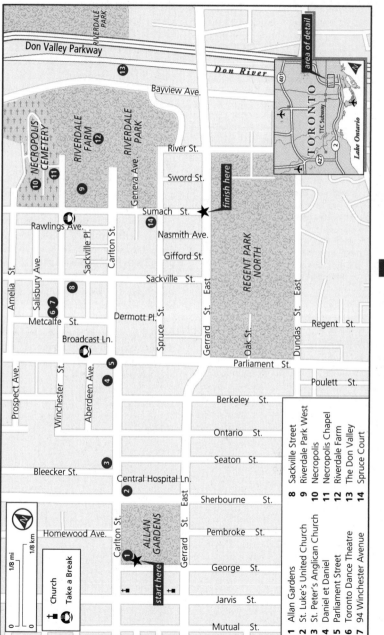

CITY STROLLS

8

CABBAGETOWN

Don Valley Parkway

Don River

area of detail

TORONTO

Lake Ontario

TTC Subway

Bayview Ave.

RIVERDALE PARK

NECROPOLIS CEMETERY

RIVERDALE FARM

Geneva Ave.

River St.

Sword St.

Sumach St.

finish here

Rawlings Ave.

Nasmith Ave.

Gifford St.

Sackville St.

Carlton St.

Sackville Pl.

Salisbury Ave.

Amelia St.

Metcalfe St.

Dermott Pl.

Spruce St.

Gerrard St. East

REGENT PARK NORTH

Dundas St. East

Regent St.

Poulett St.

Broadcast Ln.

Prospect Ave.

Winchester St.

Aberdeen Ave.

Parliament St.

Oak St.

Berkeley St.

Ontario St.

Seaton St.

Bleecker St.

Central Hospital Ln.

Sherbourne St.

Pembroke St.

Homewood Ave.

ALLAN GARDENS

Carlton St.

Gerrard St. East

George St.

Jarvis St.

Mutual St.

start here

1/8 mi
1/8 km

Church

Take a Break

1 Allan Gardens
2 St. Luke's United Church
3 St. Peter's Anglican Church
4 Daniel et Daniel
5 Parliament Street
6 Toronto Dance Theatre
7 94 Winchester Avenue
8 Sackville Street
9 Riverdale Park West
10 Necropolis
11 Necropolis Chapel
12 Riverdale Farm
13 The Don Valley
14 Spruce Court

Henry Langley built it in 1872 (he's the same person who designed the eye-catching towers at St. James' Cathedral, p. 146, and St. Michael's Cathedral, p. 146). The chapel and the adjoining porte cochere are widely considered to be two of the finest pieces of Gothic Revival architecture in Canada. (Langley is buried in the Necropolis, and his grave is on the map mentioned above in stop 10.)

TAKE A BREAK
You won't find many places to grab a snack within the residential heart of Cabbagetown. The exception is **Park Snacks** (no phone), a take-out-only spot at the southwest corner of Winchester and Sumach. In summer, you can buy drinks, ice cream, or sandwiches here. Riverdale Park West provides many benches that are well shaded by trees. Year-round, you can buy snacks at **Riverdale Farm** (see below).

On the eastern edge of the park, you'll see the entrance to:

⓬ Riverdale Farm

I love this working farm in the heart of downtown Toronto. Its setting might seem incongruous, but it's a charming place to visit, particularly if you have children in tow. Even if you don't, you can appreciate the chicks, bunnies, cows, goats, and other animals.

When you leave the farm, turn to the left and follow its perimeter; this will give you a good view of:

⓭ The Don Valley

There's been a big movement to "Bring Back the Don" in Toronto, and the valley has been revitalized by it. The Don River is no longer a mighty force, but at least its valley is green. If you look to the north, you'll see the **Bloor Street Viaduct** (one of the best viewing points in the city; p. 133).

Walk west along Spruce Street to Sumach; on the northwest corner, you'll see:

⓮ Spruce Court

This was the first public-housing project in Canada. This utopian collection of two- and three-story cottages was built in 1913 by the appropriately named architect Eden Smith. All face either onto the street or one of the leafy private courtyards. Many, though not all, of the housing blocks were designed in English Cottage style, which was intended to evoke the bucolic splendor of country life. You can't see the interiors—since 1980, these have been private family homes run by a co-op—but from the street you can appreciate the half-timbered gables, the tall chimneys, and arched brick porches.

Walk south along Spruce Street to Gerrard Street; from here, you can catch any westbound streetcar, which will take you to College Station.

Shopping

Toronto is one of the world's great shopping cities for two reasons. The first is that the usual glamorous suspects—think Prada, Chanel, and Gucci—all have outposts here. The second is that many of the homegrown boutiques and designers have such outstanding offerings that you may actually forget about the international icons.

The Eaton Centre is Toronto's most famous shopping arcade, and while I can't argue with its everything-under-one-roof mentality, I encourage serious shoppers to look farther afield. You didn't come to Toronto just to shop at Banana Republic, after all, so take note of the neighborhoods to score deals on unique clothing, housewares, and antiques (see "Great Shopping Areas," below).

Another reason to shop in Toronto is that the scene suits a wide range of budgets and tastes. There's only one bit of bad news I should share: While window-shopping is a laudable pastime, don't fool yourself that it will stop there . . . just be careful not to break the bank!

1 THE SHOPPING SCENE

While you may want to investigate the impressive array of international retailers, it would be a mistake to ignore the locals. If your passion is fashion, don't overlook Canadian labels such as Mercy, Lida Baday, Ross Mayer, Misura by Joeffer Caoc, Crystal Siemens, Brian Bailey, Mimi Bizjak, Wolves, Linda Lundstrom, and Comrags.

Toronto also has a bustling arts-and-crafts community, with many galleries, custom jewelers, and artisans. Some of the best buys are on native and Inuit art. Artwork can be imported into the United States duty-free.

Stores usually open around 10am from Monday to Saturday. Closing hours change depending on the day. From Monday to Wednesday, most stores close at 6pm; on Thursday and Friday, hours run to 8 or 9pm; on Saturday, closing is quite early, usually around 6pm. Most stores are open on Sunday, though the hours may be restricted—11am or noon to 5pm is not unusual.

Almost every establishment accepts MasterCard and Visa, and a growing number take American Express.

2 GREAT SHOPPING AREAS

DOWNTOWN

CHINATOWN It's crowded and noisy, but don't let that put you off. Sure, there's the usual touristy junk, like cheapo plastic toys and jewelry, but the real Chinatown has a lot more to offer, including fine rosewood furniture, exquisite ceramics, and homeopathic herbs. Just don't try driving here: This is traffic purgatory and best navigated on foot.

THE EATON CENTRE Okay, you're short on time, but you still want to fit in all your shopping. Head to the Eaton Centre. With more than 300 shops—including an Apple

Store, Browns, Danier, Birks, Nine West, La Vie en Rose, Femme de Carriere, Eddie Bauer, Banana Republic, Mendocino, Laura Secord, H&M, and Indigo—you'll be sure to find something.

QUEEN STREET WEST   Queen Street West, between University Avenue and Bathurst Street, is rich with boutiques for both fashion and housewares, though there are a lot of familiar names thrown in the mix. Locals complain that this neighborhood isn't what it was before The Gap moved in, but it's still a great stomping ground for fashionistas in need of a fix.

THE UNDERGROUND CITY   Subterranean Toronto is a hive of shopping activity. While you won't find too many shops down here that don't have an aboveground location, the Underground City is a popular place in winter and with those whose schedules don't allow them out of the Financial District.

WEST QUEEN WEST   Playing down its grittier roots, this hot new neighborhood has got the reputation for cutting-edge fashion that Queen Street West used to enjoy. The city has dubbed it the "Art & Design District." Starting at Bathurst Avenue and running west a few blocks past Ossington Avenue, this is where you'll find an incredible array of fashion talent, art galleries, and great new restaurants.

MIDTOWN

BLOOR STREET WEST   This strip of real estate, bordered by Yonge Street to the east and Avenue Road to the west, is where most of the top international names in fashion set up shop. If you're in the mood to see what Karl Lagerfeld is designing or to pick up a glittering bauble from Cartier or Tiffany, this is your hunting ground.

YORKVILLE   One of Toronto's best known—and most expensive—shopping neighborhoods. It's also the one under the most construction at the moment, as condo developers plonk one shiny building after another on this prime patch of real estate. The shops here tend to be small boutiques that specialize, say, in beaded handbags or fine handmade papers.

---

3 SHOPPING A TO Z

ANTIQUES, FURNITURE & HOUSEWARES
Antiques
Belle Epoque   If you're feeling pretty and looking for furniture to match, this atticlike shop is worth a look. The furnishings are luxurious, and some pieces would not look out of place at Versailles—gilt and all. Keep in mind that there are reproductions mixed in with the antiques. 1066 Yonge St. ☎ **416/925-0066.** Subway: Rosedale.

Decorum Decorative Finds   If you're going on an ocean voyage, can you resist a vintage Louis Vuitton trunk? The wares here range from tables and chaise lounges to oil paintings and old books. Wares are expensive, but also top of the line. 1210 Yonge St. ☎ **416/ 966-6829.** Subway: Summerhill.

Ethel 20th Century Living (Finds)   Technically speaking, an antique is at least a century old, which makes Ethel more of a vintage store. Still, the last century was an age of fascinating design—and if you crave 1930s Art Deco or 1960s lounge lizard chic,

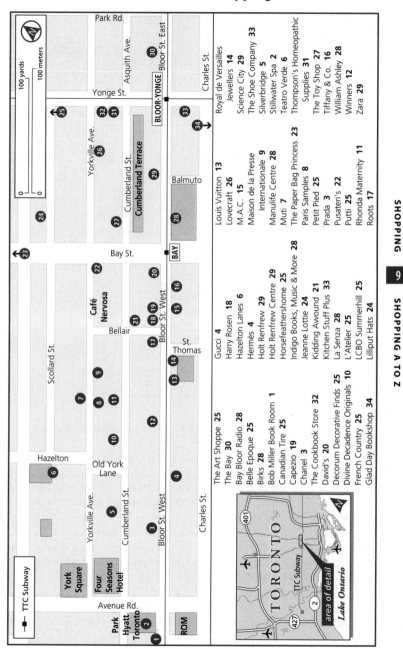

The Art Shoppe **25**
The Bay **30**
Bay Bloor Radio **28**
Belle Epoque **25**
Birks **28**
Bob Miller Book Room **1**
Canadian Tire **25**
Capezio **19**
Chanel **3**
The Cookbook Store **32**
David's **20**
Decorum Decorative Finds **25**
Divine Decadence Originals **10**
French Country **25**
Glad Day Bookshop **34**

Gucci **4**
Harry Rosen **18**
Hazelton Lanes **6**
Hermès **4**
Holt Renfrew **29**
Holt Renfrew Centre **29**
Horsefeathershome **25**
Indigo Books, Music & More **28**
Jeanne Lottie **24**
Kidding Awound **21**
Kitchen Stuff Plus **33**
La Senza **28**
L'Atelier **25**
LCBO Summerhill **25**
Lilliput Hats **24**

Louis Vuitton **13**
Lovecraft **26**
M.A.C. **15**
Maison de la Presse Internationale **9**
Manulife Centre **28**
Muti **7**
The Paper Bag Princess **23**
Paris Samples **8**
Petit Pied **25**
Prada **3**
Pusateri's **22**
Putti **25**
Rhonda Maternity **11**
Roots **17**

Royal de Versailles Jewellers **14**
Science City **29**
The Shoe Company **33**
Silverbridge **5**
Stillwater Spa **2**
Teatro Verde **6**
Thompson's Homeopathic Supplies **31**
The Toy Shop **27**
Tiffany & Co. **16**
William Ashley **28**
Winners **12**
Zara **29**

SHOPPING

9

SHOPPING A TO Z

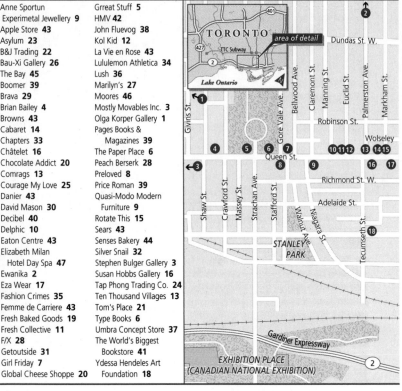

Anne Sportun
  Experimetal Jewellery **9**
Apple Store **43**
Asylum **23**
B&J Trading **22**
Bau-Xi Gallery **26**
The Bay **45**
Boomer **39**
Brava **29**
Brian Bailey **4**
Browns **43**
Cabaret **14**
Chapters **33**
Châtelet **16**
Chocolate Addict **20**
Comrags **13**
Courage My Love **25**
Danier **43**
David Mason **30**
Decibel **40**
Delphic **10**
Eaton Centre **43**
Elizabeth Milan
  Hotel Day Spa **47**
Ewanika **2**
Eza Wear **17**
Fashion Crimes **35**
Femme de Carriere **43**
Fresh Baked Goods **19**
Fresh Collective **11**
F/X **28**
Getoutside **31**
Girl Friday **7**
Global Cheese Shoppe **20**

Grreat Stuff **5**
HMV **42**
John Fluevog **38**
Kol Kid **12**
La Vie en Rose **43**
Lululemon Athletica **34**
Lush **36**
Marilyn's **27**
Moores **46**
Mostly Movables Inc. **3**
Olga Korper Gallery **1**
Pages Books &
  Magazines **39**
The Paper Place **6**
Peach Berserk **28**
Preloved **8**
Price Roman **39**
Quasi-Modo Modern
  Furniture **9**
Rotate This **15**
Sears **43**
Senses Bakery **44**
Silver Snail **32**
Stephen Bulger Gallery **3**
Susan Hobbs Gallery **16**
Tap Phong Trading Co. **24**
Ten Thousand Villages **13**
Tom's Place **21**
Type Books **6**
Umbra Concept Store **37**
The World's Biggest
  Bookstore **41**
Ydessa Hendeles Art
  Foundation **18**

Ethel's your gal. 1091 Queen St. E. © **416/778-6608**. www.ethel20thcenturyliving.com. Subway: Queen and then a streetcar east to Pape Ave.

G.U.F.F. ⟨Value⟩ The name stands for "good used furniture finds," and this Leslieville store delivers on that. Much of the stock consists of wood pieces, often with a natural finish (not just tables and chairs, but cabinets and bed frames, too). There are also framed prints and mirrors. 1152 Queen St. E. © **416/913-8025**. Subway: Queen and then a streetcar east to Bertmount Ave.

Horsefeathershome If your taste runs to English and French country-house styles, this emporium's for you. The 3,252-sq.-m (35,000-sq.-ft.) space boasts striking antique wooden pieces in walnut and mahogany, but there are modern pieces by Kartell and others. 1212 Yonge St. E. © **416/934-1771**. Subway: Summerhill.

L'Atelier This is about as glamorous as it gets. Napoleon III side tables share space with chrome bar stools and rococo Italian lamps. Many of the price tags hit four digits, but there are lovely accoutrements for moderate budgets, too. 1224 Yonge St. © **416/966-0200**. Subway: Summerhill.

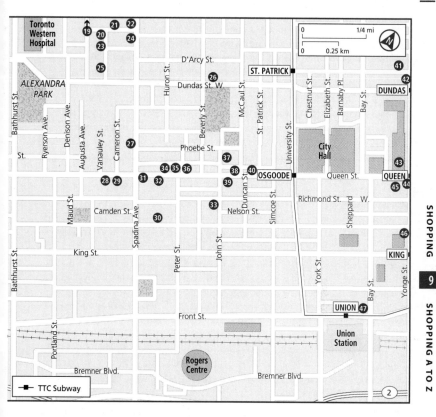

Mostly Movables Inc. This well-established shop is in new digs on the western fringe of Queen Street West. The early- and mid-20th-century Canadian and European furnishings are generally in fine form, and the prices are somewhat lower than those at many Yorkville and Rosedale competitors—a tradeoff for its remote location. 1684 Queen St. W. (*) **416/531-3565.** Subway: Osgoode and then a streetcar west to Triller Ave.

Uppity! (Finds) This colorful store is all about preservation, not restoration, so all of the painted furnishings—from graceful desks to children's furniture—are sold as is, not stripped and refinished. What's interesting is that the pieces from the 1850s through the 1930s have such a shabby chic elegance that you may want to keep them as they are. 1124 Queen St. E. (*) **647/436-0661.** www.uppity.ca. Subway: Queen and then a streetcar east to Bertmount Ave.

Zig Zag ★ (Value) This shop stocks a mélange of styles, but the specialty is early Modernist pieces. The names to watch out for are Eames, Saarinen, Arne Jacobsen, and Warren Platner. This is one store that's popular with certain uptown antiques dealers. 1142 Queen St. E. (*) **416/778-6495.** Subway: Queen and then any streetcar east to Jones Ave.

(Finds) Antiques Roadshow

On a few dates scattered throughout the calendar, more than 70 antiques dealers from Ontario and Québec descend on the Bayview Village shopping center for the **Heritage Antique Market.** The wares on sale include 19th- and 20th-century porcelains, jewelry, silver, furniture, and paintings. If you're in town when the market is, you're in luck. Be sure to call ahead or check the website (www.heritage antiqueshows.com) for the schedule. The market takes place only on Sundays or holiday Mondays. Bayview Village is located at 2901 Bayview Ave. (at Sheppard Ave.) and is accessible by subway (it's the Bayview stop on the Sheppard Line). Call ✆ **866/285-5515** or 416/483-6471 for more details.

Furniture

The Art Shoppe   This is one of the prettiest stores in the city, with top-notch furniture arranged in suites of rooms. A wide range of styles is on display, from gilty baroque to streamlined Art Deco. The price tags are high, but the store is well worth browsing. 2131 Yonge St. ✆ **416/487-3211.** www.theartshoppe.com. Subway: Eglinton.

Elte Carpet & Home   With 12,077 sq. m (130,000 sq. ft.) of showroom space, Elte has room for a lot more than rugs. This megastore is divided into boutiques displaying an astonishing array of home-design and -décor products. History-spanning reproductions abound. 80 Ronald Ave. (just west of Dufferin St.). ✆ **888/276-3583** or 416/785-7885. www.elte.com. Subway: Eglinton W. and then any westbound bus to Ronald Ave.

Nestings ★   This terrific shop delivers comfort and style in equal measure. Many of the items, from ornate iron kettles to tassel-trimmed ottomans, hark back to a more glamorous age. Pint-size furnishings are available at **Nestings Kids** at 2433 Yonge St. (✆ **416/322-0511;** subway: Eglinton.). 1609 Bayview Ave. ✆ **416/932-3704.** Subway: Eglinton and then bus no. 34 to Bayview.

Putti ★   Two generously proportioned rooms hold grand (and grandly priced) European treasures old and new: dining sets, armoires, cushions, and china. If you've ever wished you could walk into a layout from *Victoria* magazine, this shop is for you. 1104 Yonge St. ✆ **416/972-7652.** Subway: Rosedale.

Quasi-Modo Modern Furniture   With offerings for both home and office, this shop showcases some of the best of streamlined 20th-century design. Many of the items are European imports, such as the tables and chairs by Sweden's Bruno Mathsson. 789 Queen St. W. ✆ **416/703-8300.** Subway: Osgoode and then a streetcar west to Claremont St.

UpCountry   The ownership has changed, but the upscale Arts-and-Crafts and mission-style aesthetic hasn't altered. Most of the offerings are wooden or upholstered furnishings, with a few decorative elements thrown in. 310 King St. E. ✆ **416/368-7477.** www. upcountry.ca. Subway: King and then a streetcar east to Parliament St.

Housewares, Glass & Fine China

Bergo Designs ★   I'm a shelter-magazine addict, and walking into this store is like slipping into a particularly divine *Dwell* layout. Whether you're looking for a wine rack or a candlestick, you will find the most cutting-edge international design represented here (Bergo has an especially notable collection of German and Danish pieces). There's also some architecturally inspired jewelry and watches by Frank Gehry. Prices veer to the **185** high side, but that's no surprise, is it *liebchen?* In the Distillery District, 55 Mill St. © 416/861-1821. www.bergo.ca. Subway: King and then a streetcar east to Parliament St.

Châtelet (Finds)   This tiny shop brings out my girly side. There's shabby-chic painted furniture, but I barely notice it because I'm distracted by all of the beautiful baubles (bejeweled picture frames, china cups, and decorative drawer pulls). The prices are surprisingly reasonable. 717 Queen St. W. © 416/603-2278. www.chatelethome.com. Subway: Osgoode and then a streetcar west to Tecumseth.

Kitchen Stuff Plus (Value)   This housewares shop sells brand-name goods from the likes of Umbra at discount prices. It offers a good selection of picture frames, wine racks, area rugs, candles, painted ceramics, and kitchen accessories. There's also a store at 2287 Yonge St. (© 416/544-0515; subway: Eglinton). 703 Yonge St. © 416/944-2718. www.kitchenstuffplus.com. Subway: Yonge/Bloor.

Muti   Murano glass designs and cheery ceramics from Italy dominate this store. Look a little closer, and you'll find a few French tapestries and tablecloths, too. 88 Yorkville Ave. © 416/969-0253. Subway: Bay.

Tap Phong Trading Co. (Finds)   If you have only a few minutes in Chinatown, spend them here. You'll find beautiful hand-painted ceramics, earthenware, decorative items, kitchen utensils, and small appliances. Best of all, just about everything is inexpensive and of reliable quality. 360 Spadina Ave. © 416/977-6364. Subway: Spadina and then LRT to Baldwin St.

Umbra Concept Store ★ (Value)   I've long been a fan of Umbra's überstylish yet affordable designs, so the opening of its first retail outpost in 2007 is huge news. The Toronto flagship store is a 650-sq.-m (7,000-sq.-ft.) bi-level wonder that includes an expansive range of products, some furniture, and a space where you can watch members of the design team at work. 165 John St. © 416/599-0088. www.umbra.com. Subway: Osgoode.

William Ashley ★ (Value)   This is the last word in luxe, whether it be fine china, crystal, or silver. All of the top manufacturers are represented, including Waterford, Baccarat, Christofle, Wedgwood, and Lenox. Even if you're not in a buying mood, the detailed displays are fascinating. And if you *are* in a buying mood, you'll find better prices here than elsewhere. Manulife Centre, 55 Bloor St. W. © 416/964-2900. www.williamashley.com. Subway: Bay.

(Tips)   Go Where the Dealers Go

There are plenty of gorgeous antique stores in Rosedale, on that stretch of Yonge Street from the Rosedale subway station to St. Clair Avenue. True bargain hunters will gravitate to **Leslieville,** the stretch of Queen Street East between Carlaw and Coxwell, with its many small antique shops, which often contain great finds that need a little bit of fixing up. Leslieville is where the owners of some of the most glamorous antiques stores in town shop; they buy pieces here, fix them up, and sell them at uptown prices.

Bau-Xi Gallery After viewing the masterworks at the Art Gallery of Ontario, you can head across the street and buy your own. Founded in 1965, Bau-Xi features contemporary works by artists from across the country. 340 Dundas St. W. ⓒ **416/977-0600.** www.bau-xi.com. Subway: St. Patrick.

Corkin Gallery ★ Most items here are historical and contemporary photographs from around the world. They include works by Cylla von Tiedemann, Irving Penn, and Herb Ritts, plus a small collection of modernist painting and sculpture. In the Distillery District, 55 Mill St. ⓒ **416/979-1980.** www.corkingallery.com. Subway: King and then a streetcar east to Parliament St.

Eskimo Art Gallery ★ This award-winning gallery has the largest collection of Inuit stone sculptures in Toronto. At any given time, it shows more than 500 pieces. 12 Queens Quay W. (opposite Westin Harbour Castle). ⓒ **416/366-3000.** www.eskimoart.com. Subway: Union and then LRT to Queen's Quay.

Olga Korper Gallery Established in 1973, this gallery houses contemporary Canadian and international works. Artists represented include Averbuch, John Brown, Sankawa, and the estate of Louis Comtois. 17 Morrow Ave. (off Dundas St. W.). ⓒ **416/538-8220.** Subway: Dundas West.

Sandra Ainsley Gallery ★ Specializing in glass sculpture, this renowned gallery represents Canadian, American, and international artists, including Dale Chihuly, Jon Kuhn, Peter Powning, Tom Scoon, Susan Edgerley, and David Bennett. The one-of-a-kind pieces have big price tags, but you can also find some affordable items, such as paperweights, vases, and jewelry. In the Distillery District, 55 Mill St. ⓒ **416/214-9490.** www.sandraainsleygallery.com. Subway: King and then a streetcar east to Parliament St.

Stephen Bulger Gallery ★ Ⓕⁱⁿᵈˢ If you're interested in fine art photography, this is the place to go in Toronto. Bulger Gallery displays contemporary Canadian and international photography, both by established artists and up-and-comers (the gallery is one of the driving forces behind CONTACT, Toronto's Annual Celebration of Photography, which has launched many careers). The artists represented include Robert Burley, Ruth Kaplan, Vincenzo Pietropaolo, and Alex Webb. 1026 Queen St. W. ⓒ **416/504-0575.** www.bulgergallery.com. Subway: Osgoode and then a streetcar west to Ossington Ave.

Susan Hobbs Gallery Ⓕⁱⁿᵈˢ This small gallery in an unprepossessing warehouse far from the Yorkville crowd has been a major player in Canadian contemporary art since 1992. Hobbs represents some of Toronto's best artists, including Ian Carr-Harris, Shirley Wiitasalo, Robin Collyer, and Sandra Meigs. 137 Tecumseth St. (at Queen St.). ⓒ **416/504-3699.** www.susanhobbs.com. Subway: Osgoode and then any streetcar west to Tecumseth St.

Ydessa Hendeles Art Foundation ★ This is one of the most interesting contemporary art collections in the city. Hendeles features installations by international artists. Works on display include paintings, photography, and multimedia projects. 778 King St. W. ⓒ **416/603-2227.** Subway: St. Andrew and then any streetcar west to Bathurst St.

AUDIOVISUAL & ELECTRONIC GOODS

Apple Store ★ Mac geeks, take note: Toronto has *three* Apple stores. One is at the Yorkdale shopping center and another is at Sherway Gardens, both remote from the downtown core, but the Eaton Centre location provides easy access. (Yes, I'm a Mac geek.) Eaton Centre. ⓒ **647/258-0801.** Subway: Dundas or Queen.

Bay Bloor Radio   This 1,208-sq.-m (13,000-sq.-ft.) store carries the latest and greatest audio equipment, from portable units to in-home theater systems. Manulife Centre, 55
Bloor St. W. ✆ 416/967-1122. www.baybloorradio.com. Subway: Bay.

Canadian Tire   Don't be fooled by the name—this megastore carries far more than
auto parts. This is where I head when Father's Day approaches. The endless aisles over-
flow with gadgets for home, yard, office, car, and any place in between. There's another
branch just north of Bloor at 839 Yonge St. (✆ 416/925-9592). 65 Dundas St. W.
✆ 416/979-9056. www.canadiantire.ca. Subway: Dundas.

Henry's ★   This bi-level shop deals in analog and digital photography. The first floor
has electronic equipment, darkroom supplies, and a photo-processing lab. Upstairs, a
wide selection of secondhand cameras and gear is available. 119 Church St. ✆ 416/868-0872.
Subway: Queen.

BOOKS, MAGAZINES & NEWSPAPERS
Books

Atticus Books   Bookworms can while away hours in this crowded shop filled with
secondhand scholarly tomes. It stocks many volumes of philosophy, psychology, and
psychoanalysis. Antiquarian books are at the back of the store. 84 Harbord St. ✆ 416/922-
6045. Subway: Spadina and then walk south to Harbord.

Ballenford Books on Architecture   Interior designers, whether amateur or pro,
will love this well-arranged store. The books cover everything from antique furniture to
architectural theory, from urban design to landscaping. The shop also displays sketches
and drawings by local architects. 600 Markham St. (south of Bloor St. W.). ✆ 416/588-0800.
Subway: Bathurst.

Bob Miller Book Room   When I was a student at the University of Toronto, I would
come into this academic bookstore looking for a single book and end up browsing for
ages. It stocks mainly literary fiction, humanities, and social sciences. Works in transla-
tion are carefully selected. 180 Bloor St. W., lower concourse. ✆ 416/922-3557. Subway: St.
George.

Book City ★ Value   For a small chain, Book City offers big discounts—many tomes
are discounted by 10% to 30%. The selection of international magazines is particularly
good. Book City also has branches at 1950 Queen St. E. (✆ 416/698-1444), and 348
Danforth Ave. (✆ 416/469-9997). 501 Bloor St. W. ✆ 416/961-4496. Subway: Bathurst.

Chapters ★   While Indigo (see below) now owns and operates the Chapters bookstores, they retain their own particular charm. Eminently browse-worthy and well
stocked, Chapters boasts comfy chairs, a Starbucks cafe, and a host of free special events.
Celebrity authors Sophia Loren and Sarah, Duchess of York, had their Toronto engage-
ments here. The stores are open late, usually until 10 or 11pm on weeknights and midnight on weekends. 142 John St. ✆ 416/595-7349. Subway: Osgoode.

The Cookbook Store   Call it food porn: lush, gooey close-ups of scallop ceviche and
tiramisu. This store specializes in the kind of books that make a gourmet's heart go pitter-
patter. There are also tomes about wine, health, and restaurants. 850 Yonge St. ✆ 416/920-
2665. www.cook-book.com. Subway: Yonge/Bloor.

David Mason   This well-established store has moved into a new location. It stocks
many travel books, and a number of first editions of Canadian, American, and British
works. The collections of 19th- and 20th-century literature are vast. 366 Adelaide St. W.
✆ 416/598-1015. www.davidmasonbooks.com. Subway: St. Andrew.

(Value) **The Best Bargains**

Maybe you can't get something for nothing . . . but you can score some pretty fab finds on the cheap in Toronto. It's a treasure hunt of sorts, and the spoils are anything but certain, but when you find that perfect piece marked down to next to nothing, well, that makes it all worthwhile. Many Toronto retailers, including luxurious Holt Renfrew, have their own outlet shops. Here's my own little black book of favorite foraging grounds. Happy hunting!

Dixie Outlet Mall ★ Ten minutes from Pearson International Airport is the answer to bargain-shoppers' prayers. It's hard to beat the Dixie Outlet Mall for number of bargains per square foot. You can shop at more than 120 outlet shops here, including Jay Set (which carries Peter Nygard fashions), La Vie en Rose lingerie, and chocolatier Laura Secord, so you're bound to find something. There's also a large Winners store (see description below). 1250 S. Service Rd., Mississauga. (✆) **905/278-7492.** Gardiner Expwy./Queen Elizabeth Way (QEW) west to Dixie Rd. exit. Turn left; follow Dixie Rd. south to S. Service Rd.

Grreat Stuff An awful lot of men's clothes are jammed into this small retail space, but if you're not troubled by claustrophobia, dig in for some amazing deals. Business casual is this shop's mainstay, though you can find *grreat* prices on Italian silk ties and brand-name suits. 870 Queen St. W. (✆) **416/533-7680.** www.grreatstuff.com. Subway: Osgoode and then streetcar west to Shaw St.

Honest Ed's World Famous Shopping Centre ★ Ed's is a Toronto institution, having turned 60 in 2008. The store is framed with flashing red and yellow lights both outdoors *and* indoors. "Don't just stand there, buy something!" blurts out one brazen sign. This idiosyncratic store has a deal on everything from housewares to carpets, and from clothing to sundries. Crazy-making as shopping here can be, the bargains are unbeatable. In case you *do* need to refuel after shopping here, there's a **Lettieri** (see p. 223) tucked into the corner at Bloor and Bathurst. 581 Bloor St. W. (✆) **416/537-1574.** Subway: Bathurst.

Marilyn's (Finds) Here's a rare thing: knockdown prices paired with attentive service. The specialty is Canadian fashions for women, from sportswear to glamorous gowns. You can also attend in-store seminars on fashion-forward

Glad Day Bookshop ★ This was the first gay-oriented bookstore in Canada, and it remains one of the best. The shelves hold a sizable collection of gay and lesbian fiction, biography, and history books, and the offerings have expanded to include magazines, CDs, videos, calendars, posters, and cards. 598A Yonge St., 2nd floor. (✆) **416/961-4161.** Subway: Wellesley.

Indigo Books Music & More ★ (Kids) This Canadian-owned chain boasts an excellent selection of books, magazines, and videotapes. It has tables and chairs for browsing, a cafe, and a helpful staff. Best of all, special events, such as author visits, live performances, and even seminars, take place almost daily. Kids have their own series of events. The store is a favorite with night owls—it's open until 11pm or midnight every day. You'll find branches at the Eaton Centre ((✆) **416/591-3622**) and at 2300 Yonge St., at topics like traveling with just one suitcase. 200 Spadina Ave. ✆ **416/504-6777.** Subway: Spadina and then LRT to Queen St. W.

Paris Samples   This store snaps up designers' samples and marks them down 20% to 75%. The clothes range from wool pants to velvet dresses to micro-miniskirts. *One caveat:* The sizes are all under 14, and many clothes come only in the smallest sizes. 101 Yorkville Ave. ✆ **416/926-0656.** Subway: Bay.

The Shoe Company   This is every foot fetishist's dream: great shoes for men and women from Unisa, Nine West, and others, marked down to unbeatable prices. You'll find lots of trendy styles that won't be stylish for long, but it won't hurt your pocketbook to splurge. Outlets are around the city, including one at First Canadian Place. 711 Yonge St. ✆ **416/923-8388.** Subway: Yonge/Bloor.

Tom's Place ★   After more than 40 years in business, Tom's Place looks sharper than ever. While the shop devotes an entire floor to women's wear, the best buys are in the men's department: You'll find brand-name merchandise by the likes of Armani and Valentino. Tom's Place stocks sizes from 36 short to 50 tall. 190 Baldwin St. ✆ **416/596-0297.** Subway: Spadina and then LRT to Baldwin St.

Winners   This northern outpost of the U.S.-owned T.J. Maxx chain offers great deals on clothes for men and women (think Jones New York, Tommy Hilfiger, and Liz Claiborne), and top-name togs for the kiddies. There's also an ever-changing selection of housewares, cookware, linens, toiletries, and toys. The 3,716-sq.-m (40,000-sq.-ft.) outlet at College Park is always packed, but its large, airy space is filled with deals (✆ **416/598-8800;** subway: College). Winners has a smaller but longstanding location in the Fashion District which is another good bet (57 Spadina Ave.; ✆ **416/585-2052;** subway: Spadina and then LRT to King St. W.). Its new location in Scotia Plaza, in Toronto's Underground City, will hold purchases for shoppers till closing time (so lunch-time shoppers can keep their secrets, I guess): 40 King St. W.; ✆ **416/360-8162.** The outpost on tony Bloor Street West outraged some of its high-priced neighbors, but deal-obsessed shoppers love it. 110 Bloor St. W. ✆ **416/920-0193.** www.winners.ca. Subway: Bay.

Eglinton Avenue (✆ **416/544-0049**). Manulife Centre, 55 Bloor St. W. ✆ **416/925-3536.** www.indigo.ca. Subway: Yonge/Bloor or Bay.

Mabel's Fables ★ **Kids**   This charming shop is stocked with every book a child could possibly want—and a lot more. Offerings are grouped by age, going up to early adolescence. On weekends, author visits and other special events take place. 662 Mount Pleasant. ✆ **416/322-0438.** www.mabelsfables.com. Subway: Eglinton, then bus no. 34 to Mount Pleasant, and walk 2 blocks south.

Nicholas Hoare   This shop has the cozy feel of an English library, with hardwood floors, plush couches, and a fireplace. There's an extensive selection of Canadian and international fiction, as well as heavyweight art tomes and children's books. 45 Front St. E. ✆ **416/777-2665.** Subway: Union.

Open Air Books & Maps This shop caters to nature lovers and ecology buffs. It carries a vast assortment of travel guidebooks and maps. 25 Toronto St. ✆ 416/363-0719. Subway: King.

Pages Books & Magazines ★ (Finds) This shop is renowned for its books on the arts (film, design, photography, art, literary criticism), cultural studies, and alternative lifestyles. There's also a large section dedicated to books from small presses, and a gigantic selection of magazines. The store's owners have a strict policy on banned books: If a book has been banned elsewhere, they'll definitely have it in stock. 256 Queen St. W. ✆ 416/598-1447. www.pagesbooks.ca. Subway: Osgoode.

Seekers Books The focus is New Age, with new and used books on Eastern religion, mysticism, meditation, and the occult, but you'll find general-interest fiction and nonfiction, too. 509 Bloor St. W. ✆ 416/925-1982. Subway: Bathurst.

Silver Snail ★ (Kids) Remember those comic books you read as a kid? Well, they're all here, along with adult-oriented comics like the *Sandman* series. You'll see a sizable section of imported editions, and posters and movie memorabilia, too. 367 Queen St. W. ✆ 416/593-0889. www.silversnail.com. Subway: Osgoode.

Type Books (Finds) How can I describe how lovely this store and its contents are? A friend of mine, an editor at a major design magazine, told me that this is where local stylists get books to prop photo shoots. Worth a *long* browse. 883 Queen St. W. ✆ 416/366-8973. Subway: Osgoode and then streetcar west to Trinity-Bellwoods.

University of Toronto Bookstore ★ (Finds) This is one of the best-stocked independent booksellers in town. It also hosts its own Reading Series, which has featured authors such as Ann-Marie MacDonald and Roddy Doyle; check the website for details about upcoming events. In the Koffler Centre, 214 College St. ✆ 416/978-7900. www.uoft bookstore.com. Subway: Queen's Park.

The World's Biggest Bookstore ★ The debate about whether The World's Biggest is *really* the world's biggest rages on. Either way, the 27km (17 miles) of bookshelves do contain a good selection. Browsing is welcome, but the bright, bright lights are headache-inducing after a while. There are also software, video, and magazine departments. 20 Edward St. ✆ 416/977-7009. Subway: Dundas.

Magazines & Newspapers

Great Canadian News Company ★ There are many outposts around town, but the main shop on Queen St. West has the best selection, with more than 2,000 different magazines filling its shelves. 368 Queen St. West (at Spadina Ave.). ✆ 416/596-0279. Subway: Osgoode.

Maison de la Presse Internationale Although this store fills up fast on weekends, drawing expats and locals alike, it's still a great place to browse. The many international magazines and newspapers are as current as you'll find. The second floor is devoted to paperback novels *en français.* 99 Yorkville Ave. ✆ 416/928-2328. Subway: Bay.

DEPARTMENT STORES

The Bay The Hudson's Bay Company started out as a fur-trading business when the first French-speaking settlers came to Canada. Today, The Bay boasts excellent midrange selections of clothing and housewares. In the summer of 2008, the same company that owns the U.S. chain Lord & Taylor purchased The Bay, and management is considering extensive changes, including possibly renaming some stores. Of the several Toronto locations, here are the two best. (1) 176 Yonge St. (at Queen St.). ℂ **416/861-9111.** www.thebay.com. Subway: Queen. (2) 2 Bloor St. E. (at Yonge St.). ℂ **416/972-3333.** Subway: Yonge/Bloor.

Holt Renfrew   Designers such as Donna Karan, Christian Lacroix, and Yves St. Laurent figure in Holt Renfrew's four levels of merchandise. You'll also find the excellent Holt Renfrew Spa (see p. 158) and the Holt Renfrew Café (which is really a restaurant with great sandwiches and salads). The basement connects with an underground mall and features a gourmet food department and a cafe (yes, this one really is a cafe). Holt Renfrew Centre, 50 Bloor St. W. ℂ **416/922-2333.** www.holtrenfrew.com. Subway: Yonge/Bloor.

Sears   If you visited Toronto before 2000, you'll remember the gorgeous Eaton's department store, which anchored the Eaton Centre complex. Sears Canada bought the Eaton's name and opened this department store in its place. It's more upscale than your average Sears. Eaton Centre. ℂ **416/343-2111.** www.sears.ca. Subway: Dundas.

FASHION

Let's get this out of the way first: Toronto has all of the requisite big-name European boutiques along Bloor Street West between Yonge Street and Avenue Road. You'll find **Louis Vuitton** at no. 111; **Gucci** and **Hermès** at no. 130; and **Prada** and **Chanel** at The Colonnade shopping arcade at no. 131. The listings below focus primarily on shops particular to Toronto (with just a few exceptions). Also see "Hunting for Vintage" (p. 196) and the listings under "Shoes" below.

Clothing for Children

Fashion Crimes ★   Toronto designer Pam Chorley's store looks like a princess's dressing room, complete with Venetian glass and ornate chandeliers. There are clothes for women here, too, but her Misdemeanors line makes gossamer gowns and ruby slippers for little girls who dream they're really princesses. 322½ Queen St. W. ℂ **416/351-8758.** Subway: Osgoode.

Kol Kid (Finds)   West Queen West isn't just for grown-ups, you know. This charming boutique carries Canadian- and European-made clothing for kids, plus toys and furnishings. 674 Queen St. W. ℂ **416/681-0368.** Subway: Osgoode and then streetcar west to Palmerston Ave.

Lovechild   A favorite with tiny tots who are already developing fashion savvy, Lovechild offers a selection of groovy clothes in a rainbow of colors. 2523 Yonge St. ℂ **416/486-4746.** www.lovechild.ca. Subway: Eglinton.

(Finds)   **Fresh Perspective**

Let's say you're pressed for time, and you want to hit a single store that will let you shop for truly distinctive clothing and giftware. Get yourself to **Fresh Collective,** a designer-run collective at 692 Queen St. W. (ℂ **416/594-1313;** www. freshcollective.com). You will find cool designs by local up-and-coming labels— and you'll be able to talk to the people who made them, because they staff the store themselves. The focus is primarily on designs for women (sorry, guys), but the eclectic offerings at any given time will also include baby togs and jewelry.

(Finds) **Psst . . . Want a Free Yoga Class?**

If you're in Toronto on a Wednesday or Sunday morning and feel an overwhelming urge to exercise, here's a secret you need to know: Lululemon Athletica offers **free hour-long classes** (Wed is yoga at 8am, and Sun is "Pilates-yoga fusion" at 9:30am.) There's absolutely no charge or obligation to buy anything (though you may be tempted by the stylish workout gear that lines the walls). The classes take place at the store at 342 Queen St. W. (✆ **416/703-1399**). You should call the day before to make sure that the class is scheduled, but you can't make an advance reservation—participation is limited to the first 25 people to show up.

Clothing for Men & Women

Danier (Value) This Canadian chain carries suede and leather coats for men and women, as well as ladies' pants, skirts, and handbags. Most of the prices are very reasonable, and regular sales events knock the prices down 20% to 50%. Eaton Centre. ✆ **416/598-1159**. www.danier.com. Subway: Queen.

Lululemon Athletica ★ The athletically inclined—especially yoga devotees—will delight in this shop. In addition to the house label's nicely designed workout wear, you'll find Ayurvedic skin care products by Christy Turlington, yoga mats, and other accessories. 342 Queen St. W. ✆ **416/703-1399**. www.lululemon.com. Subway: Osgoode and then streetcar west to Spadina Ave.

Roots ★ This is one Canadian retailer that seems to be universally loved. The clothes are casual, from hooded sweats to fleece jackets, and there's a good selection of leather footwear. Don't overlook the tykes' department, which has the same stuff in tiny sizes. Other locations include the Eaton Centre (✆ **416/593-9640**). 95A Bloor St. W. ✆ **416/323-9512**. www.roots.ca. Subway: Bay.

Tilley Endurables ★ (Value) The Tilley hat may not be Canada's greatest style moment, but it certainly is one of the most recognizable. Tilley now offers a full range of men's and women's clothing, as well as belts, socks, and other travel gear. Everything is well made and incredibly durable. Note that Tilley has branched out into travel underwear (it admits that "sexy they may not be" but claims that two sets of its underclothes will get you around the world—*now* I'm curious). The store at Queen's Quay (207 Queen's Quay West, ✆ **416/203-0463**) is the most convenient, but the flagship store on Don Mills is unbeatable for choice. 900 Don Mills Rd. ✆ **800/363-8737** or 416/441-6141. www.tilley.com. Subway: Eglinton and then bus east to Don Mills and walk two lights north to Barber Greene.

TNT Man/TNT Woman (Finds) The acronym stands for "The New Trend," and this small chain offers just that, with fashions from Betsey Johnson and Plein Sud for *les femmes,* and Diesel and Iceberg jeans for *les hommes.* There are also locations uptown at 368 and 388 Eglinton Ave. 87 Avenue Rd. ✆ **416/975-1960** (men's shop) and 416/975-1810 (women's shop). Subway: Bay.

Zara (Value) This Spanish chain is renowned for transferring the latest looks into affordable fashions less than a month after they appear on the runway. This bi-level shop has a women's department at street level; the equally stylish men's shop is on the lower concourse. 50 Bloor St. W. ✆ **416/916-2401**. www.zara.com. Subway: Bay.

Clothing for Men

Boomer ★ Ever wonder where Barenaked Ladies or Moist get the glad rags they wear in their videos? Look no farther than Boomer, a hip shop that stocks such staples as Hugo Boss and Cinque, as well as the latest from Swedish trendsetter J. Linderberg. 309 Queen St. W. ℰ 416/598-0013. Subway: Osgoode.

Decibel This trendy shop is a terrific spot to pick up the latest and greatest in casual wear. Labels range from well-known brands like Kenneth Cole to up-and-comers such as Psycho Cowboy or Pusch (from Denmark and Calgary, respectively). 200 Queen St. W. ℰ 416/506-9648. Subway: Osgoode.

Delphic Don't like trendy? Then don't shop here. If you do, you'll be confronted by fashion favorites such as Evisu Jeans, which are imported from Japan. 706 Queen St. W. ℰ 416/603-3334. Subway: Osgoode and then streetcar west to Manning Ave.

Eza Wear (Finds) Design duo Susanne Langlois and Erin Murphy make many of their cool clothes from hemp, which looks as elegant as linen. 695 Queen St. W. ℰ 416/975-1388. Subway: Osgoode and then streetcar west to Markham St.

Harry Rosen ★ Designed like a mini department store, Harry Rosen carries the crème de la crème of menswear designers, including Hugo Boss, Brioni, and Versace. There are also a good selection of work-worthy footwear and a famous "Great Wall of Shirts." 82 Bloor St. W. ℰ 416/972-0556. www.harryrosen.com. Subway: Bay.

Moores (Value) There's something for everyone at this spacious shop. Most of the suits, sport coats, and dress pants are Canadian-made, and such international designers as Oscar de la Renta are represented, too. Sizes run from extra-short to extra-tall and oversize. The prices tend to be reasonable, and bargains abound. 100 Yonge St. ℰ 416/363-5442. www.mooresclothing.com. Subway: King.

Clothing for Women

Brian Bailey ★ This Canadian designer creates glamorous gowns, cocktail dresses, and smart suits. The shop is located in an edgy neighborhood, but the look is classic and feminine. 878 Queen St. W. ℰ 416/516-7188. Subway: Osgoode and then streetcar west to Shaw.

Comrags Designers Judy Cornish and Joyce Gunhouse create retro-inspired clothing that looks great on a variety of body types. 654 Queen St. W. ℰ 416/360-7249. www.comrags. com. Subway: Osgoode and then streetcar west to Palmerston.

Ewanika (Finds) Little Italy is famous for its nightlife, but if you happen by during the day, be sure to check out designer Trish Ewanika's boutique. Her tailored creations are perfect for women who don't like suits but want to look polished at work. 490 College St. ℰ 416/927-9699. Subway: Queen's Park and then streetcar west to Palmerston Ave.

Fashion Crimes ★ These glamorous dresses, designed by shop owner Pam Chorley, are a tribute to playful femininity and whimsical imagination. Many of the fabrics are made for Chorley in Paris, and you won't find them anywhere else. In addition to the elegant gowns, there are plenty of original accessories, including opera-length gloves, feathery boas, and glittering handbags. (Little girls have their own Misdemeanors line; see p. 191.) 322½ Queen St. W. ℰ 416/351-8758. Subway: Osgoode.

Femme de Carriere ★ For a dose of Québécois savoir-faire, look no farther than this elegant emporium. While the name translates as "career woman," the offerings range from shapely suits to evening-appropriate dresses and chic separates. Branches in shopping

SHOPPING

9

SHOPPING A TO Z

centers around town include First Canadian Place, Holt Renfrew Centre, and Fairview Mall. Eaton Centre. ✆ 416/595-0951. Subway: Dundas or Queen.

Fresh Baked Goods ★ (Finds)   Surprise—this *isn't* a bakery. Owner Laura Jean, "the knitting queen," features a line of flirty knitwear made of cotton, mohair, wool, or lace. This is a favorite haunt of the celebrity set—stars like Neve Campbell drop by when they're in town. The staff is friendly and incredibly helpful; if you like a sweater but not its buttons, they'll sew on different ones from their sizeable collection free of charge. They also do custom orders. 274 Augusta Ave. ✆ 416/966-0123. www.freshbakedgoods.com. Subway: Spadina and then LRT to Baldwin St., and walk 2 blocks west.

F/X   The significance of the name is clear from the start: This is dressing for dramatic effect. Funkier pieces from the prêt-à-porter collections of Vivienne Westwood and Anna Sui are at the back of the store. There are also cutting-edge shoes and boots, a makeup collection, and candy. 515 Queen St. W. ✆ 416/504-0888. Subway: Osgoode and then a streetcar west to Augusta Ave.

Girl Friday ★ (Finds)   Local designer Rebecca Nixon creates feminine dresses, suits, and separates for her shop under the name Girl Friday. The store also carries pieces from hip labels Nougat and Dish, but I come here for Nixon's elegant but affordable pieces. 740 Queen St. W. ✆ 416/364-2511. www.girlfridayclothing.com. Subway: Osgoode and then a streetcar west to Claremont St.

Jeanne Lottie ★ (Value)   Can you make a fashion statement with a handbag? Canadian designer Jane Ip thinks so—and she's made a convert out of me. Purses for all occasions, from zebra-patterned boxy bags for day to glittering sequin-encrusted numbers for a night out, fill her boutique. Beaded shoes and sparkly accessories are also sold. 32 Scollard St. ✆ 416/975-5115. www.jeannelottie.com. Subway: Yonge/Bloor.

Lilliput Hats (Finds)   Deep down, I long for a return of the days when people wore hats. Not winter head-warmers, but the glamorous headgear of the 1920s, '30s, '40s, and '50s. If you feel the same way, stop by Lilliput; most of the stunning hats are made by the owner, Karyn Gingras, whose designs have been worn by Celine Dion and Whoopi Goldberg. 32 Scollard St. ✆ 416/975-5115. www.jeannelottie.com. Subway: Yonge/Bloor.

Maxi Boutique   Variety is the name of the game at this long-established boutique in the heart of Greektown. Labels include homegrown talent such as Lida Baday as well as international brands like Naf Naf, Miss Sixty, and Betsey Johnson. 575 Danforth Ave. ✆ 416/461-6686. Subway: Pape.

Peach Berserk ★ (Finds)   Toronto designer (and local legend) Kingi Carpenter creates dramatically printed silk separates, dresses, and coats. Don't look for demure florals—prints range from bold martini glasses to the ironic "Do I Look Fat in This?" logo. 507 Queen St. W. ✆ 416/504-1711. www.peachberserk.com. Subway: Osgoode and then a streetcar west to Spadina.

Preloved ★   The original Toronto boutique was destroyed by a fire in February 2008. In September 2008, the store reopened in a new location across from Trinity-Bellwoods park. This is an incredible feat given that Preloved's pieces really *are* one of a kind: the shop's owners breathe new life into vintage clothing and cast-off jeans and T-shirts by changing the shapes and adding details like vintage lace. The roster of celeb fans includes Alanis Morissette. 881 Queen St. W. ✆ 416/703-1936. Subway: Osgoode and then a streetcar west to Trinity-Bellwoods.

Price Roman ★   The husband-and-wife team Derek Price and Tess Roman produces
sleek, tailored clothes with a sultry edge. They are rightly famous for their special-occa-
sion dresses. 267 Queen St. W. ⓒ **416/979-7363.** Subway: Osgoode.

Rhonda Maternity   Red-hot mamas-to-be should check out this glamorous boutique. The stylish suits, sweater sets, and sportswear are this store's exclusive designs. 110
Cumberland St. ⓒ **416/921-3116.** www.rhondamaternity.com. Subway: Bay.

Trove ★ (Finds)   I used to think of Trove primarily as a jewelry store, but now that it
has expanded into a larger space, I've started to appreciate its gorgeous selection of clothing by local designers, stylish shoes, stunning handbags, and other accessories, too. One
of the nicest things about this boutique is that it makes the effort to be size-inclusive, so
that women of all shapes can enjoy the treasures here. 793 Bathurst St. (at Bloor St. W.)
ⓒ **416/516-1258.** www.trove.ca. Subway: Bathurst.

Lingerie

La Senza (Value)   This Montréal-based chain carries moderately priced but eye-catching bra-and-panty sets and naughty-looking nighties. There are also plush unisex robes
and patterned boxers. An assortment of slippers, candles, bath mousse, and picture
frames rounds out the offerings. Holt Renfrew Centre, 50 Bloor St. W. ⓒ **416/972-1079.** www.
lasenza.com. Subway: Yonge/Bloor.

La Vie en Rose   You'll find quite the eclectic collection of undies here, from sensible
cotton briefs to maribou-trimmed teddies, retro PJs to up-to-the-minute cleavage
enhancers. The items at the front of the store are inexpensive; the farther back you go,
the pricier it gets. Eaton Centre. ⓒ **416/595-0898.** Subway: Queen.

Linea Intima ★ (Finds)   While there's no shortage of fabulous undergarments at this
boutique, the real reason to visit is owner Liliana Mann's encyclopedic knowledge of what
suits the female form. This extends to prosthetics and bras that are designed for women
who have had mastectomies. 1925 Avenue Rd. ⓒ **416/780-1726.** www.lineaintima.com. Subway: York Mills, then a bus west along Wilson Ave. to Avenue Rd. and walk 6 blocks south to
Brooke Ave.

Secrets From Your Sister ★   Thanks to Oprah, we know that the vast majority of
women in North America are wearing the wrong bra size. That won't be true of you if
you visit this store, which carries a terrific selection of bras to suit figures as dissimilar as
Audrey Hepburn and Jayne Mansfield, and everything in between. 560 Bloor St. W.
ⓒ **416/538-1234.** www.secretsfromyoursister.com. Subway: Bathurst.

Shoes (Men's, Women's, & Children's)

Browns ★   To treat your feet to fabulous footwear by Manolo Blahnik, Prada, or Fer-
ragamo, beat a path to this newly renovated shop for men and women. While you're here,
check out Browns' own house label, which is well designed *and* less pricey. There's also a
selection of leather handbags. Browns has several branches around the city. Eaton Centre.
ⓒ **416/979-9270.** www.brownsshoes.com. Subway: Queen.

Capezio   Whether you're looking for the perfect pair of ballet slippers or an up-to-the-
minute design from Steve Madden or Guess, you'll find it here. All the shoes and other
leather goods are for women. 70 Bloor St. W. ⓒ **416/920-1006.** Subway: Bay.

David's   For serious shoppers only. This high-end store stocks elegant footwear for
men and women—from Bruno Magli, Bally, and Sonia Rykiel, as well as the store's own
collection—but prices are accordingly steep. 66 Bloor St. W. ⓒ **416/920-1000.** Subway: Bay.

(Finds) **Hunting for Vintage**

I've been shopping vintage since I was 14, and I can promise you that Toronto has a truly great vintage-shopping scene. It spans the high and low points of the price spectrum. Want a pristine Chanel suit? Or a frothy chiffon concoction from the 1950s? Or maybe a now-classic rock-band T-shirt from the 1970s? Check out these treasure troves below.

Asylum   Secondhand jeans and vintage dresses line the racks in this Kensington Market stalwart. Bargains turn up in odd places, like the Anne Klein scarf at the bottom of a last-chance bin. An assortment of toys and candy only adds to the fun. 62 Kensington Ave. (C) **416/595-7199.** Subway: Spadina and then LRT to Baldwin St.

Brava (Finds)   This spacious, airy shop is a favorite among local stylists, who pick up everything from cashmere sweaters to evening wraps for ladies, and printed shirts to golf pants for gents. 553 Queen St. W. (C) **416/504-8742.** Subway: Osgoode and then streetcar west to Augusta.

Cabaret ★   Sally Bowles was right: Come to Cabaret, old chum. The shop features glamorous eveningwear of bygone eras—all in prime condition (the store employs a seamstress to make repairs and all clothing is dry-cleaned before it hits the sales floor). My only caveat is that prices have soared lately. If you're on a budget, look at the basement room for deals on off-season vintage clothing. 672 Queen St. W. (C) **416/504-7126.** Subway: Osgoode and then a streetcar west to Palmerston.

Courage My Love ★ (Value)   With its mix of vintage clothing and new silver jewelry, Courage is a Kensington Market favorite. Dresses run from '50s velvet numbers to '80s jersey, with a few bias-cut 1930s gowns appearing once in a blue moon. There are also cashmere sweaters and handbags worthy of a

Getoutside   The store doesn't look like much with its utilitarian shelving and lighting, but it stocks an amazing variety of sneakers from manufacturers around the world. Moccasins made by Laurentian Shoes, a Québec-based company, are also on show. 437 Queen St. W. (C) **416/593-5598.** www.get-out-side.com. Subway: Osgoode.

John Fluevog ★   Famous for his Goth footwear, this Vancouver designer also creates shoes and boots in a kaleidoscope of colors. These shoes aren't for shrinking violets, but their funky chic will get you attention without having to stomp your feet. 242 Queen St. W. (C) **416/581-1420.** www.fluevog.com. Subway: Osgoode.

Mephisto   These shoes are made for walking—particularly because they're made from all-natural materials. Devotees of this shop, now in its third decade, swear that it's impossible to wear out Mephisto footwear. 1177 Yonge St. (C) **416/968-7026.** Subway: Summerhill.

Petit Pied ★ (Kids)   This elegant shop carries children's shoes for newborns to adolescents. Many of the brands are European, including Minibel and Elefanten, but there are also sporty designs from Nike and Reebok. 890 Yonge St. (C) **416/963-5925.** Subway: Rosedale.

night at the Stork Club. The owners' cat makes an occasional furtive appearance. 14 Kensington Ave. © **416/979-1992.** Subway: Spadina and then LRT to Dundas St. W.

Divine Decadence Originals ★   The price tags at this glamorous shop are sky high, but the dresses are so magnificent and well maintained that Divine Decadence feels like a couture museum. Take a look at the Lanvins and Balenciagas of years gone by. 128 Cumberland St., 2nd floor © **877/295-0299** or 416/324-9759. Subway: Bay.

Gadabout (Finds   Whether you're channeling Jacqueline Kennedy or Marilyn Monroe, you'll find an outfit to match your mood at this jam-packed Leslieville shop. The quality is good, and pieces are dry-cleaned before they make it onto the racks. There is menswear too, and a wide selection of accessories and memorabilia. 1300 Queen St. E. © **416/463-1254.** www.gadabout.ca. Subway: Queen and then streetcar east to Alton Ave.

The Paper Bag Princess   L.A. has had a Paper Bag Princess boutique for several years, but only recently did its owner, Toronto native Elizabeth Mason, decide to open a location in her hometown. This store is a treasure trove, and its boudoirlike setting makes it a sexy place to shop. The mint-condition Chanel and Pucci outfits cost a bundle, but what else would you expect? 287 Davenport Rd. © **416/925-2603.** www.thepaperbagprincess.com. Subway: Bay.

Thrill of the Find (Finds   Actually, this isn't as much of a hunt as the name implies. This airy shop has well-organized women's clothing on a few racks, with designer names like Chanel featured in a separate couture section. 1172 Queen St. E. © **416/461-9313.** Subway: Queen and then a streetcar east to Jones Ave.

FOOD & WINE
Food

The Big Carrot   Who says health food can't be fun? This large-scale emporium stocks everything from organic produce to vitamins to all-natural beauty potions. Stop in at the cafe for a vegetarian snack or light meal. 348 Danforth Ave. © **416/466-2129.** www.thebigcarrot. ca. Subway: Chester.

The Bonnie Stern School   Crammed to the rafters with cooking accoutrements (such as stovetop grills) and exotic books, this store also features the raw ingredients you need to produce fine cuisine. It carries top-notch olive oil, balsamic vinegar, Asian sauces, and candied flower petals. If you take a course or seminar, you get a 10% discount on everything you buy. 6 Erskine Ave. © **416/484-4810.** www.bonniestern.com. Subway: Eglinton.

Chocolate Addict ★ (Finds   Do you know anyone who *isn't* a chocolate addict? This shop is definitely the right place to get a fix. My favorite treat is the tangy wasabi truffle, though the other housemade specialties (lavender, lemon-basil, and caramel truffles) are divinely decadent. 185 Baldwin St. ✆ **416/979-5809.** Subway: Spadina and then a streetcar to Baldwin St.

Global Cheese Shoppe ★ (Value)   Cheese, glorious cheese. More than 150 varieties are available, from mild bocconcini to the greenest of Gorgonzola, and the staff is generous with samples. 76 Kensington Ave. ✆ **416/593-9251.** Subway: Spadina and then LRT to Baldwin Ave.

House of Tea   Visitors to this shop can drink in the heady scent of more than 150 loose teas. And the selection of cups, mugs, and tea caddies runs from chic to comical. 1017 Yonge St. ✆ **416/922-1226.** Subway: Rosedale.

Pusateri's (Finds)   The Pusateri's store up at Lawrence and Avenue Road is a Toronto institution—and this younger Yorkville sibling is becoming one. The store stocks high-end sweets, meats, produce, and groceries. Travelers will appreciate the gourmet prepared meals that can be eaten on the go. 57 Yorkville Ave. ✆ **416/785-9100.** www.pusateris.com. Subway: Bay.

Senses Bakery ★   The pastries and chocolates here are simply exquisite. The bottles of maple syrup come from an Ontario family-run operation, so they're a particularly good souvenir. In the Maritime Life Tower, 2 Queen St. E. ✆ **416/364-7303.** www.senses.ca. Subway: Queen.

Simone Marie Belgian Chocolate   All of the rich truffles, colorful almond dragées, and fruit jellies in this shop are flown in from Belgium. 126A Cumberland St. ✆ **416/968-7777.** Subway: Bay.

SOMA Chocolatemaker ★ (Finds)   This is truly a temple to chocolate. The chocolate maker does all of his work on site, starting with roasting the raw cocoa beans. The results are breathtaking: chocolate bars (such as the Dark Fire, with chilies, ginger, and vanilla, or the milk chocolate with dried cherries) simply melt in your mouth. The truffles—which range from the sultry bergamot to the luscious caramel—are kept in temperature-controlled shelves until you leave the store. In the Distillery District, 55 Mill St. ✆ **416/815-7662.** www.somachocolate.com. Subway: King and then a streetcar east to Parliament St.

Sugar Mountain Confectionery   Remember Pez, candy necklaces, and lollipop rings? Sugar Mountain carries the tooth-aching sweets of youth, several of which have been elevated to cult status. Teens are drawn to this store, but the biggest customers are nostalgic boomers. 2291 Yonge St. ✆ **416/486-9321.** Subway: Eglinton.

Wine

In Ontario, Liquor Control Board of Ontario (LCBO) outlets and small boutiques at upscale grocery stores sell wine; no alcohol is sold at convenience stores. The best deals are on locally produced wines—especially the icewine, a sweet dessert wine that has won awards the world over. There are LCBO outlets all over the city, and prices are the same at all of them. The nicest shop is the **LCBO Summerhill,** 10 Scrivener Sq. (✆ **416/922-0403;** subway: Summerhill). Built out of a former train station, this outpost hosts cooking classes, wines and spirits tastings, and party-planning seminars. Other locations are at the Manulife Centre, 55 Bloor St. W. (✆ **416/925-5266**), 20 Bloor St. E. (✆ **416/368-0521**), the Eaton Centre (✆ **416/979-9978**), and Union Station (✆ **416/925-9644**). See **www.lcbo.com** for information about products and special in-store events.

   Vintages stores have a different name, but they're still LCBO outlets. Check out the one at Hazelton Lanes (✆ **416/924-9463**) and at Queen's Quay (✆ **416/864-6777**).

GIFTS & UNIQUE ITEMS

B&J Trading (Finds)   I never learned how to wrap gifts nicely, but that hasn't mattered since I discovered B&J in Chinatown. This store stocks a wide assortment of goods, but its claim to fame is the gift-prep department. The store has unusual wrapping papers, bows, and bags—but best of all are the beautiful presentation boxes that could almost be gifts themselves. 378 Spadina Ave. © 416/586-9655. Subway: Spadina and then a streetcar south to Nassau St.

French Country ★ (Finds)   Owner Viola Jull spent several years living in France, and she re-creates a Parisian atmosphere in her shop, selling such one-of-a-kind items as painted lampshades, antique silver, and framed prints. She also carries a few gourmet food products and hand-milled soaps. 6 Roxborough St. W. © 416/944-2204. Subway: Rosedale.

The Paper Place ★ (Finds)   In addition to being popular with artists, this shop has all the boxes, papers, and handmade cards you could ever need to create exquisite gift-wrappings. Better yet, it stocks instruction books! 887 Queen St. W. © 416/703-0089. www.thepaperplace.ca. Subway: Osgoode and then any streetcar west to Ossington Ave.

Teatro Verde   Life is drama, so why should the items you fill your home with be dull? That seems to be the question at Teatro Verde, where even table coasters are things of great beauty. Hazelton Lanes. © 416/966-2227. www.teatroverde.com. Subway: Bay.

Ten Thousand Villages ★   Everything at these stores arrived via fair-trade programs, so the artisans who make the items benefit directly from the sale of their work. In addition to hand-crafted housewares, there's jewelry, toys, and shea-butter skin-care products. There are branches at 474 Bloor St. West (© **416/533-8476**) and 362 Danforth Ave. (© **416/462-9779**). 709 Queen St. W. © 416/703-2263. www.tenthousandvillages. com. Subway: Osgoode and then streetcar west to Bathurst.

HEALTH & BEAUTY

Elizabeth Milan Hotel Day Spa ★   Even if you don't have time for the spa, you will appreciate the well-stocked shop in its foyer. Elizabeth Milan carries a terrific array of products by brands such as Guinot, Dr. Renaud, and Phytomer. Fairmont Royal York, 100 Front St. W. © 416/350-7500. www.elizabethmilanspa.com. Subway: Union.

Lush   This clever U.K.-based emporium stocks a selection of fizzy bath bombs, skin lotions and potions, and an ever-changing variety of soaps stacked in jagged, jewel-colored slabs. All products are sold by weight. 312 Queen St. W. © 416/599-5874. www.lush.com. Subway: Osgoode.

M.A.C. ★   M.A.C. was founded in Toronto and is now owned by Estée Lauder. This flagship store is perpetually packed, especially on weekends, but if you call ahead you can schedule an appointment for a makeup lesson. In addition to cosmetics, the store carries skin- and hair-care supplies. 89 Bloor St. W. © 416/929-7555. www.maccosmetics.com. Subway: Bay.

Noah's (Value)   This is a mecca for health nuts. Noah's boasts aisle after aisle of vitamins and dietary supplements, organic foods and "natural" candies, skin-care and bath products, and books and periodicals. The staff is well informed and helpful. A smaller but more centrally located outlet is at 667 Yonge St. (at Bloor; © **416/969-0220**). 322 Bloor St. W. © 416/968-7930. Subway: Spadina.

Thompson's Homeopathic Supplies (Finds)   This is just like an old-fashioned apothecary, with endless rows of potions behind a wooden counter. It has a homeopathic remedy for everything from the common cold to dermatitis to conjunctivitis. The staff is friendly and knowledgeable. 844 Yonge St. ✆ **416/922-2300.** Subway: Yonge/Bloor.

JEWELRY

Anne Sportun Experimetal Jewellery   Some of Sportun's sterling silver, gold, and platinum creations have won design awards. She also custom-makes engagement and wedding bands. 742 Queen St. W. ✆ **416/363-4114.** www.experimetal.com. Subway: Osgoode and then streetcar west to Claremont.

Birks ★   This Canadian institution, founded in 1879, is synonymous with top quality. Among the silver, crystal, and china is an extensive selection of fine jewelry, including exquisite pearls and knockout diamond engagement rings (the diamonds themselves were mined in northern Canada). A children's section is filled with such keepsakes as Royal Doulton Bunnykins china and whimsical picture frames by Nova Scotia's Seagull Pewter. My personal favorite is the showcase of antique estate jewelry. A smaller branch is at the Eaton Centre (✆ **416/979-9311**). Manulife Centre, 55 Bloor St. W. ✆ **416/922-2266.** www. birks.com. Subway: Bay.

Mink (Finds)   In gangsterspeak, a "mink" is a sexy woman—exactly the type who would love the fabulous fakes at this boutique. Many of the necklaces, bracelets, and rings are Canadian-designed, but a few are Euro imports. 550 College St. ✆ **416/929-9214.** Subway: Queen's Park and then streetcar west to Euclid Ave.

Royal de Versailles Jewellers   This shop carries an eye-catching assortment of pearls, gold, and platinum. The designs range from classic to funkier, playful styles. There are also watches by the likes of Piaget, Cartier, Rolex, and Tag Heuer, as well as a Bulgari boutique. 101 Bloor St. W. ✆ **416/967-7201.** Subway: Bay.

Silverbridge   Most of the necklaces, bracelets, rings, and earrings here are silver, but a few are in 18-karat gold and platinum. Designer Costin Lazar has a modern sensibility, and he will also take on custom work. Watches by Georg Jensen and Ole Mathiesen are also available. 162 Cumberland St. ✆ **416/923-2591.** www.silverbridge.com. Subway: Bay.

Tiffany & Co.   Diamonds are still a girl's best friend at this Art Deco–style shop. Precious gems and designs by Elsa Peretti and Paloma Picasso are on the first level; the second floor holds silver jewelry, stationery, and housewares. 85 Bloor St. W. ✆ **416/921-3900.** www.tiffany.com. Subway: Bay.

LEATHER GOODS

Taschen!   Exclusive designer handbags, luggage, wallets, and other accessories are mainstays here. Many are European imports, and quality is high. 162 Cumberland St. ✆ **416/961-3185.** Subway: Bay.

MALLS & SHOPPING CENTERS

Atrium on Bay   This two-level complex has more than 60 shops selling clothing, jewelry, furniture, and more. Bay and Dundas sts. ✆ **416/980-2801.** Subway: Dundas.

Bayview Village ★ (Finds)   Think that you hate malls? Visit this one before you swear them off. Elegantly designed and moderately sized, Bayview Village is home to several independent boutiques as well as some chain stores (such as the best Chapters bookstore in the city). It's also a place to come for excellent food: The Oliver & Bonacini restaurant is here. 2901 Bayview Ave. (at Sheppard Ave.). ✆ **416/226-0404.** Subway: Bayview.

College Park This shopping center was under renovation forever, but now it houses a giant Winners store (see "The Best Bargains" on p. 188). 444 Yonge St. ✆ **416/597-1221.** Subway: College.

Eaton Centre It's odd that one of urban Toronto's main attractions is a mall—but oh, what a mall. More than 285 shops and restaurants spread over four levels in the Eaton Centre, which takes up 2 entire city blocks. 220 Yonge St. ✆ **416/598-2322.** www.toronto eatoncentre.com. Subway: Dundas or Queen.

Fairview Mall This massive shopping complex with its 260 stores has been around for years, but until the Sheppard subway line opened, it wasn't easily accessible by public transit. Now that the subway brings you right to the door, you can easily shop at Toronto's first H&M store, as well as The Bay, Sears, Birks, Femme de Carriere, La Scnza, Harry Rosen, and Danier. 1800 Sheppard Ave E. ✆ **416/491-0151.** www.fairviewmall.com. Subway: Don Mills.

First Canadian Place ★ A piece of the labyrinth of the underground city, this complex houses 120 shops and restaurants, and stages free noontime events each week, with performances as diverse as Opera Atelier's Handel recital and the dancing monks of the Tibetan Drikung Monastery. Ongoing art exhibitions are also featured. King and Bay sts. ✆ **416/862-8138.** Subway: King.

Hazelton Lanes ★ A byword for elegance and extravagance, Hazelton is a two-level complex with about 90 shops, including the Whole Foods Market. The charming courtyard at the center transforms into an ice-skating rink in winter. 55 Avenue Rd. ✆ **416/968-8602.** www.hazeltonlanes.com. Subway: Bay.

Holt Renfrew Centre Anchored by the chic Holt Renfrew department store, this small underground concourse is more down to earth price-wise. It connects with the Manulife Centre and the Hudson's Bay Centre. 50 Bloor St. W. ✆ **416/923-2255.** Subway: Yonge/Bloor.

Manulife Centre ★ More than 50 posh shops—including William Ashley, Indigo Books Music & More, and a top-notch LCBO outlet (Liquor Control Board of Ontario)—occupy this complex. The Manulife connects to the Holt Renfrew Centre underground. 55 Bloor St. W. ✆ **416/923-9525.** Subway: Bay.

Royal Bank Plaza Part of Toronto's underground city, the Royal Bank Plaza connects to Union Station and to the Royal York Hotel. Its 60-plus outlets include a variety of shops, two full-service restaurants, and a food court. The building above is worth a look, too. See p. 145. Bay and Front sts. ✆ **416/974-5570.** Subway: Union.

MARKETS

Kensington Market ★ This neighborhood has changed dramatically in the past 40 years. Originally a Jewish community, it now borders on Chinatown. It contains several Asian herbalists and grocers, as well as West Indian and Middle Eastern shops. Kensington Avenue has the greatest concentration of vintage clothing stores in the city. For a full description, see "Walking Tour 1: Chinatown & Kensington Market," in chapter 8. Along Baldwin, Kensington, and Augusta aves. No phone. Subway: Spadina and then LRT to Baldwin St. or Dundas St. W.

St. Lawrence Market This market is a local favorite for fresh produce, and it even draws people who live a good distance away. Hours are Tuesday through Thursday from 8am to 6pm, Friday from 8am to 7pm, and Saturday from 5am (when the farmers arrive) to 5pm.

(Tips) **An Outlet for People Who Hate Outlets**

While I have no problem digging through mounds of dross to unearth a gem (witness my love of Kensington Market shopping), I know that lots of people feel quite differently. If you fall into that latter camp, let me suggest a place you can find deals without too much trouble. **Vaughan Mills** is a massive shopping complex 32km north of Toronto (close to Canada's Wonderland; see p. 136). This clean, modern mall is home to **Holt Renfrew Last Call** (the only Holt Renfrew discount center in the province), the world's largest **Tommy Hilfiger** store, and Canada's largest **Toys R Us/Babies R Us.** Most of the stores in Vaughan Mills aren't outlets, but there are just enough to make sure you get an easy deal (plus there's a massive **Winners** store—do you really need more?). The only catch is that you do need to drive to get here (take Hwy 401 to Hwy 400, then drive north, and exit at Bass Pro Mills Dr., which leads directly to the mall). For more information, call ✆ **905/879-2110** or visit www.vaughanmills.com.

See p. 150 for a complete description. 92 Front St. E. ✆ **416/392-7219.** www.stlawrencemarket.com. Subway: Union.

MUSIC

HMV   This is the flagship Toronto store of the British chain. (You'll find smaller outlets throughout the city.) The selection of pop, rock, jazz, and classical music is large. Best of all, you can listen to a CD before you buy it. 333 Yonge St. ✆ **416/586-9668.** Subway: Dundas.

The Music Store   On the Toronto Symphony Orchestra's home turf, this attractive shop includes several TSO CDs in its collection of classical and choral music. Roy Thomson Hall, 60 Simcoe St. ✆ **416/593-4822.** Subway: St. Andrew.

Rotate This ★ (Finds   Low-key but well stocked, this is an excellent bet if you're interested in the local indie scene. In addition to CDs (new and used), there's plenty of vinyl, with countertop turntables you can use as listening stations. 801 Queen St. W. ✆ **416/504-8447.** Subway: Osgoode and then streetcar west to Claremont.

Wild East ★ (Finds   This is a great source for new and secondhand CDs and DVDs. Wild East is a strong supporter of both local talent and international indie acts, so you'll find music here that you won't get anywhere else. 360 Danforth Ave. ✆ **416/469-8371.** Subway: Chester.

SEX TOYS

Lovecraft ★   Believe it or not, Lovecraft is downright wholesome. Sure, there are the requisite bad-girl (and -boy) lingerie and toys, but much of the shop stocks joke gifts, T-shirts with suggestive slogans, and an impressive collection of erotic literature (no porn mags). The staff is friendly and the atmosphere playful. 27 Yorkville Ave. ✆ **877/923-7331** or 416/923-7331. www.lovecraftsexshop.com. Subway: Bay.

TOYS

George's Trains (Kids   Everything the young (or young at heart) could want to set up a model train set is here, including wooden trains and train kits, tracks, stations, and

scenic backdrops. 510 Mount Pleasant Rd. 🕿 **416/489-9783.** www.georgestrains.com. Subway:
Davisville, then bus no. 11 or 28 to Mount Pleasant, and walk 1 block north.

Kidding Awound (Kids) (Finds)   Wind-up gadgets are the specialty here—hundreds of
'em. There are also some antique toys (which you won't let the kids near) and gag gifts.
91 Cumberland St. 🕿 **416/926-8996.** Subway: Bay.

The Little Dollhouse Company ★   This toy store isn't really for kids. It's beloved
by adults in search of miniature tea services and wicker furniture. It also sells nine different dollhouse kits, from a stately Victorian mansion to a ranch bungalow. 612 Mt. Pleasant
Rd. 🕿 **416/489-7180.** www.littledollhousecompany.com. Subway: Eglinton and then bus no. 34
east to Mount Pleasant, and walk 2 blocks south.

Science City ★ (Kids)   Kids and adults alike will love this tiny store filled with games,
puzzles, models, kits, and books—all related to science. Whether your interest is astron-
omy, biology, chemistry, archaeology, or physics, you'll find something here. Holt Renfrew
Centre, 50 Bloor St. W. 🕿 **416/968-2627.** www.sciencecity.ca. Subway: Yonge/Bloor.

The Toy Shop ★ (Kids)   Toronto's oldest toy shop (it was founded in 1908) carries toys,
many of them educational, from around the world. It also stocks a good selection of books,
games, and videos. 62 Cumberland St. 🕿 **416/961-4870.** www.thetoyshop.ca. Subway: Bay.

Toronto After Dark

Toronto has a vital and varied nightlife scene. Renowned local artists and troupes include the Canadian Stage Company, the Canadian Opera Company, the National Ballet of Canada, Soulpepper, the Tafelmusik Baroque Orchestra, and the Toronto Symphony Orchestra. The city is also a mecca for top-notch theater—you can sometimes see shows before they reach New York or London (the world premiere of the *Lord of the Rings* musical opened in Toronto in 2006 before heading to London's West End). Toronto's many dance and music venues also host the crème de la crème of international performers. Some of the best entertainment is in Toronto's comedy clubs, which have served as training grounds for stars such as Jim Carrey, Mike Myers, Dan Aykroyd, and John Candy. The nightclub scene moves at a frenetic pace. Martini bars are perennially popular, though lower-key pool bars are in vogue, too.

MAKING PLANS For listings of local performances and events, check out *Where Toronto* (www.where.ca/toronto) and *Toronto Life* (www.torontolife.com), as well as the *Toronto Star* (www.thestar.com). For up-to-the-minute lists of hot-ticket events, check out the free weeklies *Now* and *Eye,* available around town in newspaper boxes and at bars, cafes, and bookstores. The city website **www.toronto.com** also boasts lengthy lists of performances. Events of particular interest to the gay and lesbian community are listed in *Xtra!* (www.xtra.ca), another free weekly available in newspaper boxes and many bookstores. The **Torontoist** blog (www.torontoist.com) is also a great source for upcoming performances.

GETTING TICKETS For almost any theater, music, or dance event, you can buy tickets from **Ticketmaster** (© **416/870-8000;** www.ticketmaster.ca). To avoid the service charge on each ticket (not just every order) sold over the phone, head to a ticket center. They're scattered throughout the city; call the information line for the lengthy list of locations.

1 THE PERFORMING ARTS

Toronto's arts scene offers something for everyone year-round. The city's arts institutions are widely renowned, and many top-notch international performers pass through town.

THEATER

While it may seem that Toronto favors big-budget musicals—*The Lion King* and *Mamma Mia!* both played here for what felt like forever—a number of excellent smaller companies also exist. Many of the smaller troupes have no permanent performance space, so they move from venue to venue.

The best time to capture the flavor of Toronto's theater life is during the **Fringe Festival** (© **416/966-1062;** www.fringetoronto.com), usually held for 12 days starting in late June or early July. In July and August, try to catch the **Dream in High Park** (© **416/368-3110;** www.canstage.com). It mounts stunning productions of Shakespearean or Canadian plays from the CanStage Company in an outdoor setting.

(Value) Discount Tickets ★

Want to take in a show, but don't want to spend a bundle? Drop by the **T.O. Tix booth** (✆ **416/536-6468,** ext. 40), which sells half-price day-of-performance tickets. The booth is currently in the Yonge-Dundas Square, which is just across the street from the Eaton Centre. T.O. Tix accepts cash, Visa, and MasterCard, and all sales are final. The booth is open Tuesday to Saturday from noon to 7:30pm; it's closed Sunday and Monday (tickets for performances on those days are sold on Sat).

Landmark Theaters & Performance Venues

Canon Theatre ★ The Canon has had a tumultuous history. It got its start as the Pantages Theatre in 1920, and its opulent design (by the famous theater architect Thomas Lamb) was widely admired. However, the theater's fortunes sank in 1929—not because of the stock-market crash, but because its owner was embroiled in a legal battle. Eventually, the gorgeous space was carved into six cinemas. It was rescued and dramatically renovated by the Livent production company, which also brought back its original name, and the new 2,250-seat Pantages Theatre was home for many years to the lavish Andrew Lloyd Webber show *The Phantom of the Opera*. But after Livent collapsed, the theater went dark for a long time. Fortunately, its current owners—who have renamed it the Canon—have turned over the theater's management and programming to Mirvish Productions (owned by "Honest Ed" Mirvish, who has done more to revitalize Toronto's theater scene than anyone else). Recent productions have included *The Producers* and *Spamalot*. 244 Victoria St. ✆ **416/872-1212.** www.mirvish.com. Tickets from C$40 (£20). Subway: Dundas or Queen.

The Elgin and Winter Garden Theatre Centre ★ These landmark theaters first opened their doors in 1913, and today they vie with the Royal Alex and the Princess of Wales Theatre for major shows and attention. Recent productions have included *Avenue Q*.

Both the Elgin and the Winter Garden have been restored to their original gilded glory. They are the only double-decker theaters in Toronto. The downstairs Elgin is larger, seating 1,500 and featuring a lavish domed ceiling and gilded decoration on the boxes and proscenium. Hand-painted frescoes adorn the striking interior of the 1,000-seat Winter Garden. Suspended from its ceiling and lit with lanterns are more than 5,000 branches of beech leaves, which have been preserved, painted, and fireproofed. Both theaters offer everything from Broadway musicals and dramas to concerts and opera performances. 189 Yonge St. ✆ **416/872-5555** for tickets or 416/314-2901 for administration. Tickets from C$35 (£18). Subway: Queen.

Four Seasons Centre for the Performing Arts ★★★ Toronto's opera house, which opened in June 2006, is a beauty. Designed by architect Jack Diamond, it has a simple exterior, which looks like nothing so much as a house of glass. Inside, in the tradition of truly grand opera houses, there are three stages: main, rear, and side. But the masterstroke in the Four Seasons Centre's design is in its perfect acoustics. This was no small feat given that the structure is set on not one but two major thoroughfares, and a subway line rumbles beneath it. This is home to both the Canadian Opera Company (p. 212) and the National Ballet of Canada (p. 216). 145 Queen St. W. ✆ **416/363-8231** for tickets or 416/363-6671 for administration. www.fourseasonscentre.ca. Tickets from C$45 (£23). Subway: Osgoode.

PERFORMING ARTS
Air Canada Centre **30**
Buddies in Bad Times Theatre **49**
Canadian Opera Company **27**
Canadian Stage Company **33**
Canon Theatre **44**
The Carlu **50**
Cinematheque Ontario **4**
Distillery District **38**
The Elgin and Winter Garden
    Theatre Centre **43**
Factory Theatre **7**
Four Seasons Centre for the
    Performing Arts **27**
Glenn Gould Studio **19**
Lorraine Kimsa Theatre for
    Young People **37**
Massey Hall **42**
Molson Amphitheatre **17**
Native Earth Performing Arts
    Theatre **38**
Premiere Dance Theatre **29**
Princess of Wales Theatre **22**
Rogers Centre **18**
Roy Thomson Hall **20**
Royal Alexandra Theatre **21**
Scotiabank Theatre Toronto **13**
Sony Centre for the
    Performing Arts **32**
St. James' Cathedral **39**
The St. Lawrence Centre
    for the Arts **33**
St. Michael's Cathedral **41**
St. Patrick's Church **51**
Soulpepper **38**
Theatre Passe Muraille **5**
Toronto Mendelssohn Choir **20**
Toronto Symphony Orchestra **20**
Yonge-Dundas Square **45**

CLUBS, MUSIC & BARS
Afterlife **23**
Balzac's Coffee **38**
Barrio **40**
The Ben Wicks **46**
Byzantium **48**
Cameron House **9**
C'est What? **36**
Circa **15**
Crews, Tango and The Zone **48**
Foundation Room **35**
Gypsy Co-Op **6**
The Horseshoe Tavern **10**
Irish Embassy **31**
The Laugh Resort **14**
Laurentian Room **46**
The Library Bar **28**
The Lounge **6**
The Melody Bar **6**
Mill Street Brew Pub **38**
Park Lane **24**
Pegasus Bar **49**
Phoenix Concert Theatre **47**
Reservoir Lounge **34**
The Rex Hotel Jazz &
    Blues Bar **25**
The Rivoli **11**
Sailor **48**
Second City **16**
Sneaky Dee's **2**
Supermarket **3**
Sutra Tiki Bar **1**
This Is London **12**
The Underground **6**
Wheat Sheaf Tavern **8**
Woody's **48**
Yuk Yuk's Supper Club **26**
Zelda's **48**

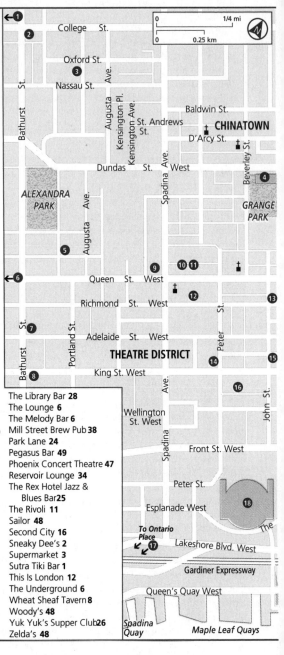

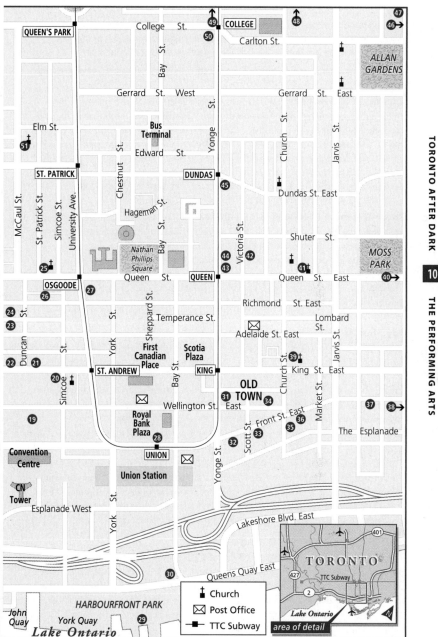

(Tips) Farther Afield

Don't forget that two major theater festivals—the **Shaw Festival** (www.shawfest. com) in Niagara-on-the-Lake and the **Stratford Festival** (www.stratfordfestival. ca) in Stratford—are only an hour or two away. See chapter 11 for details.

Princess of Wales Theatre ★   This spectacular 2,000-seat, state-of-the-art facility was built for the production of *Miss Saigon,* with a stage large enough to accommodate the landing of the helicopter in that production. Later, it was home to *The Lion King* and *Hairspray,* and in 2006 the world premiere of the stage adaptation of the epic *The Lord of the Rings* opened here. More recently, it featured *The Sound of Music.* Frank Stella, who painted 929 sq. m (10,000 sq. ft.) of colorful murals, decorated the exterior and interior walls. People in wheelchairs have access to all levels of the theater (not the norm in Toronto). 300 King St. W. ✆ 416/872-1212. www.mirvish.com. Tickets from C$45 (£23). Subway: St. Andrew.

Royal Alexandra Theatre ★★   The 1,495-seat Royal Alex is a magnificent spectacle, never mind the show! Constructed in 1907, it owes its current health to discount-store czar and impresario Ed Mirvish, who refurbished it (as well as the surrounding area) in the 1960s. Inside, it's a riot of plush reds, gold brocade, and baroque ornamentation. Recent productions here have included *Mamma Mia!,* the ABBA-inspired musical, and *Dirty Dancing,* a show inspired by the 1987 Patrick Swayze movie. Avoid the vertigo-inducing second balcony and the seats "under the circle," which don't have the greatest sight lines. 260 King St. W. ✆ 416/872-1212. www.mirvish.com. Tickets from C$45 (£23). Subway: St. Andrew.

Roy Thomson Hall ★★   This stunning concert hall is home to the Toronto Symphony Orchestra (p. 213), which performs here from September to June, and to the Toronto Mendelssohn Choir (p. 213). Since it opened in 1982, it has also played host to an array of international musical artists. The hall was designed to give the audience a feeling of unusual intimacy with the performers—none of the 2,812 seats is more than 33m (108 ft.) from the stage. 60 Simcoe St. ✆ 416/872-4255 for tickets or 416/593-4822 for administration. www.roythomson.com. Tickets from C$40 (£20). Subway: St. Andrew.

The St. Lawrence Centre for the Arts ★   For three decades, the St. Lawrence Centre has presented top-notch theater, music, and dance performances. The Bluma Appel Theatre is home to the Canadian Stage Company (p. 211), and the smaller Jane Mallet Theatre features the Toronto Operetta Theatre Company, among others. This is a popular spot for lectures, too. In 2006 and 2007, the complex was renovated and updated. 27 Front St. E. ✆ 416/366-7723. www.stlc.com. Tickets from C$30 (£15). Mon night pay what you can. Senior and student discounts may be available 30 min. before performance. Subway: Union.

Major Concert Halls & Auditoriums

The Carlu   Located on the seventh floor of College Park, this was considered one of the grandest concert halls in Canada when it opened in 1931; like so many other venues in Toronto, the Carlu was shuttered in the 1970s. Now the 1,200-seat concert hall is back in favor, and its architecture is believed to be one of the best surviving examples of Art Moderne in the world (it was created by Jacques Carlu, the architect also responsible for New York's Rainbow Room). The concerts here tend to be charity benefits, with big price tags in tickets. College Park, 444 Yonge St., 7th Floor. ✆ 416/597-1931. www.thecarlu.com. Tickets from C$150 (£75). Subway: College.

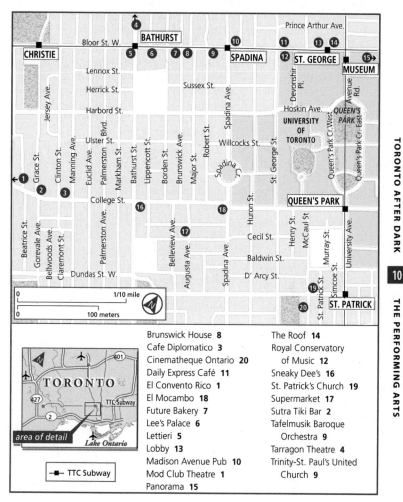

Brunswick House **8**
Cafe Diplomatico **3**
Cinematheque Ontario **20**
Daily Express Café **11**
El Convento Rico **1**
El Mocambo **18**
Future Bakery **7**
Lee's Palace **6**
Lettieri **5**
Lobby **13**
Madison Avenue Pub **10**
Mod Club Theatre **1**
Panorama **15**

The Roof **14**
Royal Conservatory
  of Music **12**
Sneaky Dee's **16**
St. Patrick's Church **19**
Supermarket **17**
Sutra Tiki Bar **2**
Tafelmusik Baroque
  Orchestra **9**
Tarragon Theatre **4**
Trinity-St. Paul's United
  Church **9**

TORONTO AFTER DARK

10

THE PERFORMING ARTS

Distillery District ★★★   This was once the home of the Gooderham-Worts Distillery, which was Canada's largest distilling company in the 19th century. The 45-building complex is an outstanding example of industrial design from the Victorian age (p. 132). In 2003, it was reinvented as the Distillery District, which includes galleries, restaurants, and shops. The district also houses several performing-arts venues, including the **Case Goods Theatre** and the state-of-the-art **Young Centre for the Performing Arts.** The Dancemakers (p. 214), Soulpepper (p. 212), and Native Earth (p. 211) troupes now perform here. 55 Mill St. ✆ **416/367-1800.** www.thedistillerydistrict.com. Tickets from C$25 (£13). Subway: King and then a streetcar east to Parliament St.

Glenn Gould Studio ★   Located on the main floor of the Canadian Broadcasting Centre, this 341-seat radio concert hall offers chamber, jazz, and spoken-word performances. Its name celebrates the great, eccentric Toronto pianist whose life was cut short by a stroke in 1982. 250 Front St. W. ☎ **416/205-5555.** www.glenngouldstudio.cbc.com. Tickets from C$25 (£13). Subway: Union.

Massey Hall   This landmark 1892 building is one of Canada's premier music venues. Its 2,753 seats aren't the most comfortable, but the flawless acoustics will make you stop squirming. The music performances run from classical to pop to rock to jazz, with recent stops by the likes of Diana Krall, Jewel, Prince, and Pink. This is also a popular stop for lectures. 178 Victoria St. ☎ **416/872-4255** for tickets or 416/593-4822 for administration. www.masseyhall.com. Tickets from C$35 (£18). Subway: King.

Premiere Dance Theatre   Part of the sprawling Harbourfront Centre (p. 125) by the waterfront, this 446-seat hall is specifically designed for dance performances. Here is where you can catch some of Toronto's leading contemporary dance companies. Queen's Quay Terminal, 207 Queens Quay W. ☎ **416/973-4000.** www.harbourfrontcentre.com. Tickets from C$35 (£18). Subway: Union and then LRT to York Quay.

Sony Centre for the Performing Arts   If you visited Toronto before 1997, you might remember this as the O'Keefe Centre; if you visited before the fall of 2007, it was the Hummingbird Centre. The Sony Centre is currently undergoing a top-to-bottom transformation. Architect Daniel Libeskind, the man responsible for the Royal Ontario Museum's crystal galleries (p. 134), has designed a 49-storey residential tower that will loom over the theater, which will also be completely overhauled. There's no information at press time about when the theatre will be closed, so check the website for updates. 1 Front St. E. ☎ **416/872-2262.** www.sonycentre.ca. Subway: Union.

Toronto Centre for the Arts   Built in 1993, this gigantic complex is home to the Toronto Philharmonia, an acclaimed classical orchestra. It also hosts international performers and shows such as *Jersey Boys* (in April and May 2009, Neil Simon's *The Sunshine Boys* will be staged here). 5040 Yonge St. ☎ **416/733-9388.** www.tocentre.com. Tickets from C$40 (£20). Subway: North York Centre.

Yonge-Dundas Square ★   Toronto's open-air entertainment venue is across the street from the Eaton Centre. Summer is its liveliest season: Events include a Tuesday-night film series and a Summer Serenades series featuring local musicians. When not in use for events, Yonge-Dundas is a public square where you can stroll or sit by the fountains. Year-round, this is home to the T.O. Tix discount-tickets booth (p. 205). Yonge and Dundas, southeast corner. ☎ **416/979-9960.** www.ydsquare.ca. Free admission. Subway: Dundas.

Theater Companies & Smaller Theaters

Buddies in Bad Times Theatre ★   Established in 1979, this "gay, lesbian, and queer" theater company produces edgy and provocative new Canadian works. Their work is not for everyone (the list of upcoming productions identifies shows that are "not for the faint of heart," and they mean it), but Buddies produces shows that you simply won't see anywhere else. The theater also stages Canadian adaptations of some well-known works, such as Ibsen's *Hedda Gabler.* American Sky Gilbert has helped build the theater's cutting-edge reputation. 12 Alexander St. ☎ **416/975-8555.** www.artsexy.ca. Tickets from C$20 (£10); some performances are pay-what-you-can admission. Subway: Wellesley.

(Finds) More Than Church Music ★

Everyone knows that a church is where you go to listen to choir music—but in Toronto, several churches double as performance spaces for classical or opera ensembles. **Trinity-St. Paul's United Church,** 427 Bloor St. W. (✆ **416/964-6337;** www.tspucc.org), is home to Toronto's acclaimed Tafelmusik Baroque Orchestra (p. 213). **St. James' Cathedral,** at 65 Church St. (✆ **416/364-7865;** www.stjames cathedral.on.ca), hosts everything from solo performances of classical cellists to youth choirs from abroad. **St. Patrick's Church,** 141 McCaul St. (✆ **416/483-0559**), is where the **Tallis Choir of Toronto** (✆ **416/286-9798;** www.tallischoir. com) often performs (the choir's repertoire is mostly Renaissance and Tudor music). And if you happen to love real church music, stop in at **St. Michael's Cathedral,** 65 Bond St. (✆ **416/364-0234;** www.stmichaelscathedral.com). Its own Boys Choir has won international competitions.

Canadian Stage Company ★★   Formerly known as CanStage, this company performs an eclectic variety of Canadian and international plays. You'll see some shows here that you won't see anywhere else (my recent favorite was *Letters From Lehrer,* a tribute to the musical genius of Tom Lehrer). They perform at the St. Lawrence Centre, seating 500 to 600, and the Berkeley Theatre, a more avant-garde, intimate space.

The Canadian Stage Company also presents open-air summer theater—traditionally Shakespeare—in High Park. It's known as the **Dream in High Park.** The company frequently stages Canadian-written works, too. Berkeley Theatre, 26 Berkeley St., and St. Lawrence Centre, 27 Front St. E. ✆ 416/368-3110. www.canstage.com. Tickets from C$30 (£15). Mon night pay what you can. Senior and student discounts may be available 30 min. before performance. Subway: Union for St. Lawrence Centre. King, and then any streetcar east to Berkeley St. for Berkeley Theatre.

Factory Theatre ★   Since it opened in 1970, the Factory Theatre has focused on presenting Canadian plays, from political dramas to over-the-top comedies. The theater likes to call itself "the home of the Canadian playwright," and all of the works staged here are by homegrown talent. Performances showcase up-and-coming scribes as well as established playwrights, so the options veer from experimental to traditional. 125 Bathurst St. ✆ 416/504-9971. www.factorytheatre.ca. Tickets from C$25 (£13). Subway: St. Andrew and then any streetcar west.

Lorraine Kimsa Theatre for Young People ★★ (Kids)   Toronto's such a theater town that even tiny tots (and the rest of the family) get their own performance center. The always-enjoyable Lorraine Kimsa Theatre (formerly known as the Young People's Theatre) mounts whimsical productions such as *Jacob Two-Two Meets the Hooded Fang* (by the late, great Mordecai Richler) and children's classics such as *Pinocchio* and *You're a Good Man, Charlie Brown.* This theater company is particularly committed to diversity in its programming and in its artists. 165 Front St. E. ✆ 416/862-2222 for tickets or 416/363-5131 for administration. www.lktyp.ca. Tickets from C$15 (£7.50). Subway: Union.

Native Earth Performing Arts Theatre   This small company is dedicated to performing works that express and dramatize the native Canadian experience. Playwright Thomson Highway, who authored *Dry Lips Oughta Move to Kapuskasing,* was one of the company's founders. The company also performs at other theaters around town. Performing at the Case Goods Theatre in the Distillery District, 55 Mill St. ℂ 416/367-1800. www.nativeearth. ca. Tickets from C$15 (£7.50). Subway: King and then a streetcar east to Parliament St.

Soulpepper ★★ Founded in 1997, this artist-founded classical repertory company presents theatrical masterpieces. The highly respected—and award-winning—group has recently staged Anton Chekhov's *Uncle Vanya* and Lorraine Hansberry's *A Raisin in the Sun*. Performing at the Young Centre in the Distillery District, 55 Mill St. ℂ 416/866-8666. www.soul pepper.ca. Tickets from C$40 (£20). Subway: King and then a streetcar east to Parliament St.

Tarragon Theatre ★ The Tarragon Theatre opened in 1971. It produces original works by such famous Canadian literary figures as Michel Tremblay, Michael Ondaatje, and Judith Thompson, and an occasional classic or off-Broadway play. There are two small theaters on site—or three, if you count the 60-seat rehearsal hall, which is occasionally used for performances. 30 Bridgman Ave. (near Dupont and Bathurst sts.). ℂ 416/531-1827 or 416/536-5018 for administration. www.tarragontheatre.com. Tickets from C$25 (£13). Sun pay what you can. Subway: Bathurst.

Theatre Passe Muraille This theater started in the late 1960s, when a pool of actors began experimenting and improvising original Canadian material. It continues to produce innovative, provocative theater by such contemporary Canadian playwrights as John Mighton, Daniel David Moses, and Wajdi Mouawad. There are two stages—the Mainspace seats 220; the more intimate Backspace, 70. 16 Ryerson Ave. ℂ 416/504-7529. www.passemuraille.on.ca. Tickets from C$25 (£13) Subway: Osgoode and then any streetcar west to Bathurst.

CLASSICAL MUSIC & OPERA

Canadian Opera Company ★★★ Canada's largest opera company, the sixth-largest in North America, was founded in 1950. Its performances take place at the Four Seasons Centre for the Performing Arts (p. 205), a venue that was built with opera aficionados in mind. To give you an idea of how popular the Canadian Opera Company is, its performances have been at 99% capacity in 2007 and 2008. More than three-quarters

---

ⓕinds   Opera Obsessed ★

It was big news in 2006 when Toronto's opera house—the Four Seasons Centre for the Performing Arts—opened its doors for the first time. The irony was that Toronto, a city that had never before possessed an opera house, was already the North American magnet for opera lovers. And while I'm a huge fan of the **Canadian Opera Company** (see above), it was just one reason to visit. Others include **Opera Atelier** (ℂ 416/703-3767; www.operaatelier.com), a renowned company that produces baroque operas (Monteverdi, Mozart, and Gluck are perennially popular). The **Toronto Opera Repertoire** (ℂ 416/698-9572; www.toronto-opera.com) is dedicated to making opera accessible to all, using supertitles in English and keeping ticket prices democratically low. **Tapestry New Opera Works** (ℂ 416/ 537-6066; www.tapestrynewopera.com) is dedicated to the production of original works of Canadian opera and musical theater. A favorite of mine is the **Queen of Puddings Music Theatre** (ℂ 416/203-4149; www.queenofpuddingsmusic theatre.com) which offers a provocative and fantastical take on chamber opera; the company has performed in London's Convent Garden.

ⓥ Value Great Music on a Budget

As the cost of concert tickets spirals ever upward, it can be frustrating to budget for an evening out. But there are some places you can count on scoring a deal. My personal best bet is **University of Toronto's Faculty of Music** (ℂ **416/978-3744;** www.music.utoronto.ca), which offers a full range of instrumental and choral concerts and recitals. They are held at various locations around the St. George Campus, and some performances are free of charge (others cost up to C$22/£11). It's also worth checking out who's performing at the **Royal Conservatory of Music,** 273 Bloor St. W. (ℂ **416/408-2825;** www.rcmusic.ca). There are concerts by well-known jazz vocalists or international ensembles (which cost about C$20/£10 per ticket), as well as free recitals given by faculty members and students.

of the tickets are held by subscribers, making this a tough "get" for visitors—so plan ahead. The Canadian Opera Company's 2008–2009 season includes productions of *Don Giovanni, La Boheme,* and *A Midsummer Night's Dream.* 145 Queen St. W. ℂ 416/363-8231 for tickets or 416/363-6671 for administration. www.coc.ca. Tickets from C$60 (£30). Subway: Osgoode.

Tafelmusik Baroque Orchestra ★ This internationally acclaimed group plays baroque compositions by the likes of Handel, Bach, and Mozart on authentic period instruments. Visiting musicians frequently join the 19 permanent performers. It gives a series of concerts at **Trinity-St. Paul's United Church,** 47 Bloor St. W., and stages other performances in Massey Hall (p. 210) and the Toronto Centre for the Arts (p. 210). 427 Bloor St. W. ℂ 416/964-6337. www.tafelmusik.org. Tickets from C$30 (£15). Subway: Yonge/Bloor for Trinity-St. Paul's; King for Massey Hall; North York Centre for Toronto Centre for the Arts.

Toronto Mendelssohn Choir ★ This world-renowned group first performed in Massey Hall in 1895. Today, it calls Roy Thomson Hall home. Its repertoire ranges from Verdi's *Requiem,* Bach's *St. Matthew Passion,* and Handel's *Messiah* to the soundtrack of *Schindler's List.* 60 Simcoe St. ℂ 416/598-0422. www.tmchoir.org. Tickets from C$30 (£15). Subway: St. Andrew.

Toronto Symphony Orchestra ★★ The symphony performs anything from classics to jazzy Broadway tunes to new Canadian works at Roy Thomson Hall from September to June. In June and July, the symphony puts on free concerts at outdoor venues throughout the city. 60 Simcoe St. ℂ 416/593-4828. www.tso.on.ca. Tickets from C$40 (£20). Subway: St. Andrew.

POP & ROCK MUSIC VENUES

Everyone comes to Toronto—even Madonna, who ran into some trouble with the obscenity police a while back (that was before her reincarnation as lady of the manor, of course). Tickets are available through **Ticketmaster** (ℂ **416/870-8000;** www.ticketmaster.ca). In addition to the previously mentioned **Roy Thomson Hall** and **Massey Hall,** these are the major pop and rock music venues.

Air Canada Centre Better known as a sports venue (it's home to the Maple Leafs and the Raptors), the Air Canada Centre also hosts popular musical acts. Neil Young has performed here, as have Ozzy Osbourne, Justin Timberlake, and Mariah Carey. 40 Bay St. (at Lakeshore Blvd). ℭ **416/815-5500.** www.theaircanadacentre.com. Subway: Union and then LRT to Queen's Quay.

Kingswood Music Theatre   From May to September, Kingswood's open-air theater plays host to diverse, top-notch talent. Don Henley, the Beach Boys, the Scorpions, Barry Manilow, and Public Enemy have all played here. The bandshell is covered, but the lawn seats aren't—so beware in bad weather. Paramount Canada's Wonderland, 9580 Jane St., Vaughn. ℭ **905/832-8131.** Subway: Yorkdale or York Mills and then GO Express Bus to Wonderland. By car: Take Yonge St. north to Hwy. 401 and go west to Hwy. 400. Go north on Hwy. 400 to Rutherford Rd. exit and follow signs. From the north, exit at Major Mackenzie.

Molson Amphitheatre ★   This is a favorite summer spot because you can listen to music by the side of Lake Ontario. Most of the seating is on the lawn, and it's usually dirt cheap. Ontario Place, 955 Lakeshore Blvd. W. ℭ **416/314-9900.** www.ontarioplace.com. Subway: Bathurst and then Bathurst streetcar south to Exhibition Place (last stop).

Rogers Centre   This is the biggest venue in the city, and it's where the biggest acts usually play. Ticket prices frequently rise into the stratosphere. This venue is about as intimate as a parking lot. If you're seated in the 400 or 500 levels, you'll be watching the show on the JumboTron unless you bring your binoculars. And remember to steer clear of the seats next to the JumboTron, or you won't see anything at all. 1 Blue Jays Way. ℭ **416/341-3663.** www.rogerscentre.com. Subway: Union.

DANCE

Dancemakers   Artistic director Serge Bennathan's nine-person company has gained international recognition for its provocative mix of stylized physical movement and theater. One of the best-known works in its repertoire is *Sable/Sand,* which won a Dora Award for choreography. Performing at the Case Goods Theatre in the Distillery District, 55 Mill Street. ℭ **416/367-1800.** www.dancemakers.org. Tickets from C$25 (£13).

Danny Grossman Dance Company   This local dance favorite is noted for its athleticism, theatricality, humor, and passionate social vision. Grossman's own choreography is witty and exuberant. The company, which celebrated its 30th anniversary in 2007, performs both new works and revivals of modern-dance classics. Performing at Premiere Dance Theatre, Queen's Quay Terminal, 207 Queens Quay W. ℭ **416/973-4000** for tickets or 416/408-4543 for administration. www.dannygrossman.com. Tickets from C$50 (£25).

National Ballet of Canada ★★★   Perhaps the most beloved and famous of Toronto's cultural icons is the National Ballet of Canada. English ballerina Celia Franca launched the company in Toronto in 1951 and served as director, principal dancer, choreographer, and teacher. Over the years, the company has achieved great renown. The legendary Canadian ballerina Karen Kain became its artistic director in 2005. The company shares the Four Seasons Centre for the Performing Arts (p. 205) with the Canadian Opera Company. Its repertoire includes the classics (you can always count on *The Nutcracker* every Dec) and works by luminaries like George Balanchine. 145 Queen St. W. ℭ **866/345-9595** or 416/345-9595 for tickets or 416/345-9686 for administration. www.national. ballet.ca. Tickets from C$45 (£23). Subway: Osgoode.

Toronto Dance Theatre   The city's leading contemporary-dance company was founded in 1968, bringing an inventive spirit and original Canadian dance to the stage. Christopher House joined in 1979 and became the company's director in 1994. House's choreography is widely acclaimed, and his *Timecode Break* won three prestigious Dora

awards in 2007. Performing at Premiere Dance Theatre, Queen's Quay Terminal, 207 Queens **215**
Quay W. ℂ **416/973-4000.** Office: 80 Winchester St. ℂ 416/967-1365. www.tdt.org. Tickets from
C$35 (£18).

2 THE CLUB & MUSIC SCENE

A few hints before you head out for the evening. The drinking age in Ontario is 19 (that's at press time—some groups are working to raise it to 21), and most establishments enforce the law. Expect long queues on Friday and Saturday after 10pm at clubs in the downtown core. Bars and pubs that serve drinks only are open Monday to Saturday from 11am to 2am. Establishments that also serve food are open Sunday, too. If you're out at closing time, you'll find the subway shut down, but late-night buses run along Yonge and Bloor streets. Major routes on streets such as College, Queen, and King operate all night. To find out what's on, see "Making Plans," earlier in this chapter.

LIVE MUSIC VENUES

C'est What?   This casual spot attracts young and old alike. It offers a wide variety of draft beers—including the perennially popular Homegrown Hemp Ale and the Chocolate Ale—and a broad selection of single malts. Half pub and half performance space, C'est What? has hosted the likes of Jewel, Barenaked Ladies, and Rufus Wainwright before they hit the big time. 67 Front St. E. ℂ **416/867-9499.** www.cestwhat.com. Cover up to–C$10 (£5). Subway: Union.

El Mocambo ★   This rock-'n'-roll institution was where the Rolling Stones rocked in the '70s, Elvis Costello jammed in the '80s, and Liz Phair mesmerized in the '90s. It has played peek-a-boo in recent years—it regularly closes and reopens and once even relocated to another site. Maybe that's why its current headliners include such acts as Vendetta Red and Harold Wartooth (of course, I'll be eating my words about them one day . . .). Its Spadina Avenue digs are open again, and because they've gone through a top-to-toe reno, maybe they'll stay open this time. 464 Spadina Ave. ℂ **416/777-1777.** Cover up to C$20 (£10). Subway: Spadina and then streetcar south to College St.

The Horseshoe Tavern   This lonstanding venue has showcased the sounds of the decades: blues in the '60s, punk in the '70s, New Wave in the '80s, and everything from ska to rockabilly to Celtic to alternative rock in the '90s. It's the place that launched Blue Rodeo, The Tragically Hip, The Band, and Prairie Oyster, and staged the Toronto debuts of The Police and Hootie & the Blowfish. 368 Queen St. W. ℂ **416/598-4753.** www. horseshoetavern.com. Cover up to C$10 (£5); tickets for major artists C$25 (£13). Subway: Osgoode.

Lee's Palace   Versailles this ain't. Still, that hasn't deterred the crème de la crème of the alternative-music scene. Red Hot Chili Peppers, The Tragically Hip, and Alanis Morissette have performed here. Despite the graffiti grunge, Lee's does boast the best sight lines in town. The audience is young and rarely tires of slam dancing in the mosh pit in front of the stage. 529 Bloor St. W. ℂ **416/532-1598.** www.leespalace.com. Cover C$6 (£3) Fri & Sat. Subway: Bathurst.

The Melody Bar ★ (Value)   This is Toronto's favorite karaoke bar, and if you show up on nights from Thursday through Sunday, that's usually what you'll get (the first Friday of every month features bands from around the globe). During the rest of the week, you'll

Comedy Clubs

Toronto must be one heck of a funny place. That would explain why a disproportionate number of comedians, including Jim Carrey and Mike Myers, hail from here. This is one authentic Toronto experience you shouldn't miss.

The Laugh Resort   If you get your kicks from incisive humor with occasional dashes of social commentary, this is your place. Gilbert Gottfried, Paula Poundstone, Ray Romano, and George Wallace have performed here. Most of the acts are stand-up solos, with the occasional inspired improv. At the Holiday Inn on King, 370 King St. W. © **416/364-5233.** www.laughresort.com. Tickets C$7–C$15 (£3.50-£7.50). Subway: St. Andrew.

The Rivoli ★   While the Riv is well known for its music performances, the Monday-night ALT.COMedy Lounge and Tuesday-night Sketch! Comedy Lounge are its biggest draws. The Riv features local and visiting stand-ups, and is best known as the place where the Kids in the Hall got their start. Shows take place in the intimate 125-seat back room. See p. 106 in chapter 6 for a restaurant review. 332-334 Queen St. W. © **416/597-0794.** www.alt comedylounge.com. Pay-what-you-can admission. Subway: Osgoode.

Second City ★   This was where Mike Myers received his formal—and improvisational—comic training. Over the years, the legendary Second City has nurtured the likes of John Candy, Dan Aykroyd, Bill Murray, Martin Short, Andrea Martin, and Eugene Levy. It continues to turn out talented young actors. The scenes are always funny and topical, though the outrageous postshow improvs usually get the biggest laughs. 51 Mercer St. © **800/263-4485** or 416/343-0011. www.secondcity.com. Tickets C$23-C$28 (£12–£14). Reservations required. Subway: St. Andrew.

Yuk Yuk's Superclub   Yuk Yuk's is Canada's original home of stand-up comedy. Comic Mark Breslin founded the place in 1976, inspired by New York's Catch a Rising Star and Los Angeles's Comedy Store. Famous alumni include Jim Carrey, Harland Williams, Howie Mandel, and Norm MacDonald. Jerry Seinfeld, Robin Williams, and Sandra Bernhard have all headlined here. Tuesday is amateur night. Another Yuk Yuk's is in **Mississauga,** not far from Pearson International Airport (© **905/434-4985**). 224 Richmond St. W. © **416/967-6425.** www.yukyuks.com. Show only from C$3–C$19 (£1.50–£9.50); dinner is available from an a la carte menu. Subway: Osgoode.

find local musicians, DJs, and open-mic events. Wednesday is queer night. At the Gladstone Hotel, 1214 Queen St. W. © **416/531-4635.** www.gladstonehotel.com. No cover. Subway: Osgoode and then streetcar west to Gladstone.

The Mod Club Theatre ★   This is one of Toronto's best live music venues. The Mod Club is co-owned by Mark Holmes, the frontman for the '80s band Platinum Blonde (c'mon, you remember them, right? "Standing in the Dark," "Situation Critical," "Sad Sad Rain" . . . I was in elementary school when they were big, but I loved them). In any case, Holmes is the DJ when the concert hall morphs into a dance club after hours. The

Killers, The Tragically Hip, and Amy Winehouse have all performed here. 722 College St.
© **416/588-4MOD.** www.themodclub.com. Cover up to C$15 (£7.50); sometimes higher prices for concerts. Subway: College Park and then streetcar west to Crawford St.

Phoenix Concert Theatre   The Phoenix is an old-school rock venue, and it has a very loyal local following. It has showcased such artists as Screaming Headless Torsos, Warrant, and Patti Smith. On the weekends, it gets the crowds dancing with a mixture of retro, Latin, alternative, and funk. Thursday is gay night. 410 Sherbourne St. © **416/323-1251.** Tickets C$12–C$40 (£6–£20). Subway: College and then any streetcar east to Sherbourne St.

Reservoir Lounge   This perennial favorite is a modern-day speakeasy. The cramped space—it seats only 100—is below street level, yet feels intimate rather than claustrophobic. Live jazz, whether Dixieland, New Orleans, or swing, belts out 7 nights a week. The epicenter for the swing dance craze in Toronto, this is still the place to watch glam hepcats groove. 52 Wellington St. E., lower level. © **416/955-0887.** www.reservoirlounge.com. Cover up to C$10 (£5). Subway: King.

The Rex Hotel Jazz & Blues Bar ★   This casual watering hole has been drawing jazz fans since it opened in 1951. Admittedly, the decor hasn't changed much since the old days, but the sounds you'll find here are cutting-edge. The Rex lures top local and international talent; Tuesday is the weekly jam night. 194 Queen St. W. © **416/598-2475.** www.therex.ca. Cover up to C$10 (£5). Subway: Osgoode.

The Rivoli ★   Currently, this is the club for an eclectic mix of performances, including grunge, blues, rock, jazz, comedy, and poetry reading. Holly Cole launched her career here, Tori Amos made her Toronto debut in the back room, and the Kids in the Hall still consider it home (see "Comedy Clubs," above). Shows begin at 8pm and continue until 2am. Upstairs there's a billiards room and an espresso bar. 332-334 Queen St. W. © **416/596-1908.** Cover up to C$12 (£6). Subway: Osgoode.

Supermarket ★   Kensington Market is famous for its grocery stores, so maybe it's appropriate that this new club is playing on the name. It does offer a wide assortment of live jazz, funk, soul, and reggae. Earlier in the evening, Supermarket is an Asian fusion restaurant, and it occasionally hosts author readings and art events. 268 Augusta St. © **416/840-0501.** www.supermarkettoronto.com. Cover up to C$10 (£5). Subway: Spadina and then streetcar south to College St.

The Underground   In the basement of the Drake Hotel, this venue was designed with flexibility in mind. It's a good thing, too, because the performers who appear here range from local and visiting musical acts to burlesque artists. At the Drake Hotel, 1150 Queen St. W. © **416/531-5042.** Cover up to C$15 (£7.50). Subway: Osgoode and then streetcar west to Beaconsfield.

DANCE CLUBS

Dance clubs come and go at an alarming pace in Toronto. My suggestions below are perennials, so they're almost certainly going to be around when you visit. That means that they're not on the cutting edge, so if you're looking for a hot, hip scene, be sure to check out the club listings in the free weekly *Now* or at **www.martiniboys.com** or **www. torontolife.com** for the latest and greatest. Some things stay constant, though. Most clubs don't have much of a dress code, though "no jeans" rules are not uncommon. And remember, it's always easier to get in earlier rather than later in the evening, when lines start to form.

(Finds) **Literary Types** ★

One of the most reliably interesting reading series in Toronto is organized by Pages Books & Magazines (p. 190). Called **This Is Not a Reading Series** (or TINARS, for short), it runs from September through May and bills itself simply as a series that presents artists and writers who have new books. It is incredibly eclectic: The TINARS Manifesto states "This is writers talking about anything and everything: late night fiction, early morning hangovers, the politics of pot, octopuses on hockey rinks, the future of poetry, the history of cyborgs, the location of the mind, the cultural significance of the comma . . ." TINARS does host events around the city, but its home base is at the **Gladstone Hotel** at 1214 Queen St. West (p. 78). Check out **www.pagesbooks.ca** for a schedule (events are also listed in *NOW Magazine,* a partner in the reading series). Readings normally take place at 7:30pm, and they are free.

Several primarily gay and lesbian clubs attract a sizable hetero contingent; one notable destination is **El Convento Rico** (p. 222).

Afterlife   Formerly the Limelight, this is truly the club that won't die. People in their early 20s have been coming in from the suburbs forever to dance, play pool, and lounge, and they show no signs of stopping. No jeans. 250 Adelaide St. W. ℂ **416/593-6126.** Cover C$10 (£5). Subway: St. Andrew.

Circa   Peter Gatien, the former club king of New York City (remember the Limelight?), is an Ontario boy. His latest venture is this four-story, 4,924-sq.-m (53,000-sq.-ft.) club. I'm not sure how to describe it but… big. Monolithically so. Theoretically, this should mean there's something for everyone, what with the multiple event spaces, art displays, dance floors, and various themed "bars." (Got a fetish? It's on display here.) Maybe I just wasn't into spending the night with a crowd 3,000 strong. 126 John St. ℂ **416/979-0044.** Cover C$15 (£8), special events C$25–C$35 (£12–£17). www.circatoronto.com. Subway: St. Andrew.

Park Lane ★ (Finds)   You don't have to tell me that the name of this club reminds you of a brunch spot your elderly auntie likes. Trust me when I say that this is one of the more upscale clubs in downtown Toronto. It opened in spring 2008, complete with velvet rope and "Red Carpet" Saturday nights. The hefty dose of attitude is tempered by a gorgeous setting and DJs who are serious about getting the lounge lizards dancing under the swirling lights 184 Pearl St. ℂ **416/217-1100.** www.parklanetoronto.com. Cover C$20 (£10). Subway: St. Andrew.

Sneaky Dee's ★   Here's the antidote to the glut of posh clubs taking over downtown. This long-established oasis of dive-bar cool boasts pool tables, Mexican food, and alternative rock spun by a DJ in the club upstairs until 1:30am. Downstairs, the bar is open until 3am on weekdays, 4:30am on weekends. 431 College St. ℂ **416/603-3090.** Cover up to C$10 (£5). Subway: Queen's Park and then any streetcar west to Bathurst St.

This Is London ★   Gentlemen, please forgive me if I say that my favorite thing about this club is its incredible ladies' room. There's a makeup artist and a hairstylist who spend the night in there, helping femmes fatales primp (I'm not joking). This Is London is more sophisticated and less frenzied than most of its peers—you might even manage a conversation. It reminds me of an old-fashioned gentlemen's club with its Oriental rugs and comfortable armchairs, though the dance floor is pretty hot. *A word to the wise:* This is a very dressy place. 364 Richmond St. W. ☏ **416/351-1100.** Cover C$20 (£10). Subway: Osgoode.

3 THE BAR SCENE

The current night scene encompasses a flock of attractive bistros with billiard tables. You can enjoy cocktails, a reasonably priced meal, and a game of billiards in comfortable, aesthetically pleasing surroundings. The cigar bar is still in vogue, and most clubs have a humidor for the stogie set. Unlike dance clubs, the bars and lounges in Toronto are a pretty stable bunch.

BARS & LOUNGES

Barrio (Finds)   The Leslieville neighborhood has changed dramatically since the march to gentrification began, but this charming lounge has been here for 7 years. It serves up a long list of martinis (try the Porn Star, a blend of vodka, raspberry, and Sprite) and microbrews. 896 Queen St. E. ☏ **416/572-0600.** Subway: Queen and then a streetcar east to Logan Ave.

Foundation Room (Finds)   Half the fun with subterranean clubs is knowing how to find them. But the Foundation Room has far more going for it than just that: The room is decked out in glorious Moroccan style, with plush lounges, hammered-brass chandeliers, and plenty of mirrors. The vibe is very sexy—and the pomegranate martinis are delicious. 19 Church St. ☏ **416/364-8368.** Subway: Union.

The Library Bar ★   This is one of the most romantic settings in town. This intimate, wood-paneled bar is the best place in the city to order a top-quality martini, which is served in a generous "fishbowl" glass. With its leopard-print couches and wingback chairs, it has an old-fashioned, almost colonial feel. At the Fairmont Royal York, 100 Front St. W. ☏ **416/863-6333.** Subway: Union.

> (Moments)   **The Legendary Laurentian** ★
>
> Back in 1935, the Laurentian Room was *the* watering hole of choice in Toronto. It was the ladies-and-escorts bar at the Winchester Hotel in Cabbagetown, a neighborhood that has had a history of topsy-turvy fortunes (p. 175). But this Art Deco–styled lounge fell upon hard times and was eventually abandoned. The space stood empty (if you don't count squatters) for 39 years. And then, in 2004, a visionary group of friends brought it back to life. The newly revived **Laurentian Room** (51A Winchester St.; ☏ **416/925-8680**) makes me feel like I'm on the set of a cool HBO show: There's a sleek 10m (35-ft.) black bar, swank red banquettes, and backlit bronzed mirrors. Sure, you can eat dinner here, but to me this is simply *the* perfect spot for cocktails. My current love is the Tickle Me Pink, an effervescent combination of champagne and raspberry liqueur with real berries bobbing about. The Laurentian Room is all about glamour, so dress up a little and soak up the retro ambience. In the golden glow of the lamplight, this is a place we can *all* pretend to be Bogey or Bacall.

Lobby   Technically, this is a restaurant, but I have yet to meet anyone who chooses it for dinner (though people do decide to stay for dinner after meeting for drinks here). Famous as the spot where Jay-Z had his bachelor party, Lobby is sleek and sophisticated, and the crowd is dressed to match. Scenesters, this one's for you. 192 Bloor St. W. ℂ **416/964-0411.** Subway: Bay or Museum.

The Lounge ★   The recently remodeled bar at the Drake Hotel is a perfect perch for sipping martinis and envisioning yourself in a glamorous bygone era. The Lounge is designed to evoke a mid-twentieth-century feel. It's dressed-up, grown-up fun, and it attracts a crowd of devoted locals. At the Drake Hotel, 1150 Queen St. W. ℂ **416/531-5042.** Subway: Osgoode and then a streetcar west to Beaconsfield.

Panorama   From this 51st-floor perch above Bloor and Bay, visitors can see north and south for 242km (150 miles)—at least on a clear day. Go for the lit skyline and the Latin music. Arrive early if you want a window seat. In the Manulife Centre, 55 Bloor St. W. ℂ **416/967-0000.** Subway: Bloor/Yonge.

The Roof ★★★   Author Mordecai Richler called this the only civilized spot in Toronto. It's an old literary haunt, with comfortable couches in front of a fireplace and excellent drinks. The walls sport caricatures of members of Canada's literary establishment. The James Bond martini—vodka with a drop of Lillet—is my personal favorite. The view from the outdoor terrace is one of the best in the city. At the Park Hyatt Toronto, 4 Avenue Rd. ℂ **416/924-5471.** Subway: Museum or Bay.

Sutra Tiki Bar ★ (Finds)   Summer never ends at this sexy, intimate Little Italy bar. The drink list is composed of the usual hot-weather suspects (mojitos, caipirinhas) and lush champagne cocktails (try the house specialty, the Sutra). In warm weather, there's a patio out back with real sand. 612 College St. ℂ **416/537-8755.** Subway: Queen's Park and then any streetcar west to Clinton St.

PUBS & TAVERNS

Allen's   Allen's sports a great bar that offers more than 80 beer selections and 164 single malts. Guinness is the drink of choice on Tuesday and Saturday nights, when folks reel and jig to the Celtic–Irish entertainment. 143 Danforth Ave. ℂ **416/463-3086.** Subway: Broadview.

The Ben Wicks (Finds)   The late Ben Wicks was a well-known local cartoonist, and he opened this eponymous pub in 1980. His artwork still adorns the walls, and the nice selection of beer and wine and the inexpensive pub menu (think Guinness-battered fish and chips) have made it a Cabbagetown institution. 424 Parliament St. ℂ **416/961-9425.** Subway: College and then a streetcar east to Parliament.

Brunswick House   Affectionately known as the Brunny House, this cavernous room is an inexpensive place to down some beer. Not surprisingly, it's a favorite of University of Toronto students. Waiters carry trays of frothy suds between the Formica tables. Impromptu dancing to background music and pool and shuffleboard playing drown out the sound of at least two of the large-screen TVs, if not the other 18. Upstairs, thoroughbred and harness racing is broadcast live from around the world. 481 Bloor St. W. ℂ **416/964-2242.** Subway: Spadina or Bathurst.

Cameron House   Since 1981, this local favorite has drawn a crowd (before then it was a divey hotel). There's a rococo bar at the front, and local bands try out in the back room. If the owners are to be believed, Prince has stopped by to jam here. 408 Queen St. W. ℂ **416/703-0811.** www.thecameron.com. Subway: Osgoode.

(Moments) A Traditional Irish Pub ★

Toronto used to be known as the Belfast of the North for its quiet, abstemious ways. The city has changed dramatically since then, though it's still got the Irish spirit . . . just a *different* kind of Irish spirit. Drop by **Dora Keogh** (141 Danforth Ave.; ℂ **416/778-1804**) to see—and hear—what I mean. Comfortable and friendly, this is a good spot for a hearty meal and a pint. But the real reason to come is the music. I love traditional Celtic melodies, and on Thursdays at 9pm and Sundays at 5pm, local musicians gather to play them. The sessions are becoming legendary, especially since famous fiddler Natalie McMaster and members of the Chieftains have come by and joined in. As my Irish relatives would say, it's good *craic!*

Irish Embassy ★　Located in a stunning 1873 bank building in the Financial District, this pub fills up after the closing bell rings at the Toronto Stock Exchange. Guinness is just one of the many brews on tap, and there's an excellent pub grub menu to tide you over. 49 Yonge St. ℂ **416/866-8282.** Subway: King.

Madison Avenue Pub　When I was a student at U of T, this was the place to hang out and enjoy a pint. Beer is still on tap here, but now there are 150 varieties to choose from. The original pub at 14 Madison has gobbled up its neighbors at 16 and 18, and now this spot is a huge complex with six separate British-style pubs. 14 Madison Ave. ℂ **416/927-1722.** Subway: Spadina.

Mill Street Brew Pub ★　This pub features an incredible array of beers, brewed in small batches (some are only available seasonally). The Tankhouse Pale Ale is a constant, with its five malts blended for a particularly complex flavor. In the Distillery District, 55 Mill St. ℂ **416/681-0338.** Subway: King and then a streetcar east to Parliament.

Pilot Tavern　This watering hole dates to the early years of World War II. Regulars who go way back mix with a suited-up after-work crowd. It's an unpretentious place with pool tables and a wonderful rooftop patio. 22 Cumberland St. ℂ **416/923-5716.** Subway: Yonge/Bloor.

Wheat Sheaf Tavern　Designated a historic landmark, this is the city's oldest tavern, in operation since 1849. For fans, eight screens show great moments in sports. The jukebox features 1,200 choices, and there are two pool tables and an outdoor patio. 667 King St. W. ℂ **416/504-9912.** Subway: St. Andrew and then any streetcar west to Bathurst St.

4 THE GAY & LESBIAN SCENE

Toronto's gay and lesbian community is one of the largest of any city in North America, so the nightlife scene is diverse (yet largely concentrated in the Gay Village around Church and Wellesley streets). The free weekly newspaper *Xtra!* (www.xtra.ca) lists events, seminars, and performances, targeted at the gay and lesbian community; also check out **Gay Toronto** (www.gaytoronto.com), and the **Gay Toronto Tourism Guild** (www.gaytorontotourism.com) for listings. Some mostly straight nightspots, such as the

Melody Bar (see p. 215), have one night a week that's gay night (in The Melody Bar's case, Wednesdays).

Byzantium ★★ (Value)   An attractive but low-key bar/restaurant, Byzantium attracts an affable gay and straight crowd. The cocktails are both excellent and reasonably priced (try either the Red Velvet or the Black Orchid—they are as delicious as the names are dramatic). You can follow drinks with dinner in the adjacent top-notch dining room. 499 Church St. ℂ **416/922-3859.** Subway: Wellesley.

Crews, Tango and The Zone ★   Located in two adjoining Victorian houses, this three-in-one club promises something for everyone. Crews is a gay bar for men, and it is known for its pubby atmosphere and its drag shows, which start at 11pm Wednesday to Sunday. The upstairs Tango bar draws a lesbian crowd to its dance floor and lounge. Then there's The Zone, which offers karaoke, drag queen and drag king shows, and dancing. 508 Church St. ℂ **416/972-1662.** Subway: Wellesley.

El Convento Rico ★★ (Finds)   The Latin beat beckons one and all—straight, gay, and otherwise—to this lively club. If you don't know how to samba, you can pick up the basics at the Friday- and Sunday-night dance lessons, but if you don't learn, no one on the jam-packed dance floor will notice. There's a substantial hetero contingent that comes out just to watch the fabulous drag queens—and don't be surprised if you encounter a bachelorette party in progress. 750 College St. ℂ **416/588-7800.** www.elconventorico. com. Subway: Queen's Park and then a streetcar west.

Pegasus Bar ★   This relaxed pub draws a gay and lesbian crowd with its four professional-size billiards tables, trivia nights, video games, pinball machines, and gigantic TV (tuned to gay dramas). The staff is warm and welcoming. 489B Church St. ℂ **416/927-8832.** Subway: Wellesley.

Sailor   This bar is attached to Woody's (see below) but has a livelier atmosphere; unlike Woody's, you won't see many women here. Every Thursday, there's a Best Chest competition; every Friday, the prize is for Best Ass. In the evening, a DJ spins an assortment of dance and alternative tunes. 465 Church St. ℂ **416/972-0887.** Subway: Wellesley.

Woody's ★   A local institution, Woody's attracts mainly men but welcomes women; the crowd is a mix of gay and hetero. It's a popular meeting spot, especially for weekend brunch. 467 Church St. (south of Wellesley St.). ℂ **416/972-0887.** www.woodystoronto.com. Subway: Wellesley.

Zelda's ★ (Finds)   This is a don't-miss spot in Toronto's Gay Village. Yes, the queues can be long—but when you get inside, it will be worth it. Zelda's has great food and a great sense of humor—ideally, you'll be there for one of the many theme nights (love those nurse outfits). 542 Church St. ℂ **416/922-2526.** Subway: Wellesley.

5 CINEMAS & MOVIE HOUSES

Check *Now, Eye,* **www.toronto.com,** or one of the daily newspapers for listings.

Cinematheque Ontario ★ (Finds)   A division of the Toronto International Film Festival, Cinematheque Ontario shows the best in world cinema. The programs include directors' retrospectives, plus new films from France, Germany, Japan, Bulgaria, and other countries that you won't find in the first-run theaters around town. Note that the screenings at the Art Gallery of Ontario's Jackman Hall continue while the rest of the

museum is closed. Screenings at the Art Gallery of Ontario, 317 Dundas St. W. ✆ 416/968-FILM.
www.cinemathequeontario.ca. Tickets C$12 (£6) adults, C$8 (£4) seniors and students. Subway: St. Patrick.

Scotiabank Theatre Toronto (Kids)   This used to be the Paramount, but the trend in Toronto lately has been to sell the naming rights to anything bigger than a park bench. In any case, this is a giant megaplex, but it's a really nice one. If you're going to see a blockbuster, it may as well be on a giant screen in a theater with plush, comfy seats, right? 259 Richmond St. W. ✆ 416/368-6089. Tickets C$12 (£6). Tues discounts. Subway: Osgoode.

6 COFFEEHOUSES

While **Starbucks** has certainly staked out plenty of territory in Toronto, the Canadian chain, the **Second Cup,** is holding its ground. It offers a full range of flavored coffees and espresso varieties, plus cakes, muffins, croissants, and gift items. Another chain, **Timothy's,** invites you to pour your own selection from about 10 varieties. My favorite coffeehouses are all independents, though.

Balzac's Coffee ★   If you're in the Distillery District, this is the place to stop for coffee. Not only is the setting dramatic (soaring ceilings, red-brick walls, and elaborate chandelier), but the in-house roasted coffees are deservedly famous. In the Distillery District, 55 Mill St. ✆ 416/207-1709. Subway: King and then a streetcar east to Parliament.

Café Diplomatico ★ (Finds)   One of the oldest cafes in Toronto, this Little Italy gem has mosaic marble floors, wrought-iron chairs, and an extra-large sidewalk patio. Many longtime area residents get their caffeine fix here in the morning; the patio attracts a trendier crowd. 594 College St. ✆ 416/534-4637. Subway: Queen's Park and then a streetcar west to Clinton St.

Daily Express Café   Near the student ghetto in the Annex neighborhood, this lively cafe draws most of its crowd from the nearby University of Toronto. 280 Bloor St. W. ✆ 416/944-3225. Subway: St. George.

Future Bakery   This rambling cafe attracts an artsy crowd with fine breads and a selection of coffees. Would-be writers tap away in well-lit corners. 483 Bloor St. W. ✆ 416/922-5875. Subway: Spadina or Bathurst.

Gypsy Co-Op   Coffee is not the only king here. Many teas and herbal infusions (for everything from stress to colds and flu) are available, as are super-rich brownies. 815 Queen St. W. ✆ 416/703-5069. Subway: Osgoode and then any streetcar west to Manning.

Lettieri ★   The house rule at this small local chain is that after 7 minutes, a pot of coffee is no longer fresh. This place takes the bean seriously. In addition to the wide range of coffees, you can order focaccia sandwiches, tarts, cookies, and pastries. There are outposts at **441 Queen St.** (at Spadina Ave.; ✆ 416/592-1360), and at the corner of Bloor and Bathurst, tucked into the beloved **Honest's Ed's** emporium (p. 188). 94 Cumberland St. ✆ 416/515-8764. www.lettiericafe.com. Subway: Bay.

Side Trips from Toronto

The good news: Some of the greatest attractions in this region are within a 2-hour drive of Toronto, making them easily accessible. The bad news: If you're trying to shoehorn all of the sights into a short stay . . . you've got some serious decisions to make. This chapter describes three of the best-known destinations—the theater town of Stratford, the wine region of Niagara-on-the-Lake, and the golf/spa/sailing resort retreat of the Muskokas—as well as the less famous city of Hamilton.

For information about the areas surrounding Toronto, contact **Ontario Tourism** (*©* **800/ONTARIO;** www.ontariotravel. net) or visit its travel information center in the Atrium on Bay (street level) at 20 Dundas St. W.—it's just across Dundas from the Sears store at the northern edge of the Eaton Centre. It's open daily from 8:30am to 5pm; hours are extended during the summer, often to 8pm. Another good resource is the **Southern Ontario Tourism Organization** (*©* **800/267-3399;** http://soto.on.ca), which has a travel-planning booklet, an e-mail newsletter, and an informative website.

1 STRATFORD ★

145km (90 miles) SW of Toronto

The grand Stratford Festival has humble roots. The idea of a theater was launched in 1953, when director Tyrone Guthrie lured the great Sir Alec Guinness to the stage here. Whether Sir Alec knew the "stage" was set up in a makeshift tent is another question, but his acclaimed performance gave the festival the push—and press—it needed to become an annual tradition. Since then, the Stratford Festival has grown to become one of the most famous in North America, and its four theaters (no more tents!) have put this charming and scenic town on the map. While visitors will notice the Avon River and other sights named in honor of the Bard, they may not realize that Stratford has another claim to fame: It's home to one of Canada's best cooking schools, which makes dining at many of the spots in town a delight.

ESSENTIALS

VISITOR INFORMATION For first-rate visitor information, go to the **Visitors' Information Centre** by the river on York Street at Erie. From May to early November, it's open Sunday through Wednesday from 9am to 5pm, and Thursday through Saturday from 9am to 8pm. At other times, contact **Tourism Stratford** (*©* **800/561-SWAN [7926]** or 519/271-5140; www.welcometostratford.com).

GETTING THERE Driving from Toronto, take Highway 401 west to Interchange 278 at Kitchener. Follow Highway 8 west onto Highway 7/8 to Stratford.

For me, nothing beats the train, and Stratford is a small and very walkable town, so unless you're planning to tour the surrounding area, call **VIA Rail** (*©* **800/VIA-RAIL** or 416/366-8411; www.viarail.ca). Canada's national rail company operates several trains

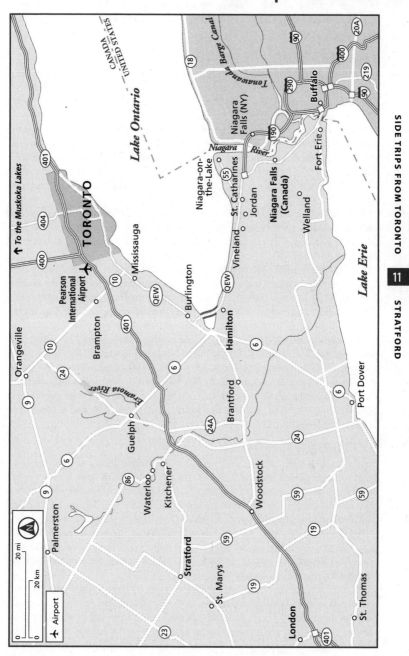

daily along the Toronto–Kitchener–Stratford route. The toll-free number works within North America; if you're traveling from overseas, you can book your rail travel in advance through one of Via's general sales agents (there's a long list of local agents on www. viarail.ca).

THE STRATFORD FESTIVAL ★

On July 13, 1953, *Richard III,* starring Sir Alec Guinness, was staged in a huge tent. From that modest start, Stratford's artistic directors have built on the radical, but faithfully classic, base established by Tyrone Guthrie to create a repertory theater with a glowing international reputation.

Stratford has four theaters. The **Festival Theatre,** 55 Queen St., has a dynamic thrust stage (a modern re-creation of an Elizabethan stage). The **Avon Theatre,** 99 Downie St., has a classic proscenium. The **Tom Patterson Theatre,** Lakeside Drive, is an intimate 500-seat theater. The newest venue—the **Studio Theatre** (attached to the Avon Theatre)—opened its doors in 2002; the 278-seat space is used for new and experimental works.

World-famous for its Shakespearean productions, the festival also offers classic and modern theatrical masterpieces. Recent productions have included *Cabaret, The Music Man,* and *The Trojan Women;* from the Bard, we've seen *The Taming of the Shrew* and *Hamlet.*

In addition to attending plays, visitors may enjoy the Celebrated Writers Series, which features renowned authors (some of whom have penned works performed at the Stratford Festival). All lectures take place on Sunday mornings at the Tom Patterson Theatre or the Studio Theatre, and they cost C$25 (£13) per person; tickets are available from the box office.

The season usually begins in early May and continues through mid-November, with performances Tuesday through Sunday nights, and matinees on Wednesday, Saturday, and Sunday. Ticket prices range from C$20 to C$109 (£10–£55), with special deals for students and seniors. For tickets, call © **800/567-1600** or visit **www.stratfordfestival. ca.** Tickets are also available in the United States and Canada at Ticketmaster outlets. The box office opens for mail and fax orders in late January; telephone and in-person sales begin in late February.

EXPLORING THE TOWN

Stratford was founded in 1832, and much of its historic heart has been preserved. Ninety-minute **guided tours of Stratford** take place Monday through Saturday in July and August, and on Saturday only in May, June, September, and October. They leave at 9:30am from the Visitors' Information Centre by the Avon river and are free of charge (call ahead to confirm). The visitor's booth also has maps for self-guided tours.

Paddleboat, kayak, and canoe rentals are available at the **Boathouse,** behind and below the information booth. It's open daily from 9am until dusk in summer. Contact **Avon Boat Rentals,** 40 York St. (© **519/271-7739**). There's also a boat, the *Juliet III,* that offers scenic half-hour tours.

Past the Orr Dam and the 90-year-old stone bridge, through a rustic gate, lies a very special park, the **Shakespearean Gardens.** In the formal English garden, where a sundial measures the hours, you can relax and contemplate the herb and flowerbeds and the tranquil river lagoon, and muse on a bust of Shakespeare by Toronto sculptor Cleeve Horne. For a picnic-friendly patch of green, visit **Queen's Park,** a stone's throw from the Festival Theatre. It has a great view of the swans on the Avon.

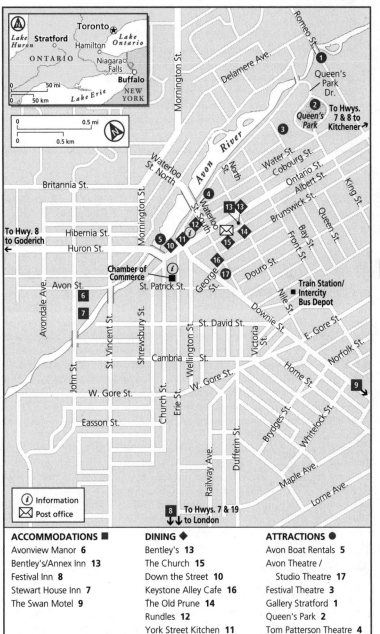

(i) Information
✉ Post office

ACCOMMODATIONS ■
Avonview Manor **6**
Bentley's/Annex Inn **13**
Festival Inn **8**
Stewart House Inn **7**
The Swan Motel **9**

DINING ◆
Bentley's **13**
The Church **15**
Down the Street **10**
Keystone Alley Cafe **16**
The Old Prune **14**
Rundles **12**
York Street Kitchen **11**

ATTRACTIONS ●
Avon Boat Rentals **5**
Avon Theatre /
   Studio Theatre **17**
Festival Theatre **3**
Gallery Stratford **1**
Queen's Park **2**
Tom Patterson Theatre **4**

(Finds) **An Open-Air Art Gallery**

Museums are grand, but who wants to spend a glorious summer day indoors? Thanks to the **Art in the Park** (www.artintheparkstratford.com), you can have both. On Wednesdays, Saturdays, and Sundays from June to September, regional artists gather at Lakeside Drive and Front Street, and put on a show from 9am to 5pm, weather permitting. The artists and artisans work in various media, so you'll find paintings, sculptures, ceramics, jewelry, and glass, among other things. While many of the works are for sale, this isn't just a market: The artists are selected through a juried process, and they are required to demonstrate their medium as part of their display.

Stratford also has a fine art museum, the **Gallery Stratford,** 54 Romeo St. (© **519/271-5271;** www.gallerystratford.on.ca). It's in a historic building on the fringes of Confederation Park. Since it opened in 1967, its focus has been on Canadian artists. Its hours change with the seasons, but mid-May through late September, it's open Tuesday through Sunday from 10am to 5pm (call ahead for hours during other times of year). Admission is C$5 (£2.50) for adults, C$4 (£2) for seniors and students 13 and up, and free for children 12 and under (admission prices change with the special exhibits on display).

A COUPLE OF EXCURSIONS FROM STRATFORD

Only half an hour or so from Stratford, the twin cities of **Kitchener** and **Waterloo** have two drawing cards: the **Farmers' Market** and the famous 9-day **Oktoberfest** (© **888/294-HANS** or 519/570-HANS; www.oktoberfest.ca). The cities still have a large population of descendents of German settlers, and many are also Mennonites. On Saturday, starting at 6am, you can sample shoofly pie, apple butter, birch beer, summer sausage, and other Mennonite specialties at the market in the Market Square complex, at Duke and Frederick streets in Kitchener. For additional information, contact the **Kitchener-Waterloo Area Visitors and Convention Bureau,** 2848 King St. E., Kitchener (© **519/748-0800;** www.explorewaterlooregion.com). It's open from 9am to 5pm weekdays only in winter, daily in summer.

Eight kilometers (5 miles) north of Kitchener is the town of **St. Jacobs.** It has close to 100 shops in venues such as a converted mill, silo, and other factory buildings. For those interested in learning more about the Amish–Mennonite way of life, the **Meetingplace,** 33 King St. (© **519/664-3518**), shows a short film about it (daily in summer, weekends only in winter). There's also the **St. Jacobs Outlet Mall** at 25 Benjamin Rd. East, open Monday through Friday from 9:30am to 9pm, Saturday 8:30am to 6pm, and Sunday noon to 5pm (closed Jan 1 and Dec 25). Call © **800/265-3353** or 519/664-2293 for more information.

WHERE TO STAY

When you book your theater tickets, you can book your accommodations at no extra charge. Options range from guest homes for as little as C$60 (£30) to first-class hotels charging more than C$200 (£100). Call the **Stratford Tourism Alliance** at © **800/561-7926** for information (note that some accommodations are open only to festival-goers, and these can be booked only through the Accommodation Bureau). You can also book

(Finds) Shopping in Stratford

I know, we're all here for the theater scene, but don't miss out on Stratford's excellent shopping options. If you were expecting touristy, overpriced, and kitschy, you're in for a pleasant surprise. Many of the stores downtown sell clothing and housewares that rival what you'll see in the best boutiques in Toronto. Prices tend to be quite reasonable. Here are some of my favorite spots.

- **For housewares:** You'll find both locally made cranberry glass and objects from Indonesia and Uzbekistan at **Watson's Chelsea Bazaar,** 84 Ontario St. ((C) **519/273-1790**). **White Oleander,** 136 Ontario St. ((C) **519/271-5616**), sells lovely linens, bedding, and tableware. Everything at **Pariscope,** 21 York St. ((C) **519/271-3316**), is French-imported or French-inspired. The venerable **Bradshaws,** 129 Ontario St. ((C) **519/271-6283**), has been in business since 1895 selling crystal and china.

- **For clothing: Elizabeth Noel,** 26 Ontario St. ((C) **519/273-4506**), sells beautiful dresses and other ladylike pieces, many of which are by Canadian labels such as Sweet Chemise. **The Green Room,** 40 Ontario St. ((C) **519/271-3240**), is actually several rooms, all jam-packed with clothing and accessories.

- **For gift items:** The fair-trade company **Ten Thousand Villages,** 14 Ontario St. ((C) **519/272-0700**), sells crafts, jewelry, housewares, and toys from artisans in developing countries. **The Wanderer,** 17 Market Place ((C) **519/271-0410**), stocks wall-hangings, carvings, and semiprecious jewelry.

- **For eclectic tastes:** One of the most interesting stores in Stratford is **The Great Dame,** 96 Downie St. ((C) **519/275-3000**), which sells sweet-smelling toiletries from Europe and a house line, Lily Josephine, that I prefer (the Blood Orange bath products are irresistible). Owner Janet Hill also sells her own artwork here, glamorous paintings of—what else?—great dames. Another wonderful find is **Gallery Indigena,** 69 Ontario St. ((C) **519/271-7881;** www.galleryindigena.com), which sells works of art by the Inuit, Iroquois, Cree, Plains, Woodland, and North Pacific Coast peoples. In business for more than 3 decades, the gallery hosts several "Meet the Artist" events throughout the summer, and it ships artwork all over the world.

a room via **Tourism Stratford's website** (www.welcometostratford.com). Rooms in Stratford are most expensive in June, July, and August; it's easier to get a discount from fall to spring. In winter, even the most opulent properties deeply discount their rates.

Hotels & Motels

Festival Inn The Festival Inn sits outside town off highways 7 and 8, on 8 hectares (20 acres) of landscaped grounds. This is the largest full-service hotel in Stratford. The place has an Old English air, with stucco walls, Tudor-style beams, and high-backed red settees in the lobby. Tudor style prevails throughout the large, motel-style rooms. Some units have bay windows with sheer curtains, and all rooms in the main building, north wing, and annex have fridges. The indoor pool has an outdoor patio.

1144 Ontario St. (P.O. Box 811), Stratford, ON N5A 6W1. ✆ **800/463-3581** or 519/273-1150. www.festival innstratford.com. 182 units. From C$159 (£80) double. Children under 16 stay for free in parent's room. AE, DC, MC, V. Free parking. **Amenities:** Dining room; coffee shop; indoor pool; Jacuzzi; sauna. *In room:* A/C, TV, fridge, coffeemaker.

Lofts at 99/The Annex Room ★

For convenience, you can't beat this spot. Formerly known as Bentley's (the on-site restaurant still goes by that moniker; see p. 232), Lofts at 99 enjoys an excellent location at the center of town. The rooms are elegant, duplex suites with efficiency kitchens. Recent remodeling of the guestrooms has done away with the period furnishings and the Victorian wallpaper; the look now is streamlined and chic. Five units have skylights.

The Annex Room Inn is in a separate building that is just a few steps away. Its rooms are described as "executive" status, and they really are—airy and bright and very elegantly decorated. Many of the rooms have a gas fireplace and a stereo system—and all have whirlpool tubs.

99 Ontario St., Stratford, ON N5A 3H1. ✆ **800/361-5322** or 519/271-1121. www.bentleys-annex.com. 13 units. Doubles start at C$195 (£98). Extra person C$20 (£10). AE, DC, MC, V. Free parking. **Amenities:** 2 restaurants. *In room:* A/C, TV, kitchen, fridge, coffeemaker, hair dryer.

The Swan Motel ★ (Value)

I don't know what "motel" means to you, but to me, it normally sounds like an unprepossessing place to stop that's right by a highway. Well, the Swan is indeed 3km (2 miles) from downtown Stratford, but its grounds are completely luxurious. This property has been run by the same family for more than 40 years, and it has a warm, gracious atmosphere. The rooms are nonsmoking, and they are simply but pleasantly arranged. The grounds are the real drawing card, with the romantic Victorian gazebo, beds of perennial flowers, and outdoor pool. *Caveat:* It's far enough from the center of town that I don't recommend staying here unless you're driving.

Downie St. South, 3765 Perth Rd. 112, Stratford, ON N5A 6S3. ✆ **519/271-6376.** Fax 519/271-0682. www.swanmotel.ca. 24 units. From C$98 (£49) double. Extra person C$15 (£7.50). Rates include continental breakfast. MC, V. Free parking. **Amenities:** Outdoor pool. *In room:* A/C, TV, fridge, hair dryer.

Bed & Breakfasts

In addition to the establishments mentioned above, extensive bed-and-breakfast listings can be found on **www.bbcanada.com**.

Avonview Manor

In a 1916 Edwardian house on a quiet street west of the downtown area, Avonview Manor offers attractive rooms. All are nonsmoking; three have queen-size beds; the suite contains four singles, a sitting room, and a private bathroom. Breakfast is served in a bright dining room that overlooks the garden. Guests have the use of a kitchen. There is also a pool and Jacuzzi.

63 Avon St., Stratford, ON N5A 5N5. ✆ **519/273-4603.** www.bbcanada.com/avonview. 4 units, 2 w/private bathroom. From C$105 (£53) double. Rates include full breakfast. No credit cards; personal checks accepted. Street parking. **Amenities:** Outdoor pool; Jacuzzi; sauna. *In room:* A/C, no phone.

Stewart House Inn ★ (Finds)

This house was built in 1870, and its owners have decorated it in appropriately opulent Victorian style. There's also a strong emphasis on old-fashioned guest service: In the morning, coffee is delivered to your room; if you want to swim in the backyard pool, you'll be supplied with robes, towels, and tumblers for drinks. A full breakfast is served every morning between 8 and 10am in what used to be the ballroom. The guest rooms themselves are outstanding. Each is individually themed to play up the romantic atmosphere, and modern convenience (flatscreen TVs, DVDs, and wireless Internet) is nicely blended in. House policies are no smoking, no children, **231** and no pets (there are two small dogs in residence).

62 John St. N., Stratford, ON N5A 6K7. © **519/271-4576.** www.stewarthouseinn.com. 7 units. Doubles start at C$180 (£90). Rates include full breakfast. MC, V. Street parking. No children. **Amenities:** Outdoor pool. *In room:* A/C, TV, hair dryer, iron.

A Nearby Place to Stay & Dine

Langdon Hall ★★   This elegant house stands at the head of a curving, tree-lined drive. Eugene Langdon Wilks, a great-grandson of John Jacob Astor, completed it in 1902. It remained in the family until 1987, when its transformation into a small country-house hotel began. Today, Langdon Hall is a Relais & Châteaux property, and its 81 hectares (200 acres) of lawns, gardens, and woodlands make for an ideal retreat. Throughout, the emphasis is on comfort rather than grandiosity. The luxurious on-site spa offers a complete range of treatments. Most rooms surround the cloister garden. Each room is individually decorated; most have fireplaces. The property has a croquet lawn and cross-country ski trails. The light, airy dining room serves fine regional cuisine. Tea is served on the veranda, and there's a bar.

R.R. 3, Cambridge, ON N3H 4R8. © **800/268-1898** or 519/740-2100. www.langdonhall.ca. 52 units. From C$259 (£130) double. Rates include full breakfast. AE, DC, MC, V. Free parking. From Hwy. 401, take exit 275 south, turn right onto Blair Rd., follow signs. Pets accepted. **Amenities:** Dining room; bar; outdoor pool; tennis courts; health club; spa; Jacuzzi; sauna; concierge; business center; 24-hr. room service; babysitting; dry cleaning; billiard room. *In room:* A/C, TV, dataport, coffeemaker, hair dryer, iron.

WHERE TO DINE
Expensive

The Church ★★ CONTINENTAL   The Church is simply stunning. The organ pipes and the altar of the 1873 structure are intact, along with the vaulted roof, carved woodwork, and stained-glass windows. You can sit in the nave or the side aisles and dine to appropriate sounds—usually Bach.

In summer, a special four-course tasting menu is offered; the a la carte menu is available throughout the year. Appetizers might include asparagus served hot with black morels in their juices, white wine, and cream; or sauté of duck foie gras with leeks and citron, mango, and ginger sauce. Among the short selection of entrees, you might find Canadian caribou with port-and-blackberry sauce and cream-braised cabbage with shallots and glazed chestnuts; or lobster salad with green beans, new potatoes, and truffles scented with caraway. Desserts are equally exciting. The upstairs Belfry is a popular pre- and post-theater gathering place and is open for lunch and dinner. To dine here during the festival, make reservations as soon as you buy your tickets. In the off season, call ahead.

70 Brunswick St. (at Waterloo St.). © **519/273-3424.** www.churchrestaurant.com. Reservations required. Main courses C$32–C$39 (£16–£20); 4-course prix-fixe menu C$90 (£45). AE, DC, MC, V. The Church: Tues–Sat 5–8:30pm; Sun 11:30am–1:30pm; off-season hours vary; closed Dec through mid-Apr. The Belfry: Tues–Sat 11:30am–midnight; off-season hours vary.

The Old Prune ★ CONTINENTAL   Situated in a lovely Edwardian home, the Old Prune has three dining rooms and an enclosed garden patio. Former Montréalers, the proprietors demonstrate Québec flair in both decor and menu. The menu changes based on what's fresh and what's in season (much of the produce comes from the region's organic farms). Appetizers might include outstanding house-smoked salmon with lobster potato salad topped with Sevruga caviar, or refreshing tomato consommé with saffron and sea scallops. Among the main courses, you might find Perth County pork loin grilled with tamari and honey glaze and served with shiitake mushrooms, pickled cucumbers, and sunflower sprouts; steamed bass in Napa cabbage with curry broth and lime leaves; or rack of Ontario lamb with smoky tomatillo-chipotle pepper sauce. Desserts, such as rhubarb strawberry Napoleon, are inspired.

151 Albert St. ☎ **519/271-5052.** www.oldprune.on.ca. Reservations required. 2-course prix-fixe menu C$60 (£30); 3-course prix-fixe dinner C$74 (£37). AE, MC, V. Fri–Sun 11:30am–1pm; Tues–Sun 5–9pm. Call for winter hours.

Rundles ★ (Value) INTERNATIONAL   Rundles provides a premier dining experience in a serene dining room overlooking the river. Proprietor James Morris eats, sleeps, thinks, and dreams food, and Chef Neil Baxter delivers the exciting, exquisite cuisine to the table. The prix-fixe dinner offers palate-pleasing flavor combinations. Appetizers might include shaved fennel, arugula, artichoke, and Parmesan salad, or warm seared Québec foie gras. Typical main dishes include poached Atlantic salmon garnished with Jerusalem artichokes, wilted arugula, and yellow peppers in a light carrot sauce; or pink roast rib-eye of lamb with ratatouille and rosemary aioli. For dessert, try glazed lemon tart and orange sorbet or hot mango tart with pineapple sorbet. In 2008, Rundles opened the Sophisto-Bistro, a more casual dining room, with a less-expensive (yet incredibly delicious) prix-fixe menu.

9 Cobourg St. ☎ **519/271-6442.** www.rundlesrestaurant.com. Reservations required. Rundles 3-course prix-fixe dinner C$80 (£40); Sophisto-Bistro 3-course prix-fixe menu C$50 (£25). AE, DC, MC, V. Apr–Oct Sat–Sun 11:30am–1:15pm, Tues and Sat 5–7pm, Wed–Fri 5–8:30pm; closed Nov–Mar.

Moderate

Bentley's CANADIAN/ENGLISH   Located in the Lofts at 99 hotel, Bentley's is *the* local watering hole and a favorite theater-company gathering spot. In summer, you can sit on the garden terrace and enjoy the light fare—grilled shrimp, burgers, gourmet pizza, fish and chips, shepherd's pie, and pasta dishes. The dinner menu features more substantial meals, including lamb curry, sirloin steak, and salmon baked in white wine with peppercorn-dill butter. The bar offers 15 drafts on tap.

99 Ontario St. ☎ **519/271-1121.** www.bentleys-annex.com. Reservations not accepted. Main courses C$15–C$20 (£7.50–£10). AE, DC, MC, V. Daily 11:30am–1am.

Down the Street ★ (Finds) INTERNATIONAL   This charming bohemian spot is a welcome sight given Stratford's delicious but pricey food scene. The softly lit interior is comprised mainly of a long, narrow dining room decked out with beautiful textiles and antique chandeliers. The menu offers selections from around the globe: Mexican guacamole and corn tortillas, Vietnamese-style roasted pork chop in the spicy chili-honey glaze, French Dijon chicken supreme. The dessert list is short but excellent (try the bittersweet chocolate tart with raspberry sorbet).

30 Ontario St. ☎ **519/273-5886.** Reservations recommended. Main courses C$18–C$28 (£9–£14). AE, DC, MC, V. Tues–Sat 11:30am–3pm and 5-9pm (bar open till 1am).

Keystone Alley Cafe ★ ASIAN/CONTINENTAL   The food here is better than at some pricier competitors. Theater actors often stop in for lunch—perhaps a sandwich, such as the maple-grilled chicken-and-avocado club, or a main dish such as cornmeal-crusted Mediterranean tart. At dinner, entrees range from breast of Muscovy duck with stir-fried Asian vegetables and egg noodles in honey-ginger sauce, to escalopes of calves' liver accompanied by garlic potato purée and creamed Savoy cabbage with bacon. The short wine list is reasonably priced.

34 Brunswick St. © **519/271-5645.** Reservations recommended. Main courses C$15–C$27 (£7.50–£19).
AE, DC, MC, V. Mon–Sat 11:30am–2:30pm; Tues–Sat 5–9pm.

Inexpensive
York Street Kitchen ECLECTIC   This small restaurant is a fun, funky spot that serves reasonably priced, high-quality food. You can come here for breakfast burritos and other morning fare, and for lunch sandwiches, which you build yourself by choosing from a list of fillings. In the evenings, expect comfort foods such as meatloaf and mashed potatoes or barbecued chicken and ribs.

41 York St. © **519/273-7041.** www.yorkstreetkitchen.com. Reservations not accepted. Main courses C$14–C$16 (£7–£8). AE, V. Apr–early Oct daily 8am–8pm; early Oct–Mar daily 8am–3pm. Closed Dec 24–Jan 5.

2 NIAGARA-ON-THE-LAKE & NIAGARA FALLS

130km (81 miles) SE of Toronto

Only 1½ hours from Toronto, Niagara-on-the-Lake is one of the best preserved and prettiest 19th-century villages in North America. Handsome clapboard and brick period houses border the tree-lined streets. It's the setting for one of Canada's most famous events, the **Shaw Festival.** The town is the jewel of the **Ontario wine region.**

Less than a half-hour drive from Niagara-on-the-Lake is **Niagara Falls,** which was for decades the region's honeymoon capital (I say this in an attempt to explain its endless motels—each with at least one suite that has a heart-shaped pink bed). While the falls are a majestic sight, I have my reservations about the town. Personally, I like to stay at an inn in Niagara-on-the-Lake and come to Niagara Falls for a day trip. By the way, the drive along the **Niagara Parkway** (p. 240) is a delight: With its endless parks and gardens, it's an oasis for nature lovers.

ESSENTIALS
VISITOR INFORMATION   The **Niagara-on-the-Lake Chamber of Commerce,** 26 Queen St., Niagara-on-the-Lake (© **905/468-1950;** www.niagaraonthelake.com), provides information and can help you find accommodations. It's open daily from 9am to 7:30pm from April through October, and from 10am to 5pm during the rest of the year.

For Niagara Falls travel information, contact **Niagara Falls Tourism,** 5515 Stanley Ave., Niagara Falls (© **800/56-FALLS [32557]** or 519/356-6061; www.niagarafalls tourism.com) or the **Niagara Parks Commission** (© **877/NIA-PARK [642-7275];** www. niagaraparks.com).

GETTING THERE   Niagara-on-the-Lake is best seen by **car.** From Toronto, take the Queen Elizabeth Way (signs read QEW) to Niagara via Hamilton and St. Catharine's, and exit at Highway 55. The trip takes about 1½ hours.

Amtrak and **VIA** (© **416/366-8411**) operate **trains** between Toronto and New York, but they stop only in Niagara Falls and St. Catharine's, not in Niagara-on-the-Lake. Call © **800/361-1235** in Canada or **800/USA-RAIL** in the United States. From either place, you'll need to rent a car. Rental outlets in St. Catharine's include **Hertz,** 350 Ontario St. (© **905/682-8695**). In Niagara Falls, **Avis** is at 5734 Valley Way (© **905/357-2847**).

(Tips) **Biking Through Wine Country**

Driving through Niagara-on-the-Lake by car is a delight, but many would argue that the region is best viewed by bicycle. Starting in 2007, Via Rail began offering a **Toronto-Niagara Bike Train,** and in 2008 the program was expanded. Passenger trains have a bike cargo car, and you can hop aboard—for C$59 (£30) per person round trip—and get to Niagara Falls in less than 2 hours. From there, you can bike to your hotel (if you're a light traveler), or arrange for pick-up for an extra fee. Call (C) **888/619-5984** or visit **www.biketrain.ca** for more details.

THE SHAW FESTIVAL

The Shaw celebrates the dramatic and comedic works of George Bernard Shaw and his contemporaries, but it also features new works by Canadian playwrights. From April till the first weekend of November, the festival offers a dozen plays in the historic **Court House Theatre,** the exquisite **Shaw Festival Theatre,** and the **Royal George Theatre.** Recent performances have included *An Inspector Calls, The Little Foxes,* and Shaw's *Mrs. Warren's Profession.*

Free chamber concerts take place Sunday at 11am. Chats introduce performances on Friday evenings in July and August, and question-and-answer sessions follow Tuesday-evening performances.

The Shaw announces its festival program in mid-January. Tickets are difficult to obtain on short notice, so try to book at least a month in advance. Prices range from C$45 to C$105 (£23–£53). For more information, contact the **Shaw Festival** ((C) **800/ 511-7429** or 905/468-2172; www.shawfest.com).

EXPLORING THE TOWN

Niagara-on-the Lake is small, and most of its attractions are along one main street, making it easy to explore on foot.

Sights

Fort George National Historic Site ★ (Kids)   The fort played a central role in the War of 1812: It was headquarters for the British Army's Centre Division. The division was comprised of British regulars, local militia, Runchey's corps of former slaves, and aboriginal forces. The fort was destroyed by American artillery fire in May 1813. After the war it was partially rebuilt, but it was abandoned in 1828 and not reconstructed until the 1930s. You can view the guardroom (with its hard plank beds), the officers' quarters, the enlisted men's quarters, and the sentry posts. The self-guided tour includes interpretive films. Those who believe in ghosts take note: The fort is one of Ontario's favorite "haunted" sites (ghost-hunting tours are available throughout the summer and in October).

Niagara Pkwy. (C) **905/468-4257.** www.parkscanada.ca or www.friendsoffortgeorge.ca. Admission C$12 (£6) adults, C$10 (£5) seniors, C$6 (£3) children 6–16, free for children 5 and under. Apr 1–Oct 31 daily 10am–5pm (open on weekends during the rest of the year).

Niagara Historical Society Museum   More than 8,000 artifacts pertaining to local history make up this collection. They include many possessions of United Empire Loyalists who first settled the area at the end of the American Revolution. The branding irons, church tuning box, portraits, maps, and other artifacts won't interest everyone, but budding historians should take note.

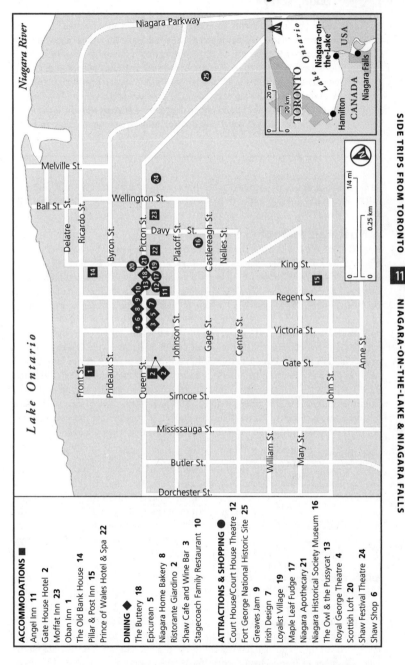

ACCOMMODATIONS ■
Angel Inn **11**
Gate House Hotel **2**
Moffat Inn **23**
Oban Inn **1**
The Old Bank House **14**
Pillar & Post Inn **15**
Prince of Wales Hotel & Spa **22**

DINING ◆
The Buttery **18**
Epicurean **5**
Niagara Home Bakery **8**
Ristorante Giardino **2**
Shaw Cafe and Wine Bar **3**
Stagecoach Family Restaurant **10**

ATTRACTIONS & SHOPPING ●
Court House/Court House Theatre **12**
Fort George National Historic Site **25**
Greaves Jam **9**
Irish Design **7**
Loyalist Village **19**
Maple Leaf Fudge **17**
Niagara Apothecary **21**
Niagara Historical Society Museum **16**
The Owl & the Pussycat **13**
Royal George Theatre **4**
Scottish Loft **20**
Shaw Festival Theatre **24**
Shaw Shop **6**

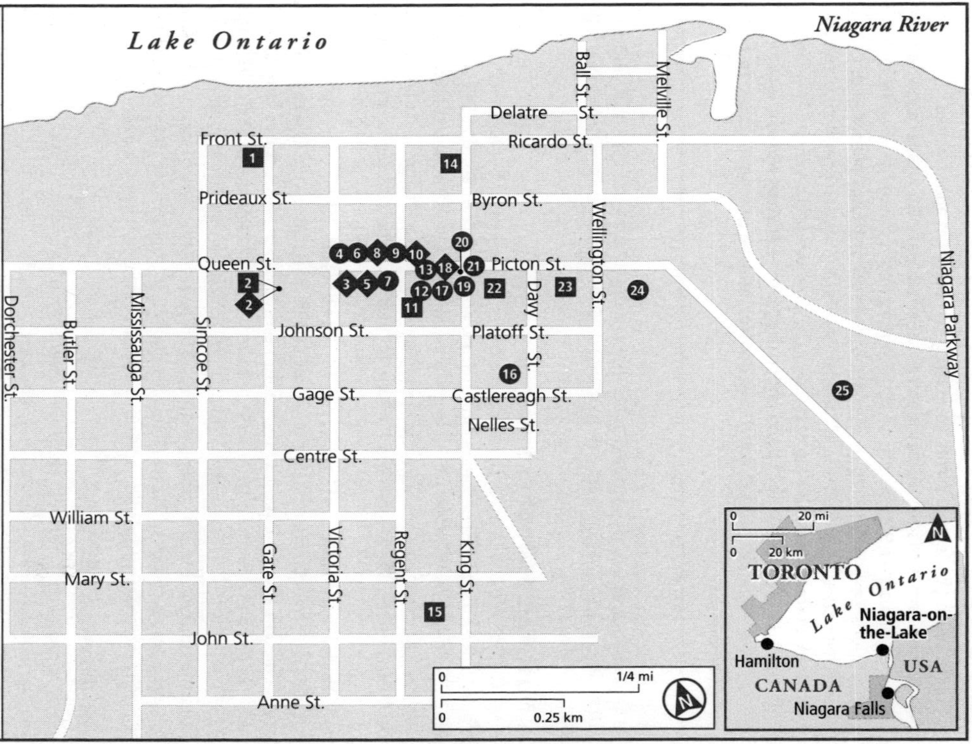
Lake Ontario
Niagara River
Niagara Parkway
Ball St.
Melville St.
Delatre St.
Front St.
Ricardo St.
Prideaux St.
Byron St.
Wellington St.
Queen St.
Picton St.
Davy St.
Johnson St.
Platoff St.
Dorchester St.
Butler St.
Mississauga St.
Simcoe St.
Gage St.
Castlereagh St.
Nelles St.
Centre St.
William St.
Mary St.
Gate St.
Victoria St.
Regent St.
King St.
John St.
Anne St.
0
1/4 mi
0
0.25 km
N
0
20 mi
0
20 km
TORONTO
Lake Ontario
Niagara-on-the-Lake
Hamilton
USA
CANADA
Niagara Falls

(Finds) Ooh, Scary

For those who believe in ghosts, Fort George is one of Ontario's favorite "haunted" sites. Reported sightings include a soldier patrolling its perimeter and a young damsel who appears in an 18th-century mirror. While I'm a skeptic about apparitions, I'm still drawn to the fun, atmospheric Ghost Tours offered at the fort. These are available on evenings from May through September, with bonus dates around Halloween. The cost is C$12 (£6) for adults and children 12 and up, and C$5 (£2.50) for children 11 and under. Contact the **Friends of Fort George** at ℂ **905/468-6621,** or visit **www.friendsoffortgeorge.ca** for a schedule and for more details.

43 Castlereagh St. (at Davy). ℂ **905/468-3912.** Admission C$5 (£2.50) adults, C$3 (£1.50) seniors, C$2 (£1) students with ID, C$1 (50p) children 5–12, free for children 4 and under. May–Oct daily 10am–5pm; Nov–Apr daily 1–5pm.

A Nostalgic Shopping Stroll

A stroll along the town's main artery, Queen Street, will take you by some entertaining, albeit touristy, shops. The **Niagara Apothecary,** at no. 5 (ℂ 905/468-3845), dates to 1866. Gold-leaf script marks its original black-walnut counters and the contents of the drawers, and the original glass and ceramic apothecary ware is on display. At no. 13 is the **Scottish Loft** (ℂ 905/468-0965), which is filled with tartans, Celtic memorabilia, candy, books, CDs, and DVDs (aside from the tartans, the products hail from England and Wales, too). **Maple Leaf Fudge,** no. 14 (ℂ 905/468-2211), offers more than 20 varieties that you can watch being made on marble slabs. At no. 16 is a charming toy store, **The Owl and the Pussycat** (ℂ 905/468-3081). At no. 35 is **Greaves Jam** (ℂ 905/468-7331), run by fourth-generation jam makers. **Irish Design,** at no. 38 (ℂ 905/468-7233), sells hand-knit sweaters, traditional gold and silver jewelry, and other treasures from the Emerald Isle. The **Shaw Shop** (ℂ 800/511-7429), no. 79, next to the Royal George Theatre, carries GBS memorabilia and more. A Dansk outlet and several galleries selling contemporary Canadian and other ethnic crafts round out the mix.

Jet-Boating Thrills

Jet-boat excursions leave from the dock across from 61 Melville St. at the King George III Inn. Don a rain suit, poncho, and life jacket, and climb aboard. The boat takes you out onto the Niagara River for a trip along the stonewalled canyon to the whirlpool downriver. The ride starts slow but gets into turbulent water. Trips, which operate from May to October, last an hour and cost C$56 (£28) for adults and C$47 (£24) for children 13 and under. Reservations are required. Call the **Whirlpool Jet Boat Company** at ℂ 888/438-4444 or 905/468-4800, or visit **www.whirlpooljet.com**.

WHERE TO STAY

In summer, hotel space is in high demand. If you're having trouble nailing down a room, contact the chamber of commerce, which provides an accommodations-reservations service. Note that the same company, Vintage Inns, owns several of the hotels in town. (Vintage Inns is known for buying upscale properties and making them even more luxurious.) Or you could opt for one of the more than 200 bed-and-breakfasts around town. The **Niagara-on-the-Lake Chamber of Commerce** (ℂ **905/468-1950;** www.niagaraonthelake.com) provides

In Town

Gate House Hotel ★   Unlike many of the Canadiana-influenced lodgings in town, the Gate House Hotel is decorated in cool, clean-lined Milanese style. Guest rooms have a marbleized look and are accented with ultramodern black lamps, block marble tables, leatherette couches, and bathrooms with sleek Italian fixtures. The Gate House's eatery, Ristorante Giardino, is one of the best places to dine in town.

142 Queen St., Niagara-on-the-Lake, ON L0S 1J0. © **905/468-3263**. www.gatehouse-niagara.com. 10 units. From C$210 (£105) double. AE, MC, V. Free parking. **Amenities:** Restaurant; concierge. *In room:* A/C, TV, hair dryer.

Moffat Inn Value   This is a fine budget-conscious choice in a convenient location. Most rooms contain brass-framed beds, and eight have fireplaces. Coffee is available in the lobby, and each room has a teakettle and supplies. There's also a restaurant, Tetley's, which serves fondue, steaks, and sushi. *One caveat:* If you have trouble climbing stairs, this hotel would not be a good choice. Most of the guest rooms are on the second floor, and there's no elevator (and no porter to handle luggage).

Touring Niagara-on-the-Lake Wineries

Visiting a local winery is one of the most delicious ways to pass an hour or two in this region. For maps of the area and information about vintners, contact the **Wine Council of Ontario** (© **905/684-8070**; www.winesofontario.org). The wineries listed below are close to the town of Niagara-on-the-Lake. Tours are free. Prices for tastings vary with the winery and the wine you're sampling, but are usually about C$10 (£5).

Take Highway 55 (Niagara Stone Rd.) out of Niagara-on-the-Lake, and you'll come to **Hillebrand Estates Winery** (© **800/582-8412** or 905/468-7123; www.hillebrand.com), just outside Virgil. It's open year-round, plays host to a variety of special events (including a weekend concert series), and even offers bicycle tours. The Hillebrand Winery Restaurant, with views of both the barrel-filled cellar and the Niagara Escarpment, is a delightful spot for lunch or dinner. Winery tours start on the hour daily from 10am to 6pm.

If you turn off Highway 55 and go down York Road, you'll reach **Château des Charmes,** west of St. David's (© **905/262-4219**; www.chateaudescharmes. com). The winery was built to resemble a French manor house, and its architecture is unique in the region. One-hour tours are given daily. It's open from 10am to 6pm year-round.

To reach the **Konzelmann Estate Winery,** 1096 Lakeshore Rd. (© **905/935-2866**; www.konzelmann.ca), take Mary Street out of Niagara-on-the-Lake. This vintner is famous for its award-winning icewines. It offers tours from May to late September, Monday through Saturday.

60 Picton St. (at Queen St.), Niagara-on-the-Lake, ON L0S 1J0. ☏ **905/468-4116.** www.moffatinn.com. 22 units. From C$125 (£63) double. AE, MC, V. Free parking. **Amenities:** Restaurant; bar; access to nearby health club. *In room:* A/C, TV, dataport, coffeemaker, hair dryer.

Oban Inn ★   In a prime location overlooking the lake, the Oban Inn is a lovely place to stay. It's in a charming white Victorian house with a green dormer-style roof and a large veranda. The gorgeous gardens are the source of the bouquets throughout the house. Each of the guest rooms is designed with comfort in mind. The sedate colors and elegant reproduction furniture lend a charming home-away-from-home feel. While the look is old-fashioned, the amenities are not: LCD plasma televisions, Bose sound systems, and individual temperature controls in all rooms.

160 Front St. (at Gate St.), Niagara-on-the-Lake, ON L0S 1J0. ☏ **866/359-6226** or 905/468-2165. www.obaninn.ca. 26 units. From C$260 (£130) double. AE, DC, DISC, MC, V. Free parking. **Amenities:** Restaurant; lounge; concierge; bike rental; room service; babysitting. *In room:* A/C, TV, dataport, hair dryer, iron.

The Old Bank House ★   Beautifully situated down by the river, this two-story Georgian was built in 1817 as the first branch of the Bank of Canada. In 1902, it hosted the Prince and Princess of Wales, and today, it's a charming bed-and-breakfast inn. Several tastefully decorated units have private entrances, and one also has a private trellised deck. Several of the rooms have private balconies. Eight units have a refrigerator and coffee or tea supplies. The most expensive suite accommodates five in two bedrooms. The extraordinarily comfortable sitting room (open to all guests) holds a fireplace and eclectic antique pieces.

10 Front St., Niagara-on-the-Lake, ON L0S 1J0. ☏ **877-468-7136** or 905/468-7136. www.oldbankhouse.com. 9 units. From C$184 (£92) double. Rates include breakfast. AE, MC, V. Free parking. **Amenities:** Jacuzzi. *In room:* A/C, no phone.

Pillar & Post Inn   The discreetly elegant Pillar & Post is a couple of blocks from the maddening crowds on Queen Street. This is one of the most sophisticated accommodations in town, complete with the 100 Fountain Spa offering the latest in deluxe treatments and a Japanese-style, warm mineral-spring pool. The light, airy lobby boasts a fireplace and comfortable seating. The style is classic Canadiana: The spacious rooms all contain old-fashioned furniture, a pine cabinet with a TV tucked inside, and historical engravings. In the back is a secluded pool. Some rooms facing the outdoor pool on the ground level have bay windows and window boxes.

48 John St. W. (at King St.), Niagara-on-the-Lake, ON L0S 1J0. ☏ **888/669-5566** or 905/468-2123. Fax 905/468-1472. www.vintage-hotels.com. 122 units. From C$240 (£120) double. AE, DC, MC, V. Free parking. **Amenities:** 2 dining rooms; wine bar; indoor and outdoor pools; spa; Jacuzzi; sauna; bike rental; concierge; business center; dry cleaning. *In room:* A/C, TV, dataport, minibar, hair dryer, safe.

Prince of Wales ★★   This is Niagara-on-the-Lake's most luxurious hotel, and it has it all: a central location across from the lovely gardens of Simcoe Park; recreational facilities, including an indoor pool; a luxurious spa; lounges, bars, and restaurants; and attractive, beautifully decorated rooms. It has a lively atmosphere yet retains the elegance and charm of a Victorian inn. Bathrooms have bidets, and most rooms have minibars. All rooms are nonsmoking.

6 Picton St., Niagara-on-the-Lake, ON L0S 1J0. ☏ **888/669-5566** or 905/468-3246. www.vintage-hotels.com. 114 units. From C$275 (£138) double. AE, DC, DISC, MC, V. Free parking. Pets accepted. **Amenities:** Dining room; cafe; bar; lounge; indoor pool; health club; spa; Jacuzzi; bike rental; concierge; business center; 24-hr. room service; massage; dry cleaning. *In room:* A/C, TV, dataport, hair dryer, iron, safe.

Inn on the Twenty and the Vintage House ★ On the grounds of the Cave Spring Cellars, one of Niagara's best wineries, these modern accommodations consist entirely of handsome suites. Each has an elegantly furnished living room with a fireplace, and a Jacuzzi in the bathroom. Seven are duplexes—one of them, the deluxe loft, has two double beds on its second level—and five are single-level suites with high ceilings. All of the suites are nonsmoking. The inn's eatery, On the Twenty Restaurant & Wine Bar (p. 240), is across the street. Its spa offers a full range of services for men and women, and has special packages for couples. Next door is the **Vintage House,** an 1840 Georgian mansion with three suites, all with private entrances. All rooms are non-smoking.

3845 Main St., Jordan, ON L0R 1S0. ℂ **800/701-8074** or 905/562-5336. www.innonthetwenty.com. 30 units. From C$259 (£130) suite. MC, V. Free parking. From QEW, take Jordan Rd. exit south; at 1st intersection, turn right onto 4th Ave., and then right onto Main St. **Amenities:** Restaurant; nearby golf course; health club; concierge. *In room:* A/C, TV, dataport, coffeemaker, hair dryer, iron.

WHERE TO DINE
In Town
In addition to the listings below, don't forget the very fine dining rooms at the **Gate House Hotel,** the **Pillar & Post,** and the **Prince of Wales,** all listed above.

The stylish **Shaw Cafe and Wine Bar,** 92 Queen St. (ℂ **905/468-4772**), serves lunch and light meals, and has a patio. The **Epicurean,** 84 Queen St. (ℂ **905/468-3408**), offers hearty soups, quiches, sandwiches, and other fine dishes in a sunny, Provence-inspired dining room. Service is cafeteria style. Half a block off Queen Street, the **Angel Inn,** 224 Regent St. (ℂ **905/468-3411**), is a delightfully authentic English pub. For an inexpensive down-home breakfast, go to the **Stagecoach Family Restaurant,** 45 Queen St. (ℂ **905/468-3133**). It also serves basic family fare, such as burgers, fries, and meatloaf, but it doesn't accept credit cards. **Niagara Home Bakery,** 66 Queen St. (ℂ **905/468-3431**), is the place to stop for chocolate-date squares, cherry squares, croissants, cookies, and individual quiches.

The Buttery ★ CANADIAN/CONTINENTAL/ENGLISH The Buttery has been a dining landmark for more than 30 years. At its weekend Henry VIII dinner theater feasts, "serving wenches" bring food and wine while "jongleurs" and "musickers" entertain; Henry and the third of his six wives, Jane Seymour, are your hosts. The meal consists of "five removes" (courses) involving broth, chicken, roast lamb, roast pig, sherry trifle, syllabub, and cheese, all washed down with a good amount of wine, ale, and mead. The regular pub menu is available every day.

19 Queen St. ℂ **905/468-2564.** www.thebutteryrestaurant.com. Reservations strongly recommended; required for Henry VIII feast. Henry VIII feast C$55 (£28); main courses C$26 (£13). MC, V. Apr–Nov daily 11am–11pm; Dec–Mar Sun–Thurs 11am–7:30pm. Afternoon tea year-round daily 2–5pm.

In Nearby St. Catharines
Wellington Court ★★ CONTINENTAL Located in an Edwardian townhouse with a flower trellis, Chef Eric Peacock's menu features daily specials along with such items as beef tenderloin in shallot-and-red-wine reduction; roast capon with a bacon, leek, and goat-cheese tart; and grilled sea bass with cranberry vinaigrette. Not surprisingly, given the location, the wine list is filled with excellent Niagara bottles.

11 Wellington St., St. Catharines. ℂ **905/682-5518.** www.wellington-court.com. Reservations recommended. Main courses C$22–C$30 (£11–£15). MC, V. Tues–Sat 11:30am–2:30pm and 5–9:30pm. From QEW, exit at Lake St., turn left, follow to Wellington Ave., turn left, follow for 1 block, turn right.

Hillebrand Estates Winery Restaurant ★ CONTINENTAL   This dining room is light and airy, and its floor-to-ceiling windows offer views over the vineyards to the distant Niagara Escarpment, or of wine cellars bulging with oak barrels. The seasonal menu features such dishes as poached Arctic char with shellfish ragout, or prosciutto-wrapped pheasant breast atop linguine tossed with mushrooms, roasted eggplant, and shallot. The starters are equally luxurious. In case the food isn't enticing enough (and it should be), the restaurant also hosts special events throughout the year, many featuring jazz musicians.

Hwy. 55, between Niagara-on-the-Lake and Virgil. ⓒ 905/468-7123. www.hillebrand.com. Reservations strongly recommended. Main courses C$30–C$38 (£15–£19). AE, MC, V. Daily noon–11pm (closes earlier in winter).

On the Twenty Restaurant & Wine Bar ★ CANADIAN   This restaurant is a favorite among foodies. The gold-painted dining rooms cast a warm glow. The cuisine features ingredients from many local producers, giving On the Twenty a small-town feel. Naturally, there's an extensive selection of Ontario wines, including some wonderful icewines to accompany such desserts as lemon tart and fruit cobbler. On the Twenty Restaurant is associated with **Inn on the Twenty** (p. 239), across the street.

At Cave Spring Cellars, 3836 Main St., Jordan. ⓒ **905/562-7313**. www.innonthetwenty.com. Reservations recommended. Main courses C$22–C$38 (£11–£19). MC, V. Daily 11:30am–3pm and 5–10pm.

Vineland Estates ★★ CONTINENTAL   This inspired eatery serves some of the most innovative food along the wine trail. On warm days, you can dine on a deck under a spreading tree or stay in the airy dining room. Start with a plate of seasoned mussels in a ginger broth. Follow with Canadian Angus tenderloin with a risotto of truffles and morel mushrooms, or pan-seared sweetbreads with a celeriac and potato mash and confit of mushrooms glazed with icewine. For dessert, try the tasting plate of Canadian farm cheeses, including Abbey St. Benoit blue Ermite; sweet tooths can indulge in the maple-walnut cheesecake in a biscotti crust.

3620 Moyer Rd., Vineland. ⓒ **888/846-3526** or 905/562-7088. www.vineland.com. Reservations strongly recommended. Main courses C$32–C$40 (£16–£20). AE, MC, V. Daily noon–2:30pm and 5–8:30pm.

ALONG THE NIAGARA PARKWAY ★★

The Niagara Parkway, on the Canadian side of the falls, is a gem. Unlike the American side, it abounds with natural wonders, including vast expanses of parkland. You can drive along the 56km (35-mile) parkway all the way from Niagara-on-the-Lake to Niagara Falls, taking in attractions en route. Here are the major ones, listed in the order in which you'll encounter them:

- The **White Water Walk,** 4330 River Rd. (ⓒ **905/374-1221**): The scenic boardwalk runs beside the raging white waters of the Great Gorge Rapids. Stroll along and wonder how it must have felt to challenge this mighty torrent, where the river rushes through the narrow channel at an average speed of 35kmph (22 mph). Admission is C$8.50 (£4.25) for adults, C$5 (£2.50) for children 6 to 12, free for children 5 and under. Open daily from 9am to 5pm (closes at 7pm or 8pm from mid-May till Labor Day).
- The **Whirlpool Aero Car** (ⓒ **905/354-5711**): This red-and-yellow cable-car contraption whisks you on a 1,097m (3,600-ft.) jaunt between two points in Canada. High above the Niagara Whirlpool, you'll enjoy excellent views of the surrounding landscape. Admission is C$11 (£5.50) for adults, C$6.50 (£3.25) for children 6 to 12,

free for kids 5 and under. Open daily May to the third Sunday in October. Hours are **241**
from 10am to 5pm (closes at 7pm or 8pm from mid-May till Labor Day).

- The **Niagara Parks Botanical Gardens and School of Horticulture** (© 905/356-8119): Stop here for a free view of the vast gardens and a look at the **Floral Clock,** which contains 25,000 plants in its 12m-diameter (40-ft.) face. The gorgeous **Butterfly Conservatory** is also in the gardens. In this lush tropical setting, more than 2,000 butterflies (50 international species) float and flutter among such nectar-producing flowers as lantanas and pentas. The large, bright-blue, luminescent Morpho butterflies from Central and South America are particularly gorgeous. Interpretive programs and other presentations take place in the auditorium and two smaller theaters. The native butterfly garden outside attracts the more familiar swallowtails, fritillaries, and painted ladies. Admission is C$11 (£5.50) for adults, C$6.50 (£3.25) for children 6 to 12, free for children 5 and under. Open daily 9am-5pm.

- **Queenston Heights Park:** This is the site of a famous War of 1812 battle, and you can take a walking tour of the battlefield. Picnic or play tennis in the shaded arbor before moving to the **Laura Secord Homestead,** Partition Street, Queenston (© 905/262-4851). This heroic woman threaded enemy lines to alert British authorities to a surprise attack by American soldiers during the War of 1812. Her home contains a fine collection of Upper Canada furniture from the period, plus artifacts recovered from an archaeological dig. Stop at the candy shop and ice-cream parlor. Tours run every half-hour. Admission is C$4.50 (£2.25) for adults, C$3.50 for children 6 to 12, free for children age 5 and under. Open Wed-Sun 11am-5pm (open daily in summer).

- Fruit farms like **Kurtz Orchards** (© 905/468-2937) and wineries such as the **Inniskillin Winery,** Line 3, Service Road 66 (© 905/468-3554 or 905/468-2187): You'll find peaches, apples, pears, nectarines, cherries, plums, and strawberries at Kurtz; you can tour the 32 hectares (80 acres) on a tractor-pulled tram. Inniskillin is open daily from 10am to 6pm June to October, and Monday through Saturday from 10am to 5pm November through May. The self-guided free tour has 20 stops that explain the winemaking process. A free guided tour, offered daily in summer and Saturdays only in winter, begins at 2:30pm.

- **Old Fort Erie,** 350 Lakeshore Rd., Fort Erie (© 905/871-0540): It's a reconstruction of the fort that was seized by the Americans in July 1814, besieged later by the British, and finally blown up as the Americans retreated across the river to Buffalo. Guards in period

SIDE TRIPS FROM TORONTO

11

NIAGARA-ON-THE-LAKE & NIAGARA FALLS

Fun Facts **The Honeymoon Capital of the World**

Seeing Niagara Falls as it today—in all of its loud, neon, carnival glory—you can't help but wonder how anyone could ever have thought it romantic enough for a honeymoon. But back in 1801, when the falls was simply a natural wonder of the highest order, Aaron Burr's daughter, Theodosia, chose it as the perfect place for her honeymoon. Napoleon's brother Jerome Bonaparte followed in her footsteps with his bride in 1804, and suddenly everybody thought Niagara Falls was the place for a newlywed couple to be. Well, not *everybody*. After that trenchant wit Oscar Wilde visited Niagara Falls in 1881, he wrote: "Every American bride is taken there, and the sight of the stupendous waterfall must be one of the earliest if not the keenest disappointments in American married life."

Tips — The Perfect Falls View

I love seeing Niagara Falls from the **Skylon Tower,** but the price of admission seems steep to me. One alternative used to be to come up to the Skylon's **revolving restaurant** for a midafternoon snack, but even that has become impossible since the place started charging a C$25 (£12.50) minimum per-adult charge at lunch and C$40 (£20) minimum at dinner. (This is a food charge— money spent on alcohol doesn't count!) There is one strategy that still works: stop by the restaurant after the dinner rush for dessert and coffee; the restaurant will usually waive the minimum charge once the mealtime crowd thins out. Just make sure you ask *before* you are seated!

costume stand sentry duty, fire the cannons, and demonstrate drill and musket practice. Open daily from 10am to 5pm from the first Saturday in May to mid-September, and weekends only to Canadian Thanksgiving (U.S. Columbus Day). Admission is C$9 (£4.50) for adults, C$5 (£2.50) for children 6 to 12, free for children 5 and under.

SEEING NIAGARA FALLS

You simply cannot come this far and not see the falls, which are the seventh natural wonder of the world. The most exciting way to do that is from the decks of the *Maid of the Mist* ★★, 5920 River Rd. (© **905/358-5781;** www.maidofthemist.com). The sturdy boat takes you right in—through the turbulent waters around the American Falls; past the Rock of Ages; and to the foot of the Horseshoe Falls, where 34.5 million imperial gallons of water tumble over the 54m-high (176-ft.) cataract each minute. You'll get wet, and your glasses will mist, but that won't detract from the thrill. Boats leave from the dock on the parkway just down from the Rainbow Bridge. Trips operate daily from mid-May to mid-October. Fares are C$14.50 (£7.25) for adults and C$9 (£4.50) for children 6 to 12, free for children 5 and under.

Go down under the falls using the elevator at the **Table Rock Centre,** which drops you 46m (151 ft.) through solid rock to the tunnels and viewing portals of the **Journey Behind the Falls** (© **905/354-1551**). You'll receive—and appreciate—a rain poncho. Admission is C$12 (£6) for adults, C$7 (£3.50) for children 6 to 12, free for children 5 and under. Another attraction at the Table Rock Centre (which has been going through a $32 million renovation lately) is **Niagara's Fury,** which opened on June 27, 2008. The details were kept tightly under wraps until just before the new attraction was unveiled. Visitors are invited to "experience" the creation of the falls in a chamber that swirls visual images over a 360-degree screen, has the ground shake beneath them, envelops them in a blizzard, and makes the temperature drop from 75F to 40F degrees (24°C to 4°C) in 3 seconds. It's an intense experience, which is why it's not appropriate for very young children. Fares are C$15 (£7.50) for adults, C$9 (£4.50) for children 6 to 12, free for children 5 and under. Open daily 9am to 9pm.

You can ride the external glass-fronted elevators 159m (522 ft.) to the top of the **Skylon Tower Observation Deck,** 5200 Robinson St. (© **905/356-2651;** www.skylon. com). The observation deck is open daily from 8am to midnight from June to Labour Day; hours vary in other seasons, so call ahead. Adults pay C$13 (£5.40), children 12 and under C$7.50 (£3.75).

SIDE TRIPS FROM TORONTO

11

NIAGARA-ON-THE-LAKE & NIAGARA FALLS

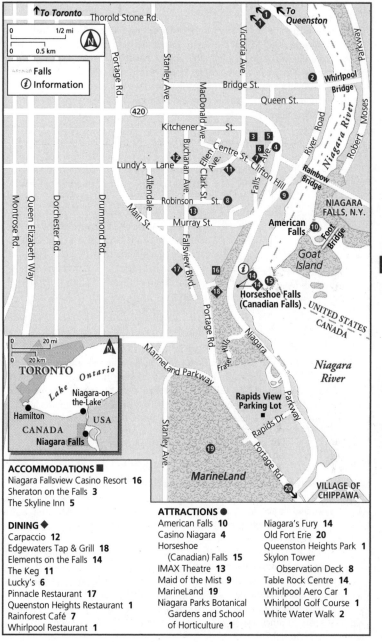

ACCOMMODATIONS ■
Niagara Fallsview Casino Resort **16**
Sheraton on the Falls **3**
The Skyline Inn **5**

DINING ◆
Carpaccio **12**
Edgewaters Tap & Grill **18**
Elements on the Falls **14**
The Keg **11**
Lucky's **6**
Pinnacle Restaurant **17**
Queenston Heights Restaurant **1**
Rainforest Café **7**
Whirlpool Restaurant **1**

ATTRACTIONS ●
American Falls **10**
Casino Niagara **4**
Horseshoe
  (Canadian) Falls **15**
IMAX Theatre **13**
Maid of the Mist **9**
MarineLand **19**
Niagara Parks Botanical
  Gardens and School
  of Horticulture **1**

Niagara's Fury **14**
Old Fort Erie **20**
Queenston Heights Park **1**
Skylon Tower
  Observation Deck **8**
Table Rock Centre **14**
Whirlpool Aero Car **1**
Whirlpool Golf Course **1**
White Water Walk **2**

A Family Adventure

If you're looking for something to keep the kids amused, visit **MarineLand** ★, 7657 Portage Rd. (© **905/356-9565;** www.marinelandcanada.com). At the aquarium-theater, King Waldorf, the walrus mascot, presides over performances by killer whales, dolphins, and sea lions. Friendship Cove, a 4.5 million-gallon breeding and observation tank, lets the little ones see killer whales up close. Another aquarium features displays of freshwater fish. At the small wildlife display, children enjoy petting and feeding the deer, and seeing bears and Canadian elk.

MarineLand also has theme-park rides, including a roller coaster, a Tivoli wheel (a fancy Ferris wheel), Dragon Boat rides, and a fully equipped playground. The big thriller is Dragon Mountain, a roller coaster that loops, double-loops, and spirals through 305m (1,000 ft.) of tunnels. You can picnic or eat at one of the three restaurants.

In summer, admission is C$40 (£20) for adults and children 10 and over, C$33 (£17) for children 5 to 9, and free for children 4 and under. Open daily July and August from 9am to 6pm; mid-April to mid-May and September to mid-October from 10am to 4pm; and mid-May to June from 10am to 5pm. Closed November through mid-April. Rides open in late May and close the first Monday in October. In town, drive south on Stanley Street and follow the signs; from the QEW, take the McLeod Road exit.

For a different view of Niagara Falls, stop by the **IMAX Theater,** 6170 Buchanan Ave. (© **905/358-3611;** www.imaxniagara.com). You can view the raging, swirling waters in *Niagara: Miracles, Myths, and Magic,* shown on a six-story-high screen. Admission is C$15 (£7.50) for adults, C$11 (£5.50) for children 4 to 12, free for children 3 and under. I consider this a lot of money to pay for a movie that is only 45 minutes long. You can save some money by buying a combination ticket with the Skylon Tower, or by purchasing your tickets online in advance.

The falls are also exciting in winter, when the ice bridge and other formations are quite remarkable.

Where to Stay & Dine near the Falls

While Niagara-on-the-Lake is a far more scenic and charming option, you may find yourself staying overnight in Niagara Falls. One good hotel bet is the **Sheraton on the Falls,** 5875 Falls Ave. (© **888/234-8410** or 905/374-4445), which offers rooms with a truly gorgeous view; many have balconies. Rates start at C$100 (£50) for a double room. If you're more interested in gambling than a view, check out **The Skyline Inn,** 5685 Falls Ave. (© **800/263-7135** or 905/374-4444), which is right by Casino Niagara. Rates here start at C$90 (£45) per night. Then there's the luxurious **Niagara Fallsview Casino Resort,** 6380 Fallsview Blvd. (© **888/325-5788;** www.fallsviewcasinoresort.com), which opened in June 2004. It boasts its own 18,580-sq.-m (200,000-sq.-ft.) casino, a performing-arts theater, a spa, and 10 dining spots. Its 368 rooms start at C$200 (£100) for a double.

Niagara Falls likes to boast about its newly invigorated dining scene, but it's a challenge to find good food that doesn't cost a small fortune. One interesting option is the **Pinnacle Restaurant,** 6732 Fallsview Blvd. (© **905/356-1501**), which offers a Continental menu and a remarkable view from the top of the Konica Minolta Tower. **Carpaccio,** 6840 Lundy's Lane (© **905/371-2063**), is surrounded by fast-food outlets, but its fine Italian cooking makes it a gastronomic oasis. **The Keg,** 5950 Victoria Ave. (© **905/353-4022**) is a reliable steakhouse chain. Over at Casino Niagara, **Lucky's,** 5705 Falls Ave. (© **888/946-3255**), serves up hearty portions of prime rib as well as burgers and pizza. The **Rainforest Café,** 5875 Falls Ave. (© **905/374-2233**), is a family favorite with its animatronic gorillas and serpents and its tried-and-true menu of pizzas, burgers, and sandwiches.

3 THE MUSKOKA LAKES

Just a 90-minute drive north of Toronto, the Muskoka region has been a magnet for visitors since the 19th century. Though the area proved futile for farming (it's located on the Canadian Shield, where you need dig only a foot or two in some places to come up against sheets of granite), its more than 1,600 lakes, unspoiled wilderness, and laid-back attitude made it an excellent place for a retreat. In the past decade, Muskoka's charms have expanded to include excellent golf courses, soothing spas, and top-notch restaurants. While the region is most popular in summer, when families congregate at the resorts and Hollywood celebrities such as Goldie Hawn and Tom Hanks lounge at their lakefront "cottages," this is a great area to visit at any time of the year.

Once accessible only by the water, Muskoka is still a boater's dream. The region also has several towns of note: Gravenhurst, Bracebridge, Port Carling, Huntsville, and Bala.

Niagara Parkway Commission Restaurants

The Niagara Parkway Commission has commandeered the most spectacular scenic spots for its restaurants. These used to be reasonably priced places serving lunch and dinner, but recent renovations have focused on creating more upscale settings, with prices to match. **Table Rock Centre,** right across from the falls, has had a complete renovation, and its expensive new restaurant, **Elements on the Falls** (© **905/354-3631**) opened in the summer of 2008. Also close to the falls is **Edgewaters Tap & Grill** (© **905/356-2217**), a more casual restaurant that's appropriate for the whole family (there's a special menu for kids). **Whirlpool Restaurant** (© **905/356-7221**), at the Whirlpool Golf Course near Queenston, is open to the public while the course is open (May to December). My favorite of the Niagara Parkway Commission's eateries is still the **Queenston Heights Restaurant,** 14184 Niagara Pkwy. (© **905/262-4274**). Set in the park among firs, cypresses, silver birches, and maples, the restaurant affords a magnificent view of the lower Niagara River and the lush, abundant land through which it flows. The restaurant also serves up an excellent duck confit and boasts a great wine list.

Located a few kilometers apart, these communities date back to the 1850s, when logging was Muskoka's primary industry. Filled with historic sites and more modern attractions, it's well worth devoting a day or two to explore them (fortunately, they are all easily reachable by car these days).

ESSENTIALS

GETTING THERE You can drive from the south via Highway 400 to Highway 11, from the east via highways 12 and 169 to Highway 11, and from the north via Highway 11. It's about 160km (99 miles) from Toronto to Gravenhurst, 15km (9 miles) from Gravenhurst to Bracebridge, 25km (16 miles) from Bracebridge to Port Carling, and 34km (21 miles) from Bracebridge to Huntsville. **VIA Rail** (© **416/366-8411;** www.viarail.ca) services Gravenhurst, Bracebridge, and Huntsville from Toronto's Union Station. An airport about 18km (11 miles) from Gravenhurst is used mainly for small aircraft. Several other landing strips and a helicopter-landing pad are at the Deerhurst Resort in Huntsville.

VISITOR INFORMATION For information on the region, contact **Muskoka Tourism** (© **800/267-9700** or 705/689-0660; www.discovermuskoka.ca).

GETTING AROUND While you won't need a car if you plan to stay close to your resort while you're here (an entirely reasonable proposition), you will need a car if you're planning to do a lot of sightseeing in the area. You could take the train to Bracebridge and then rent a car at **Budget,** 1 Robert Dollar Dr. (© **705/645-2755**). Huntsville has an **Enterprise** car rental center at 197 Main St. W. (© **705/789-1834**).

EXPLORING THE TOWNS

Both Gravenhurst and Huntsville are lovely towns that are well worth a visit. They are scenic, and they also have enough shops, restaurants, and public spaces to make them interesting. Unless you have kids and plan to visit Santa's Village (see below), there's not much of a reason to linger in Bracebridge.

Gravenhurst

Gravenhurst is Muskoka's first town—the first you reach if you're driving from Toronto and the first to achieve town status.

The **Norman Bethune Memorial House,** 235 John St. N. (© **705/687-4261**), is the restored 1890 birthplace of Dr. Norman Bethune. In 1939, this surgeon, inventor, and humanitarian died tending the sick in China during the Chinese Revolution. Tours of the historic house include a modern exhibit on Bethune's life. A visitor center displays gifts from Chinese visitors, and an orientation video is shown. In summer, the house is open daily from 10am to 4pm June through October, weekdays only from 1 to 4pm November through May. Admission is C$4 (£2) adults and C$2.50 (£1.25) for children 6 to 16, free for children 5 and under.

Sailing is one of Muskoka's greatest summer pleasures. Gravenhurst is home to the Muskoka Fleet, which includes a lovingly restored coal-powered 1887 steamship, the **RMS *Segwun.*** There are a variety of cruising options available, such as the 1-hour tour; a 2¹/₂-hour lunch cruise; and a 4-hour late-afternoon tour of **Millionaire's Row,** where you can be dazzled by the real estate as well as the natural beauty of the region. Reservations are required for all of the tours; call © **866/687-6667** or 705/687-6667 or visit **www.realmuskoka.com** for more information. Prices start at C$17 (£8.50) adults and C$10 (£5) children 12 and under for tours.

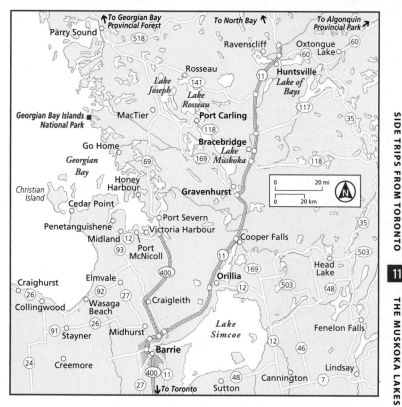

Year-round, there are theater performances at the **Gravenhurst Opera House** (© 705/687-5550), which celebrates its 108th anniversary in 2009. In summer only, there are shows at the **Port Carling Community Hall** (© 705/765-5221). For either, tickets usually cost between C$15 and C$30 (£7.50–£15).

Bracebridge: Santa's Workshop

Halfway between the equator and the North Pole, **Bracebridge** bills itself as Santa's summer home, and **Santa's Village** (© 705/645-2512; www.santasvillage.ca) is an imaginatively designed fantasyland full of delights: pedal boats and bumper boats on the lagoon, a roller-coaster sleigh ride, a Candy Cane Express, a carousel, and a Ferris wheel. At Elves' Island, kids can crawl on a suspended net and over or through various modules—the Lunch Bag Forest, Cave Crawl, and Snake Tube Crawl. Mid-June through Labour Day, it's open daily from 10am to 6pm. Admission is C$25 (£13) ages 5 and up and C$20 (£10) for seniors and children 2 to 4, free for children under 2.

Port Carling

As waterways became the main means of transportation in the region, **Port Carling** grew into the hub of the lakes. It became a boat-building center when a lock was installed connecting Lakes Muskoka and Rosseau, and a canal between Lakes Rosseau and Joseph opened all three to navigation. The **Muskoka Lakes Museum** on Joseph Street (© **705/765-5367**) captures the flavor of this era. July and August, it's open Monday through Saturday from 10am to 5pm and Sunday noon to 4pm; June, September, and October, hours are Tuesday through Saturday from 10am to 4pm and Sunday from noon to 4pm. Admission is by donation, with a suggested C$2 (£1) minimum.

Huntsville

Since the late 1800s, lumber has been the name of the game in Huntsville, and today it's Muskoka's biggest town. You can see some of the region's early history at the **Muskoka Heritage Place,** which includes **Muskoka Pioneer Village,** 88 Brunel Rd., Huntsville (© **705/789-7576;** www.muskokaheritageplace.org). It's open daily from 11am to 4pm from mid-May to mid-October. Admission is C$10 (£5) adults and C$7 (£3.50) children 3 to 12, free for children 2 and under. Muskoka Heritage Place also features the **Portage Flyer Steam Train.** Once part of the world's smallest commercial railway (running from 1904–58), it's been reborn as a tourist attraction, and you can ride its scenic route from Tuesday to Saturday for C$5 (£2.50) for adults and C$3 (£1.50) for kids.

Robinson's General Store on Main Street in Dorset (© **705/766-2415**) is so popular, it was voted Canada's best country store. Wood stoves, dry goods, hardware, pine goods, and moccasins—you name it, it's here.

WHERE TO STAY

Muskoka is famous for its lakes, but also for its resorts. While I normally like to wander from place to place when I travel to a particular area, I honestly think I could just stay put at one of the resorts here and be completely entertained for a week. Bed-and-breakfast and country-inn choices also abound. Contact **Muskoka Tourism** (© **800/267-9700** or 705/689-0660; www.discovermuskoka.ca). The prices listed below are for the peak summer season; deep discounts are available at all of these properties in early spring, late fall, and winter.

Resorts

Deerhurst Resort ★★★ (Kids)   The Deerhurst is an excellent spot for a family vacation, though it's also very popular with conference groups. This stunning resort complex rambles over 320 hectares (800 acres), and it boasts an array of amenities that boggles the mind: two 18-hole golf courses (part of the Muskoka Golf Trail) and a golf academy; a full-service Aveda spa; seemingly endless kilometers of nature trails for hiking (or snowmobiling or cross-country skiing in winter); canoeing, kayaking, and all manner of watersports; an ambitious musical revue that runs all summer; and horseback riding. (Most of the activities, including golf, the spa, and skiing, are available to visitors not staying at the resort.)

The accommodations here are spread out among several buildings on the property. They range from high-ceilinged hotel rooms in the Terrace and Bayshore buildings to fully appointed one-, two-, or three-bedroom suites, many with fireplaces and/or whirlpools. The suites come with such extras as CD players, TVs, and VCRs; some have full kitchens with microwaves, dishwashers, and washer/dryers. The most expensive suites are the three-bedroom units on the lake. The top-notch Aveda spa has some of the most talented therapists I've ever encountered.

1235 Deerhurst Dr., Huntsville, ON P1H 2E8. © **800/461-4393** or 705/789-6411. Fax 705/789-2431. www. deerhurstresort.com. 388 units. Summer from C$250 (£125) double. AE, DC, DISC, MC, V. Free parking.

> ## (Fun Facts) The Shania Connection
>
> The Deerhurst has many charms to recommend it, and whether or not you stay there, you must check out its excellent song-and-dance stage show. Now in its 26th year, it's famous in part because the phenomenally talented Shania Twain performed in it for 3 years (1988–1990). Twain has kept up her connection with the Deerhurst since, even having her wedding there. In 2002, she brought Katie Couric and a NBC film crew to reminisce about her days on its stage. Twain continues to visit the resort—and when she does, she always checks out the show. Every summer, the show is different, but it's always a pleasure.

Take Canal Rd. off Hwy. 60 to Deerhurst Rd. **Amenities:** 2 restaurants; 2 bars; 2 indoor pools and 3 outdoor pools; tennis courts; 2 18-hole golf courses; indoor sports complex; 3 squash courts; racquetball court; spa; 11 Jacuzzis; sauna; children's programs; concierge; business center; limited room service; laundry service; dry cleaning. *In room:* A/C, TV, dataport, minibar, hair dryer.

Delta Grandview Resort ★ (Kids) If the Deerhurst is for the folks on the fast track, the Delta Grandview is for those looking for a more measured pace. This smaller resort retains the natural beauty and contours of the original farmstead even while providing the latest resort facilities. Eighty accommodations are traditional hotel-style rooms, but most units are suites in a series of buildings, some down by the lake and others up on the hill with a lake view. The main dining room, the Rosewood Inn, is located in one of the resort's original buildings and overlooks Fairy Lake. In the summer, snacks are served at the Dockside Restaurant right on the shores of the lake, and the free Kidzone program provides supervision—and plenty of fun—for kids 4 to 12 from 8am to 4pm.

939 Hwy. 60, Grandview Drive, Huntsville, ON P1H 1Z4. © 888/472-6388 or 705/789-4417. www.delta hotels.com. 123 units. From C$230 (£115) double. AE, DC, DISC, MC, V. Free parking. **Amenities:** 2 restaurants; indoor and outdoor pools; 18-hole and 9-hole golf courses; 3 tennis courts; health club; children's programs; babysitting. *In room:* A/C, TV.

Taboo Resort ★★★ (Kids) Near the town of Gravenhurst in the southern Muskoka region, Taboo stands out for its sleek sophistication in a bucolic setting. Known until May 2003 as Muskoka Sands, the resort's new name may conjure up images of a hedonistic adults-only retreat. The truth is anything but: Taboo is a family-friendly zone, with a kids' club that schedules activities for every day of the week during the high season in summer. And the fact that the resort is so willing to take care of the children means that many adults can soak up spa treatments or dine at one of the on-site restaurants without a second thought.

Taboo is best known for its golf course, which Mike Weir (the 2003 Masters champion) calls his home course. The course is a major stop on the Muskoka Golf Trail. The Golf Academy can help those who want to improve their game. Another reason to come to Taboo is the excellent dining at Elements Restaurant, Culinary Theatre & Lounge (p. 250).

One of my favorite things about Taboo is that every single room, large and small alike, has its own deck or balcony. While all of the sophisticated offerings at the resort are excellent, nothing beats taking in the utterly serene and beautiful setting it enjoys.

1209 Muskoka Beach Rd., Gravenhurst, ON P1P 1R1. © 800/461-0236 or 705/687-2233. www.tabooresort. com. 157 units. From C$300 (£150) double. AE, DC, MC, V. Free parking. **Amenities:** 2 restaurants; bar; 4 pools (3 outdoor, 1 indoor); 2 golf courses (18-hole and 9-hole); 5 tennis courts; squash court; health club;

spa (in-room treatments also available); Jacuzzi; sauna; children's programs; game room; concierge; business center; limited room service; laundry service; dry cleaning. *In room:* A/C, TV, hair dryer.

Windermere House Resort ★ The appearance of the house brings you into the 1870s, with its stone-and-clapboard facade and romantic turrets. (The original building was destroyed by fire in 1996, but it was rebuilt according to its original 1870s design.) It overlooks well-manicured lawns that sweep down to Lake Rosseau. Out front stretches a broad veranda furnished with Adirondack chairs and window boxes. Rebuilding allowed the guest rooms to incorporate modern conveniences (including air-conditioning) while retaining a traditional look. Most of the rooms have gorgeous views (the best look over the lake), and a few have balconies or decks.

Off Muskoka Rte. 4 (P.O. Box 68), Windermere, ON P0B 1P0. © **800/461-4283** or 705/769-3611. Fax 705/769-2168. www.windermerehouse.com. 78 units. From C$220 (£110) double. Rates include breakfast. Weekly rates also available. AE, MC, V. Free parking. **Amenities:** Restaurant; lounge; outdoor pool; golf course; tennis courts; children's programs; limited room service; laundry service; dry cleaning. *In room:* A/C, TV, minibar.

A Country Inn

Inn at the Falls ★ (Finds) This attractive "inn" is actually a group of seven Victorian houses on a quiet cul-de-sac overlooking Bracebridge Falls and the Muskoka River. The inviting gardens are filled with delphiniums, peonies, roses, and spring flowers, plus there's an outdoor heated pool. Some units have fireplaces, Jacuzzis, and balconies; others have views of the falls. The Fox & Hounds is a popular local gathering place. In winter, the fire crackles and snaps, but in summer, the terrace is filled with flowers and umbrella-shaded tables. The more elegant Carriage Room serves upscale Continental fare. It's a perfect getaway-from-it-all spot, so I try to ignore the fact that the Inn now has Wi-Fi access. . .

1 Dominion St., P.O. Box 1139, Bracebridge, ON P1L 1V3. © **877/645-9212** or 705/645-2245. www.innatthefalls.net. 42 units. From C$110 (£55) double. Extra person C$16 (£8). Rates include breakfast. AE, DC, MC, V. Free parking. **Amenities:** 2 restaurants; outdoor pool; nearby golf course, Wi-Fi. *In room:* TV.

WHERE TO DINE

Very Expensive

Elements Restaurant, Culinary Theatre & Lounge ★★★ (Finds) CANADIAN/ FUSION It's strange to think that some Torontonians are coming to Muskoka to eat, given the big city's impressive culinary pedigree. But the chefs here have cooked at some of Toronto's famous kitchens, so perhaps it's no wonder that Elements is attracting gourmets from far and wide. The restaurant's floor-to-ceiling windows face west, so that you can take in the glorious sunset over the lake. Its a la carte menu includes wonders like Nova Scotia lobster with charred-corn-and-crab bread pudding.

The Culinary Theatre offers a unique experience. Only 18 seats are available at a time for this culinary school/live cooking show mix. Guests participate by selecting ingredients. Each meal—consisting of tasting menus of three, five, or seven courses—is cooked as you watch.

At Taboo Resort, 1209 Muskoka Beach Rd., Gravenhurst. © **705/687-2233.** www.tabooresort.com. Reservations required. Main courses C$35–C$48 (£18–£24). AE, DC, MC, V. Daily 6–10pm.

Expensive

Eclipse ★★ CANADIAN/INTERNATIONAL Recently renovated, Eclipse remains a Muskoka favorite. With an expansive lake view, this spacious dining room with a soaring ceiling of Douglas fir beams is a blend of fine dining and casual Muskoka charm.

Open for dinner, the restaurant has a lengthy menu with plenty of vegetarian options, so it's relatively easy to please different tastes. My favorite appetizer is the baked phyllo pastry filled with forest mushrooms and goat cheese, but the Sizzle—the signature dish—is the most popular (tiger shrimp sautéed in garlic, dried chiles, and white wine, and baked under mozzarella). Entrees run the gamut from breast of pheasant filled with wild rice and cranberries to a rack of lamb rubbed with fresh herbs and sourdough crumbs and served with apple-maple compote. The wine list, with its 300 selections, is just as interesting as the menu.

1235 Deerhurst Dr., Huntsville, ON P1H 2E8. © **705/789-6411.** www.deerhurstresort.com. Reservations recommended. Main courses C$26–C$36 (£13–£18). AE, DC, MC, V. Daily 5–11pm.

3 Guys and a Stove ★ (Kids) INTERNATIONAL   This is a family restaurant with a special menu for kids. But don't let the unpretentious atmosphere and the casual name fool you—the cooking is *very* fine. The curried pumpkin-and-sweet potato soup is an absolute must-have when it's on the menu; the spicy chicken stew is another surefire winner. This restaurant is also a terrific choice for vegetarians: the list of pasta and rice main-course dishes is substantial.

143 Hwy. 60, Huntsville. © **705/789-1815.** www.3guysandastove.com. Main courses C$14–C$39 (£7–£20). AE, MC, V. Daily 11am–9:30pm.

Moderate
Blondie's ★ (Finds) COMFORT FOOD/DELI/SEAFOOD   This family-run restaurant is a rare find in Muskoka. The menu has plenty of comfort foods—fish and chips, prime rib, eggs Benedict, smoked-meat sandwiches—but more exotic fare, such as sushi and various seafood dishes, is also served. Blondie's is also the official caterer to the Gravenhurst Opera House. The setting is like a country kitchen, with round wooden tables and cheery decorations, and the service is just as warm.

151 Brock St., Gravenhurst. © **705/687-7756.** Reservations recommended for dinner. Main courses C$10– C$22 (£5–£11). MC, V. Mon–Tues 9:30am–3pm; Wed–Sat 9:30am–8pm.

4 HAMILTON

75km (47 miles) SW of Toronto

A couple of years ago, a friend of mine asked for recommendations on where to go on a day trip around Toronto. When I suggested Hamilton, she was surprised. She's a lifelong Toronto resident, and she had never been there. Moreover, she'd never thought about going there. Hamilton may be Ontario's most-overlooked city, and it's a shame. Situated on a landlocked harbor spanned at its entrance by the Burlington Skyway's dramatic sweep, Hamilton has long been nicknamed "Steeltown" for its industrial roots. Since the early 1990s, however, Hamilton has been making a name for itself with its ever-expanding list of attractions. It takes roughly an hour to drive here from Toronto, and a day trip here is time well spent for the entire family.

ESSENTIALS
VISITOR INFORMATION   The **Tourism Hamilton Information Centre** is at 34 James St. S., Hamilton (© **800/263-8590** or 905/546-2666; www.tourismhamilton.com). It has a wealth of information about what to see and do, as well as where to dine and sleep. Its year-round hours run Monday to Friday from 9am to 5pm.

GETTING THERE   Hamilton is easy to reach by car. From Toronto, take the Queen Elizabeth Way (signs read QEW) to Hamilton. The drive is about an hour.

GO (Government of Ontario) Transit is a commuter train that connects Toronto and Hamilton. Call ℂ 800/438-6646 or 416/869-3200 for information, or check out www.gotransit.com. The **John C. Munro Hamilton International Airport** (ℂ 905/ 679-1999; www.flyhi.ca) has long been popular with cargo carriers and is now a hub for WestJet. In 2007, **flyglobespan** began service to Hamilton, connecting the city to 13 U.K. destinations (visit www.flyglobespan.ca for details).

WHAT TO SEE & DO

Hamilton's downtown core is best explored on foot, though you may want a car to visit attractions in the outlying areas.

African Lion Safari ★★ (Kids)   Just a half-hour drive northwest of Hamilton, you'll find a mirror image of a traditional zoo: At the African Lion Safari, visitors remain caged in their cars or in a tour bus while the animals roam wild and free. The 300-hectare (741-acre) wildlife park contains rhinos, cheetahs, lions, tigers, giraffes, zebras, vultures, and many other species. In addition to the safari, the cost of admission covers other attractions, like the cruise aboard the *African Queen,* during which a tour guide will take you around the lake and point out local inhabitants like spider monkeys, crested macaques, and ring-tailed lemurs. A train will take you through a forest populated by snapping turtles, among other wildlife.

The park has several baby Asian elephants, and the elephant-bathing event, which occurs daily, will particularly fascinate the kids. The Pets' Corner is filled with frisky otters and pot-bellied pigs. There are several play areas for children as well, including the Misumu Bay water park (bring bathing suits!).

Safari Rd, Cambridge. ℂ 800/461-**WILD** or 519/623-2620. www.lionsafari.com. Admission C$28 (£14) adults, C$25 (£13) seniors, C$23 (£12) children 3–12, free for children 2 and under; rates are discounted in spring and fall. Late June–Labour Day daily 10am–5:30pm; mid-Apr to late June and early Sept to mid-Oct daily 9am–4pm. Closed mid-Oct to mid-Apr.

Art Gallery of Hamilton ★   This art gallery first opened in 1914, but it was only when it reopened its doors in 2005 that it became one of Hamilton's greatest attractions. After a major renovation that cost more than C$18 million, the AGH is a gorgeous place to visit, with one of the most comprehensive collections of Canadian art in the country, as well as notable holdings of European and American works. The overhaul came as the result of the gallery's receiving one of the largest bequests in Canadian history—the Joey and Toby Tannenbaum Collection, which included 211 works of 19th-century art from Europe. Now when you visit, you can see a great range of works, from Jules-Elie Delaunay's astonishing *Ixion Plunged into Hades* to Alex Colville's *Horse and Train* (two of my favorites). The renovation also helped shape areas such as the open-air Irving Zucker Sculpture Garden, a green, serene space that can also be viewed from the Sculpture Atrium inside the gallery.

123 King St. W. ℂ **905/527-6610.** www.artgalleryofhamilton.com. Admission C$12 (£6) adults, C$10 (£5) students and seniors, C$5 (£2.50) children 6–17, free for children 5 and under. Tues–Wed noon–7pm; Thurs–Fri noon–9pm; Sat–Sun noon–5pm; closed Mon except on most civic holidays. Closed Jan 1, Dec 25–26.

Canadian Warplane Heritage Museum   If you're an aircraft buff like my dad, you'll love this interactive museum that charts the course of Canadian aviation from the beginning of World War II to the present. Visitors can climb into the cockpits of World War II

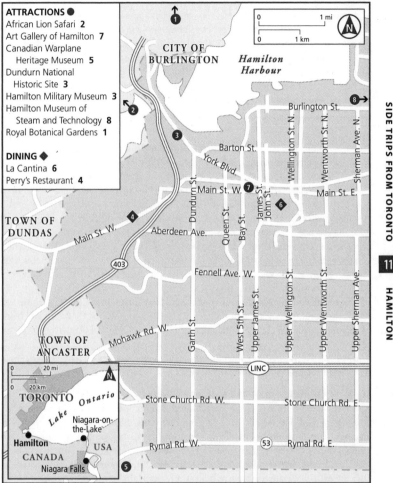

ATTRACTIONS ●
African Lion Safari **2**
Art Gallery of Hamilton **7**
Canadian Warplane
  Heritage Museum **5**
Dundurn National
  Historic Site **3**
Hamilton Military Museum **3**
Hamilton Museum of
  Steam and Technology **8**
Royal Botanical Gardens **1**

DINING ◆
La Cantina **6**
Perry's Restaurant **4**

CITY OF BURLINGTON

Hamilton Harbour

Burlington St.

Barton St.

York Blvd.

Main St. W.

Main St. E.

Wellington St. N.

Wentworth St. N.

Sherman Ave. N.

TOWN OF DUNDAS

Main St. W.

Aberdeen Ave.

Dundurn St.

Queen St.

Bay St.

James St.

John St.

403

Fennell Ave. W.

Garth St.

West 5th St.

Upper James St.

Upper Wellington St.

Upper Wentworth St.

Upper Sherman Ave.

TOWN OF ANCASTER

Mohawk Rd. W.

LINC

Stone Church Rd. W.

Stone Church Rd. E.

TORONTO   Ontario

Lake   Niagara-on-the-Lake

Hamilton   USA

CANADA
Niagara Falls

Rymal Rd. W.

Rymal Rd. E.

53

trainer crafts or a CF-100 jet fighter. The most popular attractions are the flight simulators, which allow aspiring pilots to test their skills (my favorite part). There are also short documentary films, photographs, and other memorabilia. The aircrafts on display include such rarities as the Avro Lancaster bomber and the deHavilland Vampire fighter jet.

9280 Airport Rd. (at the John C. Munro Hamilton International Airport), Mount Hope. ✆ **877/347-3359** or 905/670-3347. www.warplane.com. Admission C$10 (£5) adults, C$9 (£4.50) seniors and youths 13–17, C$6 (£3) for children 6–12, free for children 5 and under. Daily 9am–5pm. Closed Jan 1, Dec 25.

Dundurn National Historic Site ★★   This site is composed of two big attractions: **Dundurn Castle** and the **Hamilton Military Museum.** First, let's get something straight: Dundurn isn't really a castle, but a very grand manor house. But it does afford

(Finds) Architectural Gems

Hamilton has a wealth of architectural design to appreciate, and if you're a fan of Victorian red-brick buildings, you'll be in heaven—the only catch is that you need to know where to look. If this is a passion of yours, contact the **Hamilton Regional Branch of the Ontario Architectural Conservancy** (© **905/308-9790** or www.architecturehamilton.com). This not-for-profit group organizes walking tours as well as exhibitions exploring the fascinating history of the city and the people who built it.

SIDE TRIPS FROM TORONTO

11

HAMILTON

a glimpse of the opulent life as it was lived in southern Ontario in the mid–19th century. Costumed interpreters "living" in 1855 guide you through the house and tell vivid stories of what life was like there—for both the aristocrats and the servants.

Sir Allan Napier MacNab, premier of the United Canadas in the mid-1850s and a founder of the Great Western Railway, built Dundurn between 1832 and 1835; Queen Victoria knighted him for the part he played in the Rebellion of 1837. The 35-plus-room mansion has been restored and furnished in the style of 1855. The gray stucco exterior, with its classical Greek portico, is impressive enough, but inside, from the formal dining rooms to Lady MacNab's boudoir, the furnishings are rich. The museum contains a fascinating collection of Victoriana. In December, the castle is decorated splendidly for a Victorian Christmas.

The Hamilton Military Museum is on the grounds of Dundurn Castle. For those who are interested, it traces Canadian military history from the War of 1812 through World War I. Admission is included when you buy a ticket for Dundurn Castle.

Dundurn Park, York Blvd. © **905/546-2872.** Admission C$10 (£5) adults, C$8 (£4) seniors and students with ID, C$5 (£2.50) children 6–14, free for children 5 and under. Victoria Day–Labour Day daily 10am–4pm; the rest of the year Tues–Sun noon–4pm. Closed Jan 1, Dec 25–26.

Hamilton Museum of Steam and Technology (Kids) One of the things I like best about Hamilton is the city's pride in its industrial roots. This museum is a case in point. It explains—and celebrates—the technology that made urban life possible in the Victorian age. This museum has preserved two 14m (45-ft.) tall, 63,503kg (70-ton) steam engines that first pumped clean water to Hamilton (the stone-and-cast-iron Romanesque building that houses them is a gorgeous example of 19th-century public-works architecture as well). The waterworks were built to protect Hamilton from the deadly cholera outbreaks and fires that destroyed so many cities in that era. The museum also hosts a series of exhibits and special events.

900 Woodward Ave (at the QEW). © **905/546-4797.** Admission C$6 (£3) adults, C$5 (£2.50) seniors and students 13–17, C$4 (£2) children 6–12, free for children 5 and under. June 1–Labour Day Tues–Sun 11am–4pm; the rest of the year, Tues–Sun noon–4pm. Closed Jan 1, Dec 25–26.

Royal Botanical Gardens ★ Situated just north of the city, the Royal Botanical Gardens spreads over 1,214 glorious hectares (2,999 acres). The Rock Garden features spring bulbs in May, summer flowers in June to September, and chrysanthemums in October. The Laking Garden blazes during June and July with irises, peonies, and lilies. The arboretum fills with the heady scent of lilac from the end of May to early June, and

the exquisite color bursts of rhododendrons and azaleas thereafter. The Centennial Rose
Garden is at its best late June through mid-September.

The gardens host many festivals during the year, including the Mediterranean Food & Wine Festival in February, the popular Ontario Garden Show in early April, the Tulip Festival in May, the Rose Society Show in June, and the Japanese Flower Society Show in September.

Should you work up an appetite while strolling the grounds, the on-site dining options include the Gardens Café, which is open year-round, and the Rock Garden Tea House or the Turner Pavilion (both open throughout the summer).

680 Plains Rd. W., Burlington. ✆ **905/527-1158.** www.rbg.ca. Admission C$10 (£5) adults, C$7 (£3.50) seniors and children 13–18, C$5 (£2.50) children 5–12, free for children 4 and under. Daily 9:30am–dusk. Closed Jan 1, Dec 25.

WHERE TO STAY

Because Hamilton is so close to Toronto, it's easy to make a day trip here and back, rather than pulling up stakes and spending the night here. However, if you do want to stay in the area, several well-known chains have hotels here, including **Sheraton** (✆ **800/514-7101** or 905/529-5515), **Ramada** (✆ **800/2RAMADA** or 905/528-3451), and **Comfort Inn** (✆ **877/424-6423** or 905/560-4500).

WHERE TO DINE

The suggested restaurant in St. Catharines, **Wellington Court** (p. 239), is just a short drive away from Hamilton. However, Hamilton has a few restaurants worth checking out, too.

La Cantina ★ ITALIAN This is really two restaurants in one. A dining room serves up plates of veal scaloppini in a dry Marsala sauce, and seared ostrich medallions cooked with pinot noir. The casual pizzeria features more than 20 varieties of pizza, including the traditional Quattro Stagione (four seasons) with prosciutto, artichokes, olives, and mozzarella. This is a very popular spot, so try to make a reservation or arrive early, especially at lunch. If you're very lucky, you might just secure a seat in the restaurant's garden patio.

60 Walnut St. S. ✆ **905/521-8989.** Reservations recommended. Main courses C$12–C$26 (£6–£13). AE, MC, V. Tues–Thurs 11:30am–10pm; Fri 11:30am–11pm; Sat 5–11pm.

Perry's Restaurant INTERNATIONAL   This casual family-style restaurant has a large menu that has something for everyone. It borrows from a range of cuisines, including Italian, French, Mexican, Greek, and American. Offerings include chicken souvlakia, rack of ribs, hearty sandwiches, and fish and chips. There are also lighter options, such as salads, soups, and chicken fingers. There's a sunny patio at the front of the restaurant, too.

1088 Main St. W. ✆ **905/527-3779.** Main courses C$8–C$15 (£4–£7.50). MC, V. Daily 11:30am–1am.

Appendix: Fast Facts, Toll-Free Numbers & Websites

1 FAST FACTS: TORONTO

American Express There are several American Express offices in Toronto, but the most central is at Millenium Travel Canada Inc. at 77 Bloor St. W. (© **416/962-2200**).

Area Codes Toronto's area codes are **416** and **647**; outside the city, the code is **905** or **289**. You must dial all 10 digits for all local phone numbers.

ATM Networks See "Money & Costs," p. 42.

Automobile Organizations Motor clubs will supply maps, suggested routes, guidebooks, accident and bail-bond insurance, and emergency road service. The **Canadian Automobile Association (CAA)** is the major auto club in Canada, and its South Central Ontario branch is in Toronto. Within Canada, call © **800/222-4357** or 416/222-5222. If you belong to a motor club in your home country, inquire about CAA reciprocity before you leave. You may be able to join CAA even if you're not a member of a reciprocal club; to inquire, call CAA or visit **www.caa.ca**. If you are a member of the American Automobile Association (AAA), the CAA does provide emergency road service.

Business Hours Banks are generally open Monday through Thursday from 10am to 3pm, Friday 10am to 6pm. Most stores are open Monday through Wednesday from 10am to 6pm and Saturday and Sunday from 10am to 5pm, with extended hours (until 8 or 9:30pm) on Thursday and usually Friday.

Car Rentals See "Toll-Free Numbers & Websites," p. 262.

Drinking Laws The legal age for purchase and consumption of alcoholic beverages is 19 throughout Ontario; proof of age is required and often requested at bars, nightclubs, and restaurants, so it's always a good idea to bring ID when you go out.

Drinking hours run until 2am in Toronto. The government is the only retail vendor. **Liquor Control Board of Ontario (LCBO)** stores sell liquor, wine, and some beers. Most are open daily from 10am to 6pm (some have extended evening hours). The nicest shop is the **LCBO Summerhill,** 10 Scrivener Sq. (© **416/922-0403**; Subway: Summerhill). Built out of a former train station, this outpost hosts cooking classes, wine and spirit tastings, and party-planning seminars. Another good branch is at the **Manulife Centre,** 55 Bloor St. W. (© **416/925-5266**). See **www.lcbo.com** for information about products and special in-store events.

Do not carry open containers of alcohol in your car or any public area that isn't zoned for alcohol consumption. The police can fine you on the spot. And nothing will ruin your trip faster than getting a citation for DUI ("driving under the influence"), so don't even think about driving while intoxicated.

Driving Rules See "Getting There & Getting Around," p. 34.

Electricity Like the United States, Canada uses 110 to 120 volts AC (60 cycles), compared to 220 to 240 volts AC (50 cycles) in most of Europe, Australia, and New Zealand. Downward converters that change 220–240 volts to 110–120 volts are difficult to find in the Canada, so bring one with you.

Embassies & Consulates All embassies are in Ottawa, the national capital. They include the **Australian High Commission,** 50 O'Connor St., Suite 710, Ottawa, ON K1P 6L2 (© **613/236-0841**); the **British High Commission,** 80 Elgin St., Ottawa, ON K1P 5K7 (© **613/237-1530**); the **Embassy of Ireland,** 130 Albert St., Ottawa, ON K1P 5G4 (© **613/233-6281**); the **New Zealand High Commission,** 727–99 Bank St., Ottawa, ON K1P 6G3 (© **613/238-5991**); the **South African High Commission,** 15 Sussex Dr., Ottawa, ON K1M 1M8 (© **613/744-0330**); and the **Embassy of the United States of America,** 490 Sussex Dr., Ottawa, ON K1N 1G8 (© **613/238-5335**).

Consulates in Toronto include **Australian Consulate-General,** 175 Bloor St. E., Suite 314, at Church Street (© **416/323-1155**); **British Consulate-General,** 777 Bay St., Suite 2800, at College (© **416/593-1290**); and the **U.S. Consulate,** 360 University Ave. (© **416/595-1700**).

Emergencies Call © **911** for fire, police, or ambulance.

Gasoline (Petrol) At press time, in Canada, the cost of gasoline (also known as gas, but never petrol), is abnormally high. Gasoline is sold by the liter, and taxes are already included in the printed price (unlike most products in Canada). Fill-up locations are known as gas or service stations.

Holidays Toronto celebrates the following holidays: New Year's Day (Jan 1), Good Friday and Easter Monday (Mar or Apr), Victoria Day (Mon following the third weekend in May), Canada Day (July 1), Simcoe Day (first Mon in Aug), Labor Day (first Mon in Sept), Thanksgiving (second Mon in Oct), Remembrance Day (Nov 11), Christmas Day (Dec 25), and Boxing Day (Dec 26). For more information on holidays, see "Calendar of Events," in chapter 3.

Hospitals In the downtown core, the **University Health Network** manages three hospitals: **Toronto General** at 200 Elizabeth St., **Princess Margaret** at 610 University Ave., and **Toronto Western** at 399 Bathurst St. The UHN has a central switchboard for all three (© **416/340-3111**). Other hospitals include **St. Michael's,** 30 Bond St. (© **416/360-4000**), and **Mount Sinai,** 600 University Ave. (© **416/596-4200**). Also downtown is the **Hospital for Sick Children,** 555 University Ave. (© **416/813-1500**). Uptown, there's **Sunnybrook Hospital,** 2075 Bayview Ave., north of Eglinton (© **416/480-6100**). In the eastern part of the city, go to **Toronto East General Hospital,** 825 Coxwell Ave. (© **416/461-8272**).

Hotlines Poison Information Centre (© **800/267-1373**); **Distress Centre** suicide-prevention line (© **416/408-4357**); **Toronto Rape Crisis Centre** (© **416/597-8808**); **Assaulted Women's Helpline** (© **416/863-0511**); and **AIDS & Sexual Health InfoLine** (© **416/392-2437**). For kids or teens in distress, there's **Kids Help Phone** (© **800/668-6868**).

Insurance Medical Insurance Even though Canada is just a short drive or flight away for many Americans, U.S. health plans (including Medicare and Medicaid) do not provide coverage, and the ones that do often require you to pay for services upfront and reimburse you only after you return home.

As a safety net, you may want to buy travel medical insurance, particularly if you're traveling to a remote or high-risk area where emergency evacuation might be necessary. If you require additional medical insurance, try **MEDEX Assistance** (℡ **410/453-6300;** www.medexassist.com) or **Travel Assistance International** (℡ **800/821-2828;** www.travelassistance. com; for general information on services, call the company's **Worldwide Assistance Services, Inc.,** at ℡ **800/777-8710).**

Travelers from the U.K. should carry their European Health Insurance Card (EHIC), which replaced the E111 form as proof of entitlement to free/reduced cost medical treatment abroad (℡ **0845-606-2030;** www.ehic.org.uk). Note, however, that the EHIC only covers "necessary medical treatment'," and for repatriation costs, lost money, baggage, or cancellation, travel insurance from a reputable company should always be sought (www.travelinsuranceweb. com).

Travel Insurance The cost of travel insurance varies widely, depending on the destination, the cost and length of your trip, your age and health, and the type of trip you're taking, but expect to pay between 5% and 8% of the vacation itself. You can get estimates from various providers through **InsureMyTrip.com.** Enter your trip cost and dates, your age, and other information, for prices from more than a dozen companies.

U.K. citizens and their families who make more than one trip abroad per year may find an annual travel insurance policy works out cheaper. Check **www.money supermarket.com,** which compares prices across a wide range of providers for single- and multi-trip policies.

Most big travel agents offer their own insurance and will probably try to sell you their package when you book a holiday. Think before you sign. **Britain's Consumers' Association** recommends that you insist on seeing the policy and reading the fine print before buying travel insurance. **The Association of British Insurers** (℡ **020/7600-3333;** www.abi.org.uk) gives advice by phone and publishes Holiday Insurance, a free guide to policy provisions and prices. You might also shop around for better deals: Try **Columbus Direct** (℡ **0870/033-9988;** www.columbusdirect. net).

Trip Cancellation Insurance Trip-cancellation insurance will help retrieve your money if you have to back out of a trip or depart early, or if your travel supplier goes bankrupt. Trip cancellation traditionally covers such events as sickness, natural disasters, and State Department advisories. The latest news in trip-cancellation insurance is the availability of **expanded hurricane coverage** and the **"any-reason"** cancellation coverage—which costs more but covers cancellations made for any reason. You won't get back 100% of your prepaid trip cost, but you'll be refunded a substantial portion. **TravelSafe** (℡ **888/885-7233;** www.travelsafe.com) offers both types of coverage. Expedia also offers any-reason cancellation coverage for its air-hotel packages. For details, contact one of the following recommended insurers: **Access America** (℡ **866/807-3982;** www. accessamerica.com); **Travel Guard International** (℡ **800/826-4919;** www.travel guard.com); **Travel Insured International** (℡ **800/243-3174;** www.travelinsured. com); and **Travelex Insurance Services** (℡ **888/457-4602;** www.travelex-insurance. com).

Internet Access Increasingly, Toronto hotels provide dataports and even Wi-Fi access. If you don't have a computer with you, there's **Insomnia,** 563 Bloor St. W. (℡ **416/588-3907).** Another option is **FedEx Kinko's.** There are several in the city, but one sure bet is the location at 505 University Ave., at Dundas (℡ **416/970-8447).**

Laundromats **Bloor Laundromat,** 598 Bloor St. W., at Bathurst Street (📞 **416/588-6600**), and **Laundry Lounge,** 527 Yonge St., at Wellesley Street (📞 **416/975-4747**), are both conveniently located. **Careful Hand Laundry & Dry Cleaners Ltd.** has outlets at 206 Dupont St. (📞 **416/923-1200**) and 1844 Avenue Rd. (📞 **416/787-6006**); for pickup and delivery, call 📞 **416/787-9119.**

Legal Aid If you are "pulled over" for a minor infraction (such as speeding), never attempt to pay the fine directly to a police officer; this could be construed as attempted bribery, a much more serious crime. Pay fines by mail, or directly into the hands of the clerk of the court. If accused of a more serious offense, say and do nothing before consulting a lawyer. Here the burden is on the state to prove a person's guilt beyond a reasonable doubt, and everyone has the right to remain silent, whether he or she is suspected of a crime or actually arrested. Once arrested, a person can make one telephone call to a party of his or her choice. International visitors should call your embassy or consulate.

Lost & Found If you leave something on a bus, a streetcar, or the subway, call the **TTC Lost Articles Office** (📞 **416/393-4100**), at the Bay Street subway station. It's open Monday through Friday from 8am to 5pm.

Be sure to tell all of your credit card companies the minute you discover your wallet has been lost or stolen and file a report at the nearest police precinct. Your credit card company or insurer may require a police report number or record of the loss. Most credit card companies have an emergency toll-free number to call if your card is lost or stolen; they may be able to wire you a cash advance immediately or deliver an emergency credit card in a day or two. Visa's U.S. emergency number is 📞 **800/847-2911** or 410/581-9994. American Express cardholders and traveler's check holders should call 📞 **800/221-7282.** MasterCard

holders should call 📞 **800/307-7309** or 636/722-7111. For other credit cards, call the toll-free number directory at 📞 **800/555-1212.**

If you need emergency cash over the weekend when all banks and American Express offices are closed, you can have money wired to you via **Western Union** (📞 **800/325-6000;** www.westernunion.com).

Mail Postage for letter mail (up to 30 g/about 1 oz.) to the United States costs C93¢; overseas, C$1.55. Mailing letters within Canada costs C52¢. Note that there is no discounted rate for mailing postcards.

Postal services are available at convenience stores and drugstores. Almost all sell stamps, and many have a separate counter where you can ship packages from 8:30am to 5pm. Look for the sign in the window indicating such services. There are also post-office windows in **Atrium on Bay** (📞 **416/506-0911**), in **Commerce Court** (📞 **416/956-7452**), and at the **TD Centre** (📞 **416/360-7105**).

Maps Free maps of Toronto are available in every terminal at **Pearson International Airport** (look for the Transport Canada Information Centre signs), the Metropolitan Toronto Convention & Visitors Association at **Harbourfront,** and the Visitor Information Centre in the **Eaton Centre. BlogTO** produces local maps that you can pick up for free at shops and restaurants around town. At press time, they have produced maps for West Queen West, Leslieville, Parkdale, and Little Italy. Convenience stores and bookstores sell a greater variety of maps. Or try **Open Air Books and Maps,** 25 Toronto St., near Yonge and Adelaide streets (📞 **416/363-0719**).

Measurements See the chart on the inside front cover of this book for details on converting metric measurements to nonmetric equivalents.

Medical Conditions If you have a medical condition that requires **syringe-administered medications,** carry a valid signed prescription from your physician; syringes in carry-on baggage will be inspected. Insulin in any form should have the proper pharmaceutical documentation. If you have a disease that requires treatment with **narcotics,** you should also carry documented proof with you—smuggling narcotics aboard a plane carries severe penalties in the U.S.

For **HIV-positive visitors,** Canada does not require testing to enter the country on a tourist visa. However, a traveler can be denied entry to Canada if they are assessed as requiring health services during their stay. (Canada does not cover medical costs incurred by travelers.)

Newspapers & Magazines The four daily newspapers are the *Globe and Mail,* the *National Post,* the *Toronto Star,* and the *Toronto Sun. Eye* and *Now* are free arts-and-entertainment weeklies. *Xtra!* is a free weekly targeted at the gay and lesbian community. In addition, many English-language ethnic newspapers serve Toronto's Portuguese, Hungarian, Italian, East Indian, Korean, Chinese, and Caribbean communities. *Toronto Life* is the major monthly city magazine; its sister publication is *Toronto Life Fashion. Where Toronto* is usually free at hotels and some Theater District restaurants.

Passports The websites listed provide downloadable passport applications as well as the current fees for processing applications.

For Residents of Australia: You can pick up an application from your local post office or any branch of Passports Australia, but you must schedule an interview at the passport office to present your application materials. Call the **Australian Passport Information Service** at ℂ **131-232,** or visit the government website at www.passports.gov.au.

For Residents of Ireland: You can apply for a 10-year passport at the **Passport Office,** Setanta Centre, Molesworth Street, Dublin 2 (ℂ **01/671-1633;** www.irlgov.ie/iveagh). Those under age 18 and over 65 must apply for a 3-year passport. You can also apply at 1A South Mall, Cork (ℂ **21/494-4700**) or at most main post offices.

For Residents of New Zealand: You can pick up a passport application at any New Zealand Passports Office or download it from their website. Contact the **Passports Office** at ℂ **0800/225-050** in New Zealand or 04/474-8100, or log on to www.passports.govt.nz.

For Residents of the United Kingdom: To pick up an application for a standard 10-year passport (5-yr. passport for children under 16), visit your nearest passport office, major post office, or travel agency or contact the **United Kingdom Passport Service** at ℂ **0870/521-0410** or search its website at www.ukpa.gov.uk.

For Residents of the United States: Whether you're applying in person or by mail, you can download passport applications from the U.S. State Department website at **http://travel.state.gov**. To find your regional passport office, either check the U.S. State Department website or call the **National Passport Information Center** toll-free number (ℂ **877/487-2778**) for automated information.

Police In a life-threatening emergency, call ℂ **911.** For all other matters, contact the **Metro police,** 40 College St. (ℂ **416/808-2222**).

Smoking The Smoke-Free Ontario Act, which came into effect in 2006, is one of the most stringent in North America. It bans smoking in all workplaces and in all enclosed public spaces. It's all but impossible to smoke at Ontario restaurants, because the law banned designated smoking areas; even patios that have any sort of covering have also had to go smoke-free.

Taxes Ontario's provincial retail sales tax is 8%; on accommodations, it's 5%. There is an additional 5% national goods-and-services tax (GST). These taxes are added when you purchase an item, rather than being included in the original price as is common in much of Europe. The Canadian government suspended the GST Visitors' Rebate Program in 2007.

Telephones Many convenience groceries and packaging services sell **prepaid calling cards** in denominations up to C$50; for international visitors these can be the least expensive way to call home. Many public pay phones at airports now accept American Express, MasterCard, and Visa credit cards. **Local calls** made from pay phones in most locales cost C50¢ (no pennies, please). Most long-distance and international calls can be dialed directly from any phone. **For calls within Canada and to the United States,** dial 1 followed by the area code and the seven-digit number. **For other international calls,** dial 011 followed by the country code, city code, and the number you are calling.

Calls to area codes **800, 888, 877,** and **866** are toll-free. However, calls to area codes **700** and **900** (chat lines, bulletin boards, "dating" services, and so on) can be very expensive—usually a charge of C95¢ to C$3 or more per minute, and they sometimes have minimum charges that can run as high as C$15 or more.

For **reversed-charge or collect calls,** and for person-to-person calls, dial the number 0 then the area code and number; an operator will come on the line, and you should specify say whether you are calling collect, person-to-person, or both. If your operator-assisted call is international, ask for the overseas operator.

For **local directory assistance** ("information"), dial 411; for long-distance information, dial 1, then the appropriate area code, and 555-1212.

Telegraph, Telex & Fax Telegraph **and telex services** are provided primarily by **Western Union** (✆ **800/325-6000;** www.westernunion.com). You can telegraph (wire) money, or have it telegraphed to you, very quickly over the Western Union system, but this service can cost as much as 15% to 20% of the amount sent.

Most hotels have **fax machines** available for guest use (be sure to ask about the charge to use it). Many hotel rooms are wired for guests' fax machines. A less expensive way to send and receive faxes may be at stores such as the **UPS Store.**

Time Toronto is on Eastern Standard Time. When it's noon in Toronto, it's 9am in Los Angeles (PST), it's 7am in Honolulu (HST), 10am in Denver (MST), 11am in Chicago (CST), noon in New York City (also on EST), 5pm in London (GMT), and 2am the next day in Sydney.

Daylight saving time is in effect from 1am on the second Sunday in March to 1am on the first Sunday in November. Daylight saving time moves the clock 1 hour ahead of standard time.

Tipping Tips are a very important part of certain workers' income, and gratuities are the standard way of showing appreciation for services provided. (Tipping is certainly not compulsory if the service is poor!) In hotels, tip **bellhops** at least $1 per bag ($2–$3 if you have a lot of luggage) and tip the **chamber staff** $1 to $2 per day (more if you've left a disaster area for him or her to clean up). Tip the **doorman** or **concierge** only if he or she has provided you with some specific service (for example, calling a cab for you or obtaining difficult-to-get theater tickets). Tip the **valet-parking attendant** $1 every time you get your car.

In restaurants, bars, and nightclubs, tip **service staff** 15% to 20% of the check, tip **bartenders** 10% to 15%, tip **checkroom attendants** $1 per garment, and tip **valet-parking attendants** $1 per vehicle.

As for other service personnel, tip **cab drivers** 15% of the fare; tip **skycaps** at airports at least $1 per bag ($2–$3 if you have a lot of luggage); and tip **hairdressers** and **barbers** 15% to 20%.

Toilets You won't find public toilets or "restrooms" on the streets in Toronto, but they can be found in hotel lobbies, bars, restaurants, museums, department stores, railway and bus stations, and service stations. Large hotels and fast-food restaurants are often the best bet for clean facilities. Restaurants and bars in resorts or heavily visited areas may reserve their restrooms for patrons. There are also restrooms throughout the underground PATH system near the various food courts. There are restrooms at major subway stations such as Yonge–Bloor, but they are best avoided.

Useful Phone Numbers **Citizenship and Immigration Canada:** ☎ 888/242-2100 (in Canada only; available 8am-4pm weekdays). **U.S. Dept. of State Travel Advisory** ☎ 202/647-5225 (manned 24 hrs.). **U.S. Passport Agency:** ☎ 202/647-0518. **U.S. Centers for Disease Control International Traveler's Hotline:** ☎ 404/332-4559.

Visas For citizens of many countries, only a passport is required to visit Canada for up to 90 days; no visas or proof of vaccinations are necessary. For the most up-to-date list of visitor visa exemptions, visit **Citizenship and Immigration Canada** at www.cic.gc.ca.

Water Toronto's tap water is safe to drink, and it is tested continuously to guarantee public safety. For details, visit the City of Toronto's water information page at www.toronto.ca/water. However, while you'll see many locals swimming in Lake Ontario, this is not a good idea if you want to stay healthy; the lake contains high levels of E. Coli, which causes nasty bacterial infections.

2 TOLL-FREE NUMBERS & WEBSITES

CANADIAN AIRLINES

Air Canada
☎ 888/247-2262 (U.S. and Canada)
☎ 020/8750-8495 (U.K.)
www.aircanada.com

Porter Airlines
☎ 888/619-8622 (U.S. and Canada)
www.flyporter.com

WestJet
☎ 800/538-5696 (U.S. and Canada)
www.westjet.com

MAJOR INTERNATIONAL AIRLINES

Aeroméxico
☎ 800/237-6639 (U.S. and Canada)
☎ 020/7801-6234 (U.K.)
www.aeromexico.com

Air France
☎ 800/375-8723 (U.S. and Canada)
☎ 087/0142-4343 (U.K.)
www.airfrance.com

Air India
☎ 800/223-7776 (U.S. and Canada)
☎ 91 22 2279 6666 (India)
☎ 020/8745-1000 (U.K.)
www.airindia.com

Air Jamaica
☎ 800/523-5585 (U.S. and Canada)
☎ 208/570-7999 (Jamaica)
www.airjamaica.com

Air New Zealand
☎ 800/262-1234 (U.S.)
☎ 800/663-5494 (Canada)
☎ 0800/028-4149 (U.K.)
www.airnewzealand.com

Alitalia
☎ 800/223-5730 (U.S.)
☎ 800/361-8336 (Canada)
☎ 087/0608-6003 (U.K.)
www.alitalia.com

American Airlines
☎ 800/433-7300 (U.S. and Canada)
☎ 020/7365-0777 (U.K.)
www.aa.com

British Airways
☎ 800/247-9297 (U.S. and Canada)
☎ 087/0850-9850 (U.K.)
www.british-airways.com

Caribbean Airlines (formerly BWIA)
☎ 800/920-4225 (U.S. and Canada)
☎ 084/5362 4225 (U.K.)
www.caribbean-airlines.com

China Airlines
☎ 800/227-5118 (U.S.)
☎ 022/715-1212 (Taiwan)
www.china-airlines.com

Continental Airlines
☎ 800/523-3273 (U.S. and Canada)
☎ 084/5607-6760 (U.K.)
www.continental.com

Cubana
☎ 888/667-1222 (Canada)
☎ 020/7538-5933 (U.K.)
www.cubana.cu

Delta Air Lines
☎ 800/221-1212 (U.S. and Canada)
☎ 084/5600-0950 (U.K.)
www.delta.com

El Al Airlines
☎ 972/3977-1111 (outside Israel)
☎ *2250 (from any phone in Israel)
www.el.co.il

Emirates Airlines
☎ 800/777-3999 (U.S. and Canada)
☎ 087/0243-2222 (U.K.)
www.emirates.com

Hawaiian Airlines
☎ 800/367-5320 (U.S. and Canada)
www.hawaiianair.com

Iberia Airlines
☎ 800/722-4642 (U.S. and Canada)
☎ 087/0609-0500 (U.K.)
www.iberia.com

Lan Airlines
☎ 866/435-9526 (U.S.)
☎ 305/670-9999 (in other countries)
www.lanchile.com

Lufthansa
☎ 800/399-5838 (U.S.)
☎ 800/563-5954 (Canada)
☎ 087/0837-7747 (U.K.)
www.lufthansa.com

Northwest Airlines
☎ 800/225-2525 (U.S. and Canada)
☎ 870/0507-4074 (U.K.)
www.nwa.com

Olympic Airlines
☎ 800/223-1226 (U.S.)
☎ 514/878-9691 (Canada)
☎ 087/0606-0460 (U.K.)
www.olympicairlines.com

Qantas Airways
☎ 800/227-4500 (U.S. and Canada)
☎ 084/5774-7767 (U.K.)
☎ 13 13 13 (Australia)
www.qantas.com

TACA
☎ 800/535-8780 (U.S.)
☎ 800/722-TACA (8222; Canada)
☎ 087/0241-0340 (U.K.)
☎ 503/2267-8222 (El Salvador)
www.taca.com

United Airlines
☎ 800/864-8331 (U.S. and Canada)
☎ 084/5844-4777 (U.K.)
www.united.com

US Airways
   ℃ 800/428-4322 (U.S. and Canada)
   ℃ 084/5600-3300 (U.K.)
   www.usairways.com

Virgin Atlantic Airways
   ℃ 800/821-5438 (U.S. and Canada)
   ℃ 087/0574-7747 (U.K.)
   www.virgin-atlantic.com

BUDGET AIRLINES
Zoom Airlines
   ℃ 866/359-9666 (U.S. and Canada)
   ℃ 087/0240-0055 (U.K.)
   www.flyzoom.com

CAR RENTAL AGENCIES
Advantage
   ℃ 800/777-5500 (in U.S.)
   ℃ 021/0344-4712 (outside of U.S.)
   www.advantagerentacar.com

Alamo
   ℃ 800/GO-ALAMO (800/462-5266)
   (U.S. and Canada)
   www.alamo.com

Avis
   ℃ 800/331-1212 (U.S. and Canada)
   ℃ 084/4581-8181 (U.K.)
   www.avis.com

Budget
   ℃ 800/527-0700 (U.S.)
   ℃ 800/268-8900 (Canada)
   ℃ 087/0156-5656 (U.K.)
   www.budget.com

Dollar
   ℃ 800/800-4000 (U.S.)
   ℃ 800/848-8268 (Canada)
   ℃ 080/8234-7524 (U.K.)
   www.dollar.com

Enterprise
   ℃ 800/261-7331 (U.S.)
   ℃ 514/355-4028 (Canada)
   ℃ 012/9360-9090 (U.K.)
   www.enterprise.com

Hertz
   ℃ 800/645-3131 (U.S. and Canada)
   ℃ 800/654-3001 (for international
   reservations)
   www.hertz.com

National
   ℃ 800/CAR-RENT (800/227-7368)
   (U.S. and Canada)
   www.nationalcar.com

Payless
   ℃ 800/PAYLESS (800/729-5377) (U.S)
   ℃ 416/675-200 (Canada)
   www.paylesscarrental.com

Rent-A-Wreck
   ℃ 800/944-7501 (U.S.)
   www.rentawreck.com

Thrifty
   ℃ 800/847-4389 (U.S. and Canada)
   ℃ 918/669-2168 (international)
   www.thrifty.com

MAJOR HOTEL & MOTEL CHAINS
Best Western International
   ℃ 800/780-7234 (U.S. and Canada)
   ℃ 0800/393-130 (U.K.)
   www.bestwestern.com

Clarion Hotels
   ℃ 800/CLARION or 877/424-6423
   (U.S. and Canada)

   ℃ 0800/444-444 (U.K.)
   www.choicehotels.com

Comfort Inn
   ℃ 877/424-6423 (U.S. and Canada)
   ℃ 0800/444-444 (U.K.)
   www.ComfortInn.com

Courtyard by Marriott
✆ 888/236-2427 (U.S. and Canada)
✆ 0800/221-222 (U.K.)
www.marriott.com/courtyard

Crowne Plaza Hotels
✆ 800/227-6963 (U.S. and Canada)
www.ichotelsgroup.com/crowneplaza

Days Inn
✆ 800/329-7466 (U.S. and Canada)
✆ 0800/280-400 (U.K.)
www.daysinn.com

Doubletree Hotels
✆ 800/222-TREE (800/222-8733;
U.S. and Canada)
✆ 087/0590-9090 (U.K.)
www.doubletree.com

Embassy Suites
✆ 800/EMBASSY (800/362-2779)
(U.S. and Canada)
www.embassysuites.com

Fairfield Inn by Marriott
✆ 800/228-2800 (U.S. and Canada)
✆ 0800/221-222 (U.K.)
www.marriott.com/fairfieldinn

Four Seasons
✆ 800/819-5053 (U.S. and Canada)
✆ 0800/6488-6488 (U.K.)
www.fourseasons.com

Hampton Inn
✆ 800/HAMPTON (800/426-4766)
(U.S. and Canada)
www.hamptoninn.com

Hilton Hotels
✆ 800/HILTONS (800/445-8667;
U.S. and Canada)
✆ 087/0590-9090 (U.K.)
www.hilton.com

Holiday Inn
✆ 800/315-2621 (U.S. and Canada)
✆ 0800/405-060 (U.K.)
www.holidayinn.com

Howard Johnson
✆ 800/446-4656 (U.S. and Canada)
www.hojo.com

Hyatt
✆ 888/591-1234 (U.S. and Canada)
✆ 084/5888-1234 (U.K.)
www.hyatt.com

InterContinental Hotels & Resorts
✆ 800/424-6835 (U.S. and Canada)
✆ 0800/1800-1800 (U.K.)
www.ichotelsgroup.com

Marriott
✆ 877/236-2427 (U.S. and Canada)
✆ 0800/221-222 (U.K.)
www.marriott.com

Quality
✆ 877/424-6423 (U.S. and Canada)
✆ 0800/444-444 (U.K.)
www.QualityInn.ChoiceHotels.com

Radisson Hotels & Resorts
✆ 888/201-1718 (U.S. and Canada)
✆ 0800/374-411 (U.K.)
www.radisson.com

Ramada Worldwide
✆ 888/2-RAMADA (888/272-6232;
U.S. and Canada)
✆ 080/8100-0783 (U.K.)
www.ramada.com

Residence Inn by Marriott
✆ 800/331-3131
✆ 800/221-222 (U.K.)
www.marriott.com/residenceinn

Sheraton Hotels & Resorts
✆ 800/325-3535 (U.S.)
✆ 800/543-4300 (Canada)
✆ 0800/3253-5353 (U.K.)
www.starwoodhotels.com/sheraton

Super 8 Motels
✆ 800/800-8000 (U.S. and Canada)
www.super8.com

Westin Hotels & Resorts
✆ 800-937-8461 (U.S. and Canada)
✆ 0800/3259-5959 (U.K.)
www.starwoodhotels.com/westin

Wyndham Hotels & Resorts
✆ 877/999-3223 (U.S. and Canada)
✆ 050/6638-4899 (U.K.)
www.wyndham.com

INDEX

See also Accommodations and Restaurant indexes, below.

FROMMER'S® COMPLETE TRAVEL GUIDES

Alaska
Amalfi Coast
American Southwest
Amsterdam
Argentina
Arizona
Atlanta
Australia
Austria
Bahamas
Barcelona
Beijing
Belgium, Holland & Luxembourg
Belize
Bermuda
Boston
Brazil
British Columbia & the Canadian
  Rockies
Brussels & Bruges
Budapest & the Best of Hungary
Buenos Aires
Calgary
California
Canada
Cancún, Cozumel & the Yucatán
Cape Cod, Nantucket & Martha's
  Vineyard
Caribbean
Caribbean Ports of Call
Carolinas & Georgia
Chicago
Chile & Easter Island
China
Colorado
Costa Rica
Croatia
Cuba
Denmark
Denver, Boulder & Colorado Springs
Eastern Europe
Ecuador & the Galapagos Islands
Edinburgh & Glasgow
England
Europe
Europe by Rail

Florence, Tuscany & Umbria
Florida
France
Germany
Greece
Greek Islands
Guatemala
Hawaii
Hong Kong
Honolulu, Waikiki & Oahu
India
Ireland
Israel
Italy
Jamaica
Japan
Kauai
Las Vegas
London
Los Angeles
Los Cabos & Baja
Madrid
Maine Coast
Maryland & Delaware
Maui
Mexico
Montana & Wyoming
Montréal & Québec City
Morocco
Moscow & St. Petersburg
Munich & the Bavarian Alps
Nashville & Memphis
New England
Newfoundland & Labrador
New Mexico
New Orleans
New York City
New York State
New Zealand
Northern Italy
Norway
Nova Scotia, New Brunswick &
  Prince Edward Island
Oregon
Paris
Peru

Philadelphia & the Amish Country
Portugal
Prague & the Best of the Czech
  Republic
Provence & the Riviera
Puerto Rico
Rome
San Antonio & Austin
San Diego
San Francisco
Santa Fe, Taos & Albuquerque
Scandinavia
Scotland
Seattle
Seville, Granada & the Best of
  Andalusia
Shanghai
Sicily
Singapore & Malaysia
South Africa
South America
South Florida
South Korea
South Pacific
Southeast Asia
Spain
Sweden
Switzerland
Tahiti & French Polynesia
Texas
Thailand
Tokyo
Toronto
Turkey
USA
Utah
Vancouver & Victoria
Vermont, New Hampshire & Maine
Vienna & the Danube Valley
Vietnam
Virgin Islands
Virginia
Walt Disney World® & Orlando
Washington, D.C.
Washington State

FROMMER'S® DAY BY DAY GUIDES

Amsterdam
Barcelona
Beijing
Boston
Cancun & the Yucatan
Chicago
Florence & Tuscany

Hong Kong
Honolulu & Oahu
London
Maui
Montréal
Napa & Sonoma
New York City

Paris
Provence & the Riviera
Rome
San Francisco
Venice
Washington D.C.

PAULINE FROMMER'S GUIDES: SEE MORE. SPEND LESS.

Alaska
Hawaii
Italy

Las Vegas
London
New York City

Paris
Walt Disney World®
Washington D.C.

FROMMER'S® PORTABLE GUIDES

Acapulco, Ixtapa & Zihuatanejo
Amsterdam
Aruba, Bonaire & Curacao
Australia's Great Barrier Reef
Bahamas
Big Island of Hawaii
Boston
California Wine Country
Cancún
Cayman Islands
Charleston
Chicago
Dominican Republic

Florence
Las Vegas
Las Vegas for Non-Gamblers
London
Maui
Nantucket & Martha's Vineyard
New Orleans
New York City
Paris
Portland
Puerto Rico
Puerto Vallarta, Manzanillo & Guadalajara

Rio de Janeiro
San Diego
San Francisco
Savannah
St. Martin, Sint Maarten, Anguila & St. Bart's
Turks & Caicos
Vancouver
Venice
Virgin Islands
Washington, D.C.
Whistler

FROMMER'S® CRUISE GUIDES

Alaska Cruises & Ports of Call

Cruises & Ports of Call

European Cruises & Ports of Call

FROMMER'S® NATIONAL PARK GUIDES

Algonquin Provincial Park
Banff & Jasper
Grand Canyon

National Parks of the American West
Rocky Mountain
Yellowstone & Grand Teton

Yosemite and Sequoia & Kings Canyon
Zion & Bryce Canyon

FROMMER'S® WITH KIDS GUIDES

Chicago
Hawaii
Las Vegas
London

National Parks
New York City
San Francisco

Toronto
Walt Disney World® & Orlando
Washington, D.C.

FROMMER'S® PHRASEFINDER DICTIONARY GUIDES

Chinese
French

German
Italian

Japanese
Spanish

SUZY GERSHMAN'S BORN TO SHOP GUIDES

France
Hong Kong, Shanghai & Beijing
Italy

London
New York
Paris

San Francisco
Where to Buy the Best of Everything.

FROMMER'S® BEST-LOVED DRIVING TOURS

Britain
California
France
Germany

Ireland
Italy
New England
Northern Italy

Scotland
Spain
Tuscany & Umbria

THE UNOFFICIAL GUIDES®

Adventure Travel in Alaska
Beyond Disney
California with Kids
Central Italy
Chicago
Cruises
Disneyland®
England
Hawaii

Ireland
Las Vegas
London
Maui
Mexico's Best Beach Resorts
Mini Mickey
New Orleans
New York City
Paris

San Francisco
South Florida including Miami & the Keys
Walt Disney World®
Walt Disney World® for Grown-ups
Walt Disney World® with Kids
Washington, D.C.

SPECIAL-INTEREST TITLES

Athens Past & Present
Best Places to Raise Your Family
Cities Ranked & Rated
500 Places to Take Your Kids Before They Grow Up
Frommer's Best Day Trips from London
Frommer's Best RV & Tent Campgrounds in the U.S.A.

Frommer's Exploring America by RV
Frommer's NYC Free & Dirt Cheap
Frommer's Road Atlas Europe
Frommer's Road Atlas Ireland
Retirement Places Rated

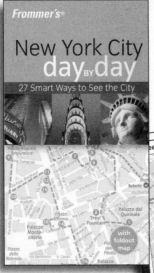
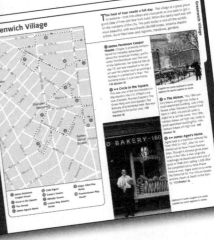